ETHNIC HERITAGE IN MISSISSIPPI

Ethnic Heritage in
Mississippi

THE TWENTIETH CENTURY

Shana Walton, *Editor*
Barbara Carpenter, *General Editor*

University Press of Mississippi
and Mississippi Humanities Council
Jackson

www.upress.state.ms.us

Publication of this book is funded in part
by a "We the People" grant from the National
Endowment for the Humanities.

The University Press of Mississippi is a member
of the Association of American University Presses.

Copyright © 2012 by Mississippi Humanities Council
All rights reserved

First printing 2012

∞

Library of Congress Cataloging-in-Publication Data

Ethnic heritage in Mississippi, the twentieth century /
Shana Walton, editor ; Barbara Carpenter, general editor.
   p. cm.
   Includes bibliographical references and index.
   ISBN 978-1-61703-262-2 (cloth : alk. paper) — ISBN
978-1-61703-263-9 (ebook) 1. Minorities—Mississippi—
History—20th century. 2. Mississippi—Race relations—
   History—20th century. 3. Mississippi—Ethnic rela-
tions—History—20th century. I. Walton, Shana, 1961– II.
Carpenter, Barbara. III. Mississippi Humanities Council.
         F350.A1E843 2012
   305.8009762—dc23   2011034329

British Library Cataloging-in-Publication Data available

CONTENTS

vii   Foreword
           —Barbara Carpenter

3   Introduction. Ethnicity in Mississippi: Stories Worth Telling
           —Shana Walton

        SECTION I
        Immigrants, Identity, and Sites of Connection

15   1. The International Immigrants of Mississippi: An Overview
           —Carl L. Bankston III

32   2. European Mississippians
           —Celeste Ray

74   3. African American Sacred and Secular Identities in Mississippi's Piney Woods
           —Joyce Marie Jackson

98   4. The Story of Mound Bayou
           —Amy L. Young and Milburn J. Crowe

122   5. Down Around Biloxi: An Overview of Ethnic and Occupational Identity in a Coastal Town
           —Aimée L. Schmidt

        SECTION II
        Ethnicity in a Biracial Culture

145   6. Mississippi Delta Chinese
           —Emily Erwin Jones and Frieda Quon

CONTENTS

172 7. Mississippi *Mahjar*: The Lebanese Immigration Experience in the Delta
     —James Thomas

193 8. Chai Cotton: Jewish Life in Mississippi
     —Stuart Rockoff

219 9. "*Chahta Siyah Ókih*": Ethnicity in the Oral Tradition of the Mississippi Band of Choctaw Indians
     —Tom Mould

     SECTION III
     Local Changes, Global Forces

263 10. The Vietnamese in Mississippi
     —Vy Thuc Dao

284 11. The Changing Face of Hindu Identity in Jackson, Mississippi
     —Devparna Roy and Lola Williamson

309 12. Filipinas in the Deep South: Reading Domestic Oral Narratives as Sites of Politicization and Community Building
     —Linda Pierce Allen

333 13. The Genesis of a New Ethnic Group?: The Meanings of Latino/Hispanic Identity in South Mississippi
     —Bridget Anne Hayden

353 Postscript. Celebrating Heritage and Recognizing Complexity and Change in Mississippi Culture
     —Shana Walton

367 Contributors

371 Index

FOREWORD

The first volume of *Ethnic Heritage in Mississippi* sprang forth almost spontaneously as part of the burst of research, scholarship, and programming surrounding the 1992 Columbian Quincentenary. Unlike the United States Bicentennial that was celebrated with general patriotic enthusiasm in 1976, the anniversary of the *entrada* provoked more soul-searching, somber, and often impassioned examinations of events, their contexts, and their consequences over five hundred years. Historians, both professionals and amateurs, anthropologists from all corners of that discipline, scholars in literature and languages, art, and even such seemingly unlikely fields as agriculture, along with teachers, students, museums, libraries, historical societies, and state humanities councils, became caught up in a frenzy of interest in events of the late fifteenth through the eighteenth centuries and concerns about how the information, artifacts, and materials should be handled and presented. Grievances and hostilities left smouldering for centuries flared forth in often anguished debates over whether to celebrate or mourn, or even what to call the event. (*Encuentro*, encounter, became the widely used term, a seemingly reasonable compromise.) Traditional histories of Mississippi abounded, but few had paid attention to issues of ethnicity beyond the most obvious areas of black and white conflict. Such a collection seemed an obvious need.

Although, as Shana Walton points out in her introduction, Mississippi is now a state with one of the smallest foreign-born populations in the U.S., it was nevertheless the scene of many of the earliest interactions among Europeans and indigenous peoples. Numerous Native American tribes lived in what is now Mississippi; encounters with Europeans devastated their populations with new diseases, warlike takeovers, and treatied removals, so that eventually the only tribe present in significant numbers was the Choctaw. Though the *Niña*, *Pinta*, and *Santa Maria* did not make it into the Mississippi Sound, fellow Spaniard Hernando de Soto passed this way some fifty years later (1542–1543), and the Canadian Pierre Le Moyne, Sieur d'Iberville, under the flag of the king of France, came ashore in what is now Ocean Springs in 1699. The Mississippi River itself was a major thoroughfare for exploration and immigration from both north and south for the next three hundred years. Interestingly, Mississippi was settled from both east and west, across the Southeast over land and along the Mississippi River from the west. The one African thought to accompany Soto was soon followed by numbers of his fellows in the bonds of slavery. When this source of labor disappeared following the Civil War, cotton planters sought to replace African Americans with Italians and Chinese in the Delta. By the late nineteenth century the Gulf Coast attracted a series of newcomers to its seafood industry: Cajun French and Creoles, Slavonians, and in the late twentieth century Vietnamese, to be followed in the early twenty-first century by Latinos, thus coming full circle. The trickle of new groups may never have been the powerful flood it was in other parts of this country, but it has been steady—and quite diverse—all the way up to the present.

In preparing volume one we made two seemingly contradictory observations: first, most people we talked to in 1990 were not consciously aware of the diversity among their fellow Mississippians; and second, at the same time, these seemingly invisible ethnic groups had had significant impact in many areas of popular culture and life in the state. Following almost every talk I gave on the topic, someone would tell about a favorite ethnic restaurant, a local mercantile store, or a family member from a generation or two back who was Lebanese, Dalmatian, Jewish, or other non–northern European. Most of their anecdotes were positive, and most of the speakers expressed surprise at themselves for not taking more note of the differences. Even more surprising was their lack of awareness of how strongly their own food, music, and everyday lives were influenced by these groups: the surprising phenomenon of hot tamales in the Delta, perhaps the most famous of them prepared by a well-known African American restaurant; the plethora of Greek-owned restaurants around the Jackson area and in other locations, with Mediterranean-influenced menus and dishes; the Native American family member whose story was perhaps not known or acknowledged until a death; the ubiquitous influence of Delta blues in every jukebox and radio station.

Perhaps one of the most memorable of these sudden moments of insight occurred on the Gulf Coast, at a program the Mississippi Humanities Council sponsored in conjunction with a photographic exhibit focusing on the seafood industry. Photographer D. C. Young had collected photos of shrimpers, fishermen, and oystermen and of the many women who worked as shuckers, packers, and in other support positions, and they were invited to the exhibit opening and asked to talk about their experiences. A succession of immigrants had worked with seafood: Cajun French; Slavonians, Croatians, Dalmatians; and, most recently at that time, Vietnamese. Relations had not always been good among these groups, with fierce competition and conflicts over many issues, from territory to the kinds of boats used. But as representatives of the various groups began to talk about their experiences, their hard work, their treatment, relating story after story of their lives, older members of the audience began to nod and murmur in obviously surprised agreement—"yes, that's the way it was for us too," "yes, that's what happened when we got here." In addition to anecdotes of hard, often ill-paid labor and social isolation, the groups found that many of them had the Catholic Church in common, even many of the Vietnamese. They had started organizations (Fleur de Lis Society, Slavonian Benevolent Society) to provide support and fellowship, had maintained strong ethnic communities, had deep family ties. It became a very enlightening and emotional experience for many present to discover commonalities with those so recently perceived as "other." The kind of spontaneous recognition of common values and community so apparent here was repeated in other places and other ways throughout the state, encouraging the council to continue its support for such projects.

The first volume was primarily historical in approach and chronological in order. It sought as a primary goal to stimulate attention to scholarship on Mississippi's indigenous peoples, a goal that has come to gratifying fruition in the last two decades, with groundbreaking work especially on the Choctaw people from a variety of perspectives. The chapters on the European backdrop, the early exploration and colonization, and the Africans who came against their will have become basic material in many classrooms. The current volume does not follow so straightforward a format or approach. Scholars are from a variety of disciplines; their approaches, their assumptions, their research techniques, even their writing styles reflect the diversity of their backgrounds and subjects. Yet this apparent quirkiness has its own value, as it mirrors the more fragmented nature of the latest newcomers and explores cultures from within as well as from outside observation.

The second goal, to develop public programming to bring information and awareness of the state's richly diverse heritage, continues to be a major emphasis of the MHC. The council has supported a statewide oral history program over the last twelve years, collecting thousands of interviews and making them available to scholars, students, and the public alike in a variety of formats. Exhibits, conferences, displays, teacher materials, Web sites and other projects address the complexity of the issues involved in relationships in the twenty-first century. The council's commitment to the present volume indicates continued dedication to this goal and its implied outcomes of acceptance and civility for all.

Currently, there is much wider recognition of the many cultures in Mississippi. Such events as the Oktoberfest in Gluckstadt, the Scottish Highland Games and Celtic Fest in Jackson, the Greek Fest on the coast, and most recently the Latino festival are well attended, as are blues and jazz and bluegrass festivals. At the same time, in this state and nationally, even internationally, conflicts and controversies over issues of diversity, multiculturalism, and immigrant populations have intensified over the last two decades. Fear, suspicion, even overt hostility toward persons of Middle Eastern descent, especially of the Muslim faith, continue to increase, exacerbated by more than a decade of wars in Iraq and Afghanistan. Perhaps more immediately apparent in Mississippi, the influx of Spanish-speaking workers from Latin American countries, especially in the construction, agricultural, and chicken and seafood industries, has heightened fears of jobs lost or funds spent on social and medical services for noncitizens. Globalization in general has aggravated incipient anxieties about environmental, ecological, economic, and cultural issues and potentially conflicting goals and values. Even a cursory glance at headlines reveals that these conflicts are universal, as, in recent months, the French government forcibly ejected the Rom, China continues to attempt to eradicate the population in Tibet, Germany is the site of fierce conflicts with Turkish and other Middle Eastern guest workers, several African countries are haunted by massive "ethnic cleansing," and even the usually staid Dutch elected an overtly xenophobic leader.

In the face of these fears and the resulting polarization and ill will they generate, the chairman of the National Endowment for the Humanities, former Congressman James Leach, has instituted a special "Bridging Cultures" initiative. In an address in Jackson he remarked that after he had announced the project, he was pleased to learn that Mississippi already has programs in place to address the issues of civil discourse and dialogue among all peoples. The Mississippi Humanities Council has prided itself since its inception on its efforts to bring all residents of this state together to work out their differences, and this volume is the latest effort in that direction. After all, as our motto proudly announces, the humanities are for everyone.

BARBARA CARPENTER
Jackson, Mississippi
December 10, 2010

ETHNIC HERITAGE IN MISSISSIPPI

INTRODUCTION

Ethnicity in Mississippi: Stories Worth Telling

—SHANA WALTON

Mississippi has one of the smallest foreign-born populations in the U.S. (see Bankston, this volume), which means that lots of the people who live here now have had their families here for generations. Even when their families were new settlers, they seldom were from foreign countries, but had "immigrated" from other parts of the eastern U.S., or nearby states like Alabama. The roots of Mississippians are started as branches off the earliest family trees in our nation. In fact, the city of Natchez had a chapter of the Daughters of the American Revolution only a few years after the national organization was founded in 1890. In Mississippi cemeteries, dozens of Revolutionary War veterans came to rest after they pulled up stakes and moved their families west to what was then the Mississippi Territory (Mississippi State Society of the DAR 2010). Their daughters and granddaughters, of course, were as as tied to the founding of the nation as were the ladies of Boston and Concord. The story of Mississippi history, however, has never sounded much like the stories of states like Massachusetts or even California, Florida, or Minnesota, where history books spin tales of waves of immigrants who left the "old country" to settle a foreign land. Part of our collective American heritage includes the stories of Ellis Island, the Pennsylvania "Dutch," or the Boston Irish. Ethnic heritages have a firm place in American history. But the story most people, including Mississippians, learn about our state has been about regional identity or racial conflict, not ethnicity.

So why a book about ethnicity? The truth is that while the majority of Mississippians today may not have had recent immigrant ancestors, both immigrants and ethnic identities—people's perceived (and real) links with other lands or groups of people—have shaped this state. There are compelling reasons that Mississippians (and others in the U.S.) should hear stories about ethnic identity in our state. First, because the common story of Mississippi often justifiably focuses on nineteenth- and twentieth-century racial strife, we often lose sight of the diversity that marked Mississippi's early years. As a frontier, Mississippi had French, Spanish, English, German, Africans, and many groups of Native Americans. Today, new populations are once again coming in record numbers, and Mississippi is returning to its early diversity. One way to understand this new change is, perhaps, to reclaim our history as a meeting ground for cultures.

The second reason ethnic identity is important is because of the influence of these groups on local areas. Immigrants and their descendents may have been small in numbers, but because Mississippi was a rural state with low population densities, groups had disproportionate local impact and formed key parts of the state's history. Each group had a big impact on some local area. If you look closely at the state, you keep finding how each region of the state was shaped and reshaped by ethnic groups. Why is the Delta famous for tamales? Who are the Sweet Potato Queens? Why does a Catholic church in Biloxi have services in Vietnamese? How did Gluckstadt get its name?[1] For example, the Vietnamese have only a small impact on the state's overall population; however, they had a powerful effect on the economic shape and cultural character of the Gulf Coast (Schmidt, this volume). Each region or small town where a group settled shows the imprint of those ethnicities—the Croatians, Lebanese, Chinese, Vietnamese, and others. Mississippi, in other words, was small enough in overall population for even small groups to become woven into the cultural history of the state. Their histories are even an important part of telling the story of racial conflict in the state. For example, having Jewish, Lebanese, and Chinese shop owners shaped the contours of black-white interaction in the Delta. And the stories of regions—the hills, the coast, the Delta—call forth tales of ethnic enclaves. In one sense, then, this book also becomes a documentation of the regional and local in Mississippi.

Clearly, then, group identities, beyond race or in addition to racial identities, have long been a part of Mississippi history and have shaped local areas for generations. This deep connection has been submerged for years, but over the last thirty years Mississippians, like Americans everywhere, have renewed an interest in their ancestry. Participation in such events as St. Patrick's Day celebrations and Oktoberfest has surged. Locals and tourists can now follow the Tamale Trail through the Delta, and Tupelo has a Cinco de Mayo festival. This renewal of interest was first flowering twenty years ago at the publication of volume one of *Ethnic Heritage in Mississippi* and continues to grow, providing a final reason to take an even closer look at ethnic identity in the state.

Of course, any book about ethnicity in Mississippi—a state where race continues to determine life outcomes more so than any other state in the nation (Burd-Sharps et al. 2009)—should not work to erase or ignore ongoing racial disparities or real-life racial issues. The hope is that carefully looking at ethnicity helps us to track and understand the evolution of the concept of identity, including race, in a more complex way. How did we get to where we are, and who are we now?

This book offers an overview of the twentieth century's most prominent ethnic groups in the state and those shaping the twenty-first century. The groups were chosen by numbers, pure and simple. That is, we tried to represent the most populous groups in the state that identify ethnically, as recorded by the U.S. Census. There are certainly groups that will be left out, and coverage of newly burgeoning populations (like the small but growing ranks of African immigrants) will be left to future volumes. This book presents some stories in an academic press for the first time. The accounts included here of the immigrations of Filipina, Lebanese, Latino, and Hindu peoples are among the first efforts to capture and present these groups, documenting their integration into Mississippi history.

Rather than being a seamless, smooth presentation of what we might call Mississippi's ethnicity story, this volume can appear rather uneven. Some chapers put forward capsule histories of a group, from first immigrants to modern times, while other groups are explored only through one aspect of their culture. Not only do the articles vary in the amount and type of information offered, but also range widely in how scholarly the approach is, how formal the writing, and even in the way the citations are noted. This volume is intended to offer the widest possible exploration of ethnicity, and one approach did not seem to fit all groups. First, some groups have simply been here longer than others or have had more attention from reseachers. These groups can have their stories told as overview histories. Such an approach is more difficult with newer groups. There are fewer documents or information. In a couple of cases, the only published article is in this volume. In the case of African Americans, few Mississippi researchers have looked at this as an ethnic or community group. While Mississippi boasts an abundance of scholars studying the state's African American history, almost all of them are focused on racial identity, political history, or specific cultural features, like unique forms of music or particular religious traditions. Few scholars look at community-based or place-based identity among U.S. African Americans. So, while scholars just now turn their research in that direction, we try to fill the gap with two articles. One article looks at music traditions that help shape or define identity (see Jackson, this volume). The second examines an African American heritage rooted in a specific place (see Young and Crowe, this volume). To fit the volume's mission, each group is approached differently, respecting depth of research or amount of time in the state.

The second major reason the articles vary is that the authors come at their topics from widely different academic disciplines. The writers include anthropologists, historians, sociologists, folklorists, archivists, and religious and cultural studies specialists. Many of the authors are themselves members of the communities about which they write. In fact, the majority of chapters are either written by or have coauthors who are members of the community or group they write about. Both inside and outside voices are always needed, and we hope we are offering a good mixture. With each author writing in the style that he/she or they feel is most suitable, the chapters vary greatly in tone and writing style. Sometimes an article provides more or less an overview of the group's history, and often, particularly with the newer groups, the author chose to look at the group through a narrow window, or link the discussion to larger theories of how ethnic identity is formed or maintained. In short, the authors gathered different kinds of information and tell different types of stories as a result.

Because the authors come from different disciplines and because the groups have quite different histories, this book also has varying approaches to the concept of "ethnicity." So far we have been talking about ethnicity without defining the term. In fact, the beginning of this introduction collapses the terms "ethnic" and "immigrant." The idea that "ethnic" equals "immigrant" is an old and easily understood definition of ethnicity—an identity you have based on which country your family immigrated from, which language and traditions you shared. Are you Irish? German? Lebanese? It seems clear enough. But that definition leaves us with lots of problems. What about Jewish people? Are they an ethnic group? Jewish people might have immigrated to the U.S. from Russia, Spain, or even Iran. So why aren't they Russian, Spanish, and Persian? Well, in fact, they are. Ethnicity is a "layered" identity. Being Jewish doesn't stop you from being Russian. We have mostly thrown out the idea that "ethnic" people have to immigrate or speak a foreign language. Anthropologists like Clifford Geertz (1973) and sociologists like Émile Durkheim (Jones 1986) found that being part of something like an ethnic group was a "social fact" for most humans, and "ethnicity" comes closer to equaling something like "birth/social community" or "heritage identity." We are born into communities other than our municipalities. In this case, "community" means the people and group of people to whom we have deep and meaningful connections. Those ties help define us and sustain us. In the past, belonging to an ethnic group often implied a separation from other groups. The communities might all live near each other, but speak different languages, eat different food or worship in different ways. "Nonethnic" people would view people with strong ethnic ties as "different" and might bar them from access to schools or social groups. That vision of ethnic enclaves and ethnic exclusion is not as meaningful in today's society. Ethnicity theorists who came along in the 1990s, like Richard Alba and Mary Waters, found that in modern cultures like ours people often have choices about expressing their ethnicity and asserted that for most people ethnic identity is "optional" or layered on, rather than being the sole, major defining identity a person has. This volume sees ethnicity as one of many layered identities people have in our complex society. But unlike, say, joining a softball league or political party, an ethnic group has ties to family, community, and shared traditions and culture for all its members. Unlike community clubs, ethnic groups are not completely optional to their members. You can quit a country club or softball team, but you can't quit being Lebanese. But, on the other hand, you could decide to not eat Lebanese food, follow any traditions, or marry a Lebanese person. In the past, because of social restrictions, people were often confined to society within their ethnic group, and their ethnicity became their defining identity and determined many of their life choices. Ethnicity has lost much of its social power, but retains a strong personal pull for many. The pull is so strong that people who once gave up their "hyphenations" to be part of the American melting pot, like many European Americans, find themselves drawn to rediscovering their heritage. This volume approaches ethnicity as deeply meaningful and sustaining to people in ways we don't fully understand.

So which groups are "ethnic" groups? Most people agree on some of the labels in this volume—the Chinese, the Lebanese, the Vietnamese. But such agreement quickly breaks down. An obvious category to outsiders is not always so obvious among insiders. For example, Latinos often don't see themselves as members of some large Latino ethnic group. Mexicans, for instance, might not see themselves as having much in common with people from Puerto Rico or Cuba. Even immigrants from the same country don't necessarily share ethnicity. For example, newly arrived Guatemalans bring with them a complicated ethnic system that includes the idea that some people from their country are not Latino at all, but are Indians. Yet, when they get to the Gulf Coast, they are seldom seen by outsiders as Guatemalans, much less as American Indians and almost never as Kaqchikel or Kiché (two of the ethnic groups). They are "Latino" to outsiders simply because they speak Spanish. Clearly, then, some of the labels we are using are not necessarily the labels the groups themselves would use. Even the word "Latino" is tricky and has political implications (see Hayden, this volume). The struggle is over what scholars call "ethnonyms," names given to ethnic groups. Ethnonyms can take on powerful meanings, helping groups see themselves as part of a larger unified whole (as in "Native American") and for accomplishing community, political, or economic goals. Many people do not take these lightly and neither do the writers in this volume. For instance, there is a debate over whether racial categories like "black" and "white" should be treated like names of ehnic groups—should they be capitalized? Why or why not? The simple question of whether names of groups should have capital letters can stir passionate arguments on both sides of the debate. The standard practice of the publisher of this volume is that racial terms are lowercased and names of ethnic groups are uppercased, despite practices of individual authors.The ethnic labels, in contrast, were chosen by the authors and are almost uniformly capitalized. Readers can notice labels created by both insiders and outsiders, each writer choosing the labels most meaningful to either the group, general readers, or, ideally, both. The politics of identity play out in discussions over naming practices, struggles over capitalization, or arguments about who's "politically correct" or "overly sensitive." In our society, when these issues become heated you can be sure that social groups and standings are in flux.

The book is divided into three sections. Section I offers an overview of immigration. This section looks at the "colonizers" of the state, both voluntary and involuntary. Carl Bankston gives a sociologist's view of the history of immigration in our state and how it compared to the rest of the U.S. South and the nation. Meanwhile, as a companion piece, folklorist Aimée Schmidt looks at how immigration played out in identities and occupations in one city in Mississippi, Biloxi. Anthropologist Celeste Ray gives an encyclopedic roundup of European ethnicities in Mississippi today. The list is extensive. To approach African American culture and identity, folklorist Joyce Jackson takes us on a tour of music and community in the Piney Woods region of the state. This section also offers two combined articles on the African American community of Mound Bayou, the first settlement founded by freed slaves in the United States. The articles are written by archaeologist Amy Young and by Milburn Crowe, an amateur historian, now deceased, who spent his life documenting Mound Bayou. In Jackson's as well as Young's and Crowe's articles, these are not cases in which people share a common country of origin, but rather situations in which people create "quasi-ethnicity" (Reed 1992) based on region, locale, and tradition. Shelton Reed, the sociologist who first advanced the idea, did so in order to suggest that white southerners shared an ethnic-like identity. In Ray's article as well, ethnicity expands to include quasi-ethnic types, like religious groups that form communities, such as Mennonites and Old Order German Baptists.

Section II deals with the groups who defined their ethnicity, in part, against the Jim Crow laws that created a society divided between black and white. The chapter by James Thomas looks at the most assimilated of these groups, the Lebanese, who for all intents and purposes were accepted into "white" society the most easily. The chapter by Stuart Rockoff on Jewish communities in Mississippi examines the particular history of the Jewish community and dedicates a section to examining how the Jewish community both was and was not accepted into white society. Emily Erwin Jones and Frieda Quon take a narrative and oral history approach to examining the story of the Chinese in the Delta. Tom Mould looks at the Choctaw use of storytelling and types of stories to maintain a distinct identity in a black-white world.

Section III offers stories about groups who have immigrated mostly since World War II or groups which have increased immigration greatly in the last thirty or forty years. These chapters tend to focus on specific aspects of each group or to look at each group through some lens, rather than approaching the groups as objects of history. The chapter on the Hindus in Mississippi by Lola Williamson and Devparna Roy looks at the growing presence of immigrants from India through the unifying force of religion. The chapter on the Vietnamese by Vy Dao reports on the community founded after the fall of Saigon and the end of the Vietnam War, and how they both have and have not melded into Mississippi society—and how they've created a society of their own. The chapter by Bridget Hayden on the growing Latino presence discusses how Latinos have long been a small part of Mississippi history (remember the Tamale Trail?) but also how they are now being perceived by themselves and by outsiders. The final ethnic group in this section is the interesting case of growing immigration from the Philippines. Many of these immigrants are women who have come to the state as part of marriages to Mississippi men. This chapter by

Linda Allen shows us the power of global communication and the ability of people to re-create community and traditions far from home.

Throughout the book, authors approach the concept of ethnicity itself differently. Some treat their groups as more or less unified through time, while others are telling stories of identity constructed in a new place, out of the materials at hand. To different degrees, several authors explore the complexity of what ethnicity is for their particular groups. The book ends with a reflection on this complicated concept of ethnicity. How do we assimilate the still-dominant race-based story of Mississippi with emerging stories of ethnicity, diversity, and difference in the state? That chapter asks us to consider what ethnicity and race mean in our modern world and how they function for us. That is, what do we "get" from having an ethnic identity? What does it mean to seek your heritage and why do people do this? And finally, how does the quest for ethnic identity mesh with racial realities in the state? Is one more "real" or more important than the other?

These brief chapter descriptions make it clear that not all communities were treated "equally" in the volume. Some chapters have a long historical section; some don't. Some have oral histories and lots of interviews; some don't. Some discuss how Hurricane Katrina impacted the group; some don't. Some groups shared photos willingly; others were reluctant. Each story, however, has at least a brief overview of the group's history and some comment on the group's status in Mississippi in 2010. But even in the best documented of communities, there are no complete stories here. For instance, the Jewish community is one that has made the greatest effort to systematically document their history. In fact, the author of our chapter "Chai Cotton" is the director of the Goldring/Woldenberg Institute of Southern Jewish Life—a whole institute to study the history and heritage of Jews across the South. The institute has an archive holding hundreds of photographs, records, and interviews. And yet, Mississippi's Jewish story is a cliffhanger. Those communities who shaped the Delta so much in the post–Civil War era are now declining in population as many of the children have moved to other states. Will the communities die out? Or will there be, as there has been with other groups, a return migration back to Mississippi?

We won't know those answers for another generation at least. The truth is that we have only partial stories, the story we can tell at this time, each story told from the perspective of one or two researchers. But the stories are ongoing and evolving. We in Mississippi will have plenty of work for the next volume.

NOTE

1. All of these questions are answered in various articles throughout the book. For tamales information, see the chapter on Latinos in Mississippi; for Sweet Potato Queens and Gluckstadt, see the chapter on European heritage; and for Catholic Church, see the chapter on the Vietnamese and the one on Biloxi.

WORKS CITED

Alba, Richard. 1992. *Ethnic Identity: The Transformation of White America*. New Haven: Yale University Press.

Burd-Sharps, Sarah, Eduardo Borges Martins, and Kristen Lewis. 2009. "A Portrait of Mississippi: Mississippi Human Development Report." American Human Development Project of the Social Sciences Research Council. Retrieved from http://www.measureofamerica.org.

Geertz, Clifford. 1977 (1973). *Interpretation of Cultures*. New York: Basic Books.

Jones, Robert Alun. 1986. *Emile Durkheim: An Introduction to Four Major Works*. Beverly Hills, CA: Sage Publications.

Mississippi State Society of the Daughters of the American Revolution. Retrieved 2010 from http://www.mississippidar.org.

Waters, Mary. 1990. *Ethnic Options: Choosing Identities in America*. Los Angeles: University of California Press.

SECTION I

Immigrants, Identity, and Sites of Connection

This section addresses the people who voluntarily and involuntarily first colonized the area now known as Mississippi. Carl Bankston presents an overview of immigration to the state and a look at the original European colonizers and how European identities play out today. Aimée Schmidt offers an article on a particular site of connection that has been unique in the history of the state as a meeting ground for disparate groups—the Gulf Coast, particularly the town of Biloxi. Also in this section are two chapters on African American heritage in Mississippi.

Very few ethnic heritage volumes—almost none—address the issue of ethnicity among one of the largest groups of Americans. But, in fact, the history of African American identity is inextricable from the growth of ethnic identity in general. There are scholars who believe that it was the shift from the usage of "Negro" and "colored" to "African American" that helped launch the "white" ethnicity movement in the U.S. in the 1970s and 1980s (cf. Alba 1992, Waters 1990). Many African Americans rejected a racial label ("black") and instead insisted on a label that identified a place of heritage and origin—"Africa." Locating which specific cultural groups their ancestors belonged to is an enormous challenge for most African Americans. In this volume, authors Jackson, Young, and Crowe approach African American identity through tradition and community. First, the article by folklorist Joyce Jackson examines the role of music in the identity of Piney Woods African Americans, and how the tradition of music, both sacred and secular, serves as an identifying force and shared language. Two *articles on the town of Mound Bayou chronicle a vibrant search by an African American community to assert identity through a search for their town's unique history and heritage. This project, "Digging for the Dream in Mound Bayou," was initiated by lifelong Mound Bayou resident Milburn Crowe, who always saw his community as an identifiable group, with a heritage firmly based in one specific place. He and Amy Young co-wrote the presentation reprinted in this volume describing how community members became amateur archaeologists. The second article was written by Dr. Young alone because Mr. Crowe passed away in 2005, before the article could be completed.*

These investigations of group, traditions, and place may not, for some, meet a strict definition of "ethnicity," because no specific country or heritage language is named. But such a narrow definition does not suit the purposes of this volume. For more than one-third of Mississippi's population, community and traditions in the U.S. are the only sure markers of heritage and identity they can claim beyond race. For further questions about identity, ethnicity, and race, see the last chapter in this volume.

—Editor

WORKS CITED

Alba, Richard. 1992. *Ethnic Identity: The Transformation of White America.* New Haven: Yale University Press.

Waters, Mary. 1990. *Ethnic Options: Choosing Identities in America.* Los Angeles: University of California Press.

1

THE INTERNATIONAL IMMIGRANTS OF MISSISSIPPI

An Overview

—CARL L. BANKSTON III

The popular stereotype of Mississippi among people in many other parts of the country is that of a conservative agrarian society, with only limited openness to outside influence. There is some basis in fact to this perception. On the surface, for example, the immigration trends that have shaped the nation as a whole since the late nineteenth century seem to have bypassed the Magnolia State. However, despite limited migration, immigrants have played notable parts in Mississippi history. Moreover, contrary to the stereotype, Mississippi did become a destination for people from other countries in the late twentieth and early twenty-first centuries.

The decades from the Civil War to World War I saw the United States change from a mainly agricultural nation to a major industrial producer. By 1890 the U.S. had outstripped the leading industrial nations of Europe to become the world's foremost producer of manufactured goods. The quickly developing industrial economy required workers, and the availability of jobs drew immigrants to American shores in unprecedented numbers and proportions. Many of these immigrants came from southern and eastern Europe, parts of the world that had previously sent few people to North America.

In 1860, about 4,140,000 foreign-born people lived in the United States. Forty years later, the number of foreign-born in the nation had grown to 14,000,000. As Figure 1.1 shows, the wave of immigration during this period brought the percentage of the American population born outside the United States to about 15 percent, or about one out of every seven Americans by the early years of the twentieth century. Restrictive immigration legislation in the early 1920s pushed immigration down after that, so that the foreign-born population reached a low of just under 5 percent (one out of every twenty Americans) by 1970.

Changes in immigration law in 1965 opened new opportunities for immigration. These opportunities were also available to new groups of people. The laws that had been enacted in the 1920s greatly favored newcomers from northern and western Europe. With the change in law, more immigrants began to arrive from Asia and Latin America. Economic and political troubles in those parts of the world, along with improved global transportation and communication, encouraged the new patterns of migration. By the 1990s and early 2000s, the United States had entered a second great migration wave, so that over 12 percent (about one out of every eight people) of the nation's people had come from elsewhere by 2005 and 2006, as Figure 1.1 shows. Most of the immigrants were from Latin America or Asia, since nearly half of the foreign-born in the early twenty-first century were from the former region and one-fourth were from the latter.

Mississippi, as shown in Figure 1.2, has always had much lower levels of immigration than the country as a whole. In the years following 1870, while the country as a whole entered a period of massive industry-driven immigration, the small immigrant proportion of the state actually decreased, and it continued to go down through the first decades of the twentieth century. Ironically, at precisely this time, Mississippi made an official effort to increase its immigration. During the post–Civil War period attempts to diversify the economy and to replace African American workers who were leaving the state led the state's political leaders to attempt to attract people from around the world. In 1878, pursuing this goal, Mississippi organized the Board of Immigration and Agriculture. During the 1880s, the state published a pamphlet in several languages advertising its employment opportunities and distributed this publication in American cities and abroad. However, these efforts met with very limited success, probably because immigrants could find greater economic opportunities elsewhere in the nation. Even at its highest level, the immigrant population in Mississippi has never reached the U.S. average at any time in our history.

International immigration to Mississippi has even been smaller than immigration to the rest of the South, which held smaller proportions of foreign-born people than any other U.S. region from the mid-nineteenth century until 1970. Moreover, while immigration to much of the South increased dramatically after 1970, Mississippi continued to hold fewer immigrants, both in absolute numbers and as a percentage of the total population, than any other southern state by 2005. Although Mississippi's

International Immigrants of Mississippi: An Overview

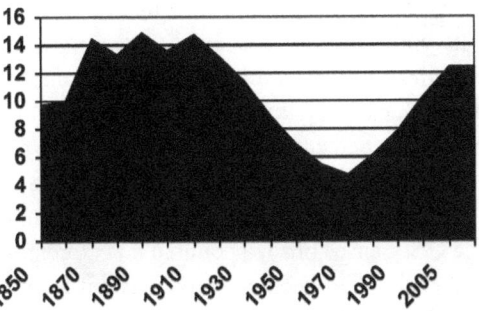

1.1. Foreign-born as a percentage of the U.S. population, 1850–2006. Source: U.S. Census, Decennial Censuses, 1850–2000; American Community Surveys, 2005 and 2006.

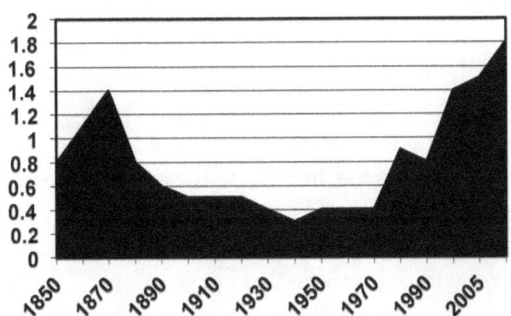

1.2. Foreign-born immigrants as percentages of the Mississippi population, 1850–2006. Source: Campbell J. Gibson and Emily Lennon, "Historical Census Statistics on the Foreign-born Population of the United States: 1850–1990," Population Division, U.S. Bureau of the Census, Table 13; Census 2000, Summary File 3, American Community Survey, 2005.

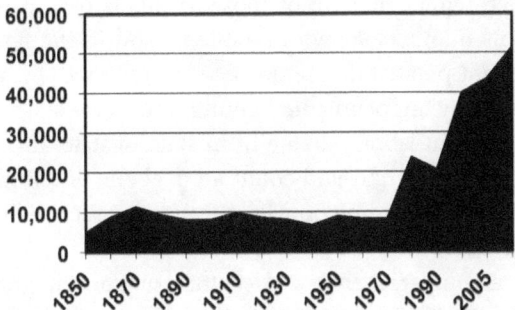

1.3. Growth in the numbers of the foreign-born immigrant population of Mississippi, 1850–2006. Source: Campbell J. Gibson and Emily Lennon, "Historical Census Statistics on the Foreign-born Population of the United States: 1850–1990," Population Division, U.S. Bureau of the Census, Table 13; Census 2000, Summary File 3, American Community Survey, 2005.

share of the foreign-born has been less than that of most other parts of the United States, its immigrant population did increase dramatically at the end of the twentieth and the beginning of the twenty-first century.

From 1990 to 2005, individuals born outside of the United States increased from under 1 percent of the state's population to over 2 percent. Since this was also a time of general population increase for Mississippi, the growth in numbers of immigrants was even more dramatic. As shown in Figure 1.3, the U.S. Census of 1970 counted 8,125 foreign-born people in the state, a number that had been roughly constant for more than a century. During the decade of the seventies, though, this number increased nearly fourfold. In the fifteen-year period from 1990 to 2005, the immigrant population of the state grew from just over 20,000 to over 43,000. By 2006, only one year later, the U.S. Census Bureau estimated that there were over 51,000 foreign-born people in Mississippi. Thus, it appears that the supposedly closed society has been rapidly opening up to the rest of the world, acquiring a much more diverse society in a short period of time.

As undocumented immigration became a topic of controversy throughout the United States in the late twentieth and early twenty-first centuries, it also became a subject of concern for Mississippi. It is difficult to estimate how much of Mississippi's growing immigrant population has arrived without immigration papers. The U.S. Census Bureau estimated that undocumented immigrants in Mississippi increased from 2,000 in 1990 to 8,000 in 2000. Five years later, in 2005, the Pew Hispanic Center gave an estimate of between 20,000 and 35,000 in the three states of Louisiana, Mississippi, and Alabama. Officials with Immigration and Customs Enforcement (ICE) have suggested that the numbers after 2005 could be much higher than all of those. If this is true, it would mean that the census numbers shown in Table 1.1 and in the figures for the recent immigrant population are drastic undercounts. One difficulty, of course, is that many undocumented immigrants in the state are probably involved in transient labor, moving from state to state for work. Therefore, even if one could find and count all of them, one would be faced with the problem of deciding how long someone must be in the state in order to count as an immigrant.

Despite the comparatively low level of international migration to Mississippi until very recent years, people from various parts of the world have helped to shape the state's demographic characteristics over the course of its history.

Table 1.1a. Major Birthplaces of the Foreign-Born Population of Mississippi, 1850–1940 (in Percentages)*

	1850	1860	1870	1880	1900	1910	1920	1930	1940
West. Eur.									
Germany	41%	24%	20%	29%	18%	10%	4%	15%	25%
Ireland	32%	42%	22%	39%	22%	11%	4%	5%	
England	14%	11%	8%	10%	9%	6%	8%	6%	1.3%
Scotland	7%	4%	12%	2%	3%	1%	2%		
France	5%	10%	10%	16%	5%	5%	1%		1%
Switzerland			2%	3%					
Netherlands					3%				
North. Eur.									
Norway		1%				1%	5%		1%
Sweden			11%	7%	8%	2%	3%		
Finland					4%	1%			
Denmark						2%		4%	1%
East. & South. Eur.									
Poland	2%		2%					5%	2%
Italy					13%	31%	24%	23%	11%
Russia					1%	6%		7%	22%
Austria					1%	3%			
Romania					3%				
Greece								3%	
Yugoslavia								4%	1%
Czechoslovakia									10%
Americas									
Canada		2%	5%		6%	8%		4%	1%
Caribbean			1%	1%		2%	4%	2%	
Brazil				1%				2%	
Mexico					1%	2%		4%	
Cent. Am.									2%
Asia									
China				1%	4%	5%	3%		1%
Africa									
Africa				1%					
Middle East									
Syria					.	4%	11%	16%	4%
Turkey							1%		
Total N	4,788	8,558	11,191	9,209	7,981	9,770	8,408	8,045	6,472*

Percentages may not add to 100 due to rounding, numbers below 1% from some countries, and immigrants from unknown places.

Source: Steven Ruggles, Matthew Sobek, Trent Alexander, Catherine A. Fitch, Ronald Goeken, Patricia Kelly Hall, Miriam King, and Chad Ronnander. *Integrated Public Use Microdata Series: Version 4.0* [Machine-readable database]. Minneapolis, MN: Minnesota Population Center [producer and distributor], 2008.

Table 1.1b. Major Birthplaces of the Foreign-Born Population of Mississippi, 1950–2005 (in Percentages)*

	1950	1960	1970	1980	1990	2000	2005
West. Eur.							
Germany				13%	16%	14%	12%
Ireland	11%	3%			1%		
England	5%	5%	2%	8%	9%	4%	4%
Scotland	4%	4%	2%	1%	1%		
France		4%	4%	2%	2%	2%	
Switzerland							
Netherlands		1%					
North. Eur.							
Norway							
Sweden		1%					
Finland	2%	2%					
Denmark							
East. & South. Eur.							
Poland	8%	1%					
Italy	16%	7%		2%	2%		
Russia	3%	4%					
Austria		1%	2%	4%			
Romania							
Greece	10%			1%			
Yugoslavia	2%		2%				
Czechoslovakia							
Albania	8%						
Spain				1%	2%	1%	
Americas							
Canada		3%	4%	6%	6%	4%	3%
Caribbean	4%						
Brazil							
Mexico	6%		2%	2%	3%	18%	25%
Honduras		1%	2%	1%	1%	1%	1%
Puerto Rico		6%					
Argentina			4%				
South America		1%				1%	
El Salvador							
Guatemala							3%
Nicaragua							1%
Panama				1%	2%	2%	1%
Cuba						1%	3%
Venezuela				1%	1%		
Jamaica							1%

Continued

	1950	1960	1970	1980	1990	2000	2005
Asia							
China	10%	1%	2%	3%	4%	4%	6%
Japan			4%	4%	5%	4%	4%
Korea		2%	15%	3%	4%	3%	7%
India	2%			2%	4%	5%	2%
Philippines				4%	6%	5%	4%
Thailand				2%			
Vietnam				5%	7%	7%	7%
Pakistan						1%	2%
Iran				1%		1%	
Africa							
North Africa			2%				
Middle East							
Lebanon	4%	5%	2%				
Syria		3%					
Turkey							
Total N	8,735	8,058	8,125	23,527	20,383	39,908	43,336*

Percentages may not add to 100 due to rounding, numbers below 1% from some countries, and immigrants from unknown places.

Source: Steven Ruggles, Matthew Sobek, Trent Alexander, Catherine A. Fitch, Ronald Goeken, Patricia Kelly Hall, Miriam King, and Chad Ronnander. *Integrated Public Use Microdata Series: Version 4.0* [Machine-readable database]. Minneapolis, MN: Minnesota Population Center [producer and distributor], 2008.

CHANGING DEMOGRAPHICS

Mississippi experienced rapid population growth during the early nineteenth century, but this was primarily a result of native-born Americans of northern European background, chiefly English and Scots-Irish, moving down into the Mississippi territory and into the coastal region of Spanish West Florida, part of which was annexed to Mississippi in 1810. These settlers also brought large numbers of slaves. Some of these slaves were undoubtedly born in Africa, but it is difficult to determine how many. Most enslaved people in the United States in the nineteenth century were born in this country, so relatively few of the slaves who arrived in Mississippi from other places were involuntary immigrants from Africa. The U.S. Census carried out every ten years shows the total population of Mississippi growing from 31,306 in 1810 to 75,448 in 1820, 136,621 in 1830, 375,651 in 1840, and 606,526 in 1850. White Mississippians slightly outnumbered black Mississippians until 1830, after which the black population became the majority for a century. The census does not provide information on the Choctaws and other Native Americans in the state, but there were probably 20,000 to 25,000 Choctaws living in Mississippi in 1830, which was the year of forced removal and westward exile. International immigration to Mississippi dates from the 1840s, when people born in Ireland and Germany began to reach the state.

Table 1.1 provides estimates of the national origins of the foreign-born population of Mississippi from 1850 through 2005. As in the rest of the United States, most immigrants to Mississippi in the middle of the nineteenth century were from Northern and Western Europe, especially from Germany, Ireland, and England. The state's immigrant population became more diverse in the late nineteenth and early twentieth centuries, especially because more people arrived from Southern and Eastern Europe. Italians, in particular, became one of the largest immigrant groups in Mississippi during the first three decades of the twentieth century. In the late nineteenth century, Mississippi also received significant numbers of Asians, from China, who first settled primarily in the Delta region. Those described as "Syrians" in this census data were often actually Lebanese, since Lebanon was a Christian Syrian province of the Ottoman Empire. The Lebanese found work in Mississippi as peddlers, traveling from place to place selling goods. They established communities in some of the larger cities, such as Vicksburg, Jackson, and Clarksdale.

The ethnic trends in migration to Mississippi, consisting mostly of Northern and Western Europeans by the middle of the nineteenth century, followed by Southern and Eastern Europeans, were similar to those of the rest of the country, although numbers of people arriving in Mississippi were much smaller. The ethnic trends in the late twentieth and early twenty-first centuries were also similar to national trends, as more Latin Americans and Asians appeared in the Deep South state. The Mexican population shot up sharply, from 3 percent of all immigrants in 1990 to one-fourth of a much larger number of immigrants in 2005. All of the Latin American national-origin groups together accounted for over one-third of the foreign-born people in the state by the middle of the twenty-first century's first decade. Among Asians, people from Vietnam, India, and China made up the largest national-origin groups, and together made up about one-fifth of Mississippi's immigrant population.

Today, foreign-born people in Mississippi are highly concentrated on the Gulf Coast and in major urban areas. As shown in Table 1.2, about

Table 1.2. Mississippi Counties with the Largest Immigrant Populations, 2005

	Number	Pct. of Miss. Immigrants	Location
Harrison	7,359	17.0	West Gulfport–Biloxi Area, Gulf Coast
DeSoto	3,990	9.2	Northwest, Memphis, Tenn., Area
Jackson	3,143	7.3	East Gulfport–Biloxi Area, Gulf Coast
Hinds	2,776	6.4	Western Jackson City Area, Center
Total	17,268	39.8	

Source: American Community Survey, 2005, U.S. Department of the Census

a quarter of Mississippi immigrants in 2005 lived in the Gulfport-Biloxi counties of Harrison and Jackson. The other large immigrant settlements were located in Hinds County, near the city of Jackson, and in DeSoto, close to Memphis, Tennessee. Altogether these four counties held almost 40 percent of the immigrants in the entire state. The Gulfport-Biloxi metropolitan area in 2006 was home to 8,309 foreign-born people (not shown in this table), or about 4 percent of the area's total population and 16 percent of all immigrants in Mississippi. The Gulf Coast region, with the greatest amount of industrial activity, had become the part of the state most likely to attract people from other locations around the world.

As Table 1.3 shows, the immigrants to Mississippi in the twenty-first century tended to be either very new arrivals or people who had been in the United States a long time. About 30 percent of the immigrants had come to the U.S. only since 2000 and 42 percent had been in this country more than twenty-one years. The census data shows marked differences between the older immigrants and the newer ones. Table 1.1 lists the home countries of the foreign-born population of Mississippi from 1850 to 2005. Among Mississippi immigrants who had been in this country over twenty years in 2005, about 90 percent were non-Hispanic (not shown in this table). The most commonly reported ancestry groups in 2005 were German (11 percent), English (10 percent), Vietnamese (7 percent), and Irish (6 percent). The Vietnamese, the only statistically prominent non-European group among these long-time immigrants, arrived during the refugee waves of the late 1970s and early 1980s. Among those who had been in the country five years or less, three-fourths were classified as Hispanic and a majority of these new arrivals (56 percent) were Mexican. As we will see below, when we look specifically at Mexican and other Latin American immigrants in Mississippi, this ethnic shift in the state's quickly growing migration became even more marked in the years

Table 1.3. Years in the United States among Mississippi Immigrants, 2005

	Percent of Immigrants
0–5 Years	29.7
6–10	12.3
11–15	7.8
16–20	8.5
21+ Years	41.6

Source: American Community Survey, 2005, U.S. Department of the Census

after 2005, as Latin Americans arrived along the Gulf Coast to rebuild after Hurricane Katrina.

The following section provides brief overviews of some of the major immigrant groups to Mississippi. Over the years, these groups have become established as part of the ethnic pattern of the state. Readers should consult the other chapters in this book for more detailed information about the ethnic groups created by this history of immigration.

A BRIEF HISTORY OF MISSISSIPPI IMMIGRANT GROUPS
Jewish Immigrants from Germany and Eastern Europe

As Table 1.1 shows, Germans constituted the largest segment of the foreign-born population of the state in 1850, and Germans continued to have a substantial representation throughout most of the following decades. This was partly a reflection of the fact that Germans in general were one of the largest national origin groups in the United States. However, it was also due to the migration of a particular group of people from German-speaking areas of Europe. Many of the immigrants to Mississippi from Germany or from German-speaking parts of Europe were Jews, who were among the large number of Jewish people arriving in the United States during the middle of the century. They were frequently motivated by the desire to flee oppression in the Austro-Hungarian Empire or in other regions.

German-speaking Jews sailed on ships to New Orleans between 1840 and 1860. Some then made the six-day trip up the Mississippi to Vicksburg, afterward moving out to other parts of the state. Jewish immigrants often went to Natchez, which had received some Jewish immigrants as early as the late 1700s, and which became a center of Mississippi Jewish life. Mississippi's first organized Jewish congregation, B'nai Israel, was established in 1840 and was soon followed by congregations in other towns (Young and Young 1992). The descendants of the nineteenth-century German Jews became members of native-born communities, so that by 1920 only 4 percent of Mississippi's immigrants were German. Proportions began to rise in 1930 and 1940 as the political situation in Europe worsened, particularly as the Nazis took power in Germany itself in 1933. Anti-Semitism in the Russian Empire and other parts of Eastern Europe also drove Russian and Eastern European Jews to settle in Mississippi, and they accounted for many of the Eastern Europeans shown in Table 1.1.

Irish

The Irish immigrants shown in Table 1.1 began to reach Mississippi during the 1840s and increased in numbers during the 1850s. As in other parts of the United States, the demand for manual laborers provided economic opportunities drawing these early foreign arrivals. These jobs involved building the nation's railroads—a common occupational concentration for early migrants from Ireland throughout the nation—and also building Mississippi's levees. One of the consequences of Irish immigration was the establishment of Catholic churches in many locations throughout a primarily Protestant state.

Chinese

Table 1.1 indicates that Chinese immigrants began to appear in Mississippi in numbers large enough to count as a recognizable group at the end of the nineteenth century. According to James W. Loewen, author of *The Mississippi Chinese: Between Black and White*, immigrants from China began to arrive in the Mississippi Delta during Reconstruction years. As newly freed slaves began trying to find better lives, many began attempting to assert their political rights and find their economic potential, moving from one plantation to another seeking better wages. In response, some plantation owners began a campaign to bring in Chinese laborers, believing that these workers would be easy to control. However, Chinese workers began moving out of the fields, often establishing small stores. The end of Reconstruction also reestablished white power over black Mississippians, ending the demand for Chinese manual labor and providing opportunities for the Chinese as members of a "middleman minority," purchasing wholesale goods from whites and selling these retail to a customer base that included many blacks.

Social and economic disruption in China following the 1910 revolution created motivation for Chinese people to leave their homeland, and they were drawn to locations that held existing Chinese networks. In his 1982 book *Lotus Among the Magnolias: The Mississippi Chinese*, Robert Seto Quan observed that the oldest Delta Chinese then living in the region had arrived between 1910 and 1930. Although there were few Chinese storeowners left by the end of the twentieth century, a third generation of Mississippi Delta Chinese, descended from the early entrepreneurial immigrants, still lived in the area.

At the end of the twentieth century, new Chinese immigrants began to arrive in Mississippi. In 1980, just over half the Chinese Mississippians in the U.S. Census had been born in the United States. By 2000, over 70 percent of the Chinese in the state were foreign-born. Over one-third of the state's Chinese immigrants had been in the country five years or less in 2000 and less than a quarter had lived in the United States more than fifteen years. In this respect, Mississippi resembled the rest of the United States, which had seen a sharp rise in Chinese immigration from 1980 onward.

The state's immigrant Chinese at the opening of the twenty-first century tended to be either highly skilled professionals, especially likely to be employed as educators, or workers in restaurants and food supply. In 2000, nearly one-fourth (23 percent) of foreign-born Chinese in Mississippi were managers, officials, and proprietors and over one in ten (11 percent) worked as professors and instructors. Nearly one in ten (9 percent) worked as cooks. Just over a fourth (26 percent) were in the education industry, while an almost equal percentage (22 percent) worked in eating and drinking places and 14 percent worked in food stores.

Lebanese (Christian Syrians)

Mississippians born in Lebanon (or the provinces of Ottoman Syria that later became Lebanon) began appearing in Mississippi as early as the 1880s. They often worked as peddlers, moving from place to place selling goods, saving money to establish small stores. Data from the 1910 through 1930 Public Use Microdata Series (PUMS) of the U.S. Census show nearly all employed people in Mississippi who were born in Syria or Lebanon working in food stores or general merchandise, and classify almost all of them as managers or proprietors, indicating a heavy concentration in self-employed entrepreneurship.

Italians

The great Italian wave of migration to the United States began at the end of the nineteenth century. As Table 1.1 shows, Mississippi's relatively small share of Italian settlement began to appear as the twentieth century opened. From 1910 to 1930, from close to one in three to about one in five foreign-born people in Mississippi were from Italy. The earliest of the Mississippi Italians, like the Chinese, came to the state during the years of Reconstruction, when plantation owners in the Delta were seeking replacements for black workers. In the early twentieth century, the growth of the seafood industries along the Gulf Coast began to draw Italians who were arriving at the port in New Orleans, particularly to Biloxi. Still, agricultural work remained a major occupational concentration for the state's early twentieth-century Italians. Data from the 1920 census, for example, give estimates of 31 percent of immigrants from Italy employed as farmers or tenant farmers (sharecroppers) and 39 percent as farm laborers working for wages.

By the end of the twentieth century, people of Italian ancestry were a native-born ethnic group in Mississippi. In 1980, only 5 percent of Mississippians who identified themselves as of Italian ancestry had been born outside of the United States and by 2000 this had gone down to only 1 percent. Mississippians who had been born in Italy were also highly acculturated by the end of the twentieth century: all Italian-born people in the state who appeared in the 2000 census either spoke English very well or spoke only English.

Vietnamese

The first Vietnamese refugees began to reach the United States in the spring of 1975, following the collapse of the South Vietnamese government. During the late 1970s and early 1980s, Vietnamese people began to move to the Mississippi Gulf Coast. Their settlement around Biloxi is usually traced to the efforts of Richard Gollott, owner of the Golden Gulf Seafood processing factory. Gollott had reportedly heard that Vietnamese workers were shucking oysters in New Orleans. Seeking low-wage manual laborers, he began to actively recruit in the growing New Orleans Vietnamese community. This type of work demanded little or no English ability, so the workers Gollott recruited were followed by others seeking employment in Gulf Coast seafood processing plants. As the Vietnamese settled in to the region, they began to move into the fishing and shrimping industry, and this became an ethnic niche business for them over the course of the 1980s.

The growing Vietnamese population frequently sought housing near the coast and in the eastern part of the East Biloxi peninsula in order to be near the harbors of Biloxi and within walking distance of the processing plants. Small Vietnamese-owned businesses grew up around East Biloxi and later in other nearby locations in order to sell foods and services to the ethnic community.

The Gulf Coast Vietnamese moved into a new ethnic occupational concentration in the 1990s, as casino gambling became a major industry. Following the acceptance of offshore gambling by the city of Biloxi in 1991, gambling became one of the most important economic activities of the region, and the Vietnamese often found jobs in or connected to the casinos. However, the casinos also encouraged the development of real estate along the coast and drove up housing prices in precisely the areas where the Vietnamese had settled.

Estimates from the 2000 U.S. Census show that nearly one out of every five (over 18 percent) employed Vietnamese people in Mississippi worked in eating and drinking places, indicating a heavy concentration in restaurant work. Another 13 percent worked in fisheries, although this was a decrease from the 18 percent of Mississippi Vietnamese who had worked in fisheries in 1990. Another 10 percent in 2000 worked in miscellaneous entertainment and recreation industries, reflecting the rapid rise of casinos along the Gulf Coast.

Mexicans and Other Latin Americans

As shown in Table 1.1, Mexicans were the fastest growing immigrant group in Mississippi during the early part of the twenty-first century. Numbers of people of Mexican origin in the state, both foreign-born and native-born, were reaching close to 50,000 by 2006. However, the numbers may be dramatic underestimates since many of the immigrants were reportedly undocumented and many native-born Mexican Americans could be children of undocumented immigrants.

In 2000, the Gulfport-Biloxi counties of Harrison and Jackson held the greatest numbers of people of Mexican origin, whether foreign-born or native-born, with 2,152 people classified as Mexican in Harrison County and 1,235 in Jackson County. Although the numbers are difficult to estimate, the Gulf Coast concentration of Mississippi Latin Americans increased greatly following Hurricane Katrina in August 2005.

The rapid growth of the Latino population of Mississippi, especially along the Gulf Coast, led to the establishment of the Mississippi Immigrant Rights Alliance (MIRA) in 2000. The organization, which has headquarters in the city of Jackson, defines its mission as providing services to immigrants, organizing, engaging in advocacy, and advancing the interests of both documented and undocumented immigrants in public education. In the field of education, MIRA has been involved in promoting bilingual education and in getting the Mississippi legislature to pass a bill guaranteeing the rights of children to enroll in public schools without regard to immigration status. The organization was especially active following Hurricane Katrina, with the dramatic rise in Latino workers involved in reconstruction work. In November 2005, MIRA submitted complaints on behalf of 150 immigrant workers who were not being compensated for the work they had done for subcontractors in restoring the Mississippi Gulf Coast. Some of the contractors, in turn, acknowledged that they had not paid their workers but said that they had been unable to meet payrolls on time because of problems in receiving payments from larger contractors. By the end of 2006, immigrant workers were able to obtain more than one million dollars in back wages.

Mississippi's Latino immigrants have tended to be concentrated in blue collar jobs, particularly in building trades or restaurant work. According to U.S. Census data on occupations, in 2000, 8 percent of the foreign-born Mexicans in Mississippi were classified as general machine operators, 7 percent as assemblers of electrical equipment, 7 percent as construction laborers, 5 percent as waiters or waitresses, 5 percent as cooks, and 4 percent as farmworkers. Considered by industry, construction was by far the greatest concentration of Latino workers, with 16 percent of Mexicans and over 12 percent of all Latinos employed in occupations in the construction industry. The concentration in construction became even greater, of course, with the influx of immigrant workers to rebuild the Gulf Coast following the 2005 hurricane.

Modern German and English Immigrants

Although the rise in Asian and Latino immigration presented a noticeable change in the foreign-born population of the state at the end of the twentieth and the beginning of the twenty-first century, a substantial portion of immigrants continued to be Europeans, particularly of German and

English background. Mississippi foreign-born people who gave their ethnicity as "German" had immigrated to the United States much earlier than Latinos or Asians: in 2000, fewer than 9 percent of the state's Germans had arrived within the previous five years and nearly two-thirds had been in the United States twenty years or more, although not necessarily in Mississippi. Accordingly, they were highly acclimated: over 90 percent spoke English very well and a majority (54 percent) spoke English in their homes.

Two-thirds of the immigrants who gave their ethnicity as "English" in 2000 had arrived in the U.S. more than twenty years earlier. Both the Germans and the English shown in the later years of Table 1.1, then, appear to have been acculturated and similar to native-born Americans in most respects.

SUMMARY

Mississippi has historically received less international immigration than other states, providing some basis to the stereotypical perception of the state as a conservative agrarian state. However, on closer examination, one can see that Mississippi has been affected by the immigration trends in the rest of the nation, and a variety of international immigrant groups have contributed to the development of the state's population. In the early years, Irish and German migrants tended to predominate. The Jewish population of Mississippi grew as a result of movement from Germany and as a consequence of people arriving from Eastern Europe.

Mississippi received some of the great wave of Southern European arrivals, especially from Italy, that came to the United States in the late nineteenth and early twentieth centuries. The state has also been part of the newest trend in international migration to the nation. About half of the legal immigrants to the United States have come from Latin America in recent years and about one-quarter from Asia. Accordingly, the Latin American and Asian populations of Mississippi have been expanding rapidly. Asians in the state date back to the arrival of the Chinese during the years after the Civil War, but their numbers became especially notable at the end of the twentieth century. The Vietnamese settled along the Mississippi Gulf Coast have been one of the most visible Asian groups.

Latin Americans, especially from Mexico, were drawn to Mississippi by economic opportunities during the last decade of the twentieth century. Following the devastation wrought by Hurricane Katrina in 2005, Latin

American labor has played an important part in the rebuilding of the Mississippi Gulf Coast. At the same time, the sudden spurt in growth of this new immigrant group has touched off controversies about undocumented migrants and about the treatment of foreign-born workers.

FOR FURTHER READING

Bankston, Carl L., III. 2007. "New People in the New South: An Overview of Southern Immigration." *Southern Cultures* 13(4): 24–44.
Loewen, James. 1971. *The Mississippi Chinese: Between Black and White*. Cambridge: Harvard University Press.
Quan, Robert Seto. 1982. *Lotus Among the Magnolias: The Mississippi Chinese*. Jackson: University Press of Mississippi.
Turitz, Leo E., and Evelyn Turitz. 1995. *Jews in Early Mississippi*. Jackson: University Press of Mississippi.

2

EUROPEAN MISSISSIPPIANS

—CELESTE RAY

America's colonial history is often told as an East Coast English experiment, yet the lands that now constitute the state of Mississippi were the scene of some of the earliest European exploration of North America (Cash 1992). Mississippi was actually a part of the West-Indies-looking, Creole society of the Gulf Coast long before it became a cornerstone state of the Deep South. A European history began there with contests between the French and Spanish who colonized the region for the better part of a century before Anglo arrivals. This chapter opens by outlining the successive endeavors and cultural legacies of the three colonial powers from 1541 until 1798 when Spain ceded the Natchez District to the United States. The second decade of the nineteenth century brought statehood and a variety of new European and European-descended immigrants to Mississippi. The essay considers how these arrivals created enduring cultural subregions. Through the lean postbellum years of the late nineteenth and early twentieth centuries, Mississippi attracted new immigrants from southern and eastern Europe. Today, in the first decade of the twenty-first century, the most common European origin for new Mississippians is Germany (as has been true for many decades of the state's history since the 1850s). What follows includes short historical overviews of each major European ethnic group that has helped shape the state. Mississippi is home to numerous European cultural festivals, and ongoing ethnic awareness is also a feature of each group overview.

COLONIAL MISSISSIPPI

Mississippi's prehistoric inhabitants arrived perhaps as early as thirteen thousand years ago. In the sixteenth century European explorers found a land well-peopled by a diversity of protostates and chiefdoms. Hernando de Soto was the first known European to visit Mississippi. His exact route is debated for several reasons (limited artifactual evidence, the subsequent mobility of the indigenous peoples with whom he made contact, and the mutability of place names over time), but he certainly traveled the current state from east to west. He crossed the Tombigbee River near Columbus and reached the Mississippi River in June of 1541. He had returned to the Mississippi River in 1542 when he caught a fever and died. His men secretly deposited Soto's body in the river somewhere between present-day Rosedale and Natchez, lest a grave site advertise Soto's death and embolden local inhabitants to attack what remained of his army. Under the leadership of Luis de Moscoso Alvarado, these men most likely spent the winter nearby before making their way to New Spain (Mexico).

The first Europeans to explore the length of the Mississippi River from the Great Lakes south were French Canadian explorer Louis Jolliet (also spelled Joliet, 1645–1700) and the French-born Jesuit priest Jacques Marquette (1637–1675). In 1673, they descended to a point between present-day Rosedale and Walls in Bolivar County. Near the mouth of the Arkansas River they received warning of hostile natives to the south and turned back just a little over four hundred miles short of reaching the Gulf of Mexico. They did learn, however, that the Mississippi's base level was near and not in the Pacific Ocean as had been hoped. Marquette drew maps on their expedition, and their journey spurred further exploration.[1]

In 1682, René-Robert Cavelier, Sieur de La Salle, became the first European to travel the Mississippi River to its mouth. He built a fort near the opening of the Arkansas River close to present-day Rosedale. He planted the Arms (national emblems) of France to claim the Mississippi valley for Louis XIV and did the same on arrival in the Delta. The area was then called La Louisiane as an administrative unit of New France which originally encompassed the Mississippi River Basin and included lands west to the Rockies, north to both the Appalachian Mountains and the Great Lakes, and south to the Gulf of Mexico. In 1683, La Salle sailed to France and obtained supplies, more men, and royal permission to govern the territory between the Gulf of Mexico and Lake Michigan. On his return in 1684 he became ill in the West Indies, sailed past the mouth of the Mississippi, and landed instead near the Brazos River in Texas. His ships were destroyed in a sudden storm and his disgruntled men killed him while going overland to find the Mississippi River.

Pierre Le Moyne, Sieur d'Iberville (1661–1706), began the first permanent European settlement in the lower Mississippi valley when in 1699

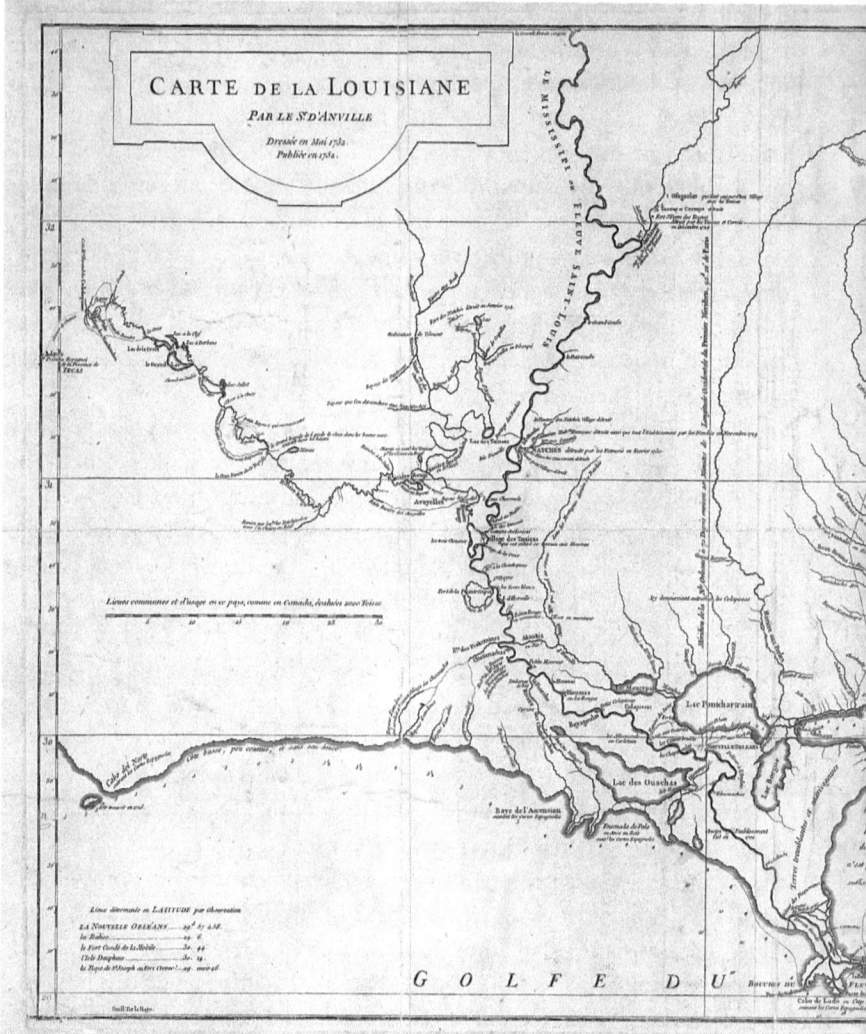

2.1. Map of La Louisiane, drawn by Jean Baptist Bourguignon d'Anville and published in Paris in 1752. Courtesy of the Mississippi Department of Archives and History.

he established Fort Maurepas (named to honor the French prime minister). On the eastern side of Biloxi Bay, the fort also became known as "Old Biloxi" and the settlement acquired its current name, Ocean Springs, in 1854 when George Austin established a convalescent resort utilizing local spring waters. When Iberville selected the site, the boundary between La Louisiane and Spanish Florida was at Perdido River near Pensacola. To prevent

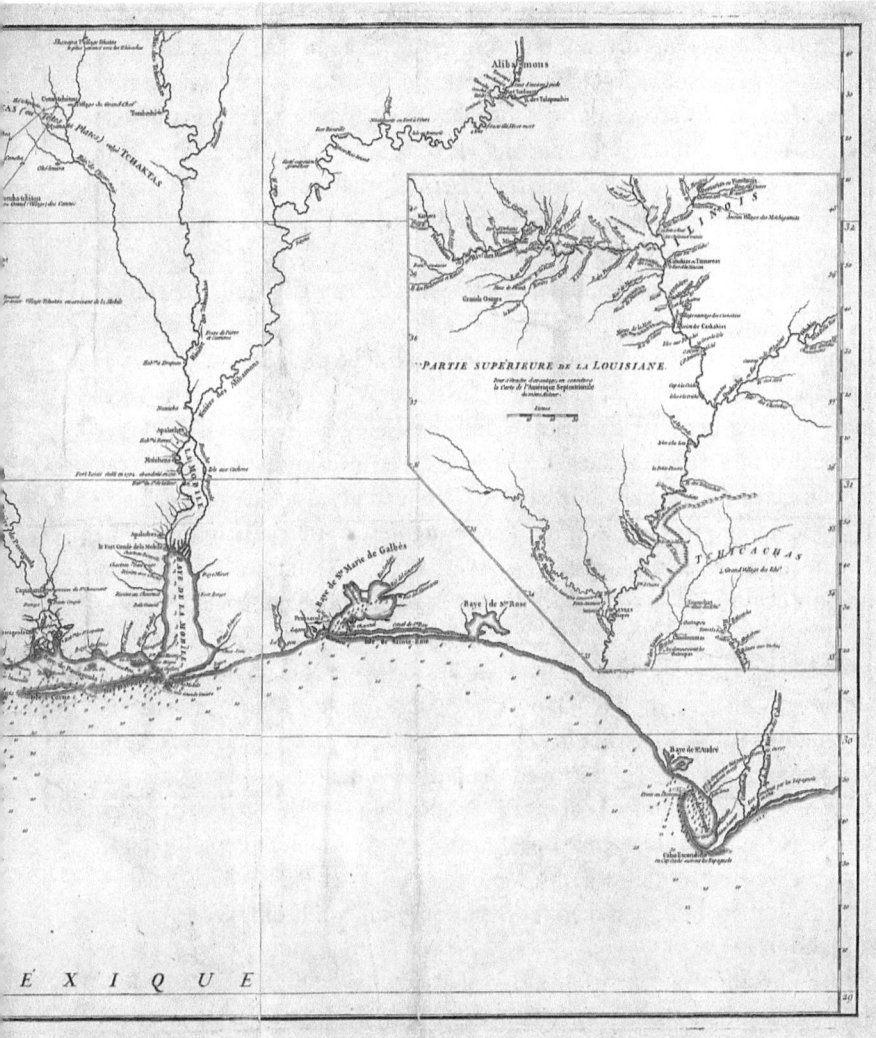

the encroachment of English and Spanish settlers, Iberville encouraged his younger brother Jean-Baptiste Le Moyne (1680–1767) to found Fort de la Boulaye fifty miles up the Mississippi in 1699 and, later, Fort Louis de la Mobile (or "Mobille") in what is now Alabama. Jean-Baptiste Le Moyne, Sieur de Bienville, lived nearly fifty years in La Louisiane and served as its governor several times beginning in 1701. Mobile became the administrative capital of La Louisiane, until this moved to Biloxi (or "Bilocci") across the bay from Old Biloxi (Fort Maurepas) in 1720 and a few years later to a new harbor town, La Nouvelle-Orléans (New Orleans) because of fears of hurricanes. Hurricane Katrina (2005) proved them right as that city remained on the "clean side" of the system (disaster was due to levees failing in the storm surge). Mississippi actually took the direct hit that destroyed portions of Old Biloxi (Ocean Springs), Biloxi, and the city of D'Iberville which took its name from Pierre Le Moyne, Sieur d'Iberville.[2]

An early French settlement that later became formative of Delta culture is Fort Rosalie, today's Natchez. Named for the wife of French naval minister Compte de Ponchartrain, it was built in 1716 by the indigenous Natchez as reparation for their defeat in the First Natchez War. Relations were never good for long between the French and the Natchez, and sporadic native attacks led to a Second Natchez War in 1722, a third in the following year, and climaxed in "the Rebellion of 1729" in which at least 250 European settlers, including pregnant women, were slaughtered. After this trauma, Fort Rosalie remained a post for French soldiers and a node in the deerskin trade, but only acquired new settlers with the arrival of British colonists.

While for most visitors to Mississippi, Vicksburg is now associated primarily with events of the Civil War, it too was part of the early French settlements. In 1719, the French built Fort Saint-Pierre on high bluffs overlooking the Yazoo River about ten miles north of present-day Vicksburg. Native American attacks destroyed the settlement about a decade later, but it again became a military post for the Spanish in 1790. The Spaniards called the site Nogales for its walnut trees, and when the Americans claimed it in 1798, they called it Walnut Hills. Methodist minister Newitt Vick began a settlement there in 1814 and, in 1825, the community officially incorporated as Vicksburg.[3]

The hostility of natives, the risk of yellow fever epidemics, and general isolation had made the current-day Mississippi portions of La Louisiane unattractive to settlers and investors. Estimates suggest that British colonists on the Atlantic coast outnumbered European settlers in La Louisiane by a hundred to one. Almost three-fifths of the settlers in what is now Mississippi came as soldiers, others as young men who were indentured servants. In 1717, John Law (1671–1729), a native of Edinburgh, Scotland, acquired a controlling interest in the Mississippi Company. Once a gambler, he had been appointed French minister of finance, and the French government granted him a monopoly on trade between the French colonies to foster economic growth and investment. Law's hyperbolic claims about the possibilities for wealth in La Louisiane led to speculation on the company's shares, followed immediately by a collapse in their value and Law's departure from France. Would-be immigrants were not encouraged.

The difficulties in recruiting labor led the French to introduce Senegambian and other West African slaves into La Louisiane in 1719. Some Swiss and German settlers also came to the colony.[4] To encourage French men to stay and to spur population growth, the king provided young French women a dowry of fifty *livres* to go to the colony for marriage. These were called *filles de la cassette* (coffin girls) for the small trunks in which they carried their provided trousseaus. Some Creole families still can trace distant grandmothers' arrivals to the Gulf Coast through this practice. Perhaps as many as 500 young women came to the frontier between about 1706 and 1720. Many of the 120 or so who came from 1719 to 1720 were orphans. These young women were distinct from the Regency era[5] banishment to the colony of another 200 women "of questionable reputation." Many in this latter group were sent abroad as a release from prison for such crimes as begging, homelessness, and prostitution. One such arrival, Marie-Anne Lescau, was the inspiration for the heroine in *Manon Lescaut* by French author Antoine-François Prévost (the Abbé Prévost). Prévost set the tale in both France and *La Louisiane*. Published in 1731, it was promptly banned as scandalous, so was of course very popular, and demonstrated a high level of romantic interest in life in New France.

In North America, the Seven Years' War was the French and Indian War (1756–1763), and its concluding Treaty of Paris required that France cede La Louisiane east of the Mississippi River (excepting New Orleans) to Great Britain. King Louis XV then sold the remainder of New France west of the Mississippi (and New Orleans) to Spain. Natchez became British. By 1770, English, Scottish, and Irish settlers were arriving and maintained relatively friendly relations with the nearby Chickasaw and Choctaw and other indigenous groups. British governors such as Peter Chester especially encouraged the arrival of Protestant settlers with free transport and large land grants. One of the most studied early planters was a Scot, William Dunbar, who kept a detailed journal from the early 1770s. Many Scots were itinerant merchants who established a base in Natchez.

Spain took advantage of the American Revolution to invade Natchez and surrounding areas in 1780 and treated British, French, German, and American colonists well (as long as they paid their taxes). Spain did not formally cede these territories to the United States until 1795 through the Treaty of San Lorenzo (although official orders to surrender the fort didn't reach the Spanish garrison at Natchez for three years). In April of 1798 the Adams administration created the Mississippi Territory and made Natchez its first capital. Mississippi became the twentieth state admitted to the Union in 1817. The capital moved back and forth between Natchez and Washington (just six miles to the east) until it moved in 1822 to Jackson. Natchez, however, located on the main transportation route of the Mississippi River, remained the economic heart of the new state through the century.

SPANISH, FRENCH, AND ENGLISH CULTURAL LEGACIES

While yielding the Natchez District to America in 1798, the Spanish continued to govern the old French settlements along the Gulf Coast (extending from Bay St. Louis to Pascagoula) from Mobile until 1813 (Coker 1972: 40). The Spanish introduced the growing of cotton, rice, indigo, and sugarcane as cash crops, as well as wheat, barley, and citrus fruits. They also brought cattle, horses, sheep, swine, and goats to Mississippi. In architectural traditions, the Spanish left stucco and tile building styles and the horseshoe arch. The raised cottage, suited to the subtropical climate, is typical of both the French- and Spanish-settled areas of the Mississippi valley and the Gulf Coast. Such houses, copied elsewhere in the state, employ a brick, aboveground basement (to avoid damp) and a wood-framed second story with a wraparound porch to keep the living space open to breezes (Cash 1992: 123). Some Spanish place names endure, particularly those later named for Hernando de Soto (DeSoto County and its city of Hernando). Additionally, later governing bodies continued to employ some Spanish laws, such as those related to property.

The French and Spanish both fostered Roman Catholicism. The French had established a Catholic diocese by 1722 in Natchez. The first known Protestant church in Mississippi had formed only in the 1770s after the departure of the French and with the arrival of new settlers from the eastern seaboard and Georgia, Virginia, and North Carolina. When the Spanish took over the area in 1780, they wished to catholicize the English settlers in the Natchez district. The Spanish government provided the area with English-speaking Irish priests from the Irish College of the University of Salamanca in 1787. While the Spanish crown continued to attract new settlers by allowing freedom of religion within the home, the only public churches permitted were Roman Catholic, and the priests were Irish. After 1792, all marriages and baptismal ceremonies for Protestants had to be performed by

Catholic priests (Holmes 1967: 169, 171–172). The end of French and Spanish rule brought a sharp decline in the Delta's Catholic communities until the arrival of Irish Catholics in Vicksburg and Natchez. These communities could not support a church until 1841 (most new immigrants were poor), but by 1850 there were over five thousand Catholics, both Irish and German, living in the diocese of Natchez alone (Wakeland 1983: 226–227).[6] Natchez was home to the largest number of Mississippi Catholics in the antebellum period. Mississippi's oldest Catholic building still in use is the neo-Gothic St. Mary's Basilica in Natchez, begun in 1842. The story of French, Spanish, and English settlers in Natchez is a featured part of the "Historic Natchez Pageant." During the annual Spring Pilgrimage tours of antebellum homes, more than two hundred costumed performers reenact high points of Natchez's history from settlement through the Civil War.

Like French Colonial Catholicism, many French contributions have become blended with later traditions so that their French origins are not always obvious. Bienville's "Black Code" of 1724 contributed to the later experience of slavery in Mississippi. More so than the Spanish, the French left an architectural legacy in their favoring of hipped roofs, casement windows, *galeries* (porches), and dormer windows. Bay St. Louis in coastal Hancock County retains some fine examples of the Creole cottage, an architectural style perhaps brought to the Louisiana coast first from the West Indies by French immigrants from Haiti.[7] Creole cottages were rectangular or square and varied in size, but on the Mississippi coast, their floor plans commonly included four rooms of equal size (each twelve to fourteen feet square) with a centrally located chimney and added-on "cabernets" (cabinets) at the rear corners which could be used for storage or for stairs to an attic sleeping space. Creole cottages often had gable roofs and were raised only one or two steps above the *banquette*, a low wall serving as a foundation (and a term which some locals use to refer to sidewalks). They usually had a front *galerie* and sometimes porches on all sides for ventilation (Oszuscik 1992: 148). Outbuildings could include *pigeonniers* where pigeons' eggs (or unsuspecting roosting pigeons) could be easily gathered. The French tended to concentrate settlements in villages, parcel land in ribbon lots, and share common pasturage, whereas the Americans who followed them dispersed in isolated farmsteads (Kniffen 1990: 16).

Enduring French influences are wide-ranging. The French introduced a particular style of boatbuilding which created the famed Biloxi schooner. Coastal Mississippians enjoy gravies and sauces made with a roux (a mix of butter, or oil, and flour) and the creolized hearty soup called gumbo.

Gumbo is based on the French *bouillabaisse* (fish stew), thickened with Native American filé powder (ground sassafras leaves) and sometimes featuring west African okra. Mardi Gras parades take place in numerous coastal towns including Biloxi, Picayune, Pass Christian, Gulfport, Long Beach, Waveland, Pascagoula, Diamondhead, D'Iberville, and Bay St. Louis. The French influence, of course, survives in place names including Amite (the county and the river), which the French named to express their reception by the indigenous people. Other place names documenting French influence include Bay St. Louis, Biloxi, D'Iberville, French Camp (a town in Choctaw County, named for a French settlement), Dedeaux, DeBuys, Beaumont, Beauregard, and Pearl (the town and the river), named for the pearl fisheries the French established there. The Creole Greenwood Leflore (1800–1865) also gives his name to both the town of Greenwood and the county of Leflore. He was an elected Choctaw chief who was the son of Rebecca Cavat (a Choctaw and niece of the famous Chief Pushmataha) and Louis LeFleur (a French explorer and trader). The French Gautier family gave their name to the town where they established a home in 1867.

Most recognizable of French legacies are, of course, the many surnames that endure especially in southern Mississippi, such as Bessey, Fournier, Gautreaux, Lambert, and Lemoine. In 2005, the U.S. Census Bureau cited 82,476 Mississippians as reporting French ancestry and another 7,044 as claiming French Canadian. While French populations do tend to be concentrated, residents of areas first settled by the French do not necessarily report the highest rates of French ancestry. Only 8 percent of Biloxi's population self-reports French descent (as many as claim English descent and 2 percent less than those who claim Irish descent). Today in Natchez, where the French settled Fort Rosalie, only 1.3 percent of the town's residents claimed French ancestry on the 2000 census, while over 9 percent claimed "American" origins, 7.4 percent English, 5.8 percent Irish, 3.6 percent German, 2.7 percent Scots-Irish, and 1.2 percent Scottish. However, the most significant and largest demographic group in the Gulf Coast's Hancock County (with its county seat at Bay St.Louis) is French (heavily Creole) at 17 percent. Ten percent of neighboring Pearl River County to the north claims French ancestry, as does 7 percent in Stone County to the east.

The English were so numerous and influential in southern history that they are sometimes wrongly dismissed as "the nonethnic norm," yet in 2000 only 8.7 percent of the U.S. population claimed English ancestry on the census (down from 13 percent in 1990). Of the three colonial powers in the South, the English do still have the largest number of descendants indicating an awareness of their ancestry. On both the 1980 and 1990 censuses, more residents of the South reported English heritage than did those of any other region. (Across the nation on the 2000 census, English was the third largest descent group after German and Irish). In 2005, the Census Bureau reported that 230,369 Mississippians considered themselves predominantly of English origins (fewer than considered themselves American or Irish, but more than considered themselves of German extraction).

The first evidence of English presence in the Mississippi valley was when René-Robert Cavelier, Sieur de La Salle, learned English traders had already made brief contact with Native Americans along the Mississippi River by 1682. After the Treaty of Paris in 1763, British troops occupied La Louisiane, and the government made generous land grants. The first of these went to British citizens who had fought in the French and Indian War. New settlers arrived from English colonies on the Atlantic through the 1760s and their numbers increased dramatically with an influx of Loyalists at the onset of the American Revolution (Greene et al. 1984: 71). Many built English "one bay" cottages (called "single pen" houses) which were simple one-room structures usually no larger than twenty feet by seventeen feet (Latham 1977: 7).[8] Under Spanish rule (1780–1798), the population remained predominantly British. The Americans who settled the area on the Spaniards' departure also brought English traditions. English influence on Mississippians is, of course, impossible to briefly summarize, even in the most reductionistic fashion. The distinctive English views of kinship and community, folkways (from foodways, ballads, and quilting to architecture and fox hunting), and legal, religious, and linguistic traditions have been manifestly formative in each of Mississippi's cultural subregions.

MISSISSIPPI CULTURE AREAS AND NINETEENTH-CENTURY IMMIGRATION

The early nineteenth century saw Mississippi's Americanization. Immigrants to the new state's existing settlements, and those who sought its frontier lands, came mainly from the eastern states. John James Audubon described their arrival in the early 1800s:

> They have crossed both the Carolinas, Georgia, and Alabama. They have been traveling from the beginning of May to that of September, and with heavy hearts they traverse the neighborhood of the

Mississippi. But now, arrived on the banks of the broad stream, they gaze in amazement on the dark, deep woods around them. Boats of various kinds they see gliding downward with the current, while others slowly ascend against it. A few inquiries are made at the nearest dwelling, and assisted by the inhabitants with their boats and canoes, they at once cross the river and select their place of habitation.... Thus are the vast frontiers of our country peopled.... (1831, 1917: 14–15)

This period of settlement shaped cultural divisions within the state that remain to some degree today. Mississippi has several geographic regions with corresponding differences in subsistence strategies and some accompanying variance in folk tradition. Mississippi encompasses a rich variety of landscapes, from the alluvial plain of the nation's mightiest river to the Appalachian foothills and coastal beaches. While Mississippians can distinguish a half-dozen or more cultural areas within the state, the four most easily recognizable to an outsider are: the Gulf Coast, the Northeastern Hills, the Delta, and the Piney Woods. Each has a different settlement and historical experience which has shaped the extent to which European identities and traditions endure.

The Gulf Coast is in some ways more similar to coastal Alabama and southern Louisiana than to interior Mississippi. The French settled the area of Ocean Springs before they settled either Mobile or New Orleans, and Biloxi was the first capital of La Louisiane. While the rest of Mississippi has been predominantly Protestant, the Gulf Coast has long been home to Roman Catholic communities (which attracted high rates of both Irish and German Catholic settlement). Commercial shrimping and the seafood industry have been central to the Gulf Coast economy, and Gulf Coast folklore and festivals relate to their importance. Cajuns, Slavonians, and Bohemians immigrated to this part of Mississippi to work as fishers and seafood processors. Gulfport is the state's second-largest city after Jackson and is county seat (with Biloxi) of Harrison County. With a population of 71,127, Gulfport's residents more strongly identify with ethnic roots than do Mississippians elsewhere. While 10.5 percent of residents claim an American ancestry, 8.6 percent cite Irish, 7.5 percent self-identify as German and the same percentage reports predominantly English heritage, 5.3 percent of the population are of French descent, and 3.1 percent of Italian.

The Northeastern Hills attracted settlers who predominantly worked mid-sized and small farms, especially situated in bottomlands along rivers and creeks. The area is often called the northern highlands, and the

Appalachian Regional Commission actually includes twenty-four of Mississippi's counties, from the Northeastern Hills to the North Central Hills, as part of Appalachia. Settlers were mainly of Scots-Irish, Irish, Scottish, Welsh, and English descent, and the majority came from other southern states (particularly Tennessee, North Carolina, northern Georgia, and Virginia). They arrived mostly between 1832 (with the Chickasaw Indian cession of Pontotoc) and the Civil War (Hudson 1928: x). In terms of folklore, subsistence, and world view, the Northeastern Hills have far more in common with other Appalachian foothills communities than with coastal or Delta Mississippi. Some ballads and Jack tales, considered Appalachian, endured into the mid-twentieth century in the area, as did moonshine production. Locals referred to stills as "kettles" and to their owners as "kettlemen." Few residents had slaves in the antebellum period and the Northeastern Hills remains the area with the fewest African American residents in the state. Electricity did not reach many settlements of the Northeastern Hills until provided in the 1930s by the Tennessee Valley Authority. Some traditions such as sacred harp singing are particularly strong in this region, especially in Calhoun County (Olson 1991).

In the northwest portion of the state is the Mississippi alluvial plain, known more commonly as the Delta. With its steamboat lore, grand plantations, and musical traditions, the Delta is what many people think of when they think of Mississippi. The Delta river lowlands, south of Vicksburg, were the most prosperous part of the state. The Natchez District, as it is called, was fully engaged in the plantation economy, growing especially tobacco and cotton. Originally settled by the French, then the British and Spanish and Americans, the Natchez district also drew many Irish and Germans. Although we do not see a plantation economy dominating the Old South until the second decade of the nineteenth century, the term "plantation" was used for the Natchez area even as early as the first portion of the eighteenth century (Kniffen 1990: 30). The most slaves lived in this district and African Americans still compose a high proportion of most county populations. The river widens north of Vicksburg, and recurrent flooding prevented the antebellum wealth found in the Natchez District from extending very far in that direction. In the 1870s however, levee construction began in earnest and drew a much larger population. Italians were one of the most significant groups to arrive in the late nineteenth century. Today, commercial fishing, catfish farming, and tourism are more economically significant than cotton.

The Piney Woods (sometimes called the Pine Hills) gained its name for abundant longleaf pines. Few European Americans settled there before the

Civil War and most were herders, especially tending cattle and pigs. Robert Baxter has noted that the early cattle in the area, called "black cattle," were largely descended from stock brought by French settlers and that cattle raising followed French practices of "running cattle on shares" or ribbon plots with extensive rules about using open range lands for grazing (1976: 4, 6). There were very few slaves in the area. Most African Americans came after the war to work in the lumber industry's sawmills or in building railroads. The rebuilding necessitated by the Civil War brought a lumber boom as did a larger market created by World War I. Exploitation of the pine forests brought prosperity to the area although today the poultry industry is more significant (Napier 1986: 21). The population is still predominantly of Scots-Irish, Anglo-American, or Irish-American descent. Sacred harp singing is one of many enduring traditions among these Mississippians (Downey 1986: 92). The Piney Woods are home to Mennonite and German settlements. Cajuns and Greeks have also brought their distinctive traditions to the southernmost counties.

POSTBELLUM IMMIGRATION

America experienced a new phase of immigration between the 1880s and the 1920s. Immigrants from southern and eastern Europe, who were Catholic or Jewish and from rural agrarian backgrounds, replaced the primarily northern and western European immigrants of Protestant and largely urban environments who had characterized immigration in the first portion of the nineteenth century. However, few immigrants came to the war-devastated South; the vast majority chose the industrial urban areas of the North or the farmlands of the Midwest and West. Mississippi received even fewer immigrants than other southern states, but small communities of Greeks, Italians, Irish, and Slavonians did form. These new immigrants settled on one side of a color line, but did not encounter the organized nativism that immigrants did in the North at the time. In fact, local governments were eager to attract immigrants with new ideas for industry and also workers to take up occupations once performed by enslaved laborers. In the 1880s, the Mississippi Board of Immigration and Agriculture issued the *Hand-Book of Mississippi*, of which thirty thousand copies were printed in English, fifteen thousand in German, and five thousand in Swedish. Campaigns also specifically sought to recruit Italian peasants as laborers for factory and farm work. By 1890, although the foreign-born population of Germans and Swedes had actually declined, the Italians had answered the call in significant numbers (Bettersworth 1959: 348). These newcomers to the postwar South started fresh in a region with the lowest standard of living in the nation.

In 1936, famed regionalist Howard Odum published *Southern Regions of the United States*, in which he analyzed social and demographic characteristics of the South compared with other regions. Odum outlined great disparities between Mississippi and the rest of the U.S. that lessened the state's appeal to new immigrants. At the time Odum wrote his report, the economic legacy of the Civil War meant that the average gross income per farm per year in the 1920s in the southern states was half or less (under fifteen hundred dollars) than that of Iowa, North Dakota, Wyoming, Nebraska, Montana, California, Nevada or Arizona. Sixty-five years after the Civil War, southern farms were the smallest in the nation—most averaging fewer than 75 acres. Georgia and Florida had a slightly higher average closer to 75–100, but only Texas had farms closer in size to those of the western and northwest central states with 150–300 acres; this partly explains why Texas attracted a higher number of immigrants in the postwar period, including Czechs, Bohemians, and Italians. Texas was more like Mississippi and the rest of the South, in that under 10 percent of farms had tractors and the percentage of its population living on farms (40 percent or more) was the greatest in the country. The South then had high percentages of its population living on the smallest and most underequipped farms and making the lowest incomes from their farms in the nation. Odum noted that between 50 and 90 percent of southern children received inadequate diets, leading to rickets, anemia, and the carious teeth found in close to 50 percent of the schoolchildren examined. Such conditions were not what motivated immigrants to cross an ocean, and kept European immigration to the region dramatically low (cf. Bankston, this volume).

Odum calculated that "foreign-born whites" constituted at least 17.5 percent of the population of the Northeast and between 12.5 and 17.5 percent of the populations of states such as California, Nevada, Washington, and those of the upper Midwest, but that less than 2.5 percent of the white population of the southern states was foreign-born in 1930. Mississippi had just over 9,000 foreign-born persons in 1910 (compared with, for example, over 57,000 in West Virginia, almost 329,000 in Connecticut, 543,010 in Minnesota, 1,202,560 in Illinois, and 1,438,719 in Pennsylvania in the same year). Only South Carolina, at 6,054, and North Carolina, at 5,942, had fewer foreign-born residents than Mississippi.[9] By 1940, Mississippi had only 5,988 foreign-born residents, the second-lowest figure in the nation after South Carolina with 4,915.[10] The discrepancies Odum calculated still hold. Few European immigrants now arrive in the state and most are seeking an inexpensive place to retire. The gulf states of Louisiana, Mississippi, and Alabama remain the poorest stretch of major coastline in the United States. As of 2004, 19.3 percent of the population of Mississippi was living below the poverty line (compared with a national average of 12.7 percent). Although Mississippi currently has the highest increase in immigration of any state, this is relative to the decades through which it attracted few immigrants rather than relative to the numbers of immigrants now arriving in other states. The demographic changes now sweeping the South are as dramatic as the colonial transitions of the seventeenth century.[11]

What do these trends mean for current ethnic awareness in Mississippi? Native Mississippians of European descent often have centuries-deep familial roots in the South and their strong identification with the region and with Mississippi means they are less likely to consider themselves ethnic than European Americans elsewhere. Over 95 percent of European American Mississippians are natives to the state. To be sure, there are many Mississippians that care fervently about their ancestry and cultural heritage (see below). The Gulf Coast counties report the highest percentages of several European ancestries in the state. However (at least on the U.S. Census), Mississippians' self-identification with the European ethnic groups considered largest in the country is far below the national average. Mississippians (of all colors) are simply some of the most American of Americans.

The tremendous distress and disruption of the Civil War hastened the loss of ethnic distinctiveness for many groups as regional loyalties reshaped ethnic identities as southern identities. In the twentieth century, Mississippians became some of the most patriotic Americans, supplying its young to the military on a per capita ratio far exceeding other states. Today, 14 percent of Mississippians report "American" for ancestry on the U.S. Census, one of the highest rates in the nation (only Texas, Kentucky, Tennessee, and Arkansas surpass Mississippi in this demographic). The U.S. Census does not indicate a generational or date range for answering its ancestry question. That, coupled with the relative lack of new immigrants to the South after the Civil War, explains in part why southern states have the highest numbers of persons reporting their ancestry as "United States" or "American." More Mississippians identified as being of American descent than those who claimed descent from a European ethnic group (Irish, 7 percent; English 6 percent; German 4.5 percent).

Mississippi has a total population of only 2,900,000 (at least one-half million persons smaller than the metropolitan area of Dallas, Texas). Percentages of the Mississippi population identifying as any particular ethnic group should be kept in perspective. Census data on ethnicity can also be misleading as the census ancestry question does not measure to what extent a person may be aware of ancestral origins. For example, a person reporting "French," may be vaguely aware of French descent through surnames, or may be actively involved in French associations and have compiled detailed genealogies or speak the French language. Census figures are also often estimates from samples and may skew the actual size of ethnic groups. Although the 2000 census recorded less than 2 percent of Mississippi's population as foreign-born (the smallest percentage of any state other than West Virginia), the Pew Hispanic Center estimated there might be as many as 50,000 illegal aliens living in Mississippi as of 2005.[12] Mississippi's population increased by 10.7 percent (approximately 27,000 persons) between 1990 and 2000, and over 2 percent between 2000 and 2006. Though considered one of the smallest in the nation, the state's foreign-born population actually almost doubled during the 1990s alone. Clearly Mississippi's demographics are changing more rapidly than they have since colonial times and population numbers are growing at the fastest rate since the "boom times" of the 1830s.

What follows are brief sketches of the major European groups to have been part of Mississippi's cultural landscape since early statehood and those who chose to make a new home in Mississippi's subregions at a time when the state received few immigrants. (The colonial arrival of Sephardic Jews and the nineteenth century settlement of Jews from Germany are considered in another chapter.)

IRISH AND SCOTS-IRISH

In the colonial era, the Irish played an important role in the Catholic history of Mississippi. As noted, the Spanish colonial government purposely sought English-speaking Irish priests to help convert the British settlers of the Natchez area. Later, Irish Catholics organized new parishes elsewhere (often in conjunction with Catholic Germans), including that in Hattiesburg (1890) centered on the Sacred Heart Church. In the early nineteenth century increasing numbers of Protestant Scots-Irish arrived from elsewhere in the United States and settled in all of the subregions of Mississippi,

2.2. Stanton Hall in Natchez, which today is home of the Natchez pilgrimage, was originally named "Belfast" by its builder, Frederick Stanton, who had immigrated to Mississippi from Ireland. Courtesy of the Mississippi Department of Archives and History.

while the newly immigrating Catholic Irish tended to come first to the Gulf Coast and the Natchez District where Catholicism was already established. Both groups eventually settled across the state. While they had distinct traditions, the friction that existed between the two groups elsewhere in the country did not characterize their experience in Mississippi.

In the Northeast, prejudice against the Catholic Irish caused immigrants to turn inward and resist assimilation. Only an estimated 10 percent of Irish immigrants to the U.S. settled south of the Mason-Dixon Line. Arriving in smaller numbers, never dominating the population of any area and never challenging the status quo, they had a greater opportunity for acceptance in the South and for social mobility despite an established class system. In the antebellum South they were particularly accepted for their contributions to the urban work force, their work in 1850s railroad construction, and their willingness to take on potentially high-mortality work deemed too dangerous for slaves. Many Irish died building canals and levees through swamp lands and along the Mississippi River, succumbing to yellow fever, malaria, cholera, or dysentery. Many Irish came without a skill. For example, in Vicksburg in 1850, Irish men and women constituted 44 percent of all foreign-born workers, but 64 percent of those were doing unskilled labor (Morris 1995: 117). However, other immigrant Irish and Irish American professionals (both Protestant and Catholic) brought valued skills to Mississippi, became quite prosperous, and, unlike elsewhere in the United States, mixed freely in society and in business with each other and with the Scots-Irish.

While in British North America (Canada) the Ulster Scots were simply known as "Irish," in the United States they became "Scots-Irish." The ethnonymn "Scotch-Irish" (Scots-Irish) was first employed to distinguish Patriot Ulster Scots from Highland Scots (mostly Loyalists) in the American Revolution and later to distinguish between Protestant Scots who had lived in Ulster and the Catholic "Famine Irish." In the colonial South, the Ulster Scots (Scots-Irish) and the Highland Scots had divergent settlement patterns and occupations. The Highland Scots arrived with their own language (Gaelic) and maintained a separate ethnic identify for some time. The Scots-Irish were quicker to assimilate within the Anglo mainstream, although in the South they also did associate with Catholic Irish in a way Scots-Irish in the North did not. In Mississippi, particularly in Natchez, Protestant Irish from Ulster and from the south of Ireland, and their descendants, associated regularly with Catholic Irish and their descendants. David Gleeson tells us that Irish Catholics in the antebellum South accepted many Irish American Protestants as truly Irish and bonded on both this and a southern identity (2006: 81–82; see also Nolan 1992). Seeking parallels between their southern experience and their Irish history, Irish immigrants' ethnic activities in the nineteenth century (fund-raisers, parades, and speeches delivered at fraternal associations) placed a celebration of Irishness firmly within a southern context.

The Irish were quick to organize Hibernian societies and other immigrant-aid organizations. The Mississippi Hibernian Society was founded in

2.3. The St. Patrick's Day Parade in Jackson now has thousands who attend and several hundred participants. Rather than purity, however, such ethnic parades often display how identity is reimagined or given new contexts. In 2011, the parade blended traditional nods toward Irish heritage with traditional Mississippi or regional culture. A green bus (top) carries signs of the blues "crossroads," the intersections of Highways 61 and 49 in the Delta. The Irish paraders (bottom) might sport shamrocks, wear green tennis shoes, and carry shillelaghs with green, orange, and white carnations, but they are marching to a traditional New Orleans African American brass band. Photos by Natalie Maynor.

1826 (less than a decade after Mississippi became a state). Other branches followed in Natchez and on the Gulf Coast. Mississippi Hibernian Societies tended to be more inclusive (accepting Catholic and Protestant Irish and Scots-Irish) than were northeastern branches of that society, so that the Orange Order (an explicitly Protestant fraternity) found very little support in the South while it prospered in Canada and for a time in conjunction with the Know-Nothing Party in the northern United States (Gleeson 89). In the year after the Mississippi Hibernian Society's founding, George W. Smyth gave the St. Patrick's Day address. Smyth was a graduate of Trinity College, Dublin, and had been on the Mississippi Supreme Court in its early statehood. His address noted the positive experience of Irish immigrants to Mississippi. The Natchez Hibernian Society has been in existence since at least 1844 and, then dominated by more prosperous citizens, began St. Patrick's Day celebrations in a local hotel in that decade. Working-class Irish also celebrated, but in more public venues.

The popularity of the St. Patrick's Day parade in Jackson (introduced only in 1982) is partly due to the Sweet Potato Queens. Self-described "fallen belles," wearing flowing red wigs, majorette boots, and sequined green dresses preposterously overstuffed to emphasize curvaceousness, the Queens occupy the featured float and toss sweet potatoes to spectators along the fourteen city blocks of the parade route. While Jackson's main event feels more like Mardi Gras than a saint's feast day, Natchez has a "krewe" to lead its parade, but sticks a little closer to the story. A member of Krewe of Killarney annually dresses as St. Patrick. As the saint rid Ireland of snakes in legend, the krewe's St. Patrick leads a procession down Main Street to the city's bluff and symbolically drives any snakes in his path into the Mississippi River.

Irish surnames are common in Mississippi's population (especially in the south and west of the state), and Irish place names dot the landscape, including Shannon, Boyle, and Limerick. The county of Coahoma has a town named Dublin. Carrollton County is named for Irish American Charles Carroll of Carrollton (1737–1832) who was the only Catholic and longest-lived signer of the Declaration of Independence. His Irish grandfather came to America in 1659. Charles Carroll was born in Maryland, but inspired place names across the country. Of Irish descent, Gerard Chittocque Brandon (1788–1850), was the first native Mississippian to become his state's governor. Brandon, the county seat of Rankin County, is named for him.

On the 2000 census, 10.8 percent of Americans self-identified as Irish and were the second-largest ancestry group nationally. In 2000, 6.9 percent of Mississippians identified Irish ancestry on the census (with common surnames including Doherty, Kelly, McGee, Murphy, and O'Donnell). While this was the third-largest reported ancestry group in Mississippi (the first two being African American and American), it was actually the lowest percentage reporting Irish ancestry in the southern states. Yet there are communities such as the small town of Bassfield in south-central Mississippi (Jefferson Davis County) where more people identify with Irish ancestry than with any other. The community grew around St. Peter's Catholic Church founded by 1850s immigrant Michael O'Rourke and other Irish natives. The church opened a parochial school in 1927 which the Sisters of Mercy ran for three decades. Twenty percent of Bassfield's 330 residents self-identify as Irish American (the largest ancestry group in town), 9 percent identify as Scots-Irish, and 3 percent as Scottish. In terms of counties, Prentiss and DeSoto each claimed 15 percent Irish, Choctaw County reported 14 percent, Smith in the central part of the state and Tishomingo in the far north both recorded 13 percent. Both Stone and Hancock counties in the south, Itawamba in the north, and centrally located Rankin (with a county seat named Brandon) noted 12 percent of their populations as Irish-derived. All of these counties rank above the national average for Irish ancestry. Newton, Attala, Lee, and Lamar counties report 11 percent, and the southern counties of Pearl River, Forrest, and Jones each report 10 percent as do Neshoba and Carroll counties in central Mississippi and Alcorn in the northern fringe of the state. Close to ten other counties report at least 9 percent Irish.[13]

Only 1.9 percent of Mississippians reported Scots-Irish ancestry despite the fact that it is actually one of the most common among European Americans. In the 1990 census, 40 percent of Americans reporting Scots-Irish ancestry resided in the southern states and many Scots-Irish immigrated to Mississippi from Tennessee, Kentucky, Virginia, Georgia, and the Carolinas. While the Scots-Irish brought folklore, musical, architectural, and religious traditions all their own, they assimilated more quickly to Anglo norms than did Gaelic-speaking Scottish Highlanders. What crossed the Atlantic and became part of their new identity related more to worldview, subsistence strategies, and farming techniques—not the artifactual material culture of Highlanders that has become emblematic as "Scottish" in heritage celebrations today. Perhaps for this reason, those of Scots-Irish descent retained less a sense of distinctive ethnic identity and self-reporting is subsequently low. Many Scots-Irish active in the Scottish heritage revival since the 1950s tend to embrace Highland shibboleths.

SCOTS

Scottish immigrants to the South were members of three distinct ethnic groups: Highland Scots, Lowland Scots, and the Scots-Irish (Ulster Scots) who had settled in Northern Ireland before immigrating to America. In 1790, America's first census identified persons of Scottish birth or descent as composing 8.3 percent of the new nation's population. The South had the largest percentage of residents with Scottish origins, with Georgia, South Carolina, and North Carolina having the highest numbers. North Carolina's Cape Fear River Valley had especially attracted Highlanders who began arriving in large numbers in the early 1730s, experienced a peak of immigration in the 1760s, but continued to arrive until the eve of the American Revolution. Second- and third-generation descendants of Cape Fear River Valley Highlanders pioneered settlement in Alabama, Tennessee, and Mississippi. Some came to the south of the state—particularly Greene County. Early residents included Laughlin McCoy and John McRae, both of whom were members of the Constitutional Convention in 1817. While North Carolina had earned the epithet "land of the God-blessed Macs," so too was Greene County peopled by an array of Scots and Scots-Irish by the names of McDuffey, McCaskill, McPherson, McLeod, McInnis, McKay, McAfee, and McLean. Fergusons, Nicholsons, and Ramseys also abounded. The Highlanders retained their Gaelic language as they had in North Carolina (Hunter 1994: 47). Early settlers of Wayne County (to the north of Greene) included McRaes, McArthurs, McDougalds, McLaughlins, McDaniels, McDonalds, and McLaurins. Many of these Highlanders came from Robeson and Moore counties in North Carolina, and settled together on the banks of Buckatunna Creek and along the Chickasawhay River. They quickly established a Presbyterian Church and the first schoolhouse in the county (in which Gaelic was the language of instruction until the 1820s). For a time, as they had been in North Carolina, the "Scots," as they still considered themselves, were inward looking and endogamous and even referred to the Americans who settled around them as "buckskins" (Wilkins 1902: 263).

After the 1803 Louisiana Purchase, land in the west of present-day Mississippi became available to Americans, and Cape Fear Highlanders headed to the Natchez District (Buie 1983: 25). At least four families arrived via the Mississippi River just a year after the Louisiana Purchase (Torreys, Curries, and Willises). Those who followed them made the dangerous journey from North Carolina to Nashville, Tennessee, and cut their way through the canebrakes down the Natchez Trace. Among them were Buies, Camerons, Carmichaels, Gilchrists, Galbreaths, McCormicks, McCorveys, McAlpines, McIntyres, McLaurins, McPhersons, Rays, Watsons, and Wilkersons. So many came that their new community in Jefferson County became known as "the Scotch Settlement." In 1806 they founded a Presbyterian church—Union Church (so called as Methodists also worshipped there). The first ministers delivered sermons in English and Gaelic into the 1830s. Some Cape Fear River Valley Scots settled in Amite County in the eighteen teens and others continued to arrive in Mississippi, to Copiah County for example, into the 1840s and 1850s—trying to settle together in the new state whenever possible. While Gaelic did not endure for more than a few generations, the Scottish identity of the community remained for more than a century. Some immigrants from North Carolina who were heading further west to Arkansas and Texas would stop at the Jefferson County Scotch Settlement into the 1850s either because they had relatives there or knew they could claim hospitality and accommodation there because of Cape Fear River Valley links.

Mississippi boasts many Scottish place names. A group of Scottish settlers in Jasper County began the town of Montrose (four miles northeast of Louin) in the 1830s. By 1841, the Scottish emphasis on education had led to the establishment of the Montrose Academy (meant to establish the town as the intellectual center of Jasper County). Much later, a neighboring community came to be called Gilchrist after the Scottish family who settled it. Monroe County's Aberdeen is named for the city on Scotland's eastern coast. Ben Lomond, a village in Issaquena County, takes its name from the southernmost Munro (a mountain over three thousand feet in height) in the Scottish Highlands. Both Washington and Issaquena counties have towns named Glen Allan. Both Neshoba and Leake counties have towns called Edinburg (for Edinburgh). Tunica County has the town of Dundee and Monroe County has Aberdeen. Lowndes and Monroe counties have towns called Caledonia (the Latin name for Scotland also popular in romantic literature of the eighteenth and nineteenth centuries). Mississippi also has two towns called Melrose (in Jones and Panola counties) and too many towns beginning with "Mc" to list. Mississippians, like most antebellum southerners, were fans of the writings of Sir Walter Scott. The towns of Waverly in both Clay and Lowndes counties were named for Scott's famous novels as was Waverley plantation (built 1852) in West Point. The plantations and mansions of Melrose, Montrose, Dunvegan, Monmouth, and Dunleith, to name just a few, also received their names from Sir Walter's appreciative readers.

The international surge of interest in things Celtic has not bypassed Mississippi. The Celtic Heritage Society formed in 1992 in Jackson as a civic and educational nonprofit organization. Its mission is to encourage the study of Celtic languages and histories of Celtic lands in addition to the preservation and performance of music, dance, and other expressive culture from Ireland, Scotland, Wales, Brittany, Cornwall, and the Isle of Man. The society sponsors several *ceilidhs* (gatherings) each year in addition to workshops on Irish dance, Gaelic language, and genealogy. The biggest event of the year is "CelticFest Mississippi" (in its seventeenth year in 2008). The annual three-day event is open to the public and takes place at the Mississippi Agriculture and Forestry Museum. The program features six stages for musical and dance performances, vendors of Celtic-themed books, artwork, and food, and multiple workshop areas (for quick lessons in Irish step or Scottish country dancing, basic greetings in Irish Gaelic, or lectures on history and Celtic art). A "kirkin' of the tartan" takes place on the Sunday of the festival weekend. A kirkin' is a church service that began during World War II, but has come to refer to any Christian worship event (in or out of doors) at which participants wear or carry their clan tartan in recognition of their cultural and spiritual heritage. The Highlands & Islands Association of Gulfport will sponsor its twenty-fifth annual Scottish Games in November of 2010. Locals and participants from across the country compete in Scottish athletics (including caber tossing, hammer throwing, and the stone putt) as well as in Highlands dancing, bagpiping, and singing. Organizers expanded the program to include performances and displays related to the expressive arts of all Celtic cultures as the Mississippi Gulf Coast Highland Games & Celtic Festival. The association holds several *ceilidhs* through the year, participates in Mardi Gras parades along the coast in which members wear their clan tartans, and gathers in celebration of National Tartan Day on April 6. Many Presbyterian churches across Mississippi hold kirkin's of the tartan, and others annually recognize their Scottish roots at church homecomings with bagpipers at the dinner on the grounds or the performance of a Gaelic hymn in the service.

ETHNIC PROTESTANTS

Many of the ethnic Protestants of Mississippi are descendants of Anabaptists whose sixteenth-century movement was particularly pronounced in the Netherlands, Germany, Switzerland, and what is now the Czech

Republic. Among the first Protestants to embrace believer's baptism (considered by some to be heretical at the time), Anabaptists were heavily persecuted in the sixteenth and seventeenth centuries. They, and their descendant groups, believe in the strict separation of church and state so that no believer can hold a governmental post. They are pacifists and do not permit any member to bear arms or join the military. Among the variety of groups which developed from the Anabaptist tradition, Mennonites, Swartzentruber Amish, and Old Order German Baptists reside in Mississippi.

Late in 1920, opposition to the proposed migration of forty thousand Canadian Mennonites to southern Mississippi made the *New York Times*. Mennonites were then considered "undesirables," in part because they had been conscientious objectors during World War I and spoke German. Members of the Mississippi Division of the American Legion complained that the Mennonites had stayed at home "while Canada was being bled white in the trenches," and that they were "unfit to live on American soil." In one of history's ironies, after Hurricane Katrina some eighty-five years later, volunteers in the Mennonite Disaster Service from across the country and Canada came to construct twenty-five new homes in the Pass Christian area. Mennonites did arrive in significant numbers in the areas of the Tombigbee Prairie west of the Northeastern Hills, the Flatwoods, and the North Central Hills. A grouping of Mennonite churches spans the area between Meridian, Macon, West Point, Choctaw, and Philadelphia. (There is also a Mennonite Church in Jackson and a Gulfhaven Mennonite Church in Gulfport.) A Mennonite retreat and recreational center is in Meridian, the 115-acre Pine Lake Fellowship Camp, which is owned and operated by the Gulf States Mennonite Conference. Mennonites also moved to Walthall County in the south of the state's Piney Woods in the 1960s. About fifteen families there, and just over the line in Marion County, are engaged in dairy and poultry farming and together attend the Darbun Mennonite Church (a conservative rather than Old Order church).

Since the mid-twentieth century, Mississippi has also been home to a few settlements of Swartzentruber Amish (an ultraconservative branch of the Old Order Amish formed in 1917). Like other Old Order groups, they do not use indoor plumbing or electricity, but also have rejected the use of the usual bright orange triangle on the back of their buggies (to indicate a slow-moving vehicle) as it is deemed "too worldly." Their buggies may employ lanterns rather than any battery-powered lights. While many Amish communities take pride in well-kept farms, Swartzentrubers consider a trim yard a sign of preoccupation with appearances and do not even use gravel on their drives. Men wear a distinctive bob-style haircut. Women wear their dresses nearly to the ground, and clothing for both sexes is always in somber colors (navy and gray) rather than bright blues.

Old Order German Baptists settled in the small community of Hot Coffee in Covington County about twenty-five years ago. Locals suggest that the area gained its name from an 1870 inn that offered coffee to travelers; the Old Order German Baptists (sometimes called Dunkers) derive from the Schwarzenau Brethren who organized in 1708. Many immigrated to America in the second two decades of the eighteenth century to escape religious intolerance. They settled in the Delaware Valley, the Carolinas, Virginia, and Maryland (from which Hot Coffee's Old Order German Baptists arrived). While sporting bushy beards, men forego moustaches. At the time of Anabaptist persecution in Europe, cavalry officers cultivated large, showy ones as part of their identity, so rejection of the moustache became a symbol of renouncing violence. Male apparel, called "the garb," is also plain and is dark or light blue with a broad-brimmed hat for out-of-doors. Women's clothing consists of "the trinity": 1) a close-fitting white cap, 2) an ankle-length dress with long sleeves, and 3) a "shawl" (a short capelike overgarment of material matching the dress). Some are engaged in growing blueberries, one of Covington County's main crops, and others run specialty businesses promoted by the county chamber of commerce to tourists. Old Order members offer baskets, furniture handcrafted by the Dill family, and satisfying country fare with homemade pies at Martha's Kitchen, run by the Diehl family. The Diehls were part of a *National Geographic* feature on Hot Coffee by Peter Gwin and Bob Sacha. Their daughter Martha (for whom they named their restaurant) plays an important role in local transport. Despite the Old Order German Baptists' rejection of car ownership, electricity, and telephones, Martha Diehl purchased and runs a Greyhound franchise in neighboring Mt. Olive. Her office is electricity- and computer-free, so passengers wishing to book a bus trip send her requests for tickets by mail.

CAJUNS

Cajuns are descendants of Catholic French Acadians who settled predominantly in French Louisiana, but also coastal Mississippi, after being expelled by the British from the eighteenth-century Canadian Maritimes. Their story caught the nation's imagination in Henry Wadsworth Longfellow's

Evangeline (1847). Cajuns are known simply as "French" in Biloxi. Most Cajuns came to Biloxi from Louisiana for work during the World War I period. Their benevolent and social organization is named the Fleur de Lis, but most locals just call it the French Club. The organization's building was destroyed in Hurricane Katrina, but the club endures. Membership is open to anyone descended from the early French settlers and to anyone with Cajun ancestry (and spouses of the same) (Schmidt 1995). Cajun cuisine is famed for spicy dishes, such as dirty rice and gumbo, and other recipes derived from local resources such as boudin (Cajun sausage) and bouille (cane syrup pie). During Lent, when Catholics cannot eat meat on Fridays, the French Club men cook up seafood jambalaya or étouffée.[14] Foodways endure, but other forms of Cajun expressive culture including language use and fiddle and accordion playing have been on the decline in the last few decades. While the Biloxi Shrimp Festival used to include a fais do-do (a Cajun dance party), and while older community members still travel together to Louisiana for Cajun music festivals, the younger generations are less interested in traditional music. Others go to Louisiana to visit a Cajun *traiteur*, or faith healer, and Catholicism remains an important part of their identity.

Both Cajuns and Slavonians (see below) lived in Biloxi's Back Bay and Point Cadet. They built their homes where cheap-rent housing had first existed under the control of the industry owners—the "seafood camps." Cajuns and Slavonians worked in the same seafood processing factories (generally teams of Slavonian women worked together as did teams of Cajun women). While they spoke different languages and had different ethnic identities, their Roman Catholicism and shared occupations furthered bonds between the communities. Both groups did, however, remain largely endogamous until the last few decades. Members of each ethnic group are now more likely to marry out at the same time the main factors that connected Cajuns and Slavonians are in decline. Fewer young people regularly attend mass now. Legalized gambling came to coastal Mississippi in 1992, and casinos have replaced the oyster and shrimp canneries both as top employers in the area and literally in terms of physical presence. In both the Cajun and Slavonian communities, the young have opted for college and the professions over fishing.

SLAVONIANS (CROATIANS)

Immigrants from the Dalmatian coast of the Adriatic Sea have come to the Gulf of Mexico since the 1830s. Some Croatians came from the Dalmatian coast and settled where they found a similar climate conducive to their skills as fishers and fruit producers. Slavonians came from a part of Croatia that is forested lowland and fertile agricultural land. A large-scale immigration of Croatians to Mississippi and Louisiana began in the 1880s. Slavonia was the name of a town that existed briefly on the Red Creek Valley in the nineteenth century (Greenwell 1971: 28). In the late 1800s, 450 Slavonian lumberjacks worked the forests of the Delta's Bolivar County with Austrian barrel-stave makers working behind them (Willis 2000: 55). A devastating hurricane in 1893 caused many Croatians to leave Louisiana's coastal marshes for Bay St. Louis and Biloxi (Bonner 1984:36). While some became involved in citrus growing, most became a part of the growing seafood industry and opened canneries and developed special skiffs for carrying oysters and tools particular to oyster-shucking. Slavonian women, and children as young as twelve, worked in the seafood factories and canneries where they processed shrimp and oysters. Surnames such as Baricev, Kuluz, Vodanovich, Gilich, Sabilich, Tesvichand, and Leckich are prominent in East Biloxi.

The all-male Slavonian Benevolent Association of Saint Nikolai that formed in Biloxi in 1913 now has close to three hundred members and has long welcomed members who had distinct ethnicities among the southern Slavs: Croatians and Slavonians (a region of eastern Croatia) and Serbians (Eastern Orthodox Slavs). The association has held an annual golf tournament and a Croatian festival each fall. In 1939, it constructed Slavonian Hall on Point Cadet. The lodge could accommodate six hundred people and was the scene of community gatherings, wedding receptions, and concerts. Elvis played the hall in 1955 and some of his first bookings in Mississippi were by Biloxi native and Croatian American promoter "Yankie" Barhanovich. The lodge was the traditional site for a Thursday evening card-playing, gossiping, "men's night out." The Ladies' Auxiliary, with fewer than two hundred members, also has regular gatherings at the lodge. One best known to the other Biloxians is their Christmas Eve sale of *pusharatas* (a fruit- and cinnamon-stuffed doughnut). Each year Slavonian women gather to visit at the lodge and fry in excess of five thousand *pusharatas* (Schmidt 1995).

While an estimated ten thousand Croatian-Americans lived along the Gulf Coast, at least two thousand resided in East Biloxi at the time of Hurricane Katrina (2005), which destroyed Slavonian Hall and St. Michael's Roman Catholic Church, attended by much of the Croatian community. The Roman Catholic faith is central to Croatian identity, and St. John's Day (June 24) was traditionally celebrated at the close of oyster season. Another concentration of Croatians settled north of Biloxi in D'Iberville where they engaged in the fishing and boatbuilding industries. Each new boat and each new fishing season required a blessing, and it was in D'Iberville in 1920, at the urging of Croatian fishers, that the first Blessing of the Shrimp Fleet took place in waters beside the Sacred Heart Catholic Church. The blessing at the beginning of the shrimping season now takes place in conjunction with the Biloxi Shrimp Festival. Festivities begin with a race of two sixty-five-foot replica Biloxi schooners of the type used to harvest seafood in the nineteenth century. A special mass for deceased fishers precedes a Saturday night community celebration with food and music and the coronation of the new Shrimp King and Shrimp Queen. The Shrimp King is selected from three nominations (one from the community in general, one from the Fleur de Lis, the French Club, and one from the Slavonian Benevolent Association). The Shrimp Queen is a young woman between the ages of sixteen and nineteen with a fishing family background. Sunday afternoon's events begin annually with a solemn memorial for deceased fishers and seafood industry workers with the dropping of a wreath into the gulf. Then a brightly decorated fleet of upwards of 150 boats processes from the Biloxi Lighthouse as the bishop of the Catholic Diocese of Biloxi performs the blessing.

HUNGARIAN AND POLISH PLACE NAMES

Mississippi is home to at least two thousand Americans claiming Hungarian descent. Some of these Mississippians moved east from a late nineteenth-century Hungarian rural settlement in Louisiana. The surname of Hungarian patriot Lajos (Louis) Kossuth became the name of a town in Alcorn County. Ten miles southwest of Corinth, Kossuth has a population of 170 as of the 2000 census. Originally called New Hope, the town changed its name to Kossuth in 1852 to honor the Hungarian revolutionary hero who led the democratic, anti-Habsburg Hungarian revolution of 1848. His goal of a democratic state was crushed and his generals executed, but the regent-president Kossuth fled abroad. In 1851, he visited America, giving well-received public accounts (in English) of the Hungarian situation. Even his facial-hair stylings (a beard without a mustache) were briefly fashionable. He became the second foreign leader (after the Marquis de La Fayette) to address a congressional joint session. La Fayette of course also has a Mississippi county named for him. La Fayette fought for the Continental Army during the American Revolution as did Thadeus Kosciusko. The town of

Kosciusko in Attala County is named for Tadeusz Andrzej Kościuszko, the Polish national hero, who also fought in the American Revolution as a colonel in the Continental Army. In 1783, in recognition of his dedicated service, the Continental Congress brevetted him to the rank of brigadier general and he became a naturalized citizen of the United States. Some Bohemians with skills essential to the seafood industry moved from Maryland to Biloxi for work in 1890. Enough arrived to occupy five "Bohemian seafood camps." Now within the Czech Republic, Bohemia once comprised Moravia and Czech Silesia, which has a minority of Polish residents, and some of the Bohemians who came to Mississippi were called Polish by locals. Polish Jews settled in the Delta and became prosperous as merchants and money lenders. Just over 11,100 Mississippians now claim Polish descent.

GERMANS

Germans were present in the colonial settlements of La Louisiane, and German ancestry reporting remains relatively high in the census. Germans did not, however, settle in areas in large enough numbers to claim their own coast as in Louisiana's Côte des Allemands where late eighteenth-century German immigrants created their own culture area in Lafourche and St. Charles parishes. Many in Louisiana, and to some extent in coastal Mississippi, have intermarried with Acadians so that their descendants claim to be German Cajuns with surnames such as Schexnayder, Toups, Folse, and Hymel. John Willis notes that by 1870, many merchants in the Delta area were foreign-born, as were half of those living in Greenville. These included Italians, Irish, French, and Polish, but most predominant were Prussians and other Germans (2000: 86).

Some twentieth-century Germans came to Mississippi for a temporary stay. Late in 1943, German prisoners of war from the "Afrikakorps" were sent from northern Africa (where shipping cargo to feed and care for prisoners was costly) to the United States. Four camps operated in Mississippi. Camp Clinton, near Jackson, housed the highest-ranking German officers of Rommel's defeated "Korps," including twenty-five generals and the man who led the Afrikakorps after Rommel, General von Arnim. However, many of the POWs were boys in their teens—the average age of prisoners was twenty-two. Near Hattiesburg was Camp Shelby, Camp Como (which originally held Italian POWs) was in the northern Delta, and close by Grenada was Camp McCain, which, as the largest of the four, housed almost eight thousand Germans. To counteract a labor shortage after the war, President Harry Truman retained POWs to work in their compounds for close to a year after the war's end. Many German POWs in Mississippi did not leave until mid-1946. Prisoners organized an orchestra and a jazz band, had intramural sports events, and put on plays. Some returned in later years to see friends they had made through working in Mississippi and to show their families where they had lived out the remainder of the war.

After Italians in the first decades of the twentieth century, Germans provided the largest numbers of foreign immigrants in the post–World War II era into the 1990s. They came in large numbers in the 1950s and especially the 1960s. English immigrants trailed second in number to Germans during that period until the early 1990s when Indians briefly became the second largest immigrant group. The German prominence in Mississippi immigration held until the 1990s when more foreign-born Mexicans began arriving than foreign-born Germans.[15] Germans have long been the largest ethnic group in the United States (23 percent of Americans claimed German descent on the 1990 census and 15 percent in 2000). While now surpassed in number by Latinos, Americans of German ancestry still count for nearly one out of every six Americans responding to the census. On the 2000 census, 4.5 percent of Mississippians identified themselves as having German ancestry (the fifth-largest ancestry group in the state).

Although dramatically outnumbered by other new arrivals, immigrants from Germany continue to come to Mississippi (especially those retiring to the Gulf Coast after military careers), and they find an assortment of German American social groups to join, including both expatriates and those of German descent. Oktoberfests are popular on the Gulf Coast and in Catholic communities further west in the state. Gluckstadt (an unincorporated community in the Jackson metro area) holds an annual German Fest each fall. Nine Catholic families of German descent from Indiana bought land at Calhoun in 1905 and renamed their community there Glückstadt, or "lucky village."[16] In 1917 they were able to attend mass in their first church building, St. Joseph Catholic Church, and their parish now has a membership of 120 families. Their annual German Fest serves hot pretzels, bratwurst, and homemade sauerkraut. An "oom-pah" band performs polkas and traditional German folk songs. Descendants of the original settlers and also others of southern German Catholic descent are active in the Knights of Columbus and its Ladies Auxiliary group.

ITALIANS

An Italian presence in Mississippi had begun with those who accompanied Hernando de Soto's expedition in 1541. Berardo Peloso, who may have come first with Soto, was the first European to see Pascagoula Bay in 1558 (Wilson 2004). Italians accompanied French explorers on the Mississippi River in the 1680s and southern Italians fought in the American Revolution. In 1850, Louisiana had the largest Italian-born population in the United States, but Vicksburg and Natchez combined probably had no more than a hundred Italians when the Civil War began. Small in number though they were, Italian Americans served in both Mississippi cavalry and infantry regiments.

Between 1880 and 1920, Italian laborers were purposely recruited to Mississippi. Many came to rural areas and worked on cotton and sugar plantations. Some worked constructing and repairing levees. Their numbers soared, and by 1910 Mississippi had 2,137 residents who were born in Italy. Some encountered anti-Catholic prejudice, and those coming from southern Italy encountered discrimination based on their darker skin color. However, Mississippians elected Andrew Houston Longino (1855–1942), a Baptist of Italian and American descent, as the thirty-fifth governor of Mississippi. Those Italians who settled along the coast, particularly in Biloxi, Gulfport, and Ocean Springs, opened shops, acquired their own farms, or became involved in the seafood industry. Some owned seafood canning operations. In the midst of shipping disruptions due to World War I, Italian native Henry Piaggio began a wooden ship construction program in Gulfport in 1916 to export Mississippi pine to Italy. Pascagoula became home to a major Italian American shipyard. The De Angelo shipyard at Moss Point built schooners for lumber export. By the mid-twentieth century, William Cruso's shipyard on Biloxi's Back Bay was home to one of the largest seafood canning plants on the coast. Charles Reagan Wilson has noted that Sicilians and Calabrians who came to the Delta settled in towns rather than agricultural areas and opened businesses such as restaurants, grocery stores, and fruit stands (Wilson 2004:3). Greenville became home to the largest population of Sicilians in the Delta, although today only 2 percent of Greenville's population claims Italian descent on the census. Other immigrants came from central Italy (especially the Marche region), and these Italians went to the Delta plantations where many had to work off debts to plantation owners for their family's transportation and living expenses. They worked as tenant farmers until able to purchase their own farms or move elsewhere and were mostly endogamous for several

2.4. Andrew Houston Longino, the thirty-fifth governor of Mississippi, served 1900–1904 and was the first Italian American to be governor of a state in the U.S. South. He was from Lawrence County and lived from 1854 to 1942. He invited President Theodore Roosevelt to bear hunt in the Mississippi Delta. Courtesy of the Mississippi Department of Archives and history.

generations. The first generation born in Mississippi continued to speak Italian (Canonici 2003: x). Well-known surnames of Italian Mississippians include Agostinelli, Botto, Bramucci, Luzietti, Malatesta, Mancini, Spadini, Tarsi, and Zepponi.

Italians in significant numbers arrived too late to shape Mississippi place naming, but Washington County has a town named for the famous Italian engineer, Egyptologist, and showman Giambattuta Belzoni (1778–1823). This, however, was because Alvarez Fisk, who developed the land on the west side of the Yazoo River, named his plantation for Belzoni and the city followed suit. (Belzoni is perhaps better known today for its Annual World Catfish Festival.) Italians, of course, readily popularized their foodways. They continued to produce homemade wine (even though the state only repealed prohibition in 1966), grow kitchen gardens, and build outdoor, wood-fired ovens (*fornos*) of brick and stone for the weekly baking of bread. While grits eventually replaced polenta for some, coastal Italians introduced seafood raviolis and combined southern and Italian cuisine for such dishes as fried chicken piccata and deep-fried asparagus. As in Louisiana and Florida, the practice of building a St. Joseph's Day altar on March 19 endured into the late twentieth century and occasionally reappears in a few communities. The altar was usually constructed in thanksgiving for some type of deliverance and required weeks of baking to prepare a colorful altar laden with *zeppole* (doughnuts sometimes called St. Joseph's Day cakes), biscotti, *pignolata* cookies, decorative breads, or breads in the shape of Christian symbols, and perhaps a dried fava bean (as fava beans saved Sicilians in a time of famine, the beans are a symbol of good luck). Friends of the family preparing the altar would be invited for food, visiting, and prayers. Leftovers, or food reserved on the altar itself, would be given to the needy.

Italian communities formed in Bay St. Louis, Clarksdale, Greenville, Jackson, Natchez, and Shaw. By the 1920s, many Italians came to the small town of Shaw from the region of Ancona in the province of Marche and, as in many communities, helped relatives and friends also settle nearby (Schuy 1991: 71). Several immigrant aid/social organizations endure, such as a statewide association in the city of Jackson and the Gulf Coast Italian American Society of Mississippi. Nationwide, 5.6 percent of Americans claimed Italian ancestry on the 2000 census, but in Mississippi only 1.4 percent of the state's population identified as being of Italian descent. While 3 percent of Natchez residents claim Italian ancestry, percentages are larger along the coast. Bay St. Louis reports, as do many towns in Hancock County, its highest percentage of European ancestry as French (14.9 percent), second being Irish at 14.7 percent, followed by German (10.2 percent); yet Italians at 9.4 percent still rank high above the national average. In 2005, the U.S. Census Bureau estimated that 50,646 Mississippians have Italian ancestry.

GREEKS

On the 2000 census, Greek Americans in Mississippi are definitely underrepresented at 2,662 (only 0.1 percent of the state's population). Mississippi's Greeks live predominantly on the Gulf Coast and in Hinds County. Greek Orthodox churches are central to Greek American life in Jackson, Biloxi, and Aberdeen, although some of these congregations include almost as many converts as Greeks. Jackson's congregation (Holy Trinity–St. John the Theologian) dates to 1951 when Greek immigrants created both the Patmian Society (for immigrants from the island of Patmos) and the Athenian Society. Together they raised the funds to bring a priest from Patmos (the Reverend Basil Kleoudis) and to purchase land for a church. They erected a building in 1957 and now have a membership of close to seventy families.

For a few decades, the church operated a Greek school to teach congregants' children the language of their ancestors, although today fewer than a dozen members have regular conversations in Greek. Part of the liturgy is in Greek, and Greek classes are offered by a native speaker to help adults participate in the service. Women of the congregation may join the church-based, charitable organization Friends of the Poor, which is also instrumental in organizing the church's annual Greek Fest. Each May, Jacksonians come to visit a temporary gift shop with Greek linens, jewelry, traditional sailor hats and cookbooks, and also to enjoy spanakopita, Greek chicken, gyros, and baklava. Congregants perform exhibition dances, dress in traditional costumes, and play traditional music on bouzoukis and klarina.

Greek communities in the South retain the celebration of name days (Greek American children are still often named for Greek saints, and families and friends will be invited to celebrate the feast day of a saint with whom one shares a name). On the Sunday closest to the name day, one's family holds an open house. Guests are greeted with a beverage and then offered a pastry and, if close to the family, invited to stay for dinner. The occasion was traditionally a much more important celebration than a birthday. Most every Sunday was someone's name day celebration, so the first three generations of Mississippi Greeks enjoyed regular socializing. While name day open houses have passed from practice in Jackson, Mississippi, friends may still be invited for cake and coffee on a name day.

Greek Easter (*Pascha*) celebrations occur at a different time from those of Protestants and Roman Catholics. The reckoning of Greek Easter is based on the Julian rather than the Gregorian calendar. *Pascha* is preceded by a fifty-day period of fasting and attendance at special services in preparation for Holy Week. A joyful celebration of the resurrection of Christ, this most important of holidays is a time when Greek Mississippians especially try to be with family, attend weekend services, and share Greek foods such as tsouréki (a sweet Greek Easter bread), which is decorated with eggs that are always dyed red to represent the blood of Christ.

Greek Orthodox communities are also located in Aberdeen (where Jackson's minister serves the Divine Liturgy once monthly) and Biloxi (The Holy Trinity Church). Mississippi is also home to other Orthodox communities with non-Greek origins. Clinton and McComb have Orthodox Church of America congregations, derived from the Russian Orthodox tradition, and a small gathering (usually less than forty) assembles at Danforth Chapel on the campus of the University of Southern Mississippi in Hattiesburg. Antiochian Orthodox communities also are to be found in Tupelo,

Vicksburg, and Madison. Epiphany services on January 6 (marking the visit of the Magi to the infant Christ) are common to all Orthodox communities. In Greece and in Greek diaspora communities, congregations gather for a service and the blessing of the waters and of boats. A bishop, or a priest, throws a cross into the water and teenage boys dive in to retrieve it. The Jackson, Mississippi, congregation participates in a blessing of the waters at Ross Barnett Reservoir in Hinds County.

ROMANI AND IRISH TRAVELERS

While Romani and Traveler communities are both known in popular culture for nomadism, they are quite distinct people, and they do have affiliations with particular areas, own homes, and are settled, at least seasonally. Settlement was in part fostered by legislation against them. Like many states, Mississippi had a law on its books until 1988 (although rarely enforced after World War II) by which encamped "gypsies" could be fined two thousand dollars (State Code of Mississippi, Section 27-17-191).

Rose Hill Cemetery in Meridian is home to the graves of Emil Mitchell (d. 1942) and Kelly Mitchell (d. 1915)—"the King and Queen of the Gypsies." Romani often use such titles to impress outsiders (the "gadjé" or "gadjó"). Nevertheless, these graves, particularly that of Kelly Mitchell, have become a site of pilgrimage. One can regularly see gifts of fruit, candy bars, vanilla wafers, sodas, and even polished stones left there. Kelly Mitchell died in childbirth in 1915 near Demopolis, Alabama, and her family brought her to Mississippi for burial. Some Romani believe that the queen has saint-like powers to intercede on one's behalf. The lore shared with outsiders is that should you come to her grave with a concern and leave a gift, such as rosary beads, jewelry, coins, food, or something related to your worry (a baby teether or cigarette lighter, for example, if you have an ill infant or are trying to quit smoking), the queen will come to you in your dreams that night with the answer to your concern. The deposition of these "votives" has increased in the last decade, but this could be attributed to the now-common visits of tourists who also leave objects, though not always appropriate in form.

Mitchell is frequently an Irish surname, but the Romanies with that surname have quite different origins, deriving ultimately from populations in India that traveled west over many centuries throughout Europe. In at least a millennium of mobile existence, ethnic divides formed among the

Romanies, and these distinctions crossed the Atlantic. Those in the South are predominantly Romanichals (who traveled to America from Britain) and the Vlax, who came from southeastern European countries. Theories on the Irish origins of the Travelers are numerous. They earned their ethnonymn through their peripatetic lifestyle. They initially retained this lifestyle in the American South, but today only a portion of the community "goes on the road." The Mississippi Traveler men earn their living in a variety of itinerant services: landscaping, construction, asphalting, roofing, and other odd jobs. Rather than cultivate a regular clientele, they generally offer services people need irregularly and solicit business door to door. When they appear in the news, it is generally in relation to perpetrating some type of scam (taking cash down payments for work they never perform and obtaining bank loans with false identification). Some Travelers will introduce themselves to outsiders as Irish Gypsies since that is what many outsiders call them. They sometimes refer to each other as "Pavee" and to non-Pavee as "country people."

Irish Travelers have large communities in Texas, South Carolina, and Georgia. A group called the Mississippi Travelers numbers perhaps more than 275 families and resides in northern Mississippi and in Whitehaven on the south side of Memphis, Tennessee. (Though some reside in northern Mississippi, they mostly likely derive their name from the river rather than the state.) While many reside in mobile home and RV parks, others build large and expensive homes near one another. Many communities in southern states have just a dozen or so surnames (even in communities like that at Murphy Village, South Carolina, which has 545 families). Endogamy is accompanied by arranged marriages (important when communities have such intricate networks of intermarriage), and a dowry is still expected. A wedding or funeral occasions the visits of hundreds or even thousands of Traveler relatives and friends from communities elsewhere.

Travelers are generally Roman Catholic and give generously to their local parishes. Women may attend mass daily, and priests play an important role in encouraging parents to educate their children (especially daughters) and in mediating between exclusive Traveler communities and outsiders. While young people frequent shopping malls and restaurants, they employ a distinctive style of dress and hairstyling and do not often mix with "country people." Many leave public school by the eighth or ninth grade, when boys generally join their male relatives on the road. Some are homeschooled. Some Catholic parishes offer GED programs especially for Traveler teens.

In most communities, but to varying practice, they retain their own form of speech which they call the "Cant" and which some scholars call "Gammon." The Cant is a derivative of the argot of Travelers in Ireland (often called "Shelta" there) which has an English-based syntax and a core vocabulary from Irish Gaelic with increasing borrowing from English. Their ability to retain linguistic and other cultural practices, as well as unified communities, for over a century and a half is interesting in itself. Their ancestors arrived at a time when assimilation was key, yet they have resisted change through maintaining protective privacy about their way of life.

DANES

There are far fewer Danish Americans than those of Swedish or Norwegian descent. The greatest periods for Danish immigration occurred in 1881–1883 and in 1903–1905. By 1900 Danes migrated to settlements that sprang up around new railroad stations such as Leland in the Delta which also attracted Italians, Germans, Irish, Greeks, and Welsh immigrants (Willis 2000: 207). In the early 1930s, a group of twenty-five Danish American families moved to Jackson County from Montana and established the "colony of Granly." The colony was the last of those encouraged by the Danish Folk Society to extend and promote Danish culture and presence in the United States. Texas had one on the Gulf Coast—now called "the Danish Capital of Texas" at Danevang (which means "Danish fields"). The minister from Danevang traveled to Granly every fifth Sunday to conduct worship services for the community. Each colony had a *Forsamlinghus* which served as a community assembly place, church, and school, until separate structures could be built for these purposes. One goal was to resist complete assimilation and retain Danish faith traditions and language. Many children of the settlers report having spoken only Danish for the first few years of their lives. Today these descendants and their children and grandchildren live mostly elsewhere but still have annual summer reunions at the *Forsamlinghus*, and many gather near Christmastime to dance around a tree and share Danish foods such as Æbleskiver, pancakes made with apple slices. Surnames of community members include Brinkman, Nygaard, Martin, and Thyssen. On the 2000 census there were approximately 2,620 persons in Mississippi self-identifying with Danish ancestry.

CONCLUSION

Mississippi has been home to Europeans and their American descendants for over three centuries. Today, European Americans in Mississippi are more likely to identify themselves as nonethnic Americans than are European Americans elsewhere in the country, in part because of their long residence and attachment to particular parts of Mississippi. However, many communities retain a strong awareness of ancestral origins, and coastal counties exhibit more ethnic identification than others. Less so than Louisiana, or perhaps Florida, but certainly more than other southern states, Mississippi's colonial culture derived from European influences beyond the British. The legacy of varying European settlement patterns and traditions persists in Mississippi's subregions. The imprint of European ethnicities is manifest in place names and surnames, in foodways, music and folklore, in religious communities and linguistic conventions, in vernacular architecture and urbanization, and in Mississippi's vibrant cultural festivals. Centuries of creolization of European cultures, and the blending of these with Native American and African folkways, have shaped the state's unique identity within the South.

NOTES

1. In 2006, a Canadian father and daughter team, river-canoe enthusiasts Denis and Myriam Lessard, retraced Jolliet and Marquette's expedition 333 years after the first European descent of the Mississippi River.

2. D'Iberville was a small village in the mid-twentieth century which Biloxi annexed and which broke away to become a city in 1988.

3. The town interestingly is eponymous for a Virginia man famed for being a conscientious objector during the American Revolution. In an area where national sovereignty had changed so frequently between French, Spanish, and British, one who refused to take a side in the Revolution could not only avoid censure, but be honored with the naming of a new town.

4. So many Germans came to Louisiana after 1720 that the parishes of St. Charles, St. John the Baptist, and St. James are still known as the German Coast (Côte des Allemands).

5. Louis XIV died in 1715 when his heir, his great-grandson Louis XV, was only age five. Philippe, Duc d'Orleans, became regent until 1723.

6. Christopher Morris notes that Father O'Reily arrived in Vicksburg in 1839 to establish a church (1995:151).

7. Of the many interpretations of "Creole," French Creole is employed here to mean Catholic, white descendants of French settlers of non-Cajun origin rather than "Creoles of color."

8. Single pen houses were often log-built, and, as horizontal log construction was not employed in England at the time, both Latham and Terry Jordan-Bychkov have made good cases to credit the design and notching of American log houses to Germans, Swedes, and Finns. See Terry G. Jordan-Bychkov's (2003) *The Upland South: The Making of an American Folk Region and Landscape* (Santa Fe, NM: Center for American Places), and (1985) *American Log Buildings: An Old World Heritage* (Chapel Hill: University of North Carolina Press).

9. Mississippi might have led over the Carolinas slightly in attracting new immigrants, as rice, one of the earliest cash crops in all three states, became more important in the Delta just as it was declining in the Carolinas.

10. (2004). Historical Census Browser. Retrieved August 14, 2008, from the University of Virginia, Geospatial and Statistical Data Center: http://fisher.lib.virginia.edu/collections/stats/histcensus/index.html.

11. For an account of colonial demographics, see Peter Wood's 1988 article "Re-Counting the Past" in *Southern Exposure* 16(2): 30–37.

12. "Estimates of the Unauthorized Migrant Population for States Based on the March 2005 CPS," Pew Hispanic Center.

13. Including Monroe in the east, Calhoun in north-central Mississippi, Tippah in the far north, Lawrence in the south-central and George and Madison. Scott, Lauderdale, Covington, and Lowndes are among the counties with 8 percent Irish ancestry.

14. Catholic practices vary. After Vatican II, many Catholics in the U.S., particularly in south Mississippi and Louisiana, began observing the traditional Friday meat fast only during Lent.

15. In the 1990 census, Mexicans had composed less than 4 percent of Mississippi's foreign-born population, but by the 2000 census that figure had risen to over 25 percent. The 2000 census records that in that one decade, Mississippi's foreign-born population also grew by just over 95 percent. At the close of the first decade of the twenty-first century, Mexicans now represent almost 40 percent of Mississippi's foreign-born population.

16. Among the purchasers were Valentine Fitsch, Henry Klaas, John Kehle, Peter Schmidt, and Joseph Weilandt.

WORKS CITED

Audubon, John James. 1831 [1917]. "Early Settlers Along the Mississippi." In *Southern Life in Southern Literature; Selections of Representative Prose and Poetry*, edited by Maurice Garland Fulton, 14–18. New York: Ginn and Co.

Baxter, Robert J. 1976. "Cattle Raising in Early Mississippi: Reminiscences." In *Mississippi Folklore Register*. Vol. 10, No. 1: 1–23.

Bettersworth, John K. 1959. *Mississippi: A History*. Austin: The Steck Company.

Bonner, Thomas. 1984. "Yugoslavs on the Gulf Coast: At Sea and Ashore." In *Mississippi Folklore Register.* Vol. 18, No.2: 35–44.

Buie, T. R., and J. S. Buie. 1983. *The Family Buie: Scotland to North America.* Arlington, TX: Chelle-Kirk Print.

Canonici, Paul V. 2003. *The Delta Italians.* Madison, Miss.: Caló Creative Designs, Inc.

Cash, William. 1992. "European Colonization of Mississippi." In *Ethnic Heritage in Mississippi*, edited by Barbara Carpenter. Jackson: University Press of Mississippi.

Coker, William S. 1972. "Research in the Spanish Borderlands: Mississippi, 1779–1798." In *Latin American Research Review*, Vol. 7, No. 2 (Summer 1972): 40–54.

Downey, James C. 1986. "Sacred Harp Singing in the Piney Woods." In *Mississippi's Piney Woods: A Human Perspective*, edited by Noel Polk, 92–102. Jackson: University Press of Mississippi.

Gleeson, David. 2006. "Smaller Differences: 'Scotch-Irish' and 'Real Irish' in the Nineteenth-Century American South." *New Hibernia Review* 10 (Summer 2006): 68–91.

Greene, Jerome, Berele Clemensen, John Paige, David Stuart, and Lawrence Van Horn. 1984. *Mississippi River Cultural Resources Survey: A Comprehensive Study Phase I.* U.S. Department of the Interior/National Park Service.

Greenwell, D. 1971. "Studies in Progress." In *Mississippi Coast Historical & Geneaological Society.* Vol. 4.

Holmes, Jack. 1967. "Irish Priests in Spanish Natchez." In *The Journal of Mississippi History*, 169–180.

Hudson, Arthur Palmer, ed. 1928. *Specimens of Mississippi Folk-Lore.* Published by the Mississippi Folk-Lore Society and Edwards Brothers Printers. Ann Arbor, Mich.

Hunter, James. 1994. *A Dance Called America: The Scottish Highlands, the United States and Canada.* Edinburgh, Scotland: Mainstream.

Kniffen, Fred B. 1990. "The Lower Mississippi Valley; European Settlement, Utilization and Modification." In *Geoscience and Man.* Vol. 27: 3–34.

Latham, James A. 1977. *Mississippi Folk Houses.* [S.l.: s.n.]. National Endowment for the Humanities.

Morris, Christopher. 1995. *Becoming Southern: The Evolution of a Way of Life, Warren County and Vicksburg, Mississippi, 1770–1860.* Oxford: Oxford University Press.

Napier, John H. III. 1986. "Piney Woods Past: A Pastoral Elegy." In *Mississippi's Piney Woods: A Human Perspective*, edited by Noel Polk, 12–24. Jackson: University Press of Mississippi.

Nolan, Charles E. 1992. *St. Mary's of Natchez: The History of a Southern Catholic Congregation, 1716–1988. Volume I: The History; Volume II: Signs of Parish Life.* Natchez, Miss.: St. Mary's Catholic Church.

Odum, Howard. 1936. *Southern Regions of the United States.* Chapel Hill: University of North Carolina Press.

Olson, Ted. 1991. "'The Voices of the Older Ones': The Sacred Harp Singing Tradition of Calhoun County, Mississippi." In *Mississippi Folklore Register.* Vol. 25 & 26 (1991/1992): 11–29.

Oszuscik, Phillippe. 1992. "French Creoles on the Gulf Coast." In *To Build in a New Land: Ethnic Landscapes in North America*, edited by Allen G. Noble, 136–156. Baltimore: The Johns Hopkins University Press.

Schmidt, Aimée. 1995. "Down Around Biloxi: Culture and Identity in the Biloxi Seafood Industry." In *Mississippi Folklife*. Vol. 28, No. 1, 2 (Winter-Spring): 6–16.

Schuy, Irmgard. 1991. "Italian American Foodways in Shaw, Mississippi." In *Mississippi Folklore Register*. Vol. 25, 26 (1991/1992): 71–85.

Wakeland, Jon L. 1983. "Catholic Elites in the Slaveholding South." In *Catholics in the Old South: Essays on Church and Culture*. Macon: Mercer University Press, 211–240.

Wilkins, Jesse M. 1902. "Early Times in Wayne County." In *Publications of the Mississippi Historical Society*, edited by Franklin L. Riley, 265–277. Oxford: Mississippi Historical Society.

Willis, John. C. 2000. *Forgotten Time: The Yazoo-Mississippi Delta after the Civil War*. Charlottesville: University Press of Virginia.

Wilson, Charles Reagan. 2004. "Italians in Mississippi." In *Mississippi History Now: An Online Publication of the Mississippi Historical Society*. http://mshistory.k12.ms.us/index.php?id=88. Accessed August 16, 2008.

Young, D. C., and Stephen Flinn Young. 1989. *Biloxi's Ethnic Heritage: Images of Change and Tradition*. Jackson, Mississippi: Mississippi Department of Archives and History.

3

AFRICAN AMERICAN SACRED AND SECULAR IDENTITIES IN MISSISSIPPI'S PINEY WOODS

—JOYCE MARIE JACKSON

INTRODUCTION

The American South is a complex phenomenon. One aspect of the South's complexity is that cultures brought here from Africa and Europe interacted with one another despite efforts to keep them separate, and so African Americans and European Americans have assimilated to a certain extent and adapted similar traditions. In this chapter, the central question is to what degree do African American cultural patterns and identities—an "ethnic" or group identity—persist in the face of changing social and economic conditions both within and outside the region. Some answers to our questions of whether and how tradition-bound southern African American society can maintain itself in the information age may be found by looking into an earlier time. For example, social and economic upheavals occurred when slave labor–intensive cotton farming supplanted the more limited plantings of rice and indigo in the 1800s. When mechanization released a surplus farm labor force, that gave momentum to the Civil Rights Movement. Each of the changes had immediate effects on the demand for unskilled labor. But each change had reverberations far beyond an increase or decrease in the number of agricultural workers. That is, the economic changes served as a catalyst for social changes. This premise also holds true for the Piney Woods (or Pine Hills) region and the logging, sawmill, and turpentine industries. As soon as the lumber companies cleared a sizeable portion of the timberland, the camps moved and the sawmills closed, leaving those employees unemployed again. Does economics exert a controlling influence on inner lives and identity? Do assimilation and modernization mean a loss of identity?

Some folklorists theorize that groups choose to maintain traditions, selecting events and heroes from their cultural past that coincide with their present conceptions of themselves (Ben-Amos 1984: 114–115, with reference to Hobsbawm and Ranger 1983). Selecting certain traditions to maintain reinforces the values and beliefs of the current group's identity. When we understand that there is a process of "selective tradition" (Raymond Williams, quoted in Ben-Amos 1984: 115), the ways in which tradition helps create or confirm a group's sense of identity become illuminated. This chapter explores some selective traditions—sacred and secular identities of African Americans in the Piney Woods of Mississippi. I am viewing the rise and spread of various traditions like sacred harp singing schools and church gatherings and the blues and boogie woogie barrelhouse entertainment as their selective traditions. Some parts of the chapter focus directly on the perspectives of current participants and performances, and other areas offer brief biographical sketches of performers (past and present) to set the historical stage. Looking at the experiences of people close to these folk traditions, we can see the historical and current structure of some African American identities in the Piney Woods and how those identities have been maintained and transformed over the years. I believe both sacred and secular music gatherings are central to how African Americans have constructed and maintained identities in the past and in modern times, despite dramatic social and economic changes.

THE PINEY WOODS REGION

Mississippi is generally divided into four geographical and cultural areas: the Delta, the hills of northeastern Mississippi, the Gulf Coast, and the Piney Woods of southern Mississippi. The Piney Woods begin at the northern tip of the DeSoto National Forest and Interstate 20 and stretch south to the Gulf Coast and Interstate 10, and from Highway 61 in the east to the Alabama border in the west. This entire area consists primarily of longleaf pine trees forming a thick green canopy over the cities and towns in their path. The designated area of the Piney Woods in Mississippi is a segment of a larger region that crosses state boundaries to include parts of Georgia, Alabama, Louisiana, and Texas. The Mississippi Piney Woods encompasses all or part of thirty-five counties. The largest city in the region, Hattiesburg, serves as a cultural dividing line. Towns north of Hattiesburg share the traditional southern personality of Jackson, while communities south of Hattiesburg lean toward the casual indulgence of the Gulf Coast. Life on the boundary line is a pleasant mix of both.

The Piney Woods region is largely rural and diverse, with the first settlers, of course, being indigenous people—the Choctaw tribe. About a century later most of the Choctaws were removed to Indian Territory in Oklahoma (Trail of Tears) following the land cessions of the early nineteenth century. Those who stayed behind and resisted removal have grown to over seven thousand and have reconstituted their tribe as the Mississippi Band of Choctaws. Today, the Bogue Homa community is located in the Pine Hills. Anglo-Americans (mainly Scots-Irish) settled in the Pine Hills after the 1805 Treaty of Mount Dexter, in which the Choctaws ceded four million acres of south Mississippi land to the U. S. government, and they also came in after the War of 1812, when West Florida, as it was called, was void of foreign claims. By 1820, the population had grown to ten thousand, of whom two thousand were African American slaves. Plantation economy did not flourish in south Mississippi because of the poor soil, so most settlers either developed small farms or turned to livestock herding for subsistence, and after 1840 most whites in the area were nonslaveholders (Bolton 1997).

Although many customs and folklife traditions are very similar to the larger upland South, including gospel, blues, bluegrass, shape note singing conventions, quilting, canning, and dinner on the grounds at churches, the region has its own distinctions. Railroad, logging, sawmill work, and cattle industries have shaped the occupations and consequently the area's folklife. Therefore, people still sit on porches and perform narratives about life at the logging camps, sing railroad songs, and have ox team contests at community festivals (Ware 1997: 6).

AFRICAN AMERICANS IN THE PINEY WOODS

African Americans in the Piney Woods did not identify with plantation culture as the majority did in other regions of the state. Mississippi, for most of its history, was a black-majority state, but the Piney Woods has historically been a white-majority region since the economy did not depend on plantation agriculture even during the antebellum period. There were virtually no free blacks (only 773 of 437,404 blacks were free in 1860) in the state, and those people were in Natchez, Vicksburg, or Jackson. Those blacks who were enslaved worked as herders and sawyers, and unfortunately they did not receive any support from the larger primary plantation communities during the antebellum period. After Emancipation, African Americans experienced little racial turmoil because of the small number in the area, but during the late 1800s large numbers migrated to the Piney Woods seeking jobs in the timber industry. They were especially concentrated in the turpentine operations that accompanied the logging work. This was one of the most difficult periods regarding race relations in light of the Jim Crow era of segregation, disenfranchisement, and racial violence.

Race relations in the Pine Hills were different from other areas of Mississippi, such as the Delta. The black population numbers still were not great enough to affect the political vote, but increasing equality in income and land ownership was a threat to the whites and often caused violent reactions towards blacks. Since the plantation system of paternalism did not exist in the Piney Woods, whites did not have any control of blacks in this manner. For example, in the Piney Woods, many blacks owned their farms while in the other regions of the state, most blacks did not own property. In most of the state, blacks were tenants or sharecroppers and subject to or dependent upon white paternalism. Racial unrest also escalated during the depression of 1907–1911 due to the competition for jobs by blacks and whites in the lumber industry. Because blacks were so independent, secret bands of white vigilantes known as "whitecaps" brutally terrorized and killed at least a dozen black landowners and tenants and ran others off their own property. Due to the extreme violence of whites during this era, thousands of blacks left the Piney Woods in the first half of the twentieth century (Bolton 1997).

During the Civil Rights Movement most of the protest in Mississippi took place outside of the Pine Hills. White opponents of the black freedom struggle used violence as well as the more subtle Citizens' Council, which intimidated blacks by economic sanctions. However, the most brutal acts of the Ku Klux Klan in the 1950s and 60s happened in the white-majority counties of the Pine Hills. The lynching of Mack Charles Parker in Poplarville in 1959 and the fatal shooting in 1961 of Herbert Lee in Amite County by E. H. Hurst, a sitting legislator, clearly gave a message that any attempt to change the racial status quo would be dealt with in a swift and violent retaliation. These deaths were prompted by the *Brown v. Board of Education* decision, the coordination of the NAACP activists and the SNCC workers to implement a voter registration drive, and deep resentment of an African American acquiring a measure of economic success (Bolton 1997).

SINGING CONVENTIONS AND FOOD SHARING: SACRED IDENTITY

In the face of a historically brutal social experience, African Americans have affirmed their humanity by creating a rich, expressive cultural system of verbal lore, rituals, crafts, dance, and music which taught techniques of transformation, adaptation, and survival. The African Americans of the Pine Hills have a particularly strong oral tradition. The oral tradition is creatively expressed through storytelling, ministers' biblical oratory, children's games passed down through generations, and through the people's music. The most important of all of the expressive forms are religion and music. These forms also gave them a strong sense of cultural identity in the sacred and secular realms.

Historically and traditionally, religion was an organizing principle of the life structure of the community. The black church has been the most significant, conservative, and dominant institutional phenomenon in African American communities. As C. Eric Lincoln and Lawrence H. Mamiya assert:

> The proscriptions of 250 years of slavery, followed by another hundred years of Jim Crow segregation, permitted only the religious enterprise among black people to become a stable, cohesive, and independent social institution. As a consequence, black churches have carried burdens and performed roles and functions beyond their boundaries of spiritual nurture in politics, economics, education, music, and culture. (1999: 92–93)

In the Piney Woods region, the church was a central structure—as a place of worship, school, forum venue, political arena, benevolent society hall, dramatic theater, conservatory of music, and ritual space for other celebrations and life cycle rites, including christenings, marriages, and funerals. With these multilevels of community involvement located within the church, it is not surprising that this was the first institution to be owned and controlled by and for blacks in this community and in many others. As Émile Durkheim has made clear, religion is a social phenomenon, a shared group experience that has shaped and influenced the cultural screens of human communication and interpretation (1965). The black sacred cosmos, or the religious worldview of African Americans, is related both to their African heritage and to their own version of Christianity during slavery and its aftermath. African heritage envisions religion as a part of everyday life; therefore, most activities in the community centered on the church. This was and still is the case in small towns and rural areas in the Piney Woods region.

Though some congregations are now integrated, especially Catholic and Full Gospel Churches, religious life in the Piney Woods continues to be divided along racial lines. The assertion that 11:00 a.m. on Sunday morning is the most segregated hour in American society is probably as valid today as it ever was. However, the segregated nature of southern religion is one that African Americans and other ethnic groups chose, in order to worship not only with a sense of dignity and independence but also in their own style.

Here, in the midst of the "Baptist Belt," Sunday morning sermons become drama as surly black ministers, in the tradition of their forebearers, recount topical events from the past as well as the current news or happenings of the week, all to coincide with biblical scriptures, events, and characters. The central figure in the religious oratory community is the folk preacher. An indispensable part of his art and skill is to be able to respond to, engage in, and raise spiritual energies during the performance of a sermon without a written text.

Another important aspect of worship that people identity with is the music, which is another factor in the ritual. Spirituals, the sacred folk songs created by enslaved African Americans during the antebellum era, are still being performed in their traditional a cappella (unaccompanied) style in many rural churches. Urban churches and some larger rural ones have added piano accompaniment as well as other forms of instrumentation, and spirituals have also been arranged as gospel songs.

Although Anglo and African American Baptists in the Piney Woods rarely share their pews, they do share some of their hymns. Common to both churches is the lining-out style and the Dr. Watts and the long-meter hymns. (Dr. Watts was an eighteenth-century English Methodist hymn writer.) Lining-out is a hymn-singing tradition that arose out of necessity. There was a lack of hymn books and an abundance of people who could not read; therefore, one person was designated to "pitch" the song for the whole congregation. In the African American tradition, the head voice and congregation overlap melodically and rhythmically and decorate the hymn tunes with various vocal embellishments and moans. This produces an extraordinary effect sometimes referred to as "surge singing." In many churches this style is still performed a cappella today.

Gospel singing is the most desired genre of religious music in the churches—soloist, choirs, and quartets. Gospel music has contributed tremendously to the Mississippi Piney Woods region's black musical heritage. This new sacred music of the twentieth century reflects the concerns of urban life and to a large extent has replaced other sacred styles like the folk spirituals, the Dr. Watts hymns, and the music style known as sacred harp in some churches. In the African American community during the 1920s the gospel tradition began to emerge in small, urban, Pentecostal "storefront" churches, then gradually in Baptist churches. Now the genre has found its way into the sanctuaries of African American congregations of virtually every religious denomination, including Catholic.

In the Piney Woods, many of the churches have gospel choirs, and daylong gospel singings are prevalent. Choirs come together and render a few songs apiece. They are usually accompanied by piano and organ and, in some churches, other instrumentation is used, including bass, rhythm guitar, and drums. In addition, there are also smaller configurations of singers including duets, mixed groups, and quartets.

A prime example of the importance of sacred music and how it forms identity can be seen in the lives of Deborah and David Wilson of Laurel. Although Deborah and David perform both gospel and rhythm and blues, they got their start in the church. They both played several instruments and could sing. David Wilson said that Sam Newsome, an elder in the church, used to play at the church and became the inspiration for learning. Then his father bought him a guitar because he knew he liked the way it sounded and strongly encouraged him to learn how to play it. Next, his grandmother bought him a bass for graduation, and so he started to learn how to play it along with singing. Deborah Wilson started with a family group singing in church. She shares with the folklorist Worth Long: "[B]ack then it wasn't but two of us, my older sister and I. My brother was playing lead guitar and then my mother she came. She had organized the group.... Well, first of all we were named the MSB Singers and then they changed it. Well, my father changed it to the Familyettes later." After singing in this family group, she started playing piano and drums. When she and her husband married, they formed a duet and now do gospel as well as rhythm and blues and popular tunes. This is how many gospel singers start before going on to secular careers, and, instead of crossing over, some stay in the sacred field and "straddle the fence" doing both.

David Wilson remembers the first time he saw a gospel quartet and gives a good example of the sacred/secular dichotomy:

But like I said, the first time I saw a gospel group that was the group down the street from my grandmom's house where I grew up at. And I hear them as I was walking by and I stopped. I said, "This I got to hear." Now they explained to me what it was. I said, "Oh, I might get to like this." Then I got together with some. I was out to one of my friend's house who's a musician up in Tupelo now though. And a guy from one of the local quartets came by and they needed a keyboard player for the night. My friend told them I played keyboard, so they invited me to go to church with them. I'll never forget it was down in McLain, Mississippi. And I got in to this church and these people got to playing all this music, I said—yeah, I said this sounds just like the blues I've been hearing. And I said hey wait a minute, I could get to like this and I've been playing quartet off and on ever since. Now them guys made big sounds big national recording artist and stuff.... They are the Holy Spiritualaires. (1999)

Although many gospel groups and quartets adhere to the sacred sound with conviction, others synthesized both, and the music emerged with a new identity—the same as the performers that have new experiences. The music that emerged serves as a mirror in which certain aspects of southern society can be examined. Indeed, the music offers a multiplicity of insights into how people view their situation, and it makes possible a much fuller understanding of why it had to change periodically. In essence, rhythm and blues music, as manifested in the gospel quartet musical genre, can tell much about the nature of life in the South, issues and conditions of the music industry, and the identity of the people who created or changed the art form.

Another style of religious music still prevalent today in the Piney Woods is the "vocal choir" or sacred harp, in which a system of four shapes—a triangle, circle, square, and diamond—is employed to designate the musical syllables *fa, sol, la, mi* (shape-note singing is also referred to as fasola and harp singing). This system, a popular and effective way of teaching people to "read" music, was an outgrowth of the eighteenth-century New England singing school movement and the Great Awakening of the 1900s. Published in Philadelphia in 1801, William Little's *The Easy Instructor or A New Method of Teaching Sacred Harmony* introduced the shape-note system to the general public to facilitate the improvement of congregational singing. Later, in the nineteenth century, the publication of books employing the shape-note system began to spread south. William Walder's

Southern Harmony (1835) and Benjamin White and B. J. King's *The Sacred Harp* (1884) have been two of the most widely used.

Although shape-note singing has been called white spiritual and white gospel singing, the system was also adapted during the 1880s by certain African American congregations in the South using texts of songs drawn from old hymns, gospel songs, and spirituals. There is only one collection of African American sacred harp compositions, *The Colored Sacred Harp* (1934), by Judge Jackson.

Sacred harp singing is normally taught in week-long "singing schools" held in some churches in Pine Hills. Some instructors move around from church to church and county to county teaching the method. Instructors traveled to lead these singing schools—usually called "institutes" and "normals" among the African Americans—which could last weeks or even months (Willis 1994). James C. Downey explains that in the Piney Woods "singing schools were taught in the [lumber] camps and in community churches, where women's voices were added" (1986: 67). In an interview with Mrs. Julia Lewis of Mount Bethel in Marion County, it appears that an itinerant singing instructor was very notable in her area:

> I learned those notes when I was a child, do-re-mi-fa-so-la-ti-do, do-ti-la-so-fa-mi-re-do. The old man's that's dead, Professor W. E. Taylor [deacon at Sunflower Baptist Church near Columbia], he died right down the road there. I'm sure he was over a hundred, at least about a hundred if not a hundred. But he would go to the next community and he'd have singing maybe about a week or two weeks here. Then he'd go to the next community.... He would go from church to church and teach you those notes. They called that normal, that's what he called it teaching the normal you know. The normal school that's what he called it teaching. He put those notes on the board and you had to learn the notes. (McGraw 1998)

Mrs. Lewis shows the researcher her book and explains the shapes:

> Okay, okay, now I'm trying to find one that the do is straight up.... Now this is do by itself. When that point is turned up it's a do. When it turns down it's a ti. And this round one is a re and the flat one like that is a la, that's a la. This is a mi, these little ones with the diamond shape that's a mi. Un-huh and this is a so. So and so and so [starts singing].... You're supposed to sing them [syllables] all the time.

> But most of the time the teacher will make you sing these until you get the tune of the song. After you get the tune of it you can sing the words without the staff. (McGraw 1998)

Normally, the group sings the song with the fa so la syllables until they learn or become more familiar with the tune; then they replace the syllables with the words. Some groups will do this every time they sing the song. Similar to the southern folk preaching tradition, emotion and volume are valued over formal training. And in the democratic spirit, just as in regular church services, all are encouraged to sing, not just those with the good voices. The unusual harmonic effect is produced partially by the fact that the high female voices are not carrying the melody as would be the case in modern congregational or gospel singing. In addition, and except for the exclusively male bass section, women or men can sing any part. For instance, women often sing the tenor part.

Musical reformers were not without their influence on shape-note singing. Some songbooks introduced a seven-shape system to reflect the more modern way of singing the scale during the mid-nineteenth century. Most of the new books published after the Civil War used seven shapes, although four-note books remain popular in some regions to the present day. Some songs in the repertoire are "Lord, I Want to Be Ready," "When I Get to Heaven, I'm Going to Have It Made," "Things Are Going to Get Better After A While," and "What a Time." They use songbooks such as *Abundant Grace, Come On Let's Sing,* and *Fountains of Praise,* along with xeroxed copies of other songs in the shape-note notation.

There is also a very strong family involvement in this tradition. Mrs. Lewis speaks of the family involvement, apprenticeship, and passing it on to another teacher:

> Like I said he'd [Professor Taylor] teach that normal [singing school] sometimes for a week and two weeks, but he'd sleep at somebody's house, you know. They would sit around the fire at night and sing. My daddy sung. My daddy sung bass and my sister sung tenor. I had two sisters that sang alto and they'd sit around the fire and sang at night. So that's the way that went.... Now he started singing under Professor Taylor. He was his assistant, un-huh. So now that Professor Taylor passed away then he moved up. He is Brother Smiley. We send for him and he come and carry us over the songs. When we get new books we send for him and he come and sit with us maybe two days

or a day or something you know and carry us over the songs....
Well, we used to get books every year but we don't do that now.
(McGraw 1998)

Founded in 1916, the Pearl River South Singing Convention brings together four African American church congregations—Little Rock Baptist Church, Sunflower Baptist Church, Mount Bethel Baptist Church, and Mount Olive Missionary Baptist Church—in southern Mississippi's Walthall and Marion counties to sing in the sacred harp musical style. They have a convention three times a year at one of the member churches for singing practice, worship, and fellowship (Ware 1997). Older members of the organization were taught by Professor W. E. Taylor in the 1930s, according to Deacon A. C. Smiley: "We sing by the counts and the beats, not by the piano.... At the time that [Professor Taylor] taught us this singing, we didn't have a piano around. This singing is on the piano, but we didn't get it that way. And we've been putting it out the way we got it all these years" (1997).

When the convention is over and people have been dismissed, what follows is another tradition—dinner on the grounds. It is a communal feast contributed to by various participants. Food is shared with everybody, and this culminating tradition is a mutually convenient meeting place for communication and sharing of common experiences and identities. Revival Sunday and dinner on the grounds after a singing were the events of the year in most rural southern communities. According to Richard M. Mirsky, "Food sharing events have been interpreted as occasions when members of a social unit join together . . . to maintain social cohesion" (1983: 129). Echoing Mirsky in another way, Joyce White remembers that Sunday was the big day and "all the families in the Negro community who were active in the church would prepare an array of dishes for the afternoon dinner" (1998: 1–3). Although the culinary competition was intense, it did not disturb another important role African American church functions played in the South. Events like revivals and harp singings followed by dinner on the grounds were "soul-satisfying" affairs where African American southerners could pass time in "comfort and security" free from "the harsh reality of our Jim Crow world ..." (1998: 1–3).

Currently the singing convention is much smaller in size than it once was, and many of its members are aging and lamenting the fact that the youth are not participating. However, it is very likely that the tradition will continue for many years because Brother Smiley is trying to teach the children the style of shape-note singing in a way where they will also love it.

Other practitioners are teaching it in an after-school program in the community of Foxworth in Marion County. The director, Dorothy Lewis of Dorothy's Day Care, explained, "We wanted to have some kind of music education in our after-school program. It occurred to us that we had the perfect opportunity to teach this old style of singing that had deep roots in our community" (Boykin 1997).

Most of the elderly practitioners base their identity on their role in the church and with the sacred harp choirs and singing conventions. It is all ingrained in their historical memory and is still what they actively participate in today—a shared cultural experience. Deacon A. C. Smiley explains it in another way: "I was born in '22, and our way, we didn't know nothing but going to church. We'd play on Saturday, but that was 'bout all because we working the rest of the days through the week. And Sunday, wasn't no doubt about it, you had to go to church..." (2000).

Mrs. Floree Smith explains:

> It [sacred harp singing] was the best experience that I've had in church with the singing of that sort when I was growing up. And ever since then, every year, I don't miss Christian Hills, because I have the remembrance of what went on with my grandmother. And it was just beautiful singing. And they probably stayed longer, because when they got the spirit, they didn't worry about going home. Everybody just wanted to stay there and praise the Lord. (2000)

Smith continues as she speaks about the music in general and how it brought them through:

> And we were working in the fields, I remember we would just strike up a tune, and everybody would just sing. You could hear somebody over on the next hill, they would just be singing. And that brought us through the rough time. You know, we didn't know anything else, but looking back on it, all of the love and singing and the carrying on that we had then, it helped us to get to where we are now. Everybody has his own ride. (2000)

A singing, such as the one at Little Rock Baptist Church, highlights the diversity of those who participate in the activity as well as the dual sacred/secular character of shape-note singing. Some singers attend because it is like a reunion, a homecoming, an event where they can fellowship with relatives, friends, and other acquaintances they have not seen in a while. It is a sanctioned form of socializing and some people attend just because others are attending. For others, it is a religious service and another way of praising God. Elderly practitioners insist it is the message in the words more than the melody in the music in the choosing of their tune selections. Admittedly for most, it is the shared love for the entire event that brings them together several times a year and keeps them coming back.

THE BLUES CLUB AND BARRELHOUSE CIRCUIT: SECULAR IDENTITY

In the introduction to Amiri Baraka's *Blues People*, the author presents his main premise: "If the music of the Negro in America, in all its permutations, is subjected to socio-anthropological as well as musical scrutiny, something about the essential nature of the Negro's existence in this country ought to be revealed, as well as something about the essential nature of this country, i.e., society as a whole" (Baraka 1963: x, 137, 153). His subsequent concern throughout the book is examining the progression of social and historical factors that brought the first African captives to the colonies of North America and, through the experience of slavery, emancipation, reconstruction, and Jim Crow, helped transformed them into African Americans with distinct cultural forms. In his discussion of the various forms of African American music (32–94), Baraka's view of meaning in music is one that sees it as purely derived from or expressive of social conditions. The blues is indicative of Baraka's major premise.

Ralph Ellison adds to Baraka's view. He looks at the notion that the blues function not only as individual expression but as a part of a ritual involving words, music, drama, and trappings of spirituality. The ritual itself synthesizes some of the most essential values of African American life with regard to survival and daily living. For him, they constitute what Albert Murray referred to as "equipment for living." In essence, Ellison asserts that each performance helps each individual performer to negotiate his or her identity vis-à-vis other musicians, the larger community, and the music's history. For Ellison, even the nonperforming participant in a musical event also partakes of those interactions with identity and history (1964: 197).

The manner in which Baraka and Ellison view the music is the way identity is played out in a blues performance. Like other American ethnic groups, blacks in the Piney Woods are part of the development of a special cultural tradition which has significantly contributed to the greater American musical heritage and identity of a people. This musical legacy is known throughout the world as the Delta blues.

The Delta blues is nationally recognized as one of the most important musical forms of the twentieth century, a major catalyst for popular music. Existing in both a folk cultural context and as a product for the commercial music industry, the Delta blues has been a major influence on many outstanding musicians who emerged during the last century. The Delta blues of Robert Johnson, B. B. King, Muddy Waters, and other venerable regional artists influenced the development of such major performers as Elvis Presley and the Rolling Stones.

The blues arising in the black secular community of the rural South drew the least from western musical traditions but was most dependent on African American folk music tradition and the inventiveness of the artists themselves. Regional styles quickly became apparent, especially among guitarists. The guitar was the most prevalent instrument because of its portability. The cotton country of the Delta, where a large black population toiled in the fertile fields on plantations, was a haven for guitarists. This region has produced some of the greatest artists in the history of the genre. In this region that has been the stronghold of the blues, the music is characterized by a heavy, stark, and intensive percussive style where every note counts. The tendency is also one where the voice is basically in unison with the guitar. Various pianists worked the lumber camps of southeast Mississippi and Louisiana in the Piney Woods circuit, but it is logical that the Delta style and aesthetics were certainly a strong influence on the bluesmen that came out of the Piney Woods, especially those that played guitar. Despite regional differences, early blues singers and instrumentalists freely borrowed ideas and techniques from one another as they moved around with their itinerant occupations.

Robert Johnson, who stands at not only the crossroads of the Delta blues but also of American music, was not actually born in the Delta region, but in the small town of Hazlehurst in Copiah County, which is located in the Piney Woods region of southwest Mississippi. Although he died in Greenwood at an early age (twenty-seven), this influential blues singer and songwriter who, as the folk legend goes, sold his soul to Satan "at the crossroads" in exchange for his extraordinary talent and prowess on the guitar, has left an indelible legacy for many aspiring to reach his heights.

As he was born in the Piney Woods, his choices for work were limited to sharecropping or working in the lumber camps, and he felt he was ill suited for both. He gravitated instead toward the itinerant lifestyle of a musician. He started playing in his teens and was tutored by some of the most esteemed blues figures of his time—Charley Patton and Son House. Johnson was a very versatile performer not only as a blues master but also of the popular songs and styles of the day. His travels took him to small towns and big cities, to juke joints, country picnics and suppers, clubs, barrelhouses in the railroad, levee and lumber camps. He died mysteriously in 1938 in Greenwood, Mississippi, but his classics, including "Terraplane Blues," "Cross Road Blues," "Love in Vain," "Preaching Blues," "Come On in My Kitchen," "Hellhound on My Trail," and "Sweet Home Chicago" will live forever. Many musicians believe that these songs are the bedrock on which modern blues and rock and roll were built. In 1986, Johnson was inducted into the Rock and Roll Hall of Fame as an early influence, and in 1994 the U.S. Post Office issued a stamp in his honor. His life has been fictionalized in novels and in Hollywood, and his songs have been covered by countless bluesmen including Muddy Waters, Elmore James, Robert Junior Lockwood, Howlin' Wolf, Sonny Boy Williamson, and Big Joe Williams, and many rock stars, including Eric Clapton and the Rolling Stones. Though he recorded only twenty-nine songs (in San Antonio and Dallas, Texas; twenty-two released on 78 rpm singles on the Vocalion label), his legacy lives on and has altered the course of American music.

Blues musicians from both the Piney Woods and the Delta claim Robert Johnson and have a strong legacy to build on and to continue. Johnson's style of playing was eclectic, contrasting a heavy bass boogie riff with light treble slides, or he used heavily strummed chords with light spaced out comments to give texture and contrast to his songs. He would sing strictly on the beat, but simultaneously let his guitar improvise freely. He had a commanding ability to make his guitar sound like two. In Johnson's multilayered style he helped to prepare the music that had been purely of the rural community for transmission into the urban inner city. His style of playing was easily adaptable to the blues band and when Mississippians migrated into Chicago in the 1940s and 1950s, the blues style of Robert Johnson came with them.

Scott Dunbar was probably the oldest person that was still around playing the unadulterated raw country blues when his album, *From Lake Mary: Scott Dunbar*, was produced and released in 1972 by Ahura Mazda. Dunbar, son of an ex-slave, was born in 1904 in Deer Park between the Mississippi River and Lake Mary in Wilkinson County. He started learning on a homemade guitar when he was eight and later taught himself to play by accompanying the old people on the plantation. Lee Baker, who lived on the other side of Lake Mary, invited him to play in his band. Dunbar had a large repertoire of originals that he maintained by memory since he was illiterate and could not write. Although he was born and raised and stayed in the Piney Woods, his music sounded more like the raw Delta sound. At the time of his first recording he had already been playing for over fifty years and was one of the most well-known men around Lake Mary (Wolfe 2004). Well after his debut recording, Dunbar stayed around and played for another twenty-two years, dying in 1994, leaving another legacy in the Piney Woods from which younger bluesmen can profit.

The Piney Woods African American secular music combines the Delta's country blues traditions with New Orleans blues piano styles. The music of pianist Charles Nelson of Franklin County reflects these influences. Nelson lives in McCall Creek on land purchased by his father in the 1930s. They still own a hundred acres, and he is still very proud of his family's legacy of being black landowners since the 1930s, which is a very rare feat. He was born into a musical family in 1919. His father, mother, and three brothers could play the guitar and piano, and he learned by the rote method. He remembers accompanying his cousin to fish fries and parties where they would provide the entertainment, playing piano blues in the style of Pinetop Perkins. After the parties they would walk several miles to a logging camp and play until dawn. Nelson played in the boogie-woogie blues piano style, featuring rhythmic left hand with melodies played with the right, largely instrumental and performed solo. He has played for decades at churches, lodges, bars, fish fries, and barrelhouses in logging camps.

Giles Oakley explains: "It was the world of the so-called barrelhouse circuit, where quasi-professional musicians could pick up the themes that ordinary people were creating and add them to their repertoire of ragtime music and popular songs. For many of these pianists the blues was their main style; for others it would be just an occasional piece. Like the guitar songsters of the time, the pianists were often all-around, eclectic musicians" (1997).

To get a better idea and understanding of the scene in the logging camp entertainment and culture, I am including the comments of Little Brother Montgomery, who was a boogie-woogie pianist from Kentwood, Louisiana, also located in the Piney Woods. His father owned a honky-tonk, and dozens of musicians like Jelly Roll Morton and many others passed through. He recalls:

> I was playing honky-tonks, barrelhouses; barrelhouses and honky-tonks same thing. That's where people gamble, shoot dice, back there. They played Marnie, Cotch, you know, Poker and, you know, put the dice through the horn, they played everything. They work all the week, Saturday night they take a bath and they go to the juke, call it the juke, the honky-tonk, barrelhouse, they go down there and gamble until Sunday morning. Well anyway then had somebody playing in the front, somebody playing the piano, me or somebody else. (Quoted in Oakley 1997: 69–70)

Oakley continues to explain the texture of camp life in the Piney Woods, or "forest belt of the South":

> Kentwood was just one of the many company towns in the South which by 1909 was producing nearly half of the nation's timber and large quantities of turpentine. Through the Piney Woods, lumber camps, logging, saw-mill and turpentine camps were set up around the little towns, usually connected by railroads along which hobos, wandering musicians and workers would ride.
> The memories of some of the earlier jazz and blues musicians suggest that blues and boogie-woogie piano styles were developed in these camps. Bunk Johnson and Lead Belly heard boogie in Western Louisiana in the early 1900's. Richard M. Jones first heard it in 1906 in a railroad camp played by a man called "Starvin Chain" (the name itself is that of a folk hero who crops up in a number of obscene folk songs and blues). Men like Starvin Chain would have been playing in the "barrelhouse" jukes installed in the camps by the companies and where drinks could be bought. It was a tough and brutal world, prone to sudden outbreaks of violence, where the work was dangerous and unhealthy and accidents were frequent. The camps were often isolated deep in the woods as the trees got hacked back further and further, and the enforcement of law was rough and ready. The housing provided by the companies was primitive, fresh water and cooking facilities minimal. (Oakley 1997: 71)

There were also "good road" camps where they were building rock roads and they were rough just like the others. The workers in these camps always liked musicians. If you were good, they would always take up for you if you got in trouble. Although pianists were the chief entertainers on the circuit, there were also guitarists. In the world of the Piney Woods, instability was paramount to the whole way of life. The forest belt of the South was rapidly being stripped of its timber by lumber companies. Despite the raucous pleasures of Saturday nights, the realities of the logging camps remained grim for many workers.

> Trees were coming down far faster than any attempt at replanting so that by 1933 over 80 million acres of timberland had been laid waste. The hills and gullies were left scarred, with great ugly gaps where trees had been ripped out or felled, leaving the soil to be eroded by wind and rain. As soon as a timber or railroad company had reduced one bit of woodland to waste, the temporary rails were shifted, the camps moved and the saw-mills closed, leaving the employees with no work. (Oakley 1997: 73)

Musicians who were not pianists also worked the sawmill honky-tonk and barrelhouse circuit and reflected some of the same influences. Guitarist Wakefield "Big Moody" Coney of McComb and Tommy "T-Bone" Pruitt of Hattiesburg are good examples. Like their counterparts in old-time music, these musicians learned from others in the community, a legacy that Wakefield Coney feels obligated to continue (Boykin 1997: 57).

Wakefield "Big Moody" Coney, guitarist and singer, is the senior blues artist of southwest Mississippi. He grew up in the East Fork community in Amite County right outside of McComb. Like many other secular artists, he received his basic training starting at five years old in his grandmother's church. In addition, he sharpened his skills while playing along with records at home and listening to his older cousins play at local gatherings. He began playing professionally at fourteen and formed his own band at eighteen. Working the circuit, he played clubs in Natchez and Kentwood, Louisiana, as well as Woodville and McComb and other towns in the region. It is fortunate that his family is directly involved with the band, including a son, three nephews, and now his grandson. Coney, whether for economic or legacy reasons, is ensuring that the blues and his own legacy live on. In addition, he has been recording some of his originals with a local group and intends to get his music widely distributed (Coney).

David Wilson of Laurel talks about his teacher, Tommy "T-Bone" Pruitt:

> Church, blues bands and all I learned a whole lot from just listening to different people. About that old blues I didn't know too much about that. See, I ran into this guy name of Tommy Pruitt. The man could play some blues, I mean this guy's good. You put him and B. B. King in a room together, if you ain't looking at who's playing you won't know. He's just that good [on guitar]. He does a pretty good job [at singing].... Yeah, he taught me [guitar]. (1999)

Wilson's mentor, Tommy "T-Bone" Pruitt, was born in 1933 and came from a musical family in Ellisville, Mississippi (Jones County). Joe Pruitt, his father, was a fiddler, harmonica player, and tap dancer. He enlisted his eleven children to sing in front of businesses in Laurel for tips. One of Pruitt's brothers played what he refers to as "Spanish music" and the older brother "Baby Ruth" traveled widely "like Robert Johnson" as an accomplished blues artist. Also like Johnson, he died very young when an acquaintance mistook him for an intruder and killed him. After his brother would not allow him to play his guitar, Pruitt made his own "diddley-bow" (ad hoc homemade string instrument) on the side of the house and played it like a string bass. He later created his second homemade string instrument (with four strings) from screen wire, a board, and a cigar box. He remembers that many aspiring bluesmen at the time played ad hoc instruments, including washtub basses, washboards, and "harmonicas" made from paper and combs. He finally received his first real guitar and amplifier after marrying his wife, Verta, in 1950. He plays mostly in the Laurel/Hattiesburg area with other bands like the Rhythm Aces out of Bogalusa, Louisiana, and his own band, the Rhythm Rockers. During the 1960s he toured with Bo Diddley, the Five Royals, and Ernie K-Doe and appeared on shows together with Ike and Tina Turner, Ivory Joe Hunter, and Solomon Burke. He notes that his band's repertoire has a wide range, from originals to covers of songs by Muddy Waters, Jimmy Reed, and B. B. King to popular standards including "Summertime" and "Misty." He states, "I mix it up ... and try to play something for everybody. I've been playing for sixty years, so I know how to feel out what people out there like." In 1975, he opened a blues club, The Blue Poodle, in Ellisville. He sold it several years later and in 2007 was renovating another building into a blues club located in Laurel (Barretta).

The country blues entered the world of popular music, although its place has been largely on the fringes of the musical mainstream as a provider of ideas and resources. The following segment consists of interview excerpts with the folklorist Worth Long and the blues musician David

Wilson. They are focusing on the changes in the blues, DJs, gospel, and hip-hop and how it relates to the Piney Woods and thus community identity.

> DAVID WILSON: [A]t this point live bands ain't really kicking. It's just the DJs taking over these days. Rap. Rap is exactly what is going on. Rap is okay. I'm just going to be honest. I ain't too much into gangsta rap. I don't like that too much but that old school rap as they used to call it. I like that. I used to do some of that myself to tell you the truth....
>
> WORTH LONG: Is there ever going to be something like a blues rap? I am talking about a fusion. I was just wondering.
>
> WILSON: I don't know, I'm just going to be honest. I'm like most other people, maybe I shouldn't be, but I still associate the blues with way back in the days. And it just don't seem, rap it just don't seem to go together with me.
>
> LONG: It was a different experience.
>
> WILSON: Yeah, very different.
>
> LONG: Different experience. Well, the blues were sung to sell liquor and to bring people into the club for live music. Rap is sung to sell intoxicants of another kind still, isn't it? You're saying they're very different.
>
> WILSON: Blues is good music. I like it. And maybe, okay, now I've gone places even some of these younger guys are getting into blues, at least listening to it if not playing it. Little old clubs out in the country towns called Hebron where young people get into everything out there.... It's in Jones County.
>
> LONG: But they can play some blues?
>
> WILSON: Yeah, yeah, they play blues at the club, they play rap. Like I was there last night, as a matter of fact, had to take somebody there. They play one song rap and the very next song was the blues. And they were getting off into that one too.

LONG: And they played it good? Was there a singer?

WILSON: No, it was a DJ doing this, and they even liked it.

LONG: Yeah. So I mean the blues is not a music that people would hate just because they're young people?

WILSON: Right. That's one thing that, how shall we say, it bridges the generation gap.

LONG: Yeah, it bridges generations, yeah.

The blues and hip-hop are different as far as the technical aspect of the music, but lyrics and sensibilities are parallel. Yes, the language and images in hip-hop are sometimes offensive, but look at the deplorable conditions that it arises from. The blues had just as much hard-core sensibilities and lyrics, albeit lyrics were not as overt and much double entendre was utilized. In Michael Grafton's article "Hip Hop Ain't Nothing But the Young People's Blues," he clearly states the main premise in a succinct way:

> With all the technology, economic resources, goodwill, and intellectual mind power within the United States of America, it makes absolutely no sense that the blues artist of yesterday and the hip-hop artist of today voice the same concerns. . . . Although the names have changed from Blues to Hip-Hop; Muddy Waters to Snoop Dog; Clarence Brown to 50 Cent; John Lee Hooker to Tupac; and Lightnin Hopkins to Dr. Dre, the hardcore language and images of both art forms reflect the same reality from which blues musicians found their songs of despair and from which hip-hop artists are inspired to give voice to and paint portraits of what they see and feel. (2007)

In their conversation, Wilson and Long address this question of inspiration, the future, and identity:

LONG: Right. What's going to be different? What's going to be the music for the future for your family? If I say five years from now what y'all figure you are going to be singing. If I visit you at your mansion, yeah, and I come by and say, "What y'all singing now?"

WILSON: If we're living in a mansion we're going to be singing R & B. I got to admit I love gospel, but I just hate it's not supported as well as R & B. They won't support it, come out and support it.

LONG: You are saying the money is in R & B?

WILSON: Right. That's where the money is.

Yes, the money is in R & B. This is one of the reasons why gospel and blues musicians crossed over to this genre.

But it is good to see the blues finally getting its due ... I just wish these young folks would decide to learn more about our history as a race.... And hey, I'm going to be honest, we black folk came up with some pretty good music styles, blues, New Orleans jazz. I'm not certain who originated zydeco, but I've heard some of that too.

LONG: It's Creole, Creole music.

WILSON: That's right, Creole.

The marginal place of the blues has enabled this music to retain an identity of its own and to have a distinct history of stylistic development for over a century. Considering all of these years, the blues is still in remarkably good shape. Even in the present-day Piney Woods, the people still have the community and regional festivals and gatherings, including the Great Day at Bude and the Labor Day Weekend Blues Festival at Percy Bryant's farm. They still experience the blues in the rural clubs where some of the DJs even mix hip-hop with the blues for a younger audience.

CONCLUSION

Along with other forms of expressive culture, black music in the Piney Woods allowed members of the community to express themselves communally and individually, to derive great spiritual and aesthetic pleasure, to perpetuate traditions and values, to create new expressions and to maintain a sense of identity. These selective traditions of worship and entertainment in the Piney Woods region constantly reunite African Americans by reminding them of their shared but multifocal heritage. Sacred and secular traditions are shaped by a collective and selective memory. The gatherings, in churches or clubs, are still binding people together with a shared identity, providing them a sense of community, and giving all members of these communities a chance to participate in the democracy of music, in which all participants are equally vital in the tradition's performance and preservation. Decisions are made by regarding fundamental and shared values. To be an active participant in these traditions is to relive and identify with the past and the present and to make it a source of power for the future.

NOTE

I am grateful to Carolyn Ware, Worth Long, and Scott McGraw for the use of their field interviews gathered while working under the auspices of the Pine Hills Culture Program. In addition, I would like to acknowledge the Center for Oral History and Cultural Heritage and the Pine Hills Culture Program of the University of Southern Mississippi for their release and permission to utilize the materials.

BIBLIOGRAPHY

Baraka, Amiri (LeRoi Jones).1963. *Blues People: Negro Music in White America.* New York: Morrow.

Barretta, Scott. Nd. Tommie "T-Bone" Pruitt. *Mississippi Folklife and Folk Artist Directory.* www.arts.state.ms.us/folklife/artist.php?dirname=pruitt_tommie.

Ben-Amos, Dan. 1984. The Seven Strands of Tradition: Varieties in Its Meaning in American Folklore Studies. *Journal of American Folklore Research* Vol. 21: pp. 97–131.

Bolton, Charles. 1997. A Brief History of Mississippi's Pine Hills. Special Issue of *Mississippi Folklife* Vol. 30, Nos. 1 and 2, pp.14–23.

Boyd, Joe D. 1971. Negro Sacred Harp Singing in Mississippi. *Mississippi Folklore Register* Vol. 5, No. 3 (Fall): pp.60–83.

———. 1970. Judge Jackson: Black Giant of White Spirituals. *Journal of American Folklore* Vol. 83, No. 330 (October–December): pp. 446–451.

Boykin, Deborah. 1997. Pine Hills Music. Special Issue of *Mississippi Folklife* Vol. 30, Nos. 1 and 2, pp.52–59.

Burke, Kenneth. 1964. Literature as Equipment for Living. In *Perspectives by Incongruity,* ed. by Stanley Edgar Hyman, pp.100–109. Bloomington: Indiana University Press.

Coney, Wakefield "Big Moody." Nd. *Mississippi Folklife and Folk Artist Directory.* www.arts.state.ms.us/folklife/artist.php?dirname=coney_wakefield.

Downey, James C. 1986. Sacred Harp Singing in the Piney Woods. In *A Human Perspective: Mississippi's Piney Woods,* ed. by Noel Polk, pp. 92–102. Jackson: University Press of Mississippi.

Durkheim, Émile. 1965. *The Elementary Forms of the Religious Life*. New York: Free Press.

Ellison, Ralph. 1964. *Shadow and Act*. New York: Random House.

Grafton, Michael O. 2007. Hip Hop Ain't Nothing But the Young People's Blues. www.mybrotha.com/hip-hop-blues.asp.

Hobsbawm, Eric, and Terence Ranger. 1983. *The Invention of Tradition*. Cambridge: Cambridge University Press.

Jackson, Joyce Marie. 1995. The Changing Nature of Gospel Music: A Southern Case Study. *African American Review* Vol. 29, No. 2, pp.185–200.

———. 2005. Working Both Sides of the Fence: African American Quartets Enter the Realm of Popular Culture. In *Bridging Southern Cultures: An Interdisciplinary Approach*, ed. by John Lowe, pp.154–171. Baton Rouge: Louisiana State University Press.

Jackson, Judge. 1992. *The Colored Sacred Harp, For Singing Class, Singing School, Convention and General Use in Christian Work and Worship*. Montgomery, Alabama: Brown Printing.

Lewis, Julia. 1998. Interview conducted by Scott McGraw, 10 September.

Lincoln, C. Eric, and Lawrence H. Mamiya. 1990. *The Black Church in the African American Experience*. Durham, NC: Duke University Press.

McGraw, Scott. Nd. Charles Nelson. *Mississippi Folklife and Folk Artist Directory*. www.arts.state.ms.us/folklife/artist.php?dirmame=nelson_charles.

Mirsky, Richard M. 1983. Perspectives in the Study of Food Habits. In *Foodways & Eating Habits: Directions for Research*, ed. by Michael Owen Jones et al. Los Angeles: California Folklore Society.

Murray, Albert. 1976. *Stomping the Blues*. New York: Da Capo Press.

Olson, Ted. 1999. The Sacred Harp Singing Tradition of Calhoun County, Mississippi. *Prospectus: An Annual of American Cultural Studies* Vol. 24, pp. 261–283.

Smiley, A. C. 2000. Interview conducted by Carolyn Ware, 3 May.

Smith, Floree. 2000. Interview conducted by Carolyn Ware, 3 May.

Ware, Carolyn. 1997. Piney Woods Folklife and Pine Hills Community Scholars. Special Issue of *Mississippi Folklife*, Vol. 30, Nos. 1 and 2, pp. 5–11.

———.1997. Piney Woods People and Traditions. Special Issue of *Mississippi Folklife*, Vol. 30, Nos. 1 and 2, pp. 82–94.

White, Joyce. 1998. *Soul Food: Recipes and Reflections from African-American Churches*. New York: Harper Collins.

Whitehead, Tony Larry. 1984. Sociocultural Dynamics and Food Habits in a Southern Community. In *Food in the Social Order: Studies of Food and Festivities in Three American Communities*, ed. by Mary Douglas. New York: Russell Sage Foundation, 1984.

Willis, Chiquita G., ed. 1994. *The African American Shape Note & Vocal Music Singing Convention Directory*. Special issue of *Mississippi Folklife*, Vol. 27, 1994. Oxford, MS: Mississippi Folklore Society and Center for the Study of Southern Culture at the University of Mississippi.

Wilson, David, and Deborah Wilson. 1999. Interview with Worth Long, 15 February, Laurel, MS.

Wolfe, Karl Michael. 1972. *From Lake Mary: Scott Dunbar*. Album liner notes, Fat Possum Records 2004. www.fatpossum.com/artists/dunbar.html.

4

THE STORY OF MOUND BAYOU

PART I: DESCENDANT COMMUNITY INVOLVEMENT IN
AFRICAN AMERICAN ARCHAEOLOGY IN MISSISSIPPI:
DIGGING FOR THE DREAM IN MOUND BAYOU
—AMY L. YOUNG
—MILBURN J. CROWE

Introduction and History of Mound Bayou[1]

In March 1998, a pubic dig was held in Mound Bayou, Mississippi. The excavation was conducted by Amy Young, Milburn Crowe, five students from the University of Southern Mississippi, and, most important, local youth. After a brief sketch of the history of this remarkable all-black town in the Mississippi Delta was given, there was a discussion of the steps taken in working with a descendant community. The purpose was to share information about what we found that works when descendant communities participate in archaeological investigations.

Mound Bayou was established in 1887 by Isaiah T. Montgomery and his cousin Benjamin Green (Hermann 1981; Hamilton 1991). It is located in Bolivar County, Mississippi, in the region known as the Delta. The Delta is renowned for its many vast late antebellum cotton plantations (Cobb 1992). Montgomery and Green established Mound Bayou to be a haven and self-sufficient black community in the midst of the white-controlled cotton kingdom. This is especially remarkable considering the violence of the post-Reconstruction era in the Deep South, particularly in the Delta. Isaiah Montgomery and Benjamin Green and the other early pioneers of Mound Bayou wanted to create a refuge for blacks in the heart of this plantation country. In the words of modern residents, "Mound Bayou was a place where a black man could run *for* sheriff instead of *from* the sheriff."

Isaiah Montgomery was born a slave on May 21, 1847, to Ben and Mary Montgomery (Hamilton 1991). Ben Montgomery was one of Joseph Davis's (brother of Jefferson Davis) favored slaves. Ben Montgomery learned special skills (farm management, reading, and writing) and managed to accumulate some wealth. His son, Isaiah, served as Joseph Davis's personal slave and secretary until Davis fled the Union Army in 1862 (Hamilton 1991).

After the war, Ben Montgomery purchased Brierfield and Hurricane plantations at Davis Bend that had been owned by Joseph Davis (Hamilton 1991). Because of financial setbacks, however, he lost the property in 1881. His son, Isaiah Montgomery, spent his life trying to bring his family back to their former state of wealth and comfort. Mound Bayou was one of the results of these efforts (Hamilton 1991).

Benjamin Green was born a slave in 1857 on the Davis Bend settlement. In 1886 he lived with his aunt, Mrs. Benjamin Montgomery (Isaiah Montgomery's mother), and learned the planting and mercantile businesses. Green was the Montgomerys' mercantile manager at Davis Bend. Benjamin Green and Isaiah Montgomery convinced other former slaves from the Davis Bend area near Vicksburg to join them in the settlement. They also attracted other black settlers to Mound Bayou, as well. Modern Mound Bayou residents feel that the success of the early colony is a clear demonstration of the potential and abilities of peoples who had been enslaved. Therefore, modern Mound Bayouans are not ashamed of their roots in slavery, but rather proud.

Mound Bayou was to be developed as part of the extension of railroads into the Deep South, and was thus placed on the Louisville, New Orleans, and Texas line (Hamilton 1991: 43). The Delta during the 1880s was still largely uninhabited and an untamed wilderness. Even in the twentieth century there were still vast tracts of Delta that remained a wilderness. The cotton plantations were located primarily on the Mississippi River, but the remainder of the Delta contained thick forests of hardwoods and pine trees, with numerous streams and bayous which made the area virtually impenetrable. "Poisonous snakes, wolves, panthers, and bears endangered adventurers . . . and settlers" (Hamilton 1991: 44). The earliest colonists of Mound Bayou were faced with the tremendous task of carving a town and community out of the wilderness with little or no economic resources. The railroad served to connect Mound Bayou with the rest of the nation. According to Hamilton (1991: 50–51), the experiences of a pioneer of Mound Bayou named Simon Gaiter seem to typify those of most of the early settlers. Gaiter arrived in 1887 with $175, but his family did not join him until the following year. Gaiter purchased a forty-acre plot, cleared a small part, and with the timber built a log house for his family. After the down payment of $40, the purchase of supplies, and the cost of transporting his family and his possessions to Mound Bayou, Gaiter was left with only $10. This was not enough to make it through the first year. Gaiter had his wife and children clear five acres of the town for $4 per acre, and Gaiter himself cut firewood for $6 per cord. Gaiter's children and wife also picked cotton for $0.50 per hundredweight. Gaiter supplemented the family's diet with hunting and fishing, but recalled many weeks without meat (Hamilton 1991: 50–51).

In the 1890s and in the first years of the twentieth century, the population of the town and surrounding black colony grew (Hamilton 1991: 53). Isaiah Montgomery, Benjamin Green, and other pioneers not only spent time in their own family pursuits establishing businesses and farms, but also continued to contact people of means around the nation to invest in Mound Bayou, with the ultimate goal of making the town self-sufficient. In 1891 there were about 500 residents in the colony. In 1893 there were 183 living in the town proper. By 1900, the town was home to 287 residents with an additional 1500 living in the hinterlands on farms (Hamilton 1991:53). A study of the 1900 census of Mound Bayou shows 65 households. It is evident that Mound Bayouans placed a priority on education. Nearly 90 percent of the population could read, according to the census. The most common occupations were farmer, farm laborer, day laborer, servant, and grocer. Most of those listed as farm laborer apparently worked on their fathers' farms. Day laborers hired out on other farms. There were two blacksmiths in Mound Bayou in 1900, two general contractors, three ministers, three carpenters, a postmaster, a stenographer, a wheelwright, a barber, two teachers, one lawyer, and one physician.

In the first years of the twentieth century, a prominent black businessman, Charles Banks, arrived in the community and founded the Bank of Mound Bayou. By 1910 the pioneers of Mound Bayou had succeeded in transforming the little community into a thriving town of five hundred people, and many more in the hinterlands, with thirteen stores, six churches, a train station, a telephone exchange, and a weekly newspaper. It appeared that the dream of Isaiah Montgomery and the other early settlers had been realized (Hermann 1981). President Theodore Roosevelt named Mound Bayou "The Jewel of the Delta" and the town had the backing of Booker T. Washington and many other prominent Americans. Various industrial endeavors were established in the town. These included several cotton gins and a cotton oil mill. The cotton oil mill was erected as an additional economic boost to the economy of Mound Bayou.

Mound Bayouans understand that their unique history has also given them a unique perspective. Mound Bayou has *always* had black officials like mayors, sheriffs, school board members, aldermen, and police, so that the fears associated with dealing with the white counterparts have been somewhat subdued in local residents. They recognized that black folks had much to fear from whites outside of town, but they have never really felt that once black officials are in place all problems are automatically solved. Also, the everyday oppression felt by many black Mississippians in the early part of this century was not the norm for Mound Bayouans; however, residents could never remain shielded from the harsh outside world. More than anything, Mound Bayouans feel that they have a special story to tell and that their town holds a very special place in local, state, and national history. They feel that their town can be a source of pride for many Americans, not just Mound Bayouans. They also strongly feel that their youth need to be exposed to their own history and culture, but because of encroaching economic conditions, this is becoming more and more difficult. Mound Bayouans are proud of their history and want to share it. Also, because Mound Bayouans do not want Isaiah Montgomery's dream to fade, the project was entitled "Digging for the Dream: Archaeology at Mound Bayou."

To our knowledge, this is the first archaeological project designed and implemented by a black community. The public outreach, plus the involvement of the community in discovering and interpreting their past, then relating that history to outsiders, makes this project another example of the pioneering efforts of the citizens of Mound Bayou.

Working with Descendant Communities

Involvement of descendant communities is an increasingly visible topic in historical archaeology (McKee 1998; McDavid 1997; Derry 1997; Blakey 1997; Singleton 1997). Within African American archaeology the issue of involving descendant communities has gone beyond an interesting, and possibly productive, idea to being a necessity. The political, social, and economic effects of archaeological investigations (and the resulting interpretations) on the descendant community and the entire nation must be considered by archaeologists (Blakey 1997). Suggestions by archaeologists for involving descendant communities have run the gamut from informing these groups after the fact (e.g., give a public slide presentation), to having descendant communities involved in earlier stages of research (Edwards-Ingram 1997). Further, many archaeologists have been confronted by difficulties trying to involve descendant communities in the archaeological research (McDavid 1997; Derry 1997). Clearly, involvement of descendant communities is complex and time consuming for archaeologists, but also very important in African American archaeology.

The remainder of this paper describes the process, which is on-going, of public archaeology in Mound Bayou, Mississippi. The effort is a sustained collaboration between a professional archaeologist and the local citizens. We will outline the steps we have taken, and the issues we have faced to accomplish a public dig.

The Steps

The archaeology at Mound Bayou began as a chance encounter between the two authors of this article. Milburn Crowe was a native and historian of Mound Bayou. Amy Young met him as he served as the president of the Mississippi African American Historic Preservation Council. Crowe invited Young as soon as he understood her research area was African American archaeology. Crowe had been thinking about the possibility of archaeology in his town. What made this first step easy was that Crowe already had some understanding of historical archaeology, which is remarkable in itself. He had met Theresa Singleton when she was involved in the conference "Digging the Afro-American Past." While that conference was held in Oxford, Mississippi, it also included a tour of Mound Bayou. Most nonarchaeologists have no understanding of the profession of archaeology and often equate archaeology with Indiana Jones. Without a basic understanding of the potential and limitations of modern archaeology, collaboration between professional archaeologists and others is very difficult.

Despite the knowledge that Crowe had an understanding of historical archaeology, when Young first visited Mound Bayou, she made a slide presentation of her work on other African American sites so that he and other local residents might know something about the kinds of information obtained in the work. This was very important because it made the descendant community aware of the potential and the limits of archaeology. This step, educating the descendant community, is absolutely critical for public archaeology and for involvement of a descendant community in archaeology. It is somewhat unfortunate that nonarchaeologists have such a limited understanding of archaeology and often equate it with treasure hunting.

During this first visit, Crowe and other residents began educating Young about the history of their town. The history presented in the first part of this article is the story of Mound Bayou from the perspective of local residents. All referenced material was checked with residents for accuracy. Learning the history from the perspective of the descendant community was the second step for the archaeologist in working with a descendant community. In this case, because of the pride Mound Bayouans feel for their history and culture, this second step was also easy. Understanding the history and the source of pride that Mound Bayou provides to residents was critical for the archaeologist who was often reminded by the residents that history is a very personal thing and that archaeologists are actually digging up (through excavations and through interviews) intimate aspects of their past. Interestingly, while Young was taught the history of Mound Bayou, she also learned of the diversity of opinions within the community and how this affects modern cultural traditions like their annual Heritage Festival. Recognizing the diversity within a descendant community is the third step in working with a descendant community. For example, there are Mound Bayouans who are descended from the original pioneers. There are Mound Bayouans who are descended from later immigrants. This is a source of potential conflict, even if it is only friendly competition. Knowledge of the history and culture of another community from the perspective of the descendant community is also critical for a successful project.

Once it was decided that a dig was to take place, then the fourth step was to find the right site. Because of the potential divisiveness within the community based on descent from early pioneer or later immigrant, Young encouraged a focus on a site with which all Mound Bayouans could identify. In other words, we decided not to excavate at the home of one of the founding families, but on a public or commercial site. In this case, the choice was relatively simple. Mound Bayouans recognize that they have several important buildings, including the Bank of Mound Bayou, constructed in 1904 by Charles Banks, a later immigrant. The old bank building is in a state of disrepair because the current owner cannot afford to fix it. The Mound Bayou Historic Preservation Council hopes eventually to acquire the building and obtain funds to stabilize and reconstruct it. Some hope it can be used as a cultural center.

The Bank of Mound Bayou is a two-story brick structure standing on the corner of West Main and Green streets (Lot 1, Green's Square). It is listed on the National Register of Historic Places. The first floor contained the bank, and the second story held offices, including the office of a physician, Dr. Scott Harris, and offices of the Mound Bayou Oil Mill. The building served as the headquarters of the Knights and Daughters of Tabor, a black fraternal organization aimed at helping widows and orphans and supporting black business endeavors. Charles Banks organized the Mississippi Negro Business League as a chapter of Booker T. Washington's national organization, also located in the Bank of Mound Bayou (Hermann 1981). The building occupies almost the entire lot, and it was thought that Lot 2 might contain refuse from the building, as it was vacant until 1919 or 1920. The refuse may help in understanding the daily activities that took place in the bank building, and many of these activities are associated with the early organization and business activities of the town.

The lot on which we excavated, besides being immediately adjacent to the Bank of Mound Bayou, was eventually the site of the first city hall and mayor's office. The building which served as the first city hall was constructed in 1919 or 1920 by Benjamin A. Green, Benjamin Green's son and first child born in Mound Bayou. Benjamin A. Green served as mayor of Mound Bayou from 1920 until around 1970. All of these factors made the lot ideal for an archaeological excavation. Choosing the site together with the descendant community is absolutely necessary so that the archaeologist has the support of residents.

Many residents of Mound Bayou felt that the local youth had a poor-to-marginal understanding of the history and culture of Mound Bayou. They felt that it was necessary to involve young people in the archaeological project. Thus the public aspect of this project was born. We decided where to dig and that this was to be a local effort. Crowe and Young wrote a grant proposal to fund a public dig, and because it would involve school-age children, the excavation was scheduled for spring break. The fifth step in working with a descendant community is to directly involve local people in the work. In this case, the youth of Mound Bayou excavated with us. The decision to involve the youth of Mound Bayou in the archaeology was one of the wisest decisions we made. Instead of strangers coming into town to excavate, it put control in the hands of the descendant community. Furthermore, in a community that has experienced continual oppression from whites and made some local residents reluctant to share memories, it opened the door to additional information in the form of oral histories shared more with the youth than with strangers. After the excavation and the processing and identification of the artifacts, the story of this public dig and what we found will be disseminated throughout Mississippi in the form of a traveling exhibit, "Digging for the Dream in Mound Bayou."

The last step in working with a descendant community is to make sure all interpretations are approved by that community. In this case, Young made a subsequent visit to Mound Bayou to meet with the mayor and the Historic Preservation Council where she laid out ideas for the exhibit, which they commented upon and approved. Most of her suggestions were greeted warmly and the input added detail and richness to the exhibit. This last step is the most important of all, because who owns the story of Mound Bayou but Mound Bayouans. The "Digging for the Dream" project culminated in a final public forum to disseminate the findings during Mississippi's Archaeology Week. Young gave a brief slide presentation of the dig, and Theresa Singleton came and talked about the place of Mound Bayou in state, national, and international history. Dr. Alferdteen Harrison from Jackson State University also spoke, as did the mayor of Mound Bayou and Milburn Crowe.

Conclusions

The public excavations at Mound Bayou were a tremendous success for a number of reasons. First, Mound Bayouans initiated the project and had control over the site and the subsequent interpretations. Second, a dialogue between Mound Bayouans and professional archaeologists was facilitated through mutual interests and through involvement of the youth of Mound Bayou. Third, involvement of the youth of Mound Bayou in the excavations tended to open the doors (and memories) to outsiders. In this way, elderly residents felt they were sharing their memories and oral histories with their younger residents rather than outsiders who might not understand. Third, Mound Bayouans are proud of their history and want to share this history with everyone. They believed that archaeology would be an effective way of gaining the attention of the public to educate them about Mound Bayou.

Because of the work of the volunteers, those who excavated and those who shared their knowledge, we now know more about the activities that took place within the Bank of Mound Bayou and city hall. We have a secure date of ca. 1920 for the construction of the city hall building. But perhaps even more important, the youth of Mound Bayou have a deeper appreciation of the history of their important community and can now share that history with others across the state.

The overall success of the "Digging for the Dream" project is, in part, attributable to the unique character and culture heritage within the community of Mound Bayou. This case study of working with descendant communities, therefore, is ideal. However, in archaeological and cultural investigations of black life in and around Natchez, Mississippi, the same basic principles were adopted and also have been successful. One of the biggest problems to overcome in working with African American descendant communities is the perspective shared by part of the community that there is something shameful in the history of slavery. In other words, there is some degree of shame within the black community concerning slavery and descent from slaves. In the case of Mound Bayou, this was not an issue. However, through trust, respectful discussion, and mutual education, this can be overcome. Building trusting relationships, though, is very time consuming for the archaeologist and for members of the descendant community. One final step in working with descendant communities is not to force any beliefs or issues on that community until there is a general willingness to be open and trusting in the exchange of information.

PART II: AN ARCHAEOLOGICAL AND ARCHITECTURAL STUDY OF MODERNIZATION IN MOUND BAYOU, MISSISSIPPI, 1887–1940
— AMY L. YOUNG

The majority of African Americans held in bondage in the Southeast lived and labored on farms and plantations. Thus a rural, self-sufficient agricultural existence defined the African American experience in slavery (Young 2004; Young et al. 2001). Most of what was needed to survive, namely food, water, fuel, materials for shelter, and means to dispose of waste, was produced or contained within the farmstead or plantation. Further, previous studies indicate that survival for African Americans depended largely on establishing cooperative, reciprocal ties within the slave quarter community (Webber 1978; Young 1995; Young 1997). However, between Emancipation and civil rights, a radical shift in southeastern African American lifeways occurred, slowly at first, and then more rapidly with the onset of farm mechanization. The shift was from rural to urban, from extended family and community-based relationships to emphasis on the individual, and from self-sufficiency to heavy dependence on industrially produced goods. In the Delta region in Mississippi, just after the Civil War over 90 percent of the African American population was rural. Though the details of this dramatic transformation are not fully documented, by 1890 nearly 70 percent of the African American population in the Delta shifted to municipal residences (Aiken 1987, 1990). This study examines the transformational processes between the 1880s and the mid-twentieth century in Mound Bayou, Mississippi. Mound Bayou, located in the heart of the Delta, was specifically built as a cooperative all-black town to serve as a center of industry and commerce in the midst of white-controlled cotton plantations in the region.

Mound Bayou presents an interesting opportunity to explore modernizing processes because the town, founded by former slaves, was conceived as an industrial and commercial center. Nevertheless, the majority of the residents of the colony lived in the hinterlands surrounding the town as sharecroppers and tenant farmers. In addition to many other problems experienced by African Americans after freedom, not the least of which included escalating threats and instances of attacks by white mobs (Foner 1988; Kolchin 1992; Litwack 1979; Magdol 1977; McMillen 1989; Powdermaker 1993), Woodman (1997) suggests that many former slaves between 1880 and the 1930s were attempting to climb the agricultural ladder to farm ownership, but often at the expense of better incomes. The racialized agricultural system in the Southeast offered essentially two choices for most former slaves: working as croppers/wage laborers under close supervision of plantation owners that might yield more income, or tenancy/ownership of small farms often with inferior land but without close supervision. This latter option was preferred by many because it removed black families from the scrutiny of white owners and overseers and offered some opportunity for self-sufficiency, but it often meant that former slaves began the climb up the agricultural ladder without tools, work animals, or capital to invest in fertilizer or larger plots of land. Typically, the small plots of land they could afford could not support a family, so many had to have nonfarm work, or work as croppers to supplement income from their own farm. Modernization under these circumstances would have been quite difficult. Mound Bayou, because it was conceived explicitly to be modern and was home to a broad range of residents, from poor farmers and sharecroppers to successful business people and industrialists, seems an ideal case study for the examination of modernization processes. Also, because Mound Bayou was founded by former slaves who, during slavery, relied on strong kin-based community relationships for survival, rather than concentrating effort on individual residences, processes of modernization might best be illuminated through the examination of two community sites, the Bank of Mound Bayou and the first town hall. These two institutions occupied contiguous lots in town.

Modernization Theory

Recently a number of archaeologists have effectively utilized modernization theory to examine the shift to modern life in North America (Ahlman

1996; Cabak and Inkrot 1997; Cabak et al. 1997; Groover 1992; Groover and Cabak 1992). Modernization theory, a product of the cold war in the industrialized West, attempted to both explain and encourage economic development in Third World countries. Modernization is conceptualized as a cultural, political, and economic process whereby societies adopt characteristics of Western industrialized culture (Haviland 2003; Levine 1963; Preston 1981; Rostow 1960). Within this school of thought, developing societies are characterized as progressing through transformational stages culminating in a society heavily dependent on consumption and industrialized production. Scholars often classify societies as either modern or traditional.

Modern societies are characterized as those that exhibit high levels of mass consumption (Rostow 1960) and value technological innovations, formal education, secular rationality, and scientific thinking (Ferraro 2002; Miller 2002). Traditional societies, in contrast, tend to be defined as those emphasizing ascribed or inherited rather than achieved status, and instead of embracing innovation and technology, are resistant to change. Rather than being based on complex social, economic, and political structures, traditional societies are predominantly kin-based.

Both modern and traditional life have a material reality, but are defined in part by what exists in the minds of members of those societies: ideas, beliefs, and values. In this context, modernization theory is highly suitable for historical archaeology with a long and successful history of addressing both material culture and the cultural information encoded in that material culture (Deetz 1977; Leone 1984).

There are drawbacks to modernization theory, however. The theory assumes a progressive, unilinear track (Cabak and Inkrot 1997; Cabak et al.1999). As Cabak et al. (1999) indicate, modernization theory has been highly criticized for Eurocentric and Americancentric biases. Also, because modernization theory is a generalizing explanatory model, scholars have tended to ignore specific historical processes or recognize that modernization can occur in different ways and at different rates. Therefore, like Cabak et al. (1999), this study utilizes aspects of modernization theory rather than adopting it whole cloth.

This examination of modernizing processes in Mound Bayou focuses on architectural data from a standing structure and the archaeological record. The Bank of Mound Bayou, established in 1904, is still standing and is located adjacent to the archaeological site of the first town hall built ca. 1920.

Vernacular, National, and Academic Architecture: Traditional, Transitioning, and Modern Societies

Buildings, especially ordinary buildings, constitute one of the most common and most important artifacts encountered by historical archaeologists. As Carter and Cromley (2005) indicate, vernacular structures (ordinary buildings) have a material reality, but like other types of material culture, are excellent indicators of cultural ideas, values, and beliefs. They define vernacular architectural studies as the examination of those human actions and behaviors that are manifest in commonplace architecture (Carter and Cromley 2005). Where buildings are placed on the landscape, their form or design, and the kinds of materials used in their construction are especially useful in deciphering the meaning of those buildings. In other words, a building is an object with both substance and content, evoking images, ideas, and meanings for its users (Carter and Cromley 2005: vi–xv). For example, emphasis on privacy or the role of the individual is expressed in architecture through such things as single-purpose rooms, individual sleeping chambers, or even individual bathrooms. Conversely, dwellings with one or two multipurpose rooms such as a saddlebag log house or a hall-and-parlor home with no private sleeping chambers reflect ideals of communal life. Emphasis on the value of achieved status and material progress is expressed through fashionable styles of buildings that utilize up-to-date construction materials.

Scholars of American architecture often classify buildings as either folk or academic. Folk architecture is "built to provide basic shelter with little regard for changing fashion" (McAlester and McAlester 1976: 63). Folk houses are typically built by the future occupants, though sometimes with the help of local contractors. Also, folk house construction uses locally available materials such as wood, stone, or brick burned just off site in clamps or scove kilns. Folk building traditions are handed down through generations and change very little. For this study, folk housing is characteristic of traditional lifeways.

An excellent example of folk housing comes from the diary of William B. Scothern, a contractor who built for planters in the Natchez, Mississippi, area in the late antebellum period. He indicates slave and overseer dwellings should be:

> Double cabins, with 12 feet open passage (floored) between the cabins to be 10½ feet high from top of sill to top of plate. To be planked, with

plank 10–12 inches wide, 1½ inches thick (up & down) & joints covered, with Laths, 3 inches wide, ¾ inches thick. The flooring planks to be jointed & laid on Laths, so that the joints may be covered.

The upright plank to project high enough above the plates to come close up to the shingles, & the gable ends weatherboarded so close as to exclude the air *entirely*. The houses to be raised on brick pillars, 3 feet from the surface of the earth to the top of the sills. To be covered with 3 feet boards, & the eaves to project 10 or 12 inches over the sides of the house, & the ends to project 12 inches over the gables.

16 cabins of this size, 8 on each side of the center, & a space of 120 feet left between the to center cabins.

The overseers' house, to be of the same size and description, raised 5½ feet above the earth, & to have a gallery 10 ft. wide in front and rear, & 2 windows in front and 2 in rear, & 2 rooms 12 by 10, taken off the back gallery, one at each end. The height from floor to ceiling to be 11 feet. (Eisele 1985)

Clearly this document represents fairly typical slave and overseer dwellings, dogtrots that once dotted the landscape of the Southeast, and represents ideas handed down through generations. The cabins described by Scothern would have been built with local materials. Also of interest is the information encoded in the material culture. In this case, the relative building heights and the presence or absence of a gallery are used to graphically represent (and most likely reinforce) the plantation hierarchy, where the overseer could stand on his gallery and literally oversee the slave quarter community.

National housing is a special category of folk housing (McAlester and McAlester 1986: 89). National housing became increasingly popular in the second half of the nineteenth century and dominated the American landscape through the first half of the twentieth century. National forms often adapted folk housing traditions by altering construction techniques such as using balloon framing with nail joinery instead of log construction or timber-framing with mortise-and-tenon joinery. Standardized lumber from lumber yards was very common. The use of modern construction materials such as concrete and machine-made brick from distant brick yards is characteristic as well.

National housing, for the purposes of this study, includes folk houses modified with the addition of stylistic (academic) features as well as through use of modern building materials. Glassie describes Irish houses modified through the use of metal roofs rather than thatch roofs and the painting of houses bright white (Glassie 2000: 25–36). Academic embellishments such as Queen Anne spindle posts on a folk house porch or the mixing of academic elements are also considered here as characteristic of national housing. An example of mixing academic elements is provided by Glassie who describes a house in Bibb County, Georgia, as a "Georgian box with a Greek memory and Queen Anne aspirations" (Glassie 2000: 77). For this study, national housing is equated with societies that are modernizing, or transitional from traditional to modern.

Academic housing is characteristic of modernity, being built with "at least some attempt at being fashionable" (McAlester and McAlester 1986: 5), and thus communicating status and reflecting the achievements of the occupants. Academic buildings are designed and built by formally educated professionals using blueprints or plans from pattern books authored by professional architects. Most American academic housing is modeled on four formal architectural traditions: ancient classical, Renaissance classical, medieval, or modern. Georgian, Greek Revival, Italianate, and Queen Anne are a few of the many examples of academic housing (McAlester and McAlester 1986).

Mound Bayou: A Historical Overview

The history of Mound Bayou is extraordinarily well documented (Crocket 1979; Hamilton 1991; Hermann 1979, 1999; Jackson 2000). The town is located near the center of the Delta, a physiographic province in northwest Mississippi between the Mississippi and Yazoo rivers. The colony was founded predominantly by former slaves, many of whom came from Davis Bend, Mississippi, plantations owned by Joseph Davis, elder brother of Confederate president Jefferson Davis. Two prominent men, Isaiah T. Montgomery and Benjamin Green, both from Davis Bend, were instrumental in the establishment of Mound Bayou in 1887. At this time, the Delta was still largely covered by thick forests and swamps and was so impenetrable in many areas that cotton plantations initially were located along major streams where transportation was more feasible. Even in the twentieth century, there remained expansive tracts of undeveloped forested land (Hamilton 1991). Nevertheless, when Montgomery and Green established Mound Bayou as a stop on the Louisville, New Orleans, and Texas Railroad that was under construction, it was clear that the Delta was destined to be cotton plantation country. At this time, sharecropping was on the increase, especially for African Americans (Woodman 1997). The intent was for the Mound Bayou community to be a self-segregated, self-sufficient railroad town with a strong industrial and commercial base (Hermann 1999: 219–245). The pioneers wished to create a haven for African Americans in the midst of white-controlled cotton plantations. Isaiah Montgomery fervently believed that the only way for African Americans to succeed in the late postbellum period was through self-segregation and by proving to whites that they could govern themselves and produce commodities that whites as well as African Americans would buy (Hermann 1999: 219).

The first pioneers of Mound Bayou faced the tremendous challenge of carving a community out of the wilderness with few or no economic resources. Most lived on small farms surrounding the emerging hamlet, so during the initial phase of settlement, modernization had not yet begun for the majority of Mound Bayouans.

Despite the earliest struggles, however, within a few years of establishment, Mound Bayouans worked to modernize. Only three years after its founding, a school was begun where a teacher taught in a room located in Isaiah Montgomery's home. One of Isaiah Montgomery's major concerns was to provide the best possible educational facilities. In 1892, he and Benjamin Green donated land in town for the Mound Bayou Normal and Industrial Institute (Hermann 1999: 237).

Mound Bayou's population exhibited significant growth in the early years. In 1891 there were approximately five hundred residents in the colony, about two hundred town dwellers and three hundred farm residents. By 1900, the town was home to nearly three hundred residents with an additional fifteen hundred in the hinterlands (Hamilton 1991: 53). Analysis of the 1900 census shows sixty-five households in town, and nearly 90 percent of the town population could read (United States Bureau of Census 1990, Bolivar County, Mississippi). The census also shows that there were two blacksmiths in Mound Bayou, as well as two general contractors, three ministers, three carpenters, a postmaster, a stenographer, a wheelwright, a barber, two teachers, one lawyer, and one physician. Most of the colony's population, however, consisted of sharecroppers, tenant farmers, and subsistence farmers.

In 1904, Charles Banks, a prominent African-American businessman and son of two poor slaves, arrived in the community and founded the Bank of Mound Bayou (Jackson 2000). Historian Janet Sharp Hermann (1999: 224) describes the bank as the heart of the business community. Banks, an important lieutenant of Booker T. Washington, also organized the

Mississippi Negro Business League as a chapter of Washington's national organization. He was also instrumental in establishing a cotton oil mill in Mound Bayou (Crockett 1979; Hermann 1999; Jackson 2000).

Banks was especially devoted to helping African American farmers in the Delta, and all across the state, to prosper. In 1910, he praised farmers who raised their own meat, corn, and hay and produced surplus to sell, and chastised those who did not. He urged African American farmers to practice scientific farming by subscribing to at least one farm paper and to stop borrowing money at exorbitant rates from white establishments (Jackson 2000:281).

According to historian Jackson, Banks "went to extraordinary lengths to familiarize the black farmers in Mississippi with the latest advances in that industry to provide them with access to people who could give them technical advice" (Jackson 2000: 282). Banks, along with Thornton Montgomery (Isaiah T. Montgomery's brother), established the Mound Bayou Loan and Investment Company as a means of preventing the intrusion of white ownership in the colony (Hermann 1999: 225). The Louisville, New Orleans, and Texas Railroad held mortgages on much of the farmland in the Mound Bayou colony since its founding, and when Illinois Central purchased the railroad, there were rumors that the new owners planned a wholesale foreclosure of Mound Bayou mortgages. The loan and investment company was a response to the fear that Mound Bayouans would lose their property, but also was established to finance new settlers, thus controlling more business within the community rather than letting it fall into potentially hostile white hands (Hermann 1999:225).

Unfortunately, by about 1900, the position of African Americans in Mississippi had worsened considerably (Woodman 1997; Hermann 1999). Southern whites regained control of local and state government, and African Americans were regularly terrorized by white mobs. Isaiah Montgomery received numerous appeals for assistance from African Americans across the state who were being threatened because they had managed to accumulate some wealth. In one of his responses, Montgomery urged a terrorized African American to sell his property and move to Mound Bayou. Booker T. Washington described Mound Bayou as a "place where a Negro may get inspiration by seeing what other members of his race have accomplished ... [and] where he has an opportunity to learn some of the fundamental duties and responsibilities of social and civic life" (Hermann 1999: 233). By all appearances, around 1900 the Mound Bayou experiment was an enormous success, but the success of the colony came with heavy costs. For example, Montgomery became indignant about the inequitable distribution of county education funds which were drawn primarily from the poll tax. In 1909, seven thousand dollars for Bolivar County schools came from Negro poll taxes, but only thirteen hundred dollars came from whites. Nevertheless, the funds were divided equally so that thirteen hundred white children received the same education allotment as twelve thousand African American children. Most African American schools could only pay teachers fifteen to thirty-five dollars each month for four-month terms while white teachers received fifty-five dollars or more each month for a six-month term (Hermann 1999: 238).

Success in Mound Bayou continued. By 1910, there were numerous grocery and dry goods stores, several restaurants, a brick factory, two gins, three schools, six churches, a train station, a telephone exchange, and a weekly newspaper (Crockett 1979; Hermann 1999). The second story of the Bank of Mound Bayou housed the offices of a physician, and served as the headquarters of the Knights and Daughters of Tabor, an African American fraternal organization.

In an effort to include residents in sharing the wealth from this growth, in 1908 Isaiah Montgomery and Charles Banks began selling shares of stock in the Mound Bayou Oil Mill and Manufacturing Company. The stock was to be offered at only one dollar per share so that all African Americans in Mississippi might be able to invest in the venture. They chose a cotton seed oil mill because the demand was high and most African Americans were engaged in growing cotton. Oil mills at that time were earning between 15 and 40 percent on their investments. Mound Bayou was considered the natural location for the mill since it was considered the "racial capital" of Mississippi. Construction of the oil mill began in 1910 (Crockett 1979; Hermann 1999).

Unfortunately, the organizers of the mill failed to raise sufficient capital. Isaiah Montgomery and Booker T. Washington turned to white capitalists for additional funds. Despite a grand dedication on November 25, 1912, where Booker T. Washington gave an impressive speech praising Mound Bayouans, the mill did not begin operations until the following year. The recession of 1914 and problems with creditors ultimately spelled failure for the oil mill (Jackson 2000).

The Bank of Mound Bayou also experienced devastating problems. In 1914 the Bank of Mound Bayou was shut down, and between 1915 and 1922 was the Mound Bayou State Bank. Conditions in Mound Bayou continued to deteriorate. In 1920, the price of cotton plummeted and the value of farmland around Mound Bayou dropped from $300 to $175 per acre. Colonists were moving to northern cities in the boom associated with World War I. In 1922, the Farmer's Cooperative Mercantile Company in Mound Bayou failed. A financial blight settled on Mound Bayou. Men were forced into sharecropping on big plantations, and women were forced into domestic service for whites in nearby towns. The result was depopulation and broken homes (Hermann 1999: 241).

Overall, the period between 1910 and 1920 was a bleak one for Mound Bayou. Businesses failed, colonists migrated to northern states, and the colony struggled for existence. Modernization processes that had begun about 1900 had ceased.

Hope for improvement, however, came as Benjamin A. Green, son of founder Benjamin Green and graduate of Fisk University and Harvard Law School, attempted to revive the dream of his father and Isaiah T. Montgomery (Hermann 1999: 243–245). Green was elected town mayor in 1920. He strove to persuade young people to remain in the colony and re-create the earlier success of Mound Bayou. It was at this time the first town hall was erected in Mound Bayou. But Green was unable to persuade young people to remain in the colony. By this time, the dream of creating and sustaining a cooperative modern community appears to have ended (Hermann 1999: 243). A visitor described Mound Bayou in 1940 as a "dilapidated, depopulated town with little left to excite race pride." Benjamin A. Green insisted in 1940 that the failure of Mound Bayou "proves nothing about the Negro. It proves plenty about humanity" (Hermann 1999: 245).

In summary, between its founding and 1910, Mound Bayou was a thriving and modernizing town with all appearances of financial success and economic and political opportunity for Mississippi African Americans. The sawmills, bank, newspaper, train depot, schools, and churches attest to this success. Isaiah Montgomery's dream of a cooperative and modern African American town was realized, at least for a time. However, between 1910 and the 1940s, Mound Bayou began experiencing an economic and demographic collapse. One would conclude based on document analysis that Mound Bayou experienced a single episode of modernization that ceased about 1910.

The Archaeological and Architectural Record

The Bank of Mound Bayou, still standing, is a two-story brick building that fronts a major thoroughfare that runs through town. The brick was laid in

American common bond and the structure has a decorative brick corbelled cornice. The windows exhibit classic Italian-inspired arches. The arches over the windows and the decorative brick cornice are both characteristics of Italian Renaissance architecture that was popular between 1890 and 1935 (McAlester and McAlester 1986: 397). McAlester and McAlester suggest that Italian Renaissance was principally "a style for architect-designed landmarks in major metropolitan areas prior to World War I" (McAlester and McAlester 1986: 398). While Mound Bayou was not a major metropolitan area, town leaders and residents worked to make the colony a major commercial and industrial center.

The bank is listed on the National Register of Historic Places under Criteria A—a site that is associated with events that have made a significant contribution to the broad pattern of our history. Specifically the National Register form states that "it stands as the only historic commercial building testifying to an active, independent community of African Americans in the Mississippi Delta during the early twentieth century."

The Bank of Mound Bayou in 1904 was certainly the most formal and imposing structure in the colony. Its solid brick edifice with Italian Renaissance embellishments must have engendered confidence in the economic power of Mound Bayou to inhabitants as well as visitors and outside investors. Charles Banks labored to provide a stable financial base for Mound Bayou, no longer a frontier colony, but a thriving, modern town. The bank seems a fitting symbol of the new era that Mound Bayouans were envisioning for themselves and for the entire race.

The first town hall was built on a vacant lot around 1920. A new brick town hall was constructed around 1970 about a block away, and the first town hall was used for other purposes, including a juke joint. It was razed after a fire in the mid-to-late 1970s.

A partial footprint of the original town hall was still visible when the archaeological testing occurred in 1998. Students from the University of Southern Mississippi, assisted by Mound Bayou volunteers, conducted archaeological testing. Volunteers included youth from Mound Bayou, and the project was accomplished under the auspices of a grant called "Digging for the Dream" funded by the Mississippi Humanities Council. We had only one week to conduct the field investigations.

Because a footprint of the building was visible on the surface, five 1-x-1 m units were placed to investigate the town hall and the lot behind the building. The footprint of the building indicates it was two rooms wide and two rooms deep, though the rear rooms were smaller. Oral history confirms this design and reports that there were two front doors and that the rear rooms were in what appeared to be a shed addition that was either part of the original construction or perhaps added very soon after the original construction and contained a bathroom. Three units were placed within the town hall structure, and two tested the rear lot. Unfortunately, a 1970s brick wall bisected the town hall building, so that only the rear portions were tested.

It was hoped that archaeological testing might reveal five distinct episodes of the lot's use. The first would be the construction of the Bank of Mound Bayou dating around 1904. Next, we were interested in recovering evidence of the activities within the bank reflected in debris behind the building dating between 1905 and 1920. Subsequent to that is the construction of the town hall circa 1920, then between 1920 and the early 1970s debris reflecting activities within the town hall. The last episode would be the fire, abandonment, and demolition of the structure in the 1970s.

Unit 1 was opened in the interior of the town hall and placed to determine whether a structural foundation was placed to separate the reported two rooms at the rear of the building. Unit 2 was placed to test the outer foundation of the town hall. Unit 3 was placed approximately 2.5 m east (to the rear) of the town hall. Unit 4 was placed in the rear lot, and Unit 5 was situated within the structure of the town hall in the location of the front rooms. Excavations proceeded in 5 cm levels unless distinct soil color or texture differences indicated natural stratigraphic deposits.

Unfortunately, five distinct episodes of the lot use were not completely apparent in the field excavations, nor in the analysis of the artifacts. A graph showing the frequencies of artifacts by levels recovered from the two units in the rear yard really only clearly show two episodes. Levels 7, 8, and 9 contain high frequencies of artifacts and appear to be associated with the construction and use of the Bank of Mound Bayou. One such artifact is a heavy porcelain vessel that was likely a mortar typically associated with druggists and physicians. No pestle was found. Additionally, two small medicine vials were identified. Such artifacts could very well be associated with the physician's office on the second floor of the bank. Levels 1–4 appear to be associated with the construction, use, and destruction of the town hall, but may also contain deposits from the continuing intermittent use of the Bank of Mound Bayou.

Two important architectural features of the town hall were investigated archaeologically: the foundation and a water pipe with an associated trench. The foundation was concrete block, and the trench associated with the water pipe contained artifacts that date about 1920 suggesting that the building was plumbed when built. The deposits associated with the building foundation contained asbestos siding fragments, light bulb fragments, and wire nails. Clearly, modern materials were used in the construction of the town hall.

The use of the old town hall after about 1970 was also quite visible in the archaeological deposits. Numerous beer bottles and cans and liquor bottles were recovered, which relates to the use of the structure as a juke joint. Also, the destruction of the building was visible in the thick deposits of partially burned asphalt shingles, numerous wire nails, asbestos siding, window glass, and concrete that were found in four of the five units.

Oral traditions and a photograph that shows a small portion of the town hall provide information about the form of the town hall structure. Interestingly, the first town hall was a modest structure that looked very much like an ordinary house. A portion of the town hall is visible in a ca. 1940 photograph. In fact, the town hall looked like a Cumberland-style house with two primary front rooms (each with a front door) and a covered front porch. The first town hall must be classified as a national form of architecture, adapting a folk building by use of modern, industrial materials.

In many ways, the first town hall bears a resemblance to the type of house many Mound Bayouans occupied in the hinterlands of the settlement. The late Milburn Crowe, long-time resident of Mound Bayou, described his boyhood home outside of town as a simple wooden, side-gabled two-room house without plumbing or electricity. What stands in stark contrast to those simple folk houses is that the town hall was constructed using the most modern, industrial materials available, and was plumbed and electrified when first built. Perhaps this homey yet progressive building symbolized the kind of home that Mound Bayouans felt they could achieve in their lives. When most folks in and around Mound Bayou were living in very modest folk houses, they built a thoroughly modern town tall with all the amenities, symbolizing the aspirations of its citizens and a commitment by Mound Bayouans to continued modernization.

Conclusions

Early residents of Mound Bayou explicitly sought modernization, something they equated with progress and economic opportunities for African Americans. They eagerly pursued access to the industrialization processes that were sweeping across America, and focused much effort on education within their community. They labored to portray themselves as educated, progressive, economically stable, and modern, and this self-expression is encapsulated by the Bank of Mound Bayou. Rather than drawing on the traditional extended family resources typical of slave-quarter communities, Mound Bayouans sought to extend the sense of community through industrialization and economic development. They did this by defining themselves through their institutions like the bank, which offered a portrait to residents, visitors, and potential investors as modern, progressive, successful, and tied into the national industrial economy.

After 1910, Mound Bayou experienced depopulation and devastating economic problems, primarily as a result of the fact that complete segregation was impossible. What this study probably best illuminates is that Mound Bayouans did not give up the dream of a modern community. With more humble aspirations, in 1920, Mound Bayouans constructed their first town hall with thoroughly modern materials, yet in a style resembling residences inhabited by colonists in the hinterlands of the town. The town hall symbolized the modernization that all citizens hoped to achieve, both rural and urban.

From archaeological data, it is clear that Mound Bayou experienced at least two distinct episodes of modernization between its founding and the 1940s. The first is expressed in the architecture of the Bank of Mound Bayou, and the second in the construction of the modern, yet homey town hall. Further, studies like this that focus on recent archaeological sites have much to offer in a better understanding of cultural and historical processes. Recent sites, especially twentieth-century sites, rarely receive sufficient attention from archaeologists. Yet without archaeological investigations, the two episodes of modernization that occurred in Mound Bayou would have been entirely overlooked.

Acknowledgments

The historic preservation in Mound Bayou owes much to the late Milburn Crowe. I was so honored to have had the opportunity to work with (for) him in Mound Bayou. Like Isaiah Montgomery, Benjamin Green, and Hon. Benjamin A. Green, Milburn Crowe was devoted to educating the world about his town and achieving the initial dream of the early pioneers. Thanks go to the many Mound Bayou volunteers who spent a miserably cold week in the field and to those citizens who opened their hearts and homes to visitors from USM. A special thanks also goes to my students, without whom this project would never have been accomplished. The project, "Digging for the Dream," was funded in part by the Mississippi Humanities Council.

NOTE

1. Part I was originally a talk presented at the First Annual South Central Historical Archeology Conference held in Jackson, Mississippi, 1998. At the time the paper was given, the archeological project was still in progress, and because Mr. Crowe is now deceased and not available to update this work, we have maintained the original language with minimal copyediting.

REFERENCES CITED

Ahlman, Todd. 1996. Backwards Farmers or Modernizing Farms? The Tennessee Valley Farms of East Tennessee in the Early Twentieth Century. Master's thesis, Department of Anthropology, University of Tennessee, Knoxville.

Aiken, Charles S. 1987. Race as a Factor in Municipal Underbounding. *Annals of the Association of American Geographers* 77: 564–579.

———. 1990. A New Type of Black Ghetto in the Plantation South. *Annals of the Association of American Geographers* 80:223–246.

Cabak, Melanie, and Mary Inkrot. 1997. Old Farm, New Farm: An Archaeology of Rural Modernization in the Aiken Plateau, 1875–1950. Savannah River Archaeological Research Papers 9, Occasional Papers of the Savannah River Archaeological Research Program, South Carolina Institute of Archaeology and Anthropology, University of South Carolina.

Cabak, Melanie A., Mark D. Groover, and Mary M. Inkrot. 1999. Rural Modernization During the Recent Past: Farmstead Archaeology in the Aiken Plateau. *Historical Archaeology* 33 (4): 19–43.

Carter, Thomas, and Elizabeth Collins Cromley. 2005. *Invitation to Vernacular Architecture: A Guide to the Study of Ordinary Buildings and Landscapes*. University of Tennessee Press, Knoxville.

Crocket, Norman L. 1979. *The Black Towns*. Regents Press of Kansas, Lawrence.

Deetz, James. 1977. *In Small Things Forgotten: The Archaeology of Early American Life*. Doubleday, New York.

Derry, Linda. 1997. Pre-Emancipation Archaeology: Does It Play in Selma, Alabama. *Historical Archaeology* 31 (3): 18–26.

Edwards-Ingrarn, Ywone. 1997. Toward "True Acts of Inclusion": The "Here" and the "Out There" Concepts in Public Archaeology. *Historical Archaeology* 31 (3): 27–36.

Eisele, Florence. 1985. Ante-Bellum Slave Dwellings on Plantations of Southern United States. Manuscript on file, Historic Natchez Foundation, Natchez, Mississippi.

Ferraro, Gary. 1995. *Cultural Anthropology: An Applied Perspective*, second edition. West Publishing, Minneapolis/St. Paul.

Foner, Eric. 1988. *Nothing but Freedom: Emancipation and Its Legacy*. Louisiana State University Press, Baton Rouge.

Franklin, Maria. 1997. "Power to the People": Sociopolitics and the Archaeology of Black America. *Historical Archaeology* 31 (3): 36–51.

Glassie, Henry. 2000. *Vernacular Architecture*. Indiana University Press, Bloomington.
Groover, Mark D. 1992. Illinois Farmstead Archaeology: Past Issues, Future Goals. Midwestern Archaeological Research Center, Illinois State University, Normal.
Groover, Mark D., and Melanie A. Cabak. 1992. Phase II Archaeological Investigations for the Bloomington-Normal Airport Runway Extension, McLean County, Illinois. Report to Illinois Department of Transportation, Springfield, from Midwestern Archaeological Research Center, Illinois State University, Normal.
Hamilton, Kenneth M. 1991. Black Towns and Profit: Promotion and Development in the Trans-Appalachian West, 1877–1915. University of Illinois Press, Urbana.
Haviland, William A. 2003. *Anthropology*. Thomson/Wadsworth, Belmont, CA.
Hermann, Janet Sharp. 1979. The Black Community at Davis Bend: The Pursuit of a Dream. Ph.D. dissertation, Department of History, University of California, Berkeley.
———. 1999. *The Pursuit of a Dream*. University Press of Mississippi, Jackson.
Jackson, David H., Jr. 2000. Charles Banks: "Wizard of Mound Bayou." *Journal of Mississippi History* LXII (4): 269–292.
Kolchin, Peter. 1992. The Tragic Era? Interpreting Southern Reconstruction in Comparative Perspective. In *The Meaning of Freedom: Economics, Politics, and Culture after Slavery*, edited by Frank McGlynn and Seymour Drescher, pp. 291–311. University of Pittsburgh Press, Pittsburgh.
Litwack, Leon F. 1979. *Been in the Storm So Long: The Aftermath of Slavery*. Knopf, New York.
Magdol, Edward. 1977. *A Right to the Land: Essays on the Freedmen's Community*. Greenwood Press, Westport.
McAlester, Virginia, and Lee McAlester. 1986. *A Field Guide to American Houses*. Alfred A. Knopf, New York.
McDavid, Carol. 1997. Decisions, and Power: The Public Interpretation of the Archaeology of the Levi Jordan Plantation. *Historical Archaeology* 31 (3): 114–132.
McKee, Larry. 1998. Some Thoughts on the Past, Present, and Future of the Archaeology of the African Diaspora. Paper presented at the Plenary Session "Where Are We and Where Do We Need to Go" at the annual meeting of the Society for Historical Archaeology, January 1998, Atlanta, GA.
McMillen, Neil. 1989. *Dark Journey: Black Mississippians in the Age of Jim Crow*. University of Illinois Press, Urbana.
Miller, Barbara D. 2002. *Cultural Anthropology*, second edition. Allyn and Bacon, Boston.
Powdermaker, Hortense. 1993 [1939]. *After Freedom: A Cultural Study of the Deep South*. University of Wisconsin Press, Madison.
Rostow, W. W. 1960. *The Stages of Economic Growth: A Non-Communist Manifesto*. Cambridge University Press, Cambridge, England.
Woodman, Harold D. 1997. Race, Class, Politics, and the Modernization of the Postbellum South. *Journal of Southern History* 63 (1): 3–22.
Young, Amy L. 2004. The Beginning and Future of African-American Archaeology in Mississippi. In Transcending Boundaries, Transforming the Discipline: African Diaspora Archaeology into the New Millenium, edited by Larry McKee and Maria Franklin. *Historical Archaeology* 38 (1): 66–78.
Young, Amy L., Michael Tuma, and Cliff Jenkins. 2001. The Role of Hunting to Cope with Risk at Saragossa Plantation, Natchez. *American Anthropologist* 103 (3): 692–704.

5

DOWN AROUND BILOXI

An Overview of Ethnic and Occupational Identity in a Coastal Town

—AIMÉE L. SCHMIDT

Biloxi is located on a peninsula about eight miles long and four miles wide on the far east side of the Mississippi Gulf Coast. To the north is the Bay of Biloxi and Big Lake where the Biloxi and Tchoutacabouffa rivers empty. To the south is the Mississippi Sound, and beyond the barrier islands lies the Gulf of Mexico, the fertile grounds for the commercial and recreational fishing industries. Among the many towns of Mississippi, Biloxi—and to some extent its coastal neighbors—is unusual in that it grew from a small fishing community and vacation spot to a multiethnic city built around a thriving seafood industry. The black/white dichotomy has long been the approach of cultural and racial study for most of the state. In contract, Biloxi has a long history of ethnic and racial diversity. Usually, ethnic groups are studied as isolates. That is, scholars tend to look at one ethnic group at a time. However, sometimes it is beneficial to look at a place. In the case of Biloxi and the Gulf Coast, the geographic characteristics are partly responsible for the unique culture. East Biloxi is surrounded by water on three sides. Access to the water made working the water (shrimping, fishing, oystering) an attractive livelihood. With its economy centered on seafood and tourism, the port city attracted diverse peoples, thus creating avenues of cultural exchange.

IMMIGRATION, ETHNICITY AND THE SEAFOOD COMMUNITY

In the study of ethnicity, one must distinguish between an ethnic group and an immigrant group.[1] Certainly many of the customs and traits of an ethnic group stem from earlier immigrant traditions. However, in a new environment and over time an immigrant group adapts its customs to fit the surroundings, resources, and social mores of the broader community. Thus, second, third, and subsequent generations are not part of an immigrant group, but part of an ethnic group. This is true among Biloxi Slavonians and Cajuns and is proving so among Vietnamese, particularly younger generations who conduct business in English, and adopt the American customs of dress, music, and speech.

An ethnic group shares common beliefs and patterns of living—religion, customs, literature, cuisine, and language. Ethnic studies in the South have in large measure concentrated on the region's Anglo and African American traditions and relations, particularly in terms of the South's agricultural history.

Biloxi's seafood community formed a folk cultural group whose members share a common knowledge, belief system, experience, and set of traditions. The occupational and ethnic identities of the seafood community go hand in hand and are mutually dependent. Their influence extends beyond the immediate seafood industry participants to residents of Biloxi and the greater coastal community who experience this culture in different ways—by purchasing local seafood or dining at a local seafood restaurant, by attending the Blessing of the Fleet, or by embracing the symbols (the schooner and the lighthouse) that have come to identify the city.

As with any folk group, the Biloxi seafood community has boundaries—those created by participants themselves and those created by others. Boundaries help define who they *are* and who they *are not*. Just as culture is dynamic and changing, so too are the boundaries, which can shift to accommodate or exclude new forces.

These boundaries help the group exist within the wider community as they position people, actions, and attitudes into an identifiable context. (What is your family name? What language do you speak?) Boundaries were defined along both ethnic and occupational lines. Boundaries could include not only abstract concepts, but also real, physical locations. For example, neighborhood boundaries once identified a person's economic and social background. In Biloxi the neighborhoods of Point Cadet and Back Bay have long been identified as the places where working-class fishermen of various ethnic backgrounds live.

While neighborhoods were divided by occupation, organizations were divided by ethnicity. When founded, the Slavic Benevolent Association and the Fleur de Lis Society provided financial assistance to newcomers, served as a social network, and provided a framework for inclusion in the group. These organizations fixed certain cultural boundaries, reinforced their own values and traditions, and afforded a means of expressing their own culture within the broader community.

Membership in a folk group is complicated. Membership status is determined not only by the individual—to what degree he or she identifies with the group—but also by the other members of the group—what criteria and standards *they* set. The more strongly a person identifies with a particular group the more it determines his concept of himself, with whom he interacts, and his cultural outlook.[2] By the same token, the group determines whom it will allow to be a member. The stronger the identification the more likely that person is to create stringent boundaries and exclude those he perceives as lacking the qualities of a full member. For example: being of a certain ethnic background may not be enough to make you a full-fledged member of a group. While many of Slavonian and Cajun backgrounds remain in Biloxi, not all those work in the seafood industry. During my research I interviewed a man who identified with his Slavonian fisherman heritage. However, he was raised in Uptown Biloxi and never worked on the boats. He was an active and respected member of the Slavonian Lodge, but a few of the older members joked about his claim. "He never stepped foot on a shrimp boat," they said. They narrowed the boundaries of inclusion by placing occupational experience on par with ethnic background.

How then do members of the Biloxi seafood community construct an identity, and how do they maintain that identity? Furthermore, how do they influence and how are they influenced by the larger community? Noting the dynamic interaction and adaptation of incoming national and cultural groups in New Orleans, Louisiana, George F. Reinecke used the term "creolization" to refer to the result of the interactive forces which led to the creation of a local ethnicity.[3] Though on a smaller population scale, Biloxi claims a similar history. Interaction among ethnic groups because of shared neighborhoods, occupations, religion, etc., helped create and reinforce a community identity. The multiethnic nature of the seafood industry was present in its beginnings and continues today. Slavonians, Cajuns, and Vietnamese each contributed to the cultural landscape of Biloxi. Their livelihood has always been their shared culture, but they also strive to maintain their separate ethnic identities. Biloxi's history illustrates a continuum of ethnic influence in one southern port city and how those diverse elements fashioned a community identity.

BACKGROUND AND HISTORY OF THE TOWN

This modern city was founded in 1699 by Canadian explorer Pierre Le Moyne, Sieur d'Iberville, who claimed the land for France. In the succeeding three hundred years, the flags of France, England, Spain, and the Republic of West Florida flew over the city until 1811 when Biloxi became part of the U.S. territory.

When French explorers of the eighteenth century arrived on the Gulf Coast, Native Americans taught them how to tong for oysters and fish for flounder and other species indigenous to the gulf waters. Descendants of these early French settlers—Ladner, Moran, Necaise—still live along the coast. They were the first to learn the tools of the trade of the industry. They developed the Biloxi boatbuilding tradition and later passed this knowledge on to Slavonian immigrants.

The natural landscape of the Biloxi area was conducive to the growth of the seafood industry. The city sits on a peninsula between Biloxi Bay and the Mississippi Sound. The land on the bay side is Back Bay, and the land on the sound in the eastern part of the city is Point Cadet. The barrier islands—Petit Bois, Horn, Ship, Cat, and Deer—separate the Mississippi Sound from the Gulf of Mexico. West of the islands lay the fertile shrimping and fishing grounds of the Louisiana waters and marshes. The sound, a broad area of shallow water, is an important ecosystem that supports the food chain essential to the seafood fisheries. Though some harvesting does occur in the sound, today most of the commercial catch comes from gulf waters.

For much of its early existence, Biloxi was a small fishing town with a few resorts for summer visitors. Fresh seafood was available on the coast but not inland. The 1869 opening of the railroad that linked Biloxi to inland markets, coupled with the mass production of ice and the introduction of the process of commercially canning shrimp, made it possible for the Biloxi seafood industry to expand and earn the title "Seafood Capital of the World."

When John O. Seeligman, the city engineer of Biloxi in 1900, surveyed and drew the official city map, he called Biloxi "the recognized metropolis of the Mississippi Sea Shore." The city owned about twenty-five miles of streets "all of which are shelled and well adapted for vehicles and bicycles." Biloxi boasted a lovely seashore drive "passing all the beautiful summer residents of the Southern privileged class." Furthermore, the city boasted "two ice houses and one cold stores house which answered all the requirements of a modern city."[4]

As early as the 1850s Biloxi was one of the nation's premiere resorts. Grand hotels graced the waterfront, steamers from New Orleans and Mobile made regular stops in Biloxi, and fresh seafood was always available. The cool gulf breezes and sandy beaches lured tourists and summer residents to Biloxi, but the seafood industry was at the core of the city's economy.

THE CITY BUILT ON SEAFOOD

The first seafood cannery on the coast opened in 1881 in Biloxi. The combined talents and investments of several coast businessmen laid the foundations for the seafood industry. With eight thousand dollars and a sound business plan, F. William Elmer, William Gorenflo, Lazaro Lopez, and James Maycock formed Lopez, Elmer and Company. The other pioneer in the early industry was W. K. M. DuKate from Fredericksburg, Indiana. DuKate traveled to Baltimore, then the nation's leading city in seafood packing, to study the packing process and equipment.

These early ventures paved the way for Biloxi's economic development. As the industry steadily grew, Point Cadet, then virtually uninhabited, and Back Bay underwent enormous expansion. The population grew along with new construction. Initially Biloxi's population was not large enough to support the rapid growth and demand for factory employees. Faced with a shortage in the labor force, owners began hiring experienced laborers from Baltimore to fill the plants. These Polish or, as they were known locally, "Bohemian" seasonal workers were the first large group to move into the city. The factory owners provided transportation and housing for the workers to make the move to Biloxi.

The Biloxi seafood camps were self-contained, self-sufficient communities. The owners provided their employees with basic needs and in return had a readily available source of workers. The workers lived among their family and friends, and this arrangement continued later as Slavonians and Cajuns moved into the same neighborhoods to work in the factories. East Biloxi would soon become synonymous with the seafood industry and with these ethnic groups.

As the industry steadily grew, so too did the population, which doubled in a ten-year period to reach more than three thousand by 1890. By the turn of the century, Biloxi had five canneries, nine oyster dealers, and five "Bohemian camps." Barataria employed five hundred people—half in the factory and half on the boats, and Lopez and DuKate had a fleet of sixty vessels (*Biloxi City Directory*, 1905). Through their complete control over production and distribution, and their influence over the workforce, the factory owners held the reins on the economic growth and social and cultural development of the industry. It would take another twenty years before the industry began to decentralize. Toward the end of World War I as the workforce size increased, a growing number of workers challenged the existing structure by becoming boat owners and began working for themselves.

This increase in the workforce was largely due to the arrival of two immigrant groups: those from the Dalmatian coast of what became Yugoslavia, and Cajuns from south Louisiana. Though port cities such as Dubrovnik had established ties with the gulf and Atlantic states as early at the eighteenth century, the greatest immigration occurred during the early twentieth century and immediately following World War I. They were mainly Croats, with Serbs and Slavonians making up a smaller percentage of the group. Croats and Serbs are south Slavic groups that populated the Dalmatian coast along the Adriatic Sea and the inland areas of Croatia, Bosnia-Herzegovina, and Serbia. It is difficult to determine how many of the immigrants belonged to each group, because nineteenth-century immigrants identified themselves according to the region from which they came (e.g., Dalmatia, Bosnia-Herzegovina, Slavonia). Rather than distinguish between the different ethnic groups, Biloxians today use the terms interchangeably or more frequently use "Slavonian" to describe all the groups.

Many of the immigrants to Biloxi were rural landless peasants, political refugees, sailors, and fishermen whose experience served them well in their new home. They formed a close-knit community and over the years kept their ties to the homeland, often returning to visit or bring over fellow family members. Following the recent war in Bosnia during the early 1990s, the Biloxi Slavonian community hosted two men who were injured in the war and provided them with free medical care.

The migration of the Cajuns to Biloxi occurred around the same time. Cajuns are descendants of exiled Acadians (from Canada) who settled in Louisiana in the mid-1700s. The Acadians' intermarriage with other ethnic groups helped create the distinctive Louisiana Cajun culture. Most of those who migrated to Biloxi were small farmers and sharecroppers, many leaving after the failure of the sugarcane crop in the 1920s left them destitute. The crop failures coincided with a period of enormous growth in the Biloxi seafood industry. Biloxi factory owners even went to south Louisiana cities such as New Iberia, Lafayette, and Broussard to recruit workers. Economic opportunity drew Cajuns to Biloxi where they worked and lived alongside Slavonians and other ethnic groups.

Biloxi and other coast fishermen designed boats specifically suited to their needs and the gulf waters. Initially, flat-bottom, double-sail boats called "catboats" were most common. When an 1893 hurricane destroyed a large portion of the fleet, boatbuilders replaced their losses with a new type of boat known as the Biloxi schooner. Ranging in size from fifty feet to sixty feet and similar to the Chesapeake and Baltimore schooners, the Biloxi had a broad beam for large crews, a shallow draft suited to inland bodies of water, and sail power enough to drag the oyster dredges and shrimp nets. Although they were good work boats and heavy haulers, they earned the nickname "white winged queens" because of their grace and beauty under sail. Today Biloxi's Maritime & Seafood Industry Museum operates two reproductions of these great schooners, the *Glen L. Swetman* (1989) and the *Mickey Sekul* (1994).

Off-season months were spent in the repairing and cleaning of boats and equipment. They were also the time for schooner racing—a true community event. Work boats became competitive machines, and the races became as important as working itself. Proving one's mettle during the races was a crucial step in becoming a good fisherman. Rivalry was keen, as the fastest boat from each cannery competed against the others. By the mid-1930s, the "white winged queens" had virtually disappeared as engine power replaced sail power. Many fishermen simply converted their schooners to power boats by cutting off the masts and installing engines. Boatbuilders later designed a boat known as the Biloxi lugger on which the cabin rests astern and the foredeck is clear for unloading and culling the catch.

While shrimping and oystering were almost exclusively male tasks, the factory work was predominantly the female domain. Some men did work in the factories, and most children, including boys, began their working lives here. Sea Coast, Kaluz's, Gulf Central, Dunbar and DuKate, and other factories lined Point Cadet and Back Bay. The factory owners wanted the fastest pickers and shuckers, so they took care of their employees, and employees in turn felt loyalty to the factory. The work in the factories was equally as rigorous and demanding. A worker spent long hours in cold conditions and was paid based on the individual quantity she picked or shucked.

Slavonians and Cajuns both entered the industry as fishermen or factory workers. Each group had to adapt to different working and living environments, which meant daily contact with each other—on the boats, in the factories, in the camps and neighborhoods. As many Biloxians remember, the Slavonians and Cajuns mingled freely, but in the early years tended to keep to themselves. Such measures enabled them to better preserve their customs and traditions.

Occupations shaped their identity as well. From harvesting to processing the catch involved the work of many hands, each with a particular task and each with a different working knowledge. Entire families worked together, often side by side with families of different ethnic backgrounds. Their mutual experience as fishermen and factory workers cut across ethnic lines and bound them together in a common livelihood. Their daily lives were both an affirmation of ethnic identity and a continual cultural exchange. Their shared occupational experience reinforced their distinct ethnic identities and distinguished them from Biloxians of other ethnic backgrounds, neighborhoods, and occupations.

Clubs and societies based on ethnic identity are not unique to Biloxi. Exclusivity based on family and heritage is a conscious effort both to serve the particular community (for example, providing life insurance or burial plots) and a public expression of ethnic pride (e.g., parades or musical events). The clubs helped actualize a group identity and excluded those who fell outside the prescribed boundaries.

The Slavic Benevolent Association (or the Slavonian Lodge, as it is commonly known) was founded in 1913 in the Point Cadet neighborhood. Outside the lodge stood a statue of their patron saint, St. Nicola, and flanking the statue cement tablets inscribed with the names of all the Slavic families who have settled on the coast. In its earliest days, only full-blooded Slavonian men could join. However, as membership gradually declined, the lodge amended its membership requirements (thus broadening the boundaries) by allowing sons of Slavonian men, and eventually sons of Slavonian women, to join. Slavonian women formed the Ladies' Auxiliary, which is perhaps best known for the delicious *pusharatas* (Slavonian doughnuts) sold throughout the community on December 23.

Just a few blocks west is the Fleur de Lis (or French) Club, which serves as a benevolent and social organization for the city's French population. "French" in Biloxi includes both descendants of the early French settlers and Cajun French. People use the term interchangeably, but most of the members are of Cajun descent. Membership is open to anyone with patrilineal or matrilineal lines or through marriage. As with the Slavonian Lodge, broadening of boundaries of inclusion was necessary for the growth of the organization.

BOUND TOGETHER BY RELIGION

In addition to ethnic identity, occupation, and neighborhood, religion has been a coalescent factor. In a heavily Protestant state, Biloxi is a city with a strong Catholic history. Along the Gulf Coast, the sacred and secular mix freely, and religious heritage and events rooted in a Christian tradition, such as the Blessing of the Fleet and Mardi Gras, have close ties to the seafood industry.

One of the oldest community traditions and most public expressions of faith is the Blessing of the Fleet, a tradition that has roots in Europe. "The Blessing of the Fleet is for the fishermen a public petitioning of Almighty God's favor on his boat, his work, his family, his life," wrote the late Rev. Herbert J. Mullin. This tradition is commonly found in cities along the eastern and western seaboard and other gulf communities. Biloxians first held the blessing in 1929, and thereafter it became an annual celebration. The ritual developed into a public celebration in which the whole city, regardless of religious affiliation or occupation, participates. The blessing takes place each year usually at the beginning of May before the opening of shrimp season in Mississippi waters.

The festivities begin with a Saturday evening mass for the fishermen at St. Michael Catholic Church. If any one building embodies the spirit and influence of the seafood industry in Biloxi, it is St. Michael Catholic Church on Point Cadet. Built in 1969, St. Michael's architectural features reflect many coastal themes. The roof resembles a huge clam shell, and the interior stained-glass windows depict fishermen, anchors, and nets.

On Sunday afternoon the boats gather between the small craft harbor and Deer Island. The fishermen drop a wreath in the water in remembrance of those who have gone before them. Then the pastor of St. Michael and the bishop of the Diocese of Biloxi stand astern an anchored shrimp boat and bless the passing boats, sprinkling them with holy water. Friends and family board the boats to share in the parade, while crowds gather along the harbor or on the island to watch.

The board of directors selects the Shrimp King to lead the blessing festivities. The king is chosen from three candidates: one from the Slavic Association, one from the Fleur de Lis Society, and one from the community at large. Usually the king is an older fisherman, one who has earned the title from his many years at sea. In recent years, however, as a sign of the changing times, the average age of the king has decreased. Fewer Slavonians and Cajuns are going into the industry and fewer fishermen are participating.

Young women around the ages of eighteen to twenty contend for the title of Shrimp Queen. Local factories nominate the candidates, who must be descendants of fishermen in order to enter the contest. Candidates compete in a beauty pageant, an interview, and must submit a short essay on why they wish to become queen. The essays are rich with such phrases as "tradition" and "family heritage." The young may not enter the profession as they once did, but they continue to identify with it and show an appreciation for it. As one queen contestant wrote in her essay, "People come from all around the United States to visit here, and I want them to see the pride of the people here, pride in their community, hardworking and dedicated to improving and helping our area to prosper."

THE VIETNAMESE INFLUX

For almost sixty years the Slavonians and Cajuns formed the backbone of Biloxi's seafood industry. The boats, the factories, the churches and neighborhoods of Point Cadet and Back Bay were easily identified with these two groups. Beginning in the late 1970s and early 1980s, Vietnamese immigrants, many of them refugees from war-torn nations, began moving to south Mississippi. The shift was not easy—for the Vietnamese or established Biloxians. In some respects, the Vietnamese experience is similar to that of other immigrants to Biloxi: they settled in Point Cadet and Back Bay and they worked in the seafood industry. However, their refugee status with its real and perceived government aid and benefits alienated them from native Biloxi fishermen who saw them as economic competition. Their culture and very presence has sometimes placed them at odds with the larger Biloxi community. In Biloxi and other Gulf Coast towns they confronted racial prejudice and cultural and language barriers. However, they also met with compassion from people who sponsored their entry into the United States, assisted them in locating housing, and provided them educational and employment opportunities.

While the integration of the Vietnamese into the Gulf Coast community is complex, their entrance to Biloxi is a story of simple supply and demand. In 1977, Richard Gollot, owner of Golden Gulf Seafood on Back Bay, could not find enough experienced workers for the factory. He heard that there were Vietnamese in New Orleans who had experience shucking oysters in seafood factories. He drove a van over one day and brought back a dozen Vietnamese to work for him. After a week he persuaded one family to move to Biloxi and others soon followed. By 2005, more than twenty-five hundred, or one-third of Mississippi's Vietnamese population, lived in Biloxi, and the vast majority of those in East Biloxi.

The seafood industry offered the Vietnamese employment best suited to their needs at that time. The men became fishermen working together on the boats and pooling their resources. Women and children worked in the factories where they did not worry about their English deficiency because most of their co-workers were also Vietnamese. More important than financial success is the independence and freedom they attain for themselves and their families. Liem Tran, owner of a Biloxi trawl shop, said, "This is my business. I run by myself... I am working hard, but I save my money. I do not think for me. I think for my wife, but I think for my children."

The influx of Vietnamese in the late 1970s and 1980s coincided with a stretch of several poor shrimp seasons on the coast. Unfortunately, the Vietnamese received the blame for the economic woes of coast fishermen. Cultural differences and misunderstandings compounded by an increase in boats in an already competitive field strained the relations between Vietnamese and established coast fishermen. Rumors spread that the Vietnamese were receiving free boats and welfare checks. Some fishermen complained that many Vietnamese owned boats illegally because they were not properly documented. They called for legal measures to protect their livelihood. In some cases their protests took the form of ethnic bashing. There were instances of shooting nets and sabotaging boats, but the Vietnamese rarely reported the crimes for fear of retaliation.

Most residents, the fishermen included, wanted to help the Vietnamese and wanted peaceful solutions to the problems. Some residents, including established seafood families, went out of their way to help the Vietnamese get started with their boats. The Covacivich family, a long-time Biloxi boatbuilding family, rented space in their boat yard to Vietnamese builders. These Biloxians rightfully felt betrayed when the press, the public, and the Vietnamese made the American fishermen out as the villains in the ordeal.

Exacerbating the situation were the cultural differences and the language barrier. Since many Vietnamese could not read or speak English, they could not understand the Coast Guard regulations regarding boat operation or interpret the gauges on their boats. They also had different methods for shrimping and oystering. Americans nicknamed Vietnamese-style boats "chopsticks" because they rigged the nets on two poles extending from the bow of the boat and pushed the nets through the water rather than the standard American method of pulling them. They continued the

Vietnamese practice of working the waters north to south, but the American fishermen trawled east to west. In close quarters such as the Mississippi Sound (twelve miles wide and twenty-nine miles long), this often resulted in tangled nets. Traditionally, Gulf Coast oystermen worked the oyster beds in circles, and they claimed that the Vietnamese damaged reefs with their method of dredging back and forth.

A committee composed of Vietnamese and American fishermen, and various city and marine officials, formed to address these problems. In addition to hosting public forums and dispelling rumors about government aid to Vietnamese, they took necessary practical steps to improve relations. They translated and distributed Coast Guard rules including instructions and maintenance of boat equipment and stressed the importance of abiding by established local fishing practices in order to avoid equipment damage and to conserve the crop.

Gone are the days when the seafood unloading docks turned away Vietnamese fishermen for fear of losing their local customers. Over time, both sides have reached an understanding and acceptance of each other. A number of Vietnamese businesses opened in Biloxi to support the growing community. These were family-run operations as well. On Howard Avenue one can buy food from a Vietnamese grocery, rent a Vietnamese video, eat lunch at a Vietnamese restaurant, and buy a tape of Vietnamese music from a department store. The Vietnamese community in Biloxi, now thirty years old, will continue to change—to influence and be influenced by the broader community in which it lives. The Vietnamese in Biloxi have not withdrawn completely. They are a community within a community, but they are *in* and are becoming more so.

DOCKSIDE GAMBLING

In the early 1990s, Biloxi experienced a cultural and economic transformation with the legalization of dockside gambling. The 1990 Mississippi Gaming Control Act legalized casino gambling in counties along the Gulf Coast and the Mississippi River. Voters had to approve the measure, and Harrison County voters overwhelmingly did. With gambling came an explosion of construction, employment, and a new workforce arriving to fill the need. Prior to legalized gambling, the coast hosted a million visitors a year. That number has climbed to ten to twelve million. The Gulf Coast became the third most popular gambling destination.

Proposed legalization of dockside gambling was heated both in the Biloxi community and statewide. The concerns over crime, stress on city infrastructure, and the moral argument against the practice could not outweigh the prospect of new jobs and increased city revenue. When dockside gambling was approved in Harrison County, those historical seafood industry neighborhoods Point Cadet and Back Bay became magnets for gaming interests. All the seafood dealers and canneries on the beach sold out to casino and condominium development. They relocated their operations to Back Bay or simply closed down.

The introduction of gambling coincided with an already declining seafood industry. To many coast residents gambling seemed to be the economic panacea that the area needed. Economists and researchers at the Mississippi Coastal Research and Extension Service have shown that numerous factors—some influenced by the introduction of gaming—have adversely affected the seafood industry. The reduction in the size of the fleet, the reduction in volume and value of the goods, the competition from foreign markets (particularly Vietnam and Thailand), and rising domestic costs for fuel and maintenance, as well as the normal fluctuations in the seafood population, affect the industry. Today a fifty-to-sixty-foot steel-hull boat may require more than a hundred thousand dollars for fuel alone. Add in labor and supply expenses and the investment for merely leaving the dock is substantial.

The gaming industry brought somewhat of a renaissance to Biloxi and the Gulf Coast, at least in terms of economic growth. While Highway 90 was transformed into casino row, the seafood industry held on, and the neighborhoods of Point Cadet and Back Bay witnessed an increase in traffic, property value, and rent. For better or for worse, the city had a firm reliance on the gaming industry. It was earning almost fifty-five thousand dollars in tax revenue per day. Recognizing what a loss this would be to the city coffers, Mayor A. J. Holloway approved the ninety-two-thousand-dollar purchase of a "business interruption" insurance policy in June 2005. It was arguably one of the singular best decisions of his tenure.

DISASTERS STRIKE—HURRICANE KATRINA AND THE DEEPWATER HORIZON OIL RIG EXPLOSION

On August 29, 2005, Hurricane Katrina made landfall in Louisiana, Mississippi, and Alabama. This Class 3 hurricane brought a thirty-to-thirty-five-foot storm surge and raged for more than eight hours. It wiped thousands of homes and buildings down to their foundations, moved hulking casino barges across Highway 90, destroyed city roads and bridges, and claimed more than 230 lives in Mississippi alone. Hurricane Camille, which hit the coast in 1969, had long been the standard by which to judge other gulf storms. Despite her lesser intensity, Katrina was a wider storm than Camille. She exacted damage without regard to location, to floodplain elevation, to economic importance, or to historic significance. A new unimaginable benchmark had been set.

Much of the area of East Biloxi, particularly Back Bay and Point Cadet, lay in the existing one-hundred-year floodplain. The Maritime & Seafood Industry Museum, the Fleur de Lis Club and Slavonian Lodge, St. Michael Catholic Church, and countless homes and businesses, including the casinos, were flooded, washed from their foundations or entirely washed away. The nation's response was quick and overwhelming: food, water, money, first responders, medical personnel, volunteers, and organizations poured into the region and into the city of Biloxi. Within days following the hurricane, the city issued newsletters informing the citizens of vital information: where to obtain water, food, and ice; health hazard warnings; and calls for volunteers. Relief workers and first responders distributed the newsletters to key points in the city such as churches, supply centers, and city facilities.

It is difficult to comprehend the scale of destruction to life, personal property, city infrastructure, and the environment. Consider these statistics and how they relate to the seafood industry: more than 85 percent of the commercial fishing fleet and 97 percent of the seafood processing plants sustained significant damage; the storm caused thirty-five million dollars in damages to the seafood industry and put almost two thousand people out of work; more than 80 percent of the near shore reefs—a natural habitat for fish, shrimp, and oysters—were damaged or destroyed; marinas, ice houses, docks, wholesalers and retailers were effectively out of business, and the Mississippi Sound was littered with debris caused by the storm surge.

In the aftermath of the hurricane, the public, the press, and government officials often used the term "clean slate" when they spoke of rebuilding the coast. The damage was so extensive that it did offer the opportunity to correct old mistakes and rebuild with a cohesive master plan in mind. On the other hand, the slate that was wiped clean was people's homes, businesses, places of worship, and neighborhoods where they had lived for generations. These places were invested with emotional, cultural, and historical capital. Any effort toward rebuilding would have to take this into account and make a place at the table for everyone. This would require strong, visionary leadership and a committed, engaged, energized community to reimagine their city.

In the decade prior to Katrina, Biloxi was enjoying an economic boom time—a renaissance, as Mayor A. J. Holloway would describe it. The mayor called upon the citizens to recommit to that spirit and "revive the Renaissance." Just months after the storm, Holloway established a Reviving the Renaissance steering committee, led by retired Air Force Lt. Gen. Clark Griffith, a former commander of Keesler Air Force Base in Biloxi. The committee, serving in an advisory capacity only, was to research and develop specific recommendations for recovery with a realistic price tag and realistic timeline.[5] It modeled itself after the Governor's Commission on Recovery, Rebuilding and Renewal, which brought in architects, engineers, and city planners to work with each of the coast communities to envision a comprehensive approach to renewal, covering specific topics such as housing, transportation, education, tourism, and business. Through open forums, community brainstorming sessions called *charrettes*, the public was invited to voice suggestions, ask questions, and critique plans.

Federal and state assistance would be critical to starting the process, but long-term success depended upon the individual communities, their financial commitment and their ability to draw private investment. Commenting on the situation on the Gulf Coast, Mayor Holloway said, "We survived an unprecedented event and it has made us a stronger community. We are now in a position where we can realize unprecedented potential. Personally, these are tragic times, but exciting times. Working together, we will make our home the envy of the nation."[6]

In February 2006, Holloway announced the formation of the committee. More than five hundred people attended the first public meeting and two hundred volunteered to serve as committee members. The committees addressed infrastructure (affordable housing, transportation, land use, and historic preservation), economic development (tourism, small business seafood industry/marine resources, military/government contracting), and human services (education, health and human services, nongovernmental organizations). Within three months the committees issued their recommendations to the city. In addition, a second report, *Moving Forward*, addresses rebuilding recommendations specifically in East Biloxi. *Moving Forward* is the work of Living Cities: The National Community Development Initiative and the Boston-based Goody-Clancy, an architectural, planning, and preservation firm. Living Cities is a nonprofit consortium of major financial, philanthropic, and public sector organizations whose mission is "to increase the vitality of cities and urban neighborhoods and improve the lives of people who live there."[7] The recommendations and renderings made in *Moving Forward* embrace the philosophy espoused by the New Urbanism movement, an urban planning approach which stresses pedestrian-friendly, mixed-used, mixed-income neighborhoods to counter sprawl.

New Urbanism has received its share of criticism among architects and planners, for embracing a "mythical" past, creating "Disneyesque" towns, and lacking a modernist vision. Many developers, however, embrace the New Urbanism ideals because this type of development (e.g., multiple stories, shared greenspace) is cost effective.

The planning process included informal discussions with community stakeholders, community meetings, and coordination with community planning processes within the city and technical analyses. During these discussions and meetings, several key themes emerged: residents preferred single-family housing as a model for rebuilding; residents were concerned that the new FEMA flood elevations would prohibit many, especially the elderly, from rebuilding homes; they welcomed new commercial and residential development that was in keeping with the historic identity of the area; and they felt that public access to the waterfront was a high priority.

Among the recommendations put forth in this proposal:

- A new tourism, entertainment, and gaming district
- Expansion of East Biloxi's housing stock
- A vital, attractive downtown
- Seafood Village, a new destination on Back Bay
- A great public waterfront with access all along the water's edge
- A new central park at the heart of the peninsula
- A new "loop" boulevard linking all the major destinations
- New development sympathetic to Biloxi's character and heritage
- An overall approach to land use that mitigates the potential for future flood damage

The plan creates a strategy for rebuilding that divides East Biloxi into distinct areas based on use and potential for future flooding. The waterfront mixed-use area would incorporate larger gaming and entertainment facilities, including boating. The central redevelopment area, a low-lying area that flooded heavily in Katrina, would focus around a great central park and contain high-density, high-elevation housing. The Seafood Village on Back Bay would house the commercial fishing fleet and processing plants as well as dining and shopping. The downtown area, commercial mixed-use corridor, and neighborhood conservation and infill housing areas, all located on higher elevations, would be opportunities for new commercial, government, and residential development.

The shortage of affordable housing is one of the most pressing issues on the coast. This affects employment, as jobs go unfilled because of the lack of housing.

East Biloxi was a low-to-middle-income area with longtime homeowners and affordable rental properties. About 70 percent of the city's Vietnamese population lived inside the flood zone in East Biloxi. Here, as elsewhere, rising building and insurance costs and revised FEMA elevation requirements will cut out some longtime residents, many of them renters (ineligible for Community Development Block grants) or underinsured homeowners.

Gaming facilities will more than likely further expand in East Biloxi. This became evident less than two months after Katrina. In a special session the state legislature reassured gaming interests of the safety of their investment on the coast by approving a measure which allowed casinos to build on land within eight hundred feet of shore. This effectively opened the whole coastline to potential gaming development. Land ownership, rezoning, and approval from the gaming commission are required as well, but the expansion appears almost inevitable.

The city council had mixed reactions to the Living Cities plan, but accepted it in September 2006. Without some sort of plan, they could not apply for federal and state aid. Many residents have reservations as well, particularly with regard to affordable housing, land use, and the future of longtime neighborhood residents. One such organization, the Steps Coalition, was founded in June 2006 by community leaders and activists to focus on equitable recovery. The Steps Coalition, whose members include the NAACP, Coastal Women for Change, Back Bay Mission, and Boat People S.O.S, espouses the idea that successful community building relies upon five key values: affordable housing, economic justice, environmental justice, preservation of historical communities, and human rights. In a recent report on Mississippi's spending of CBDG disaster recovery funds, the coalition faulted the state for redirecting funds away from lower-income storm victims and lacking a plan to deal with an impending housing crisis once the FEMA assistance program ended in March 2009.

Less than five years after Katrina, another disaster threatened the Mississippi Gulf Coast and the slowly reviving seafood industry. On April 20, 2010, the Deepwater Horizon oil well, leased and operated by BP Oil, exploded. The well was located forty miles off the Louisiana coastline and was drilling in water almost a mile deep. Investigators later determined that methane gas escaped from the well, shot up through the well column and ignited. The explosion killed eleven rig workers, injured seventeen, and caused the rig to sink two days later. With a damaged well head and no immediate method to contain it, the oil began flowing into the gulf. The resulting disaster would become the largest offshore oil spill in the United States.

Confusion and misinformation surrounded the initial reports of the oil spill. BP officials greatly underestimated or underreported the amount of oil pumping from the broken well. The oil flowed unceasingly for months. It first hit the Louisiana coastline, then by late June had appeared on the Mississippi coast and barrier islands. BP and the Coast Guard worked simultaneously to contain the spilled oil and stop the flow. BP used several tactics to contain the leak, including a containment dome, a "top kill," and a "junk shot" (an attempt to clog the blowout preventer with junk such as golf balls and pieces of rubber), but none were successful. By early June BP had managed to stem the oil flow through a temporary cap, and containment ships on the surface captured or burned the oil. In mid-July, with a new cap in place, the oil flow stopped completely for the first time, and on September 19 the relief well operation succeeded in sealing the broken well permanently. Meanwhile, for three months the oil flowed—an estimated 206,000,000 *gallons*. The oil plumes, some on the surface and some under, threatened the shores, the barrier islands, and the rich ecosystem of the gulf. While coastal communities, including Biloxi, used inflatable booms to protect beaches and inland waterways, those in the seafood industry braced for the worst. The oil and the chemical dispersants used to break up the oil threatened rich oyster beds and the shrimp and sport fishing population, as well as the breeding grounds for birds, turtles, and other sea life.

The spill had far-reaching effects in a region where tourism and the seafood industry are vital to the economy. Restaurants, hotels, charter boat operations, and numerous large and small businesses felt the rippling effects. While BP employed commercial and recreational fishermen in the clean-up efforts through the "Vessels of Opportunity" program and paid more than $31 million in claims to Mississippi residents alone, the damage was done. The long-term effects remain unknown, and coastal communities are facing a Catch-22: promoting the sale of seafood from waters they are not sure are truly safe.

The environment reveals itself as complex and fragile, but resilient and enduring. The same holds true for the coastal communities. Biloxi faces a daunting task in rebuilding. The "clean slate" created by Katrina is now full of proposals, concerns, and pressure from divergent groups. The future of the seafood industry in the wake of the oil spill remains uncertain. Whatever rebuilding efforts the city makes, what should remain most important is a concern for community and its cultural and historical significance. Biloxi's maritime heritage and ethnic diversity are valuable assets that have shaped the city for more than three hundred years. Witness the Slavic Benevolent Association, which recently acquired land elsewhere in Point Cadet and will rebuild their lodge, and the Maritime & Seafood Industry Museum, which operates from a trailer on the barracks site, but has plans for a new facility on the beach. In the wake of disasters the city has the opportunity to rebuild with a plan that values these assets and the people and environment that maintain them today.

NOTES

Portions of this article previously appeared in *Mississippi Folklife*, Vol. 28, No. 1 and No. 2, 1995. Thank you to the University of Mississippi and the Center for the Study of Southern Culture for permission to reprint.

    1. Rosan A. Jordan, "Folklore and Ethnicity: Some Theoretical Considerations," in *Louisiana Folklife*, ed. Nicholas Spitzer (Baton Rouge: Louisiana Folklife Program/Division of the Arts, 1985), 51.
    2. Ibid.
    3. "Creolization" as defined by Reinecke is the synthesis of the various cultures in the unique New Orleans melting pot as they interacted one by one with the original French, Franco-American, or Afro-French population. George F. Reinecke, "The National and Cultural Groups of New Orleans," in *Louisiana Folklife*, ed. Nicholas Spitzer (Baton Rouge: Louisiana Folklife Program/Division of the Arts, 1985).
    4. John O. Seeligman, City of Biloxi, City Map, 1900.
    5. Lt. Gen. Clark Griffith, USAF Ret., Chairman, "Building Our Future, Embracing Our Past," final report, Reviving the Renaissance Steering Committee, 3.
    6. Ibid., 7.
    7. Living Cities: The National Community Development Initiative, http:www.livingcities.org (accessed July 15, 2008).

SELECTED BIBLIOGRAPHY

Griffith, Lt. Gen. Clark, USAF Ret., Chairman, "Building Our Future, Embracing Our Past," final report, Reviving the Renaissance Steering Committee, Biloxi, Mississippi, 2006.

Gutierrez, Paige C. *The Cultural Legacy of Biloxi's Seafood Industry*. Biloxi, Mississippi, 1984.

Jordan, Rosan A. "Folklore and Ethnicity: Some Theoretical Considerations," in *Louisiana Folklife*, ed. Nicholas R. Spitzer. Baton Rouge: Louisiana Folklife Program/Division of the Arts, 1985.

Sun Herald. "The People Within: How the Vietnamese have Adapted to Life on the Coast." Biloxi, Mississippi, 1993.

SECTION II

Ethnicity in a Biracial Culture

This section offers a description of three groups—the Chinese, Lebanese, and Jewish communities—who immigrated to Mississippi primarily after the Civil War and continued to have vibrant communities until after World War II. Their journey from the late nineteenth through the mid-twentieth century was one of finding a middle path, a third identity, in a society divided into white and black.

Included in this section are the Choctaws, who were obviously not immigrants but instead were indigenous occupants of what is now Mississippi. They are in this section because they also faced the problem of being neither black nor white in a society that only recognized two categories.

The four groups share the fact that dominant racial labels did not apply to them, and there are some similarities in their stories of moving between black and white. However, the groups are each quite different in how their communities and social identities evolved and how they now self-identify.

—*Editor*

6.1. Frieda Sue Quon reading. Courtesy of Delta State University Archives and Museum, Cleveland, MS, John and Frieda Quon Collection.

6

MISSISSIPPI DELTA CHINESE

—EMILY ERWIN JONES AND FRIEDA QUON

"To be in between was to be invisible."[1]

In simply meeting and exchanging pleasantries with Frieda Seu Quon, one has had a personal encounter with the rich and complex culture and heritage that is symbolic of the fabric of the Mississippi Delta. On the surface, Mrs. Quon presents a person of Chinese heritage; yet with her voice and her mannerisms, she is entirely southern, Mississippi, and Delta. Her roots reach back across a nation and an ocean, but her branches, her childhood and heirs, are profoundly American. It is in Mrs. Quon's very being that the terms "melting pot" and convergence of cultures become evident. Although Frieda Quon is particularly significant in local Mississippi Delta Chinese heritage, she is not alone. There are dozens of individuals and families who share similar familial links from the alluvial Delta plains back to the ancestral towns and villages in China. Although it is unusual for the author of a history chapter to also be a character in the chapter, we use firsthand, personal stories, photographs, and documented evidence reviewed to present a blend of historic facts and personal accounts.

FROM ONE LAND TO ANOTHER...

To understand why the Chinese settled in the Mississippi Delta, an understanding of the geography and history of the area is necessary. Layered on top of historic reference and documentation, personal, firsthand accounts and photographs provide evidence of lives lived to the fullest, with determination to succeed and family values at their core.

Historian James Cobb has referred to the land as "the most southern place on earth" and countless other historians and authors have offered their perspectives on the stark contrasts that permeated the history of the Delta.[2] Situated in the northwest corner of the state and bordered by the Mississippi and Yazoo rivers, which run contiguously down the east and west sides of the alluvial plain, is the land known best as the Mississippi Delta.

With the earliest settlers, an economic heritage was born out of the system of taking resources from the natural landscape that could be immediately used by the settlers and then sold or traded to other parts of the country. By the late 1880s, the Delta boasted acres of hardwood timber, which provided a financial base for many with the clearing and planting operations for Delta settlers. Cleveland, Mississippi, had four lumber mills in one small town as a result of the positive economic impact of the timber industry on the area, as well as the easier transportation system of the railroad that ran through the middle of town, as it did with most Delta towns. However, once the bottomland hardwoods had been harvested from the Delta, the timber industry moved on to other parts of the state, leaving behind rich soil perfect for growing cotton.

Best known for its economic history and effects on the Delta's social order is cotton farming, in which a wealthy planter aristocracy coexisted with an impoverished labor class. As evidenced by the economic disparities, racial and class differences would plague the Delta's environs.

Unwritten rules dictated the culture, establishing boundaries between the black and white societies which dominated the population. Although the black/white dichotomy would monopolize the attentions of historians for decades, other ethnic groups such as Lebanese, Italians, Mexicans, and Jews did live and prosper within this social melting pot. In the midst of the amalgamation of all of these new ethnic groups, one of the most dramatic stories of assimilation is that of the Chinese population in the Mississippi Delta and how they would define their place "between black and white."[3]

CHINESE IMMIGRATE TO THE DELTA

In 1865, a decades-long system of slave labor was abolished along with the Confederacy, and the Delta planters were left with a sense of panic as to how to address the immediate four-million-strong emancipation of their primary labor force. Given that slave labor had been the linchpin of the Delta's agricultural economy, Delta planters were eager to find ways to sustain productivity and their way of life. As they would come to find, there would be no easy or quick solution to their labor needs.

Looking beyond their local borders, Delta planters supported and held conventions and public discussions in the hopes that ideas on possible labor sources could be brought to light. Not only were the planters interested in where they could find a suitable labor force; they were also interested in finding the best way to recruit and import them into the Mississippi Delta. The most prominent idea to develop from the immigration and labor conventions was to recruit "European and Yankee white" immigrants as a possible source of labor to replace the freed slave population.[4] Blatantly evident was the fact that white immigrants would be uninterested in settling in an area with a depressed economic level. The attraction to look to other populations became even more evident when securing black labor proved difficult and a laborious task.[5]

Creative ideas were tossed about concerning using Chinese, and later Italian, populations to solve the labor problems. To explore these and other solutions, planters organized themselves into collaborative groups to search out the truly feasible and reasonable solutions. Organizations such as the Arkansas River Valley Emigration Company, established in June 1869, met with the express purpose of attracting Chinese labor. The Chinese population was an attractive alternative labor force for many reasons. Members of the organizations felt that this group of people could be attracted to the Mississippi Delta in "great numbers and at cheap rates, and made efficient in the cultivation of cotton," and prove to be resistant to malaria infections.[6] Delegates from many of the southern states, representing railroad, planting, and business interests, met in the Greenlaw Opera House in Memphis, Tennessee, to devise the "best and cheapest means of procuring Chinese laborers."[7] In addition to the conventions held in Arkansas and Memphis, others sought to encourage migration of Chinese, predominately men, in order to create a reliable source of steady labor in the post–Civil War South. Also, recruiters carried into China the stories of America as the "Gold Mountain," where the Chinese could come, earn a great sum of money, and then return to their ancestral lands. The lure of economic prosperity was a strong draw for many Chinese, specifically men.

In 1870, two ships, the *Ville De St. Lo* and the *Charles Auguste*, landed at the port in New Orleans, introducing approximately four hundred Chinese to America and a new way of life. Although there is limited actual proof that these four hundred new immigrants actually made their way to the plantations of the Mississippi Delta, what can be confirmed is that a small contingency of Chinese laborers is noted in the 1870 U.S. Census records as arriving in Bolivar County and working as farm laborers.[8]

Expectations were high for both the plantation owners and the Chinese. The planters saw this new immigrant group as a resource to populate their plantations and solve their labor issues. The Chinese looked upon their situation as sojourners. This new land and opportunity would provide a financial resource for them to send money back to families in China, as they had every intention of returning to their ancestral lands. However, the costs associated with recruiting and transporting them directly from China would prove to be more than the post–Civil War South economy could withstand and would come to an end.[9]

Because of the efforts of various conventions, recruiters would travel to China and either directly solicit or run ads to attract workers. These publicized solicitations for immigrant work attracted some Chinese workers to the States. However, other Chinese came to the Mississippi Delta from other parts of the United States, seeking relief from the arduous work on the Central Pacific Railroad in California. In the early twentieth century still other groups of Chinese sought refuge from the domestic turmoil in China after the downfall of the Imperial Manchu Dynasty in 1911.[10]

Immigration to the United States may have appeared as simple as boarding a ship; however, the Chinese Exclusion Act of 1882 barred the legal naturalization and possible immigration of Chinese into the United States. That law would not be repealed until 1943, when Chinese finally were allowed to immigrate legally as well as purchase and own property. A rather unfortunate event developed into one of the most successful ways Chinese immigrated into the United States or, for those already in the country, claimed citizenship. In 1906 an earthquake and subsequent fire consumed the public records offices in San Francisco, California. Without access to the public records, many officials could not determine if the Chinese people already in the United States had been granted citizenship legally or not. They also could not determine family lineage or connections, which allowed the Chinese in the United States to fabricate familial ties on paper, creating the term "paper sons" or, less popular, "paper daughters."

George Seu, Frieda Quon's father, was a "paper son." Her father had come to the United States by claiming that he was the son of a Chinese man already a United States citizen. "My dad's 'paper son' name was Pang, which became our name until in the 1950s when Dad was able to apply for his actual name and we were all allowed to use our real name, Seu. Explaining the name change was a bit confusing at school, doctors, and other necessary places," Mrs. Quon remembered. Other Chinese in the Mississippi Delta tell much the same type of story of how one member of the family would come to the United States under a "paper son" name and then gradually bring the rest of the family over time. In some cases, the "paper son" name would remain the family name, and in other cases, like Mrs. Quon's, the family would revert back to their original name. This was just one of the many concessions Chinese immigrating to the United States would agree to in order to provide for their families.

Even with immigrant status, there was always the fear of being discovered and deported. Frieda Quon had a relative, Third Uncle, who joined the family from South America and was terrified of being deported. One time, he was sick and had to be admitted to a hospital in Memphis. Convinced that authorities would discover his true identity and deport him, Third Uncle jumped out of a third-story window of the hospital. Fortunately, he landed in some bushes and was not injured or deported.

Records indicate that there was already a well-established community of Chinese in the Mississippi Delta by the 1880s. Census records show that of the fifty Chinese listed in Mississippi, twenty-eight were in Washington County as "farm laborers, grocers, launderers, farm hands, and hucksters."[11] Local newspaper reports indicate that near Prentiss in Bolivar County sixteen "coolies" had been recruited directly from Hong Kong to serve as the labor on the Hughs plantation.

There is little documentation, other than oral history and stories passed down from one generation to the next, that suggests that the original Chinese laborers introduced into the Mississippi Delta are the ancestors of the Delta's current Chinese community. However, several Chinese in the Mississippi Delta believe that their families are connected to these first immigrant settlers.[12] Edward Joe, currently of Jackson, comments that he was taught that the Chinese he knew and grew up with had arrived in the Delta for the express purpose of working on the plantations and then would return to China. It would be the next generation, the children born to the immigrant Chinese men and women, who would abandon the sojourner ideas and establish the Mississippi Delta as their home, viewing a return to China as less important than their parents' generation.[13]

Personal stories recounted through oral histories and correspondences illustrate how many of the Mississippi Delta's Chinese came to the area prior to the establishment of the Chinese Exclusion Act of 1882. Bobby Jue recounts that his grandfather first came over to the United States to work on the railroads in California but found his way to Arkansas and then ended up in Mayersville, Mississippi, where he worked in a grocery store. Bobby's father would open his own grocery store in the mid-1930s, first in Rolling Fork, then Greenville, and finally settle in Hollandale.[14]

Luck Wing recounts that his father arrived in the Mississippi Delta by way of Paducah, Kentucky. He explains that his father traveled from Kentucky to Greenville because of the concentration of Chinese in the Mississippi Delta. There was also an older Chinese gentleman, Joe Bing, who his father knew would help get Luck Wing's father established in the grocery business.[15]

Frieda Quon recounts the story of how her father arrived first in America and then found his way to the Mississippi Delta.

> George Seu (Tuck Chon) was my father and the youngest of three brothers born in Canton (Guangdong) China. In 1925, my father was thirteen years old and made his way on his own to Chicago where his brothers had established a laundry business. Even though his middle-class family owned and operated a mercantile business in China, they believed the stories which had trickled back to China that greater opportunities existed in the United States, or *Gam San* as it was called by the Chinese. *Gam San* translates to "Gold Mountain."
>
> As was becoming the custom, my father's family sent him to the United States in order to earn enough capital and return to China. When he arrived in Chicago, my father went straight to work in the laundry with his brothers. Arriving as a young teenager, my father became the ward of Great Uncle, twenty years his senior. My father learned all the skills necessary for survival in this new environment as well as the ins and outs of operating a laundry: cooking, washing, sewing, ironing. It was here in Chicago where my dad completed his junior high education. He and my uncles were avid readers and subscribed to the American newspapers and would wait anxiously for any news from China.

BECOMING MERCHANTS

The Chinese who came to the Mississippi Delta as laborers soon learned that the economic prosperity they sought could not be found in the fields. In searching for a better way to earn a living, the Chinese moved from being field laborers to being merchants.

Following Reconstruction, southern blacks had to establish purchasing power independent of the commissary credit system[16] that had historically dictated their lives. The Chinese saw an opportunity to provide a service and in turn make a more profitable living by opening small businesses. Basic economics influenced the decision for the Chinese to open grocery stores. Although African Americans—their major customers—were finally earning a wage, there was little extra money to support expenditures on anything beyond food, shelter, and clothing. A grocery store seemed the logical choice for the Chinese sojourner.

The transition from working as laborers in the fields to becoming grocery and mercantile owners was not as easy as simply moving from one place to another. A great deal of research has brought to light the immigrant patterns of the early Chinese settlers in the United States. More research has explored how the Chinese in the Mississippi Delta assimilated into the culture of the Delta. However, there has been relatively little attention turned to the transition from farm laborer to entrepreneur.

In his book *Chopsticks in the Land of Cotton*, Dr. John Jung suggests several ways the Chinese in the Mississippi Delta came to own grocery stores. A primary method the Chinese first chose for entering the economic setting in the Delta was to copy successful patterns of Chinese immigrants' work in other places in the U.S. and open a laundry, which would require very little overhead. The only supplies needed to operate such a business would be fairly inexpensive (washboard, tub, soap, and brushes). The 1927 Greenville City Directory indicates that Hop Lee was operating a laundry on Walnut Street.[17] Fairly quickly, the Chinese turned from laundries to grocery stores. One reason for this trend may have been because in the rural, agrarian South, there was very little need for fresh, starched shirts and suits as had been the case in the more urban locations like Chicago and San Francisco.[18]

A second method of establishing economic prosperity in the Delta was to generate a financial base outside of the Delta and then relocate to the area. Frieda Quon confirms that her father had immigrated to the United States to work in a laundry in Chicago with his older brothers in the early 1900s. Their family in China had provided a small sum of money to get them started in the United States and then the brothers pooled their resources to increase their economic gains. By the mid-1920s, the oldest brother, Great Uncle, traveled to the Mississippi Delta because he had heard that they could open a grocery store there which would be much more lucrative than the laundry business in Chicago. By 1928, the Min Sang store

6.2A and 6.2B. Min Sang storefront in Greenville (older and newer). The older photo dates from the 1940s and the newer one from the late 1950s. Courtesy of Delta State University Archives and Museum, Cleveland, MS, John and Frieda Quon Collection.

had opened on Alexander Street in Greenville and the brothers were doing a very good business.

> Great Uncle, Shui Tuck Hi, would learn about the opportunities in the Mississippi Delta. In the late 1920s he left Dad and a cousin in charge of the laundry to investigate the possibility of moving to the

South. All along the Mississippi Delta from Memphis to Vicksburg, in every town and hamlet the demand for grocery stores was needed to provide staples to the thousands of farm workers. Plantation owners wanting to concentrate on raising crops had no interest in operating commissaries. Operating grocery stores was definitely preferred over working in the cotton fields. The Chinese found this to be an ideal economic opportunity for which they were well suited. Again the Chinese viewed the grocery stores as an expedient way to establish self-owned businesses that would potentially earn enough capital to attain their goal of supplying money to family members in China and eventually retiring.

My father and great-uncles knew that moving to the segregated South would be a challenge, as they fit in neither category of "white" or "black." The Chinese became a class unto their own, wanting to maintain their own Chinese culture and heritage. They were dependent on the blacks for business, but recognized that the whites controlled the privileges and economic power. It behooved the Chinese to walk a fine line between the blacks and whites. In many of the Delta towns the Chinese located their businesses in the black parts of town and were unobtrusive citizens. However, Chinese stores were not limited to black clientele only, as there were Chinese stores in Cleveland, Indianola, Inverness, and Greenville that enjoyed a loyal following of white customers. In some smaller towns, Chinese stores may have been the only store to shop, so the business became a necessity for all.

Min Sang Company established in 1928 was strategically located on a major thoroughfare, Alexander Street, which ran the entire length of Greenville from the levee downtown to the city limits on Highway 82. Initially there were two separate stores, facing diagonally on the corners of Alexander and Eureka streets, one mainly serving white customers and the second serving blacks. With the uncles, my parents, and cousins drifting in and out, there was always manpower.[19]

Established before supermarkets, Min Sang Company prospered. Black customers came from Alexander Street north to Nelson Street and white customers from the southern direction toward Highway 82. Customers could phone in grocery orders that were delivered by porters on bicycles, and cold items were placed in the resident's refrigerator. Min Sang Company took pride in their premium meat department. The clientele included blacks and prominent whites. Mr. and Mrs. Blum, owners of Nelms and

Blum, a fine department store on Washington Avenue, ordered a seven-bone roast every week. Howard Dyer, the Koestler family, and Judge Solomon's family were regular customers. In the 1950s the two old store buildings that had made up Min Sang Company were combined and replaced by a new brick structure that was air-conditioned and had an adjoining home. Min Sang opened for business 365 days a year, including Christmas Day; later the store would close half a day on Sundays. Juanita Dong recalls of her family's store, "We sold everything! We had everything from nails to oilcloth. We had twenty-five-pound sacks of flour. We had garden dust. We had anything you could name. We had washtubs. We had scrub boards."[20]

BUILDING COMMUNITY

The Chinese had achieved a level of success and created a community which could support other Chinese relatives and friends coming to the United States. Building strong bonds of support and help was important to the first-generation immigrants. Freeda Lee remembers that as a small child she would travel with her father from family to family so that he could visit and check on the newcomers. Her father had faced many of the challenges of establishing himself and he had much advice to offer.[21] Slowly the sojourner mentality was beginning to wane, and the Chinese were building community foundations and families that were tied to the Mississippi Delta. Acknowledging the Delta as their home, the Chinese then faced the challenge of a continued economic involvement with the black community while seeking acceptance by the white community. "Not inclined toward assimilation with the black minority, and rejected by the prejudice of the white majority, the Chinese found themselves victims of social isolation."[22]

In the Mississippi Delta, the Chinese had to redefine themselves. They had created a life that was wedged in a polarized segregated society, and they were determined to make the best life they could for themselves.[23] Frieda Quon remembers, "The Chinese are in a strange land . . . I don't know if it was the attitude; they just accepted it the way it was. We were the ones who made the choice to come over here. We are in the lands where all the Caucasians are, and so we had to make the best of the situation."[24] Their economic lifeline was tied to the black community, while they preferred the social freedoms and acceptance that association with the white society would allow.

6.3. A one-room schoolhouse in Greenville. Courtesy of Delta State University Archives and Museum, Cleveland, MS, Sidney Collection.

CHINESE EDUCATION

One of the most dramatic ways this "in between" culture became quickly visible in the Delta was in education. Backed with a tradition of high value placed on education and more specifically on the quality of teachers, the Chinese desired the best quality of education for their children. The Mississippi Constitution drew a clear line, establishing a dual education system for blacks and whites; however, there were no clear mandates on the educational options for the Chinese population. Rejecting the black public schools as a viable educational option, many Chinese families chose to homeschool their children, create their own Chinese school, or send their children to the white public schools.

The question as to which public school the Chinese children would attend was answered differently in each town in the Delta, and often the solution was that the Chinese were the exception to the rule. The Chinese had faced the overt discrimination devised by the federal government with the Chinese Exclusion Act of 1882 and would again face discrimination in the court case *Lum v. Rice* in 1927. As the Chinese were trying to define for themselves a middle place between the black and white societies, their concern for their children's education was paramount. When it came to education and a question of "white" or "black," the Chinese were dealt with

6.4. An Oriental school in the Greenville Public Library, 1946. Courtesy of Delta State University Archives and Museum, Cleveland, MS, Shepherd Collection.

as an exception to the rule in many cases. For instance, schools in Boyle, Greenville, Merigold, Pace, and Ruleville allowed the Chinese students to attend the white public schools. For the Chinese of Rosedale and Cleveland, the issue would not be so clearly defined.

In Greenville, the Chinese children originally attended school in a one-room schoolhouse known as "Oriental School" by the townspeople. This school provided one teacher for all students in the first through the twelfth grades. The school was located on Nelson Street across the street from the old Trigg School in downtown Greenville, near the levee. C. W. Sidney recalls that in this one-room school in Greenville they had regular school in the mornings and then Chinese lessons in the afternoons.

As an alternative to a public school or home school and following landmark cases such as *Lum v. Rice*, Chinese mission schools were established which were residential, with no set grade levels for different ages and with blended curriculum based on a traditional U.S. model and some Chinese education. Rejecting the black schools and finding no acceptance in the white schools, Chinese accepted the invitation to partner with white churches to establish an educational curriculum based on traditional public school curriculum but which also included lessons in religion for their children. In some cases, afternoon instruction would include tutoring from Chinese instructors. It would be churches in the Delta that would not only provide an avenue for educational enrichment of their children but also provide the Chinese an opportunity to gather together socially, as well as establish that, while their children did not attend the black schools, they were deserving of a level of social acceptance from the white community.

Frances Wong states that although every town in the Delta did not deny Chinese access to white school education, many towns compromised by building Chinese schools where Chinese and English lessons were taught. In her town of Louise, the 98 percent white population voted to keep her brothers and sisters and herself from attending the white school; therefore, she attended the Louise Consolidated School from 1937 to 1945.[25] Frieda Quon recounts:

> The question as to whether Chinese children could attend white public school was different in each town. Some towns would not allow Chinese children to attend white public schools. When I started first grade in Greenville in 1948, I believe it was the first year that Chinese students of *all* grades were permitted to attend white public schools. Previously, Chinese students, grades one to twelve, were taught by a single teacher in a one-room schoolhouse at the end of Nelson Street. As parents valued education highly, this situation was not acceptable. Parents stressed to their children that a good education was vital to a better future. Leaders from the First Baptist Church appealed to the school board on behalf of the Chinese. On a trial basis Chinese students attended junior high and high school and were model students; subsequently all Chinese students were allowed to attend white public schools.[26]

Chinese parents valued education and sought many alternatives to find appropriate education for their children. John Paul Quon remembers that his brothers and sisters were not allowed to enter the white public schools in Moorhead; therefore, his father employed a private tutor for them.[27] Fay Dong recalls a similar situation for him and four other families in his town. "When I went to school, we did not have any actual public school for us. We had three or four families together at a small makeshift school. There used to be a librarian. She taught us whatever she knew. I stayed with this system through the first few grades. Then after that I went to the public schools. This was right at the time of World War II."[28]

The 1890 Mississippi Constitution had adopted many of the Jim Crow laws including that "separate schools shall be maintained for children of the white and colored races."[29] The constitutionality of that law was taken all the way to the United States Supreme Court, in a landmark case which originated out of Rosedale, Mississippi—*Lum v. Rice* in 1927.

The Gong Lums had settled in the port city of Rosedale along Bolivar County's riverside, opened a grocery store frequented by both blacks and whites, and had joined and become active in one of the local churches and developed many white friends. They also sent their daughter, Martha Lum, to the public white school in town. Sometime during the fall of 1924, the family was notified that the school district would no longer allow Martha to attend classes at the white school. The Lum family challenged this decision and filed suit on October 28, 1924.[30]

Some evidence suggests that the reason for the Lum children being excluded from the Rosedale school was that when other Chinese families learned that the Lum children had not faced any adversity in attending the white public schools, those families tried to move into the Rosedale area in order to send their children to the white school. It was at this time that the white parents voiced their objections over sharing the public school with the Chinese children, and the Lum sisters were no longer allowed to attend the school.[31]

The Lums filed a suit against the school district, which would travel from the circuit court of Bolivar County to the Mississippi Supreme Court and finally with an appeal to the U.S. Supreme Court. Of primary concern for each party in the suit was the determination of whether Chinese citizens counted as "colored" or white. Following this, the debate was over whether the 1890 Constitution requirement of separate school systems was for only two races, white and "colored." Hugh F. Causey, who was president of the school board in Cleveland in 1950, offered his opinion on interpretation of the Mississippi Constitution in a letter to Mississippi House Representative Walter Sillers, Jr., as well as other members of the legislature:

> Rice vs. Gong Lum [139 Miss. 760, 104 So. 105 (affirmed U.S. Supreme Court, 275 US 78, 72 Law Ed. 172)] and Bond vs. Tij Fung [148 Miss. 462, 114 So. 332] has held that since Chinese children are not members of the white race they fall within the general classification of colored children as mentioned in the above Section 207 of the Constitution, and cannot attend the white schools. I am of the opinion that since only two classifications of the races are named in the Constitution,

6.5. The Cleveland Chinese Mission School, circa 1940s. Courtesy of Delta State University Archives and Museum, Cleveland, MS, Chow Collection.

"white" and "colored", the Legislature has the right to define the word "colored" as not including Chinese children. In other words, the Legislature always has the right to interpret the Constitution where the Constitution itself does not admit of a contrary interpretation. In this instance the Constitution does not say that Chinese children are colored, but leaves the matter wide open for the Legislature to define the word "colored."³²

Had the framers of the 1890 Constitution been only concerned with "white" and "black"? Or had they intended that no nonwhite race be integrated into the school system with white children? From the Bolivar County Circuit Court, the judgment ruled in favor of the Lums; however, the school officials and the state of Mississippi followed this ruling with an appeal to the Supreme Court of Mississippi. There, the ruling was that the Lums were not entitled to attend a white school, reversing the ruling of the lower court. This moved the Lums' attorneys to file an appeal with the next highest court, the U.S. Supreme Court. It was in this environment that Chief Justice William Howard Taft delivered an opinion affirming the ruling of the Mississippi Supreme Court, rejecting the notion that Chinese citizens were denied equal protection of the law by being classified among the colored races and stating that the Chinese were provided an "education equal to that offered to all, whether white, brown, yellow, or black."[33]

Faced with the U.S. Supreme Court's final decision on their educational options, the Chinese rejected the black schools. Instead they turned to the only other organization willing and able to assist them in their plight to educate their children. Many Chinese had become members of white churches, and their alternative answer to black schools was to partner with their churches to create Chinese mission schools.

The Chinese were motivated to find the best possible education for their children. They also wanted to ensure that they remained as neutral as possible in associating with the black and white communities. Fighting for the best possible education, the Chinese not only found a balance between the black and white schools but they also demonstrated to the white communities that the Chinese were deserving of social acceptance. As one white Delta resident recounted, "A war is bad, but after the Second World War, a lot of people came back. They accepted Chinese a lot more."[34] This newfound acceptance brought down much of the racial and social barriers which had excluded Chinese from a quality public education.

As the walls of educational exclusion began to crumble, the insulated world of Chinese cultures in the Delta also became less attractive to a younger generation. While the grocery stores had provided a safe environment through the early part of the twentieth century, with a wider realm of economic and social possibilities before them the Delta Chinese "baby boomer" generation was now ready to experience their more Americanized opportunities.

THE CHINESE CHURCH

The option to develop and attend mission schools had grown out of the relationship that many Baptist churches had cultivated with the Chinese communities in the early part of the 1900s when the Chinese were eager to find alternatives for educating their children. Baptist churches often supported "Chinese church," which was usually held on Sunday afternoons after regular church services had ended. One historian reports that attending a white Baptist church afforded Chinese in the community one more opportunity to define themselves by white standards. Dr. John Jung suggests, "The Chinese also used religious conversion to Christianity, which, combined with carefully maintained public neutrality toward the racial tensions between blacks and whites, allowed them to gain acceptance and improve their place in the Delta society."[35]

However, even more Chinese were motivated to attend and become members of the Baptist Chinese churches for truly religious purposes. Frieda Quon recounts her memories of Chinese church in the First Baptist Church, Greenville, Mississippi.

> Church became a very important factor in our lives mainly because the First Baptist Church was so diligent in getting the Chinese involved. Since the Chinese opened their stores seven days a week and were reluctant to close, the First Baptist Church offered a special service for the Chinese on Sundays at 2:30 PM, which continues even today. When the Chinese Mission was chartered in 1934, my father, George Seu, and Great Uncle were among the original members. Attending church became a regular routine and opportunity for Chinese to see each other. Other church activities involved children in Sunbeams, Girls Auxiliary (GA) and Boys Auxiliary (BA), and Vacation Bible School in the summer. Through church and school our world expanded to learn about American customs. The Chinese women attended Women's Missionary Union (WMU), which broadened their view on Western culture when they visited the homes of the white churchwomen. As Chinese families mainly lived in the back of their stores, visiting in these homes gave them insight on how American families lived and also they experienced desserts—a new concept, as the Chinese diet seldom included sweets. I will always be grateful to the church staff of the First Baptist Church who gave their time and energy to accommodate the Chinese community. Many volunteered their Sunday afternoons and other times to provide services and programs for the Chinese. From the very beginning there were so many who provided support and stepped forward when necessary to aid the Chinese. In Greenville the Chinese came to rely on Rev. Ted Shepherd, longtime pastor of the Chinese Mission, First Baptist Church. It has been said often that in times of emergency, the Chinese would call Rev. Shepherd before calling 911. He has been a true friend of the Chinese.
>
> At the time I was growing up in Greenville during the forties, fifties, and sixties, regular attendance at the Chinese Mission would be over a hundred. An added bonus for me was the William Alexander Percy Library located across the street from the church. When I

learned to read, my world expanded even more from frequent visits to the library where I developed a lifelong love for books.

Penney Gong shares her memories of the Chinese Mission in Cleveland, Mississippi:

> The Chinese church played a very big role in trying to keep the Chinese community together—to try to keep instilling their ideals. We were very fortunate to have a pastor that came in. His name was Dr. Jachin Chan. He was very educated. He came in, and he had certain ideas about how he wanted the church to bring all the Chinese community together. He is the one who made us go to Chinese school during the summer months while we were off from regular school. So we could learn the language. Learn how to write it, and to learn the Chinese culture and teachings. Also he wanted to make sure we were able to live within the American society with these same values. After he retired, he retired back to Hong Kong. He became the head of the English department at the University of Hong Kong. As I said, we were very fortunate to have him. I think he played a major part in helping the youth grow up and be able to function well.[36]

The church setting also provided the Chinese community an opportunity to socialize with other families in their towns. Children could play with other Chinese children. Mothers could interact with other women their age, sharing stories and homemade remedies for the latest ailment in a family. The church also offered many adult Chinese the opportunity to learn English. Frieda Quon recounts that in her church in Greenville, the Sunday school lessons were often taught in either Cantonese or Mandarin and then in English. Then, following Sunday school and the church service, some members gathered again to study the English language further.

SOCIAL LIFE

The Delta Chinese families depended on the network of social gatherings, weddings, red egg parties for new babies, birthdays, and funerals as a way to keep in contact with other Chinese families and provide their children an opportunity to meet potential mates from other towns. Chinese maintain close family ties and gather for many occasions. In life there are great

Mississippi Delta Chinese 163

Established -1913-. Located behind Cypress Hills Tennis Club, which is on Oakwood Drive.

Established -1931-. Located on Crescent St. next to Liveoak Cemetery, which is behind Village Shopping Center on Main Extended.

6.6. Greenville Chinese cemetery. Courtesy of Delta State University Archives and Museum, Cleveland, MS, Shepherd Collection.

moments: birth, marriage, and death. These are recognized with much ceremony, all of it usually involving food. Traditionally, funerals were limited to simple fare and strong traditional practices, such as after the burial service the postfuneral procession passing the deceased member's home and place of business. Once gathered at the cemetery, family members exited the cars before other members of the funeral congregation. After the graveside service, as attendees left the cemetery, they were given envelopes, *lai see*, containing a coin and a piece of candy, symbolizing good fortune and health. In Greenville, there are two Chinese cemeteries with restrictions that only Chinese may be buried there. In the future, this restriction may need to be reevaluated as more Chinese families are a blend of other cultures.

For joyous occasions, Chinese cooks from Delta towns would gather to serve traditional and blended meals for hundreds of guests. Particularly, weddings were a chance for members of the Chinese communities throughout the Delta to get together and the families of the wedding party to share with their friends and family the joy of the wedding occasion. Frieda Quon shares her memories of her courtship and marriage to John Paul Quon:

> When I accepted John Quon's wedding proposal after completing my undergraduate degree in three years, I took a semester off from graduate school to prepare for a June wedding in 1964. I had no idea that the wedding would suddenly be completely out of my control and become such a huge gala. On John's side, Ray Joe, also known as the "Chinese Godfather" and a close personal friend of the Quon family, orchestrated the entire event; he consulted a Chinese almanac to select an appropriate date; Chinese moon cakes were distributed; a roasted pig was delivered to my parents; there was a dowry; all manner of Chinese customs were observed. John's family was related to one of the largest Chinese clans, Lo Joe, which must have been seven hundred people; on the Seus' side there were three hundred guests. With Ray Joe by his side John hand-addressed all the wedding invitations from the Quons' guest list; George Chu Lin (Ray Joe's son-in-law) addressed the bride's guest list. Ray Joe, a member of the governor's staff, even called on Senator Jim Eastland to pass a special bill that would expedite John's grandmother's visa to enter the United States to be here in time for the wedding.
>
> John's family welcomed the opportunity to host the wedding banquet for their friends and relatives. As they had been guests at other Chinese parties, then this was their opportunity to reciprocate. The wedding banquet was planned months in advance. Since John's father, in addition to their grocery store, had a five-hundred-acre farm, they were able to enlist the help of farm labor, raising capons (neutered chickens, which are meatier), preparing other meats and vegetables for the event; rice bowls, serving dishes, soup spoons, and chopsticks were ordered. John's oldest brother-in-law, along with a team of Chinese men from the Delta area, set up an outdoor kitchen so food

could be prepared on location in Greenville at the American Legion Building. A nine-course meal was served for a thousand wedding guests. Ray Joe presided as the emcee for the joyous event as he did for all Chinese parties. Lengthy introductions in Chinese and English were given for both sides of the families.

As Cleveland was centrally located, many of the gatherings were held at the Veterans of Foreign War (VFW) and the American Legion buildings in that town. Chinese from small towns throughout the Delta would travel to different cities in order to provide a social atmosphere for their children to get to know other Chinese. However, oftentimes the traditional Chinese cultures and that of the Mississippi Delta were at odds and created a sense of confusion for the first and second American-born generations. This gap between immigrant parents and American-born children would create many challenges. In an interview with Randy Kwan, Randy speaks of having to confront not only the social issues of the 1970s Mississippi Delta but also finding a balance between the two worlds in his home. Randy shares that the experience was very confusing: "[A]s a child of immigrant Chinese father and a second generation Chinese mother, I was exposed to a clash of cultural mores and social etiquette that I did not fully grasp until I went to college and then moved away from Mississippi."[37] At a reception in 2006, Randy told an audience that it was the challenges he faced in defining his own identity that encouraged him to find out more about his Chinese heritage and spurred his trip back to his father's village in China where he met members of a family that he would never have known, if not for that one trip.

Trey and Shannon Quon, grandchildren of immigrant grandparents and the second generation of American-born parents, are examples of how subsequent generations of Chinese Americans assimilated into their communities and how their choices were received by their families. In marriage, for instance, Trey met Lisa Lou and, after a six-year courtship, married her in 1996 at the First Baptist Church in Greenville. Their parents, John and Frieda Quon, were careful to observe traditional Chinese customs. While Lisa purchased her beautiful red dress, *cheung sam*, a traditional Chinese dress for weddings embroidered with a sequined dragon, and other Chinese accessories for her wedding trousseau, her future father-in-law, John Quon, kept a record of RSVP's to the wedding on an Excel spreadsheet. In a blend of heritage with current culture trends, a traditional American wedding was held at the First Baptist Church, followed by a reception. The second ceremony of the day had the bride and groom perform the Chinese traditional tea ceremony where Lisa wore her red *cheung sam*. Frieda recounts, "Trey and Lisa served tea to grandparents, parents, uncles and aunts; they received jewelry, *lai see* (red envelopes containing money). John and I hosted the Chinese banquet at the Washington County Convention Center for seven hundred fifty guests. By this time, Chinese weddings with banquets were rare events."[38]

Regarding their second son, Shannon, and his engagement and marriage to Elizabeth Doiron of French American descent, Frieda said that she and John were very happy for their son and not surprised at his choice of mate. "Shannon never had the opportunity to be with Chinese kids, so we were not surprised. They loved each other and that was the most important thing for John and me. Shannon has spent all of his life surrounded by Euro-Americans and probably gives little thought to being Chinese."[39]

With each generation, the traditions of Chinese culture become more blended with the American cultures in which they live. Remembering traditions and incorporating them into daily life is essential to the Chinese in the Mississippi Delta. Frieda Quon is very proud of her daughters-in-law and their efforts to instill in their children traditional Chinese values and to remind them of their special heritage. She says, "Both Trey and Shannon each have two children now who will carry on Chinese traditions as their parents encourage them to eat Chinese foods, speak Chinese, and learn about Chinese customs."[40]

DECLINING POPULATIONS AND TRADITIONS

Cultural memory carried on in each generation will be the key to preserving the Chinese American experience in the Mississippi Delta. As would be the fate of the family-run Chinese grocery stores, Chinese churches would experience a decline in membership and activity. The 1950s through the 1970s had seen a very strong membership in Chinese churches. Chinese church allowed the Chinese to uphold traditions and provided citizens an opportunity to gather, talk, learn, and worship. However, it would not take many more years before the influence of the Chinese church would decline along with the membership. As one resident states, the peak population of about 1,200 Delta Chinese in 1960[41] had declined to 782 in 1990.[42] While the membership in the Greenville and Cleveland Chinese churches was dwindling, the entire congregation of Clarksdale's mission church closed by the mid-1990s. It would be merely fifteen years before the Chinese school building would be destroyed and the congregation in Cleveland would sell its church building, remove the cornerstone, hymnals, artwork, and other signage and move on. Memories and oral history passed from one generation to the next would be all that was left of many of the early Chinese settlers' efforts to build a new community in the Mississippi Delta.

As the grocery stores, churches, and schools diminish and the children of Chinese in the Delta continue to find their way in the world outside of the Delta, the history of the Chinese experience in the Mississippi Delta could potentially be forgotten. Educational opportunities had created a path from the agrarian, rural South into a wider world of opportunity. The choices for the next generation of Chinese Americans were not the same as for their parents and grandparents before them. As the younger generation moves away from the family-oriented business and local communities into larger arenas of professional pursuits, those family members remaining in the Delta are left to deal with the declining population and questions about each family's future generations. As one Chinese merchant from Greenville said in 1994, "Two hundred years down the road, my bloodline won't exist anymore. We'll lose our heritage as we become more Americanized."[43] The fear of loss and disconnect to the immigrant and first generations is founded on the factual information of population decline evidenced in such sources as census reports and newspaper coverage. For instance, the *Clarion-Ledger* often reported on accomplishments within the Chinese communities, which were juxtaposed against the disappearing evident culture. Chinese churches, which had been the cornerstones of many Chinese communities, were experiencing a diminishing population, and the Chinese grocery stores which once dotted the downtown landscape of many towns were dying out. Americanization of Chinese communities has been viewed as the catalyst for these changes as many Chinese joined mainstream white churches and left the "family store" behind. As the Chinese populations decline in the Mississippi Delta, another wave of Asian immigrants is arriving in the region. As of 2000, the census reports that Mississippi's Asian population has seen an increase at a rate of 50 percent. These new residents are emigrating from China, Taiwan, and other Pacific Rim countries and finding their new homes in the Mississippi Delta. The opportunities that the early Chinese immigrants sought as they entered the Mississippi Delta are the same draw for this new wave of immigrants. Take-out restaurants and grocery stores are seeing a new merchant population in the Asian immigrants, and the Mississippi Delta Chinese who see themselves as American now find themselves viewing the newcomers as "foreigners." As one longtime Delta resident explains, "They look like us, but that's about it. We don't have much in common."[44]

PRESERVING HISTORY AND CULTURE

However, as evidenced by their parents and grandparents before them, the Chinese of the Mississippi Delta are diligent in their efforts to take active steps to preserve their own heritage. Their contributions to the development of the Delta both in economy and cultural affairs are invaluable and essential to understanding the rich and complex history of this area. Chinese have taken on roles of leadership within their communities, have given back to these communities through philanthropic efforts, and are committed to excellence in education. As is true for so many of the worthwhile projects that have taken root in the Delta, it has been a collaborative effort to preserve the Chinese cultural heritage in this area. From the initial oral history project funded by the Mississippi Humanities Council and directed by Dr. John Thornell to the dozens of families and individuals who participated in the project, it has taken a community of effort to build the resources available in the Delta State University Archives. These resources only begin to tell the stories of the immigration and settlement of the Delta Chinese. For John Paul Quon, establishing a cultural heritage center for the Chinese in the Mississippi Delta became a mission he would spend a lifetime trying to achieve. He found encouragement and support in Raymond Wong for this effort. Although John Paul Quon passed away in 2006, Raymond Wong and other members of the Chinese community have taken on the mantle of preserving their heritage, if not for their own benefit, then for the generations of Chinese to come. They arrived in the Mississippi Delta through a variety of ways and created a place for themselves and their families. Although their presence may dwindle on the census records and school and church rosters, their heritage has left an indelible mark on the development and culture of the Mississippi Delta. To not remember them would be to not know ourselves.

NOTES

1. Vivian Wu Wong, "Somewhere Between White and Black: The Chinese in Mississippi," Organization of American Historians online, accessed October 2008; available at http://www.oah.org/pubs/magazine/asianamerican/vivian-wong.html.

2. James C. Cobb, *The Most Southern Place on Earth: The Mississippi Delta and the Roots of Regional Identity* (New York: Oxford University Press, 1992).

3. James W. Loewen, *The Mississippi Chinese: Between Black and White* (Long Grove, IL: Waveland Press, 1988).

4. Ibid., 22.

5. Ibid.

6. Lucy M. Cohen, *Chinese in the Post–Civil War South* (Baton Rouge: Louisiana State University Press, 1984), 78.

7. Ibid., 67.

8. Robert Seto Quan, *Lotus Among the Magnolias: The Mississippi Chinese* (Jackson: University Press of Mississippi, 1982); Cohen, 144.

9. Cohen, 76–81.

10. Quan, 10–11.

11. Cohen, 144.

12. Loewen, 24–26.

13. Edward and Annette Joe, interview by Kimberly Lancaster and Jennifer Mitchell, 1 May 2000, transcript, Delta State University Archives, Cleveland, MS, 6.

14. Bobby Jue, interview by Kimberly Lancaster, 4 February 2000, transcript, Delta State University Archives, Cleveland, MS, 3.

15. Luck Wing, interview by Kimberly Lancaster, 1 March 2000, transcript, Delta State University Archives, Cleveland, MS, 3.

16. The commissary credit system was one in which people would purchase all of their food, clothing, and other goods at a plantation store, usually at inflated prices, on credit and pay the entire bill at harvest time. Because of unethical practices, sharecroppers could often remain in debt to the plantation store for much of their lives.

17. John Jung, *Chopsticks in the Land of Cotton: Lives of Mississippi Delta Chinese Grocers* (Ying & Yang Press), 3, chapter 3.

18. Ibid., 4, chapter 3.

19. Frieda Quon, 2009 interview. Delta State University Archives, Cleveland, MS.

20. Juanita Dong, interview by Kimberly Lancaster and Jennifer Mitchell, 1 May 2000, transcript, Delta State University Archives, Cleveland, MS.

21. Freeda and Hoover Lee, interview by Kimberly Lancaster, 24 April 2000, transcript, Delta State University Archives, Cleveland, MS.

22. John Thornell, "Struggle for Identity in the Most Southern Place on Earth: The Chinese in the Mississippi Delta," *Chinese America: History and Perspectives* 17 (Jan. 1, 2003).

23. Loewen, 23.

24. Frieda Seu Quon, oral history interview, 2009.

25. Francis Wong, interview by Kimberly Lancaster and Jennifer Mitchell, 19 January 2000, transcript, Delta State University Archives, Cleveland, MS.

26. Frieda Quon, interview by Kimberly Lancaster and Jennifer Mitchell, 12 January 2000, transcript, Delta State University Archives, Cleveland, MS.

27. John Paul Quon, oral history interview, Delta State University Archives, Cleveland, MS.

28. Fay Dong, oral history interview, Delta State University Archives & Museum, Cleveland, MS.

29. James W. Loewen, *The Mississippi Chinese: Between Black and White* (Cambridge, MA: Harvard University Press, 1971), 67.

30. Loewen, 66.

31. Florence Sillers Ogden Collection, Box 14, Folder 123, Delta State University Archives, Cleveland, MS.

32. Correspondence from Hugh F. Causey to Senator Oscar Wolfe, Honorable Walter Sillers, Jr., and Honorable J. A. Thigpen, 18 January 1950, Walter Sillers, Jr., Papers (MSS), Box 29, Folder 15, Delta State University Archives, Cleveland, MS.

33. Harold Horowitz and Kenneth Karst, *Law, Lawyers and Social Change: Cases and Materials on the Abolition of Slavery, Racial Segregation, and Inequality of Educational Opportunity* (Indianapolis: Bobbs-Merrill Company, 1969), 159.

34. Edward Joe and Annette Joe, interview by Kimberly Lancaster and Jennifer Mitchell, Capps Archives, Delta State University, Cleveland, MS, 1 May 2000.

35. John Jung, *Chopsticks in the Land of Cotton: Lives of Mississippi Delta Chinese Grocers* (Ying & Yang Press, 2008).

36. Penney Gong, interview by Georgene Clark, 7 October 1999, transcript, Delta State University Archives, Cleveland, MS.

37. Jung, chapter 3, p. 2.

38. Frieda Quon, personal interview.

39. Ibid.

40. Ibid.

41. Somini Sengupta, "Cleveland Journal; Delta Chinese Hang on to Vanishing Way of Life." *New York Times* online, 1 November 2000. Accessed 1 November 2009. http://www.nytimes.com/2000/11/01/us/cleveland-journal-delta-chinese-hang-on-to-vanishing-way-of-life.html?pagewanted=1.

42. "New Era Challenges Chinese Heritage," Jackson (MS) *Clarion-Ledger*, 9 September 1994.

43. Ibid.

44. Sengupta, "Cleveland Journal," 1 November 2000.

SOURCES

Cobb, James C. 1992. *The Most Southern Place on Earth: The Mississippi Delta and the Roots of Regional Identity*. New York: Oxford University Press.

Cohen, Lucy M. 1984. *Chinese in the Post–Civil War South*. Baton Rouge: Louisiana State University Press.

Dong, Fay, and Juanita Dong. 2000. Interview by Kimberly Lancaster and Jennifer Mitchell, Capps Archives, Delta State University, Cleveland, MS, 1 May.

Gong, Penney. 1999. Interview by Georgene Clark, transcript, Delta State University Archives, Cleveland, MS, 7 October.

Horowitz, Harold, and Kenneth Karst. 1969. *Law, Lawyers and Social Change: Cases and Materials on the Abolition of Slavery, Racial Segregation, and Inequality of Educational Opportunity*. Indianapolis: Bobbs-Merrill Company.

Joe, Edward, and Annette Joe. 2000. Interview by Kimberly Lancaster and Jennifer Mitchell, Capps Archives, Delta State University, Cleveland, MS, 1 May.

Jue, Bobby, and Laura Jue. 2000. Interview by Kimberly Lancaster and Jennifer Mitchell, Capps Archives, Delta State University, Cleveland, MS, 4 February.

Jung, John. 2008. *Chopsticks in the Land of Cotton: Lives of Mississippi Delta Chinese Grocers*. Ying & Yang Press.

Lee, Freeda, and Hoover Lee. 2000. Interview by Kimberly Lancaster and Jennifer Mitchell, Capps Archives, Delta State University, Cleveland, MS, 24 April.

Loewen, James W. 1988. *The Mississippi Chinese: Between Black and White*. Long Grove, IL: Waveland Press.

"New Era Challenges Chinese Heritage." 1994. Jackson (MS) *Clarion-Ledger*, 9 September.

Ogden, Florence Sillers. MSS017 Collection (1935–1972), Box 14, Folder 123, Delta State University Archives, Cleveland, MS.

Quan, Robert S. 1982. *Lotus Among the Magnolias: The Mississippi Chinese*. Jackson: University Press of Mississippi.

Quon, John Paul. 1999. Interview by Margaret Tullos, transcript, Delta State University Archives, Cleveland, MS, 2 December.

Sau-Fong, Siu. 1992. "Toward an Understanding of Chinese-American Educational Achievement: A Literature Review." Boston: Center on Families, Communities, Schools and Children's Learning. ED 343713, microfiche.

Sengupta, Somini. 2000. "Cleveland Journal; Delta Chinese Hang on to Vanishing Way of Life." *New York Times* online, 1 November Accessed 2009. http://www.nytimes.com/2000/11/01/us/cleveland-journal-delta-chinese-hang-on-to-vanishing-way-of-life.html?pagewanted=1.

Sidney, Audrey. 2000. Interview by Kimberly Lancaster and Jennifer Mitchell, Capps Archives, Delta State University, Cleveland, MS, 4 February.

Sillers, Walter, Jr., Papers. MSS004, Box 29, Folder 15. Delta State University Archives, Cleveland, MS.

Thornell, John. 2003. "Struggle for Identity in the Most Southern Place on Earth: The Chinese in the Mississippi Delta." *Chinese America: History and Perspectives* 17 (January).

Wing, Luck. 2000. Interview by Kimberly Lancaster, transcript, Delta State University Archives, Cleveland, MS, 1 March.

Wong, Vivian Wu. "Somewhere Between White and Black: The Chinese in Mississippi." Organization of American Historians online. Accessed October 2008; available at http://www.oah.org/pubs/magazine/asianamerican/vivian-wong.html.

7

MISSISSIPPI *MAHJAR*

The Lebanese Immigration Experience in the Delta

—JAMES THOMAS

The Lebanese began immigrating to Mississippi in the last two decades of the nineteenth century. Between the 1880s and the end of World War I, a combination of famines, epidemics, extreme poverty, and religious and political genocide had led to over one hundred thousand Lebanese deaths in the Mount Lebanon region of the Islamic, Ottoman Empire–controlled Syria, and during that period over one hundred thousand Lebanese residents of the predominantly Christian region participated in a mass emigration that scattered them across the globe to places such as Australia, Brazil, Mexico, and the United States. While most of these Lebanese intended to emigrate just long enough to return home with enough money to improve the quality of life for their families, many eventually realized that the life of an emigrant was preferable to their lives on Mount Lebanon (also known as simply "the Mountain"). Thus, the story of the Lebanese in Mississippi is one of a group of people who came to the state fleeing hardship and oppression, and who settled primarily in the caste-based, Jim Crow Delta, a place where they were considered neither black nor white. Their story involves looking at how they negotiated the complex color line by working between the two predominant races and how they ultimately used economic power to assimilate into white society while maintaining their Lebanese cultural identity.

THE FIRST LEBANESE IN THE DELTA

The earliest report of a Lebanese immigrant entering the Mississippi *mahjar* (roughly translated, "the land of immigration" in Arabic) is of young Elias Naseef Fattouh, from the coastal village of Al Munsif (also known as El Munsif), disembarking in the southern port of New Orleans in 1884. Traveling alone, Elias knew he needed to make contact with other Lebanese or Syrians, so he stood on the dock and cried out, "Kibbee, kibbee, kibbee!!!" (Kibbee, or kibbeh, commonly considered the national dish of Lebanon, is a mixture of ground lamb, bulgur wheat, and spices. Anyone who had grown up in Mount Lebanon or Syria would have undoubtedly understood Elias's cry.) A Syrian merchant soon approached him and offered to help by supplying him with enough merchandise to begin peddling. Shortly thereafter, Elias found himself traveling the Louisiana and Mississippi landscape northward along the Mississippi River with a suitcase full of notions and household necessities to peddle to rural farms and in small towns. Elias walked the rural roads peddling his wares for a few years, and after saving enough money and acquiring a bit of credit, he was able to open his own dry goods store in the small town of Hermanville, Mississippi (about forty miles south of Vicksburg), becoming the first known Lebanese immigrant to settle in the state (Schechla 1985).

In 1888, Elias was joined by his brother, Ameen Naseef Fattouh. By then Elias had shortened his name by dropping Fattouh altogether, and he had anglicized Elias Naseef to Ellis Nasif. Ameen, taking his brother's example, changed his name to Ameen Nasif and, possibly with Ellis's help, he purchased a horse and buggy and began peddling around the rural Mississippi countryside. Within three or four years Ameen had saved enough money to open his own dry goods store in nearby Port Gibson.

Other Lebanese immigrants followed Ellis and Ameen to the area and set up shops and home bases out of which to peddle. Sometime within the next couple of years, however, Ameen relocated to the Mississippi River port city of Vicksburg, becoming one of that city's first Lebanese immigrants (Schechla 1985). Within a few short years, other families from Al Munsif—with names such as Khory, Jabour, Thomas, Maroon, and Zahlout—immigrated to Mississippi, and by the turn of the century few were returning to the Mountain for good, although members of most families made occasional trips between the two countries (Schechla 1985).

PEDDLING IN THE DELTA

The vast majority of first-generation Mississippi Lebanese started out by peddling goods door to door to black and white farm families across the region. Although they were familiar with farming and farming practices, this original generation chose to neither farm nor work in fields. Sharecropping in Mississippi was hardly lucrative, and the advantages of peddling were comparably numerous. Unlike sharecropping, peddlers could avoid falling into the debt-peonage life of sharecroppers, and they could begin work right away. No training was necessary, and advanced English-language skills were not essential. The products they sold—which included everything from notions like pins and needles, buttons, lace, bolts of cloth, and kitchen utensils to jewelry, perfume, fancy mirrors, bric-a-brac, and holy items, such as rosaries and crucifixes—could sell themselves. Also, peddling suited the Lebanese individualistic nature. It let the peddler operate on his own terms, without having to answer to an overseer or submitting to the daily confinement and drudgery of factory work. Gregory Thomas of Vicksburg, whose grandfather came to Mississippi from Lebanon in 1920, recalled, "I remember my grandfather always telling me, 'Son, I don't care if you have to sell peanuts on the street, you work for yourself. Don't make another man rich.' I remember him telling me that all the time" (Thomas 2007).

Peddlers were, as Alixa Naff describes in her book *Becoming American*, "indefatigable men and women of steely determination who trekked along, laden like beasts of burden. A heavy suitcase strapped to the back, a *kashshi* [a notions case] to the chest, and one satchel in each hand" (Naff 1985). Wadi N., who was born at the turn of the twentieth century and who came to Vicksburg in 1911, reflected on the early peddlers whom he had grown up knowing and whose stories he had grown up hearing:

> [They] would start out . . . with their packs worth from $100 to $300—as much as a man could carry. You strap your heavy pack on your back and cover it with oil-cloth and the strap had a hook to which you hooked a small notions case. In it were scissors, razors, pins, buttons, and it weighs thirty pounds in addition to the heavy one on your back. The notions case would hang on your chest and you could rest your hand on it, but that makes it heavier, and you walked from one place to another. (Naff 1985)

Chafik Chamoun of Clarksdale, whose grandfather peddled around Brookhaven, Mississippi, in the late 1800s, discussed his grandfather's work: "Oh, they go probably about twenty-five, thirty miles, walk, and they spend the night in the black people's homes. They ain't got no vehicle, no donkey, no horse, nothing. They were tough. They put something on their back, and they go house to house. They sold clothes and socks and different things" (Chamoun 2007). As such, a peddler's store encompassed the entire countryside, come rain or shine. If a peddler was unable to secure lodging for the night in a farmer's home or barn, he or she slept under the stars. Since it was necessary to draw an income year-round, the pack-peddler preferred a climate that accommodated year-round outdoor work. Wadi N. recalled: "They peddled their way south from New York. The climate was more moderate and they liked it and stayed.... They peddled in Louisiana, Mississippi, east Texas, Tennessee, Kentucky, and Virginia which was thickly populated by Negroes, and there were farmers to whom they peddled" (Naff 1985).

In addition to the accommodating weather, the South—the Mississippi Delta in particular—provided an even more welcoming economic environment, providing a large rural market for the pack-peddler, and during the busy farming seasons, men and women alike found shopping from peddlers especially convenient (Jones 2002). Said William A., "My father's customers were farmers who lived in isolated areas, and if they needed a pair of overalls, they'd rather buy it from a peddler than go into town" (Naff 1985).

One way to bridge the cultural chasm that lay between Mississippi and the Mountain, and simultaneously strike a sympathetic chord with their customers, was by the selling of holy items. "They used to carry the rosaries suspended on a stick or arranged on their arms," wrote Salloum Mokarzel, "and they would in this way present them to a woman or the people of the house" (Naff 1985).[1] The selling of rosaries, icons, and crucifixes was an entrée to discussion of where the peddler was from and his experiences of religious persecution there. An unfortunate Christian peddler from the Holy Land, whose family still lived back home among the Muslim "infidels," would surely elicit some amount of sympathy—and a purchase—from good Christian folks within the rural countryside. Also, items from the Holy Land contained a goodly amount of attraction for God-fearing Christians in the so-called "Baptist back-waters of the South" (Mencken 1926). By linking their Middle Eastern heritage to their religious persecution, the Lebanese were able to translate their experience, draw sympathy, and hold onto a central part of their cultural identity.

In addition to bridging the cultural gap between themselves and their customers, peddlers across the South brought together blacks and whites in unconventional ways. In this passage from Lu Ann Jones's book *Mama Taught Us to Work*, a peddler arrives at a white woman's home in the South Carolina Piedmont and the whole community—both white and black—join in the rare "collective activity" that at-home shopping created.

When the peddler arrived at the home of Caroline Coleman's grandmother, the older woman invited him to turn her parlor into a showroom for the fine shawls, towels, tablecloths, pillow shams, combs, and beads that he pulled from his pack. Word of the peddler's visit traveled the "grapevine telegraph," and soon "every colored woman on the place" came to examine his stock and to join the "fine art" of trading with him. Buying turned into a collective activity, and having several women match bargaining wits with a peddler might have afforded them some advantage. After the dickering had ended, Coleman's grandmother offered to board the peddler for the night, her gesture of hospitality repaid with stories "of his home country in the great world beyond our doors" and with a gift such as fine linen towels. (Jones 2002)

In addition to showing how peddlers brought blacks and whites together, this passage illustrates how these Lebanese peddlers were typically able to trade with both races, putting each consumer on an equal footing with the merchant as the linking middle man, and in a white-dominated space (the white woman's home), no less. In few other places in the South did whites and blacks come together in the same space to enjoy something so equally—especially when the equality of economics was involved. In an even broader view of the scene played out in the parlor of Caroline Coleman's grandmother, it is important to note that not only two different ethnic groups are represented there, but three, each playing an equal role in what would under most other circumstances be taboo.

For the black farmer, peddlers provided a great deal more than the convenience of shopping at home. They also provided an opportunity to get a fair deal. Lebanese peddlers were known for extending credit on fair terms to those who needed it. Pack-peddlers also often traded for goods, such as food, meals, and for lodging. White shopkeepers, on the other hand, while welcoming black dollars, did little in the way of welcoming blacks as customers. The credit they extended came with high rates of interest and strict supervision on what they could and could not purchase. Storeowners even encouraged black customers to buy inferior products. They made black customers feel unwelcome within the store by providing little or no assistance and by making them wait until all whites had been helped before purchasing their goods. Often white customers shoved them aside or hurled vicious racial epithets at them (Jones 2002). Any chance for a black man or woman to do his or her shopping at home or from someplace other than the white-owned or plantation store was a welcomed opportunity. Hassan Mohamed, who immigrated to Clarksdale in 1911, provided this opportunity to black sharecropping families across the Delta, counting on one woman customer in particular. If, upon reaching the woman's cabin, he found that she and her family were out working in the fields, he would wait beneath the shade tree in their yard. When she returned, "he would go up on the porch and she would have some of the neighbors come, and they'd buy everything out of his suitcase right there. [S]he would run her hand up under the rug and get the money she had hid in the house.... And so that was her bank ... and that was his store" (Mohamed 1987). With a seven-to-one black/white ratio, coupled with the blacks' negative experience of shopping at the white-owned or plantation store, it is likely that these peddlers appreciated and depended upon black business as much as or more than that of the white. "I tell you," said Chafik Chamoun, speaking of his experience as a peddler, "I made my living from the black people. It was special relationship between Lebanese and black community. The people I was dealing with, doing business with, they were my friends. I have a feeling for them. I think we needed the black people and the black people needed us. It was a business relation, and we look at them as a human being not as a slave or as second-class citizen. We didn't look at them like that" (Chamoun 207).

These stories of Lebanese peddlers repeatedly crisscrossing social color lines are important to understanding that these early Lebanese peddlers successfully, yet precariously, lived lives that their customers could never imagine. The immigrant peddler was constantly aware of the fine line he walked between black and white cultures and just how easily misery could befall a man. Between 1888 and 1901, thirty-four of the ninety-three black lynchings in Mississippi occurred wholly or partially within counties located in the Delta (Cobb 1992), and any peddler would have known that he was living and working in a culture of violence and extreme prejudice. Haseeb George Abraham, a peddler who came to the Delta in 1885, was nearly lynched as a result of an innocent misunderstanding. According to Gregory Thomas, Haseeb's grandson, when Abraham, knowing little English, unintentionally asked the lady of a plantation to "sleep with me" instead of asking if she could provide shelter for the night, he soon found himself upon the back of a horse with a noose around his neck, prepared for hanging. Only when another Lebanese man came along and inquired as to what had happened was the mistake made clear and Abraham's life spared (Thomas 2007). Abraham's experience was a crash course in learning the ways of the Delta, but generally itinerant peddling provided immigrants the opportunity to gradually learn and adapt to the prevailing social customs of the South, despite its stringent social codes and harsh practices for meting out justice. Interaction with the rural farmers and, occasionally, the townsfolk, gave peddlers the chance to view the culture as somewhat passive observers, in the sense that they were perpetually "passing through."

These Lebanese peddlers were part of an informal network made up of other Lebanese immigrants. They swapped stories and news from home, and some even traded subscription-available, American-published, Arabic-language newspapers among each other, such as *Al-Bayan* (New York), *Al-Hoda* (New York), and *Syrian World* (also New York). They, often with their families, formed small peddler settlements in places like Hermanville, Brookhaven, Greenville, and Vicksburg, and within the household and settlement Lebanese elders would have spoken and read Arabic almost exclusively. Lebanese children could understand the spoken word, and some even learned to read it. Other aspects of Lebanese culture were also easily enough retained, such as the Middle Eastern food culture. Many of the spices and ingredients for Lebanese foods, such as black pepper, cinnamon, various grains, rice, onions, peppers, squashes, mint, parsley, chicken, beef, and lamb, were readily available and were part of the daily food consumption. Immigrants brought musical instruments to America, and for peddlers on the road and within Lebanese settlements, music was a chief form of entertainment. Through music, language, and food, as well as through the community of their families and kinsmen, these immigrants could bring with them to the *mahjar* those cultural elements that they had most treasured on the Mountain. As the number of Lebanese immigrants flocking to the Mississippi Delta grew, and as those newcomers acquired more and more capital, it was less important for them to return to the Mountain to maintain their ethnic culture and identity. By the late years of the first decade of the twentieth century, many peddlers were sending for their entire families and setting down roots in town.

FROM PEDDLER TO STOREOWNER

After 1908, the occupation of peddling was in a period of steady decline. One reason was that over time families grew larger, necessitating a less mobile, more stable home. Another reason was that, because of the racial terror to which blacks were being subjected, the years between 1915 and

The Lebanese Immigration Experience in the Delta

7.1. Commour Ellis (seated) and sons (l to r) James, George, Michael, and Sam. In 1892 Commour immigrated to New London, Connecticut, from Mount Lebanon, Syria, with sons George and Michael. In 1901 she and her five sons moved to Meridian, Mississippi, where they joined her brother. (Commour's son John is not pictured.) In 1908, they moved to Port Gibson, Mississippi, where they opened a mercantile business on Main Street. Courtesy of James G. Thomas, Jr.

7.2. James Ellis in front of his dry goods store in Port Gibson. The building was originally the Washington Hotel in the early 1800s. Courtesy of James G. Thomas, Jr.

7.3. George Thomas of Greenville, Mississippi, proudly wearing his Freemason pin. Courtesy of James G. Thomas, Jr.

7.4. The Ellises, mother with children, Port Gibson, Mississippi, 1921. Courtesy of James G. Thomas, Jr.

1920 saw the mass exodus of a hundred thousand blacks from the state (Woodruff 2003). The stream of cash that had been flowing into the pockets of the peddlers was now drying up. As their rural customer base dwindled, the peddlers abandoned life on the road and took the next logical step: they opened grocery and dry goods stores. James Ellis, who came to America from Al Munsif with his mother in 1901, peddled around central Mississippi for several years before opening a general merchandise store in Port Gibson with his brothers, who also peddled (Nasif 1998). The brothers lived together above the store until each got married, gathered more savings, and moved into their own homes. They collected a sizable amount of real estate, and in 1927 Jim's brother Mike built and opened a dry goods store of his own; another brother, George, opened a dry goods store/grocery around the same time. Jim's third brother, Sam, moved to Texas to open his own business. The Ellis brothers' sister, Nazera, married a Lebanese man named George Thomas, and they opened a grocery store behind their house on College Street (Ellis 2003).

Similarly, around 1911, at age twelve, Anees Mafrij and his father, Abu Anees Mafri, came to the Delta from Bishmezzine to begin peddling around the Greenville area. On the eve of World War II, as the Ottoman Empire had allied itself with Germany and large sections of Syria became military bases, Abu Anees understood that the political situation was dangerous. He returned to Bishmezzine to collect his family and make his move to Mississippi permanent. Back in Mississippi, Abu Anees resolved to take on not only a new home but a new name as well. He chose "Thomas," the name of a Mafrij family elder. His family's last name would henceforth be Thomas, and he would be known as George. George and his family settled in Greenville, and he opened a grocery store. When his eldest son, Anees, renamed Ernest, was old enough, he and his wife, Emma Ellis Thomas, opened a grocery store of their own on Nelson Street. By 1927, the grocery store had flourished, but when the levees of the Mississippi River broke, causing the Great Mississippi Flood of 1927, the store was flooded to the roof, and his business was wiped out. Ernest packed what belongings he could salvage, and he and Emma moved to Vicksburg, Emma's hometown (Schechla 1985). The rest of the Thomas family remained in Greenville and in the nearby town of Leland, opening grocery stores and dry goods stores of their own.

As Lebanese families like the Ellises and Thomases moved out of peddler settlements and into neighborhoods within towns, they congregated in multiethnic neighborhoods, such as the neighborhoods surrounding Greenville's Nelson Street. Rents were cheaper and, for the most part, the

Lebanese had yet to find social acceptance among whites. "My mother used to tell us that we were not accepted fully as citizens really," said Pat Davis, Sr., of Clarksdale. "They were called names and, you know, looked down upon, but not like the African American people. We were able to go to the white schools. We were able to drink out of white fountains and go to the white restrooms." In Clarksdale, the early Lebanese immigrants lived in the black neighborhood of Riverton. "My grandmother and a lot of the Abrahams and Gattises all lived in Riverton in the beginning," he said. "African American, Italian American, and Lebanese American living together in Riverton, side by side" (Davis 2007).

For the same reasons that blacks enjoyed the opportunity to make purchases from peddlers at home, they enjoyed the opportunity to shop at Lebanese-owned (and Chinese-, Jewish-, and Italian-owned) stores. As immigrant merchants opened dry goods or grocery stores that either catered to blacks or were located directly in black neighborhoods, those black shoppers found that they had an alternative to shopping in white-owned stores. "In the older white stores," wrote John Dollard in his 1937 sociological study, *Caste and Class in a Southern Town*, "when a Negro went in, the owner would say to him, 'Well, boy, what do you want?' even if the Negro in question were eighty years old. The Jews [and other immigrants], on the contrary, let the Negro know that his dollar was as good as anyone else's" (Dollard 1937). Subsequently, white merchants received less and less black business and were often crowded out of town by immigrant stores whose owners treated blacks with courtesy—or at least without discourtesy. It might stand to reason that whites would take umbrage in losing business to immigrants, but since whites often found that dealing directly with blacks—and relying on their business—was beneath them, the loss of a trade may not have been resented by the white community after all (Dollard). Of course, white stores were not completely wiped out. Like most other social arrangements in Jim Crow Mississippi, stores became subject to those segregated conditions, spoken or unspoken. Whites may have needed black dollars, but they certainly did not encourage them (Hale 1998).

In the 1920s, most southern whites' attitudes toward blacks were acrimonious at best, and the moderate racial tolerance that immigrants had experienced in the South before World War I was slowly fading. After World War I the South began embracing a religious and ethnic nativism that had fast turned into xenophobia. Urban centers in other parts of the country would have given the newcomers more cover from white racism, but as the pattern has been shown, these immigrants followed each other to the *mahjar*, many already having a support system of family and friends in Mississippi, a place where ugly racial epithets were thrown around freely, often aimed directly at the Lebanese whose dark skin and dark hair made them stand out. Despite what racism they did encounter, it was minor compared to the treatment they had experienced back home and slight in comparison to what blacks were suffering in Mississippi.

ASSIMILATION INTO WHITE SOCIETY

Now that the Lebanese had committed to living in Mississippi, they faced a pressing dilemma. Since the Delta would be their permanent home, they realized the economic and social necessity of assimilating into the dominant, white society. Assimilation into white society meant better housing, social and economic advancement, and a brighter future for future generations. In fact, it was not until the mid-1920s that Syrians in the United States achieved a legal "free white" status, which allowed them naturalization. Until then their voting rights had been repeatedly challenged because they were "Asian," and thus not members of the white race (Ferris 1928). But in the early decades of the twentieth century, whites and Lebanese in the Delta rarely mixed socially. Other ethnic groups, such as the Chinese, Italians, and Jews, fared just as poorly in terms of assimilation into white society, explaining, in part, why immigrants congregated in mixed-ethnicity neighborhoods. Assimilation would be difficult for these newcomers, especially since they derived their main source of revenue through a close association with the group against which whites were most prejudiced. But, caught between two cultures and needing both, the Lebanese remained loyal to their black customers out of economic need and a common understanding of what it meant to be oppressed. "It was a lot more than here's the merchant and here's the customer," said Gregory Thomas of Vicksburg. "One thing about my grandfather, he never forgot where he had been. Never did" (Thomas 2007).

In addition, Lebanese merchants new to the region had found blacks to be helpful in gaining an understanding of the southern culture, mores, and even the language. Gregory Thomas continues, speaking of his grandfather's experience in his first grocery store facing the railroad tracks in Vicksburg: "It was a black man who helped him in the store who helped to teach them English. He told me somebody would come in and ask for one thing and he'd show them a plug of tobacco and the black fella would take his hand and say, 'Naw, this is what they were asking for.'" The Lebanese extended fair lines of credit to blacks and made trades for goods when cash was simply unavailable. Gregory recalled his grandfather, many years later, trading goods for clothes at Abraham Bros. Department Store: "I remember once seeing a catfish hanging in the back of the store. A man brought that in trade for clothes" (Thomas 2007). To some extent, a result of the Lebanese/African American relationship was that the Lebanese began to achieve considerable economic success in places like Greenville, Port Gibson, Clarksdale, and especially Vicksburg during the middle decades of the twentieth century. Subsequently, Lebanese businessmen were able to move their families into more affluent, thus white, neighborhoods and their businesses into prosperous business districts. Soon the proximity between the Lebanese and black communities began to widen, loosening the bonds between the two groups. Lebanese storeowners still owned and operated stores in black neighborhoods, but the dependence on black dollars lessened.

Despite the close relationship shared between the Lebanese and black communities, it would be inaccurate to describe the relationship in terms other than primarily economic. The Lebanese were empathetic to the black struggle in the Jim Crow and pre–civil rights Mississippi Delta, but being the "other" in a xenophobic culture, the Lebanese were only able, or willing, to ally themselves with the black community so much. For the Lebanese businessman, it was easy—advantageous, in fact—to deal fairly and without prejudice, but losing a business or social standing, or even a loved one, to violence was a price that a Lebanese merchant making his way in a new culture could not afford. Few, if any, Lebanese attempted to join white supremacist groups like the Citizens' Councils in an attempt to garner whites' favor, but neither did they join voter-registration drives during the civil rights era of the 1960s in order to advance black civil rights.

As early as the 1940s, the process of Americanization began to gain a stronghold on the American-born children of immigrant parents, and because of the prosperity that their parents had begun to enjoy, Lebanese children and adults were becoming increasingly accepted in white society. The peasant and peddler pasts of Lebanese children's parents became a source of embarrassment and a stumbling block on the path to white social acceptance, and as a result, fewer children were learning to speak Arabic. Fewer were learning to read it. A woman who grew up in Vicksburg in the 1950s recalled, "We were too busy trying to get our friends to like us for five minutes that we didn't wanna be speakin' a foreign language; and we didn't want our parents speakin' it ta us. We were tryin' so hard to be accepted. And that's why we didn't learn—not that we were ashamed, mind you, but we were just fightin' a different battle. Y'all know how kids are" (Schechla 1985). Lebanese youth and adults alike adopted American dress and participated in "American" cultural activities when able, and although most Lebanese immigrants wanted to instill within their children a Lebanese identity, they also knew that any overt difference between their children and the children of whites would only slow the process of assimilation into the white Delta culture. Slowly, with each successive generation, the Lebanese, along with the Jews and Italians, were becoming untethered from the "marginalized middle" and were drifting into whiteness, leaving behind their "otherness," as well as the marginalized African Americans whose history has proved that their journey to social equality was far more arduous.

Despite their children's desire to be accepted into Anglo-American culture, Lebanese-immigrant parents attempted to preserve some sense of Lebanese identity within their children. Parents still spoke Arabic at home and, despite their apathy, the children still managed to learn a great deal of the language. At the dinner table Lebanese children gained a love and appreciation of Lebanese food, and in the kitchen they learned to make tabouleh, roll grape leaves, and stuff eggplant. Naming patterns continued, with the firstborn son being named after the father and the second son taking the first names of the grandfathers. At special events, such as weddings and baptisms, guests played traditional music with traditional instruments and danced traditional dances, such as the *dabke*. As well, Lebanese families maintained a vigorous religious life that reflected their Christian religious practices on the Mountain. In 1910, the Vicksburg Lebanese community purchased the Gibson Memorial Church and transformed it into an Orthodox temple. In 1924, the temple received its official charter as St. George Antiochian Orthodox Church.[2] By 1983, St. George could boast a congregation of 150 Lebanese families (Skipper 1983). In most other Delta Lebanese communities, where there existed a stronger Maronite Catholic presence, Lebanese immigrants attended Roman Catholic churches.

Marriages within the Lebanese culture were pressed upon children until the 1940s and 1950s, and the Lebanese practiced an informal system of arranged marriages until then. Communities sponsored singles' mixers and established Lebanese clubs, such as the Cedars of Lebanon in Clarksdale, Greenville, Jackson, and Vicksburg. The Southern Federation of Syrian-Lebanese American Clubs was established in 1931, and the following year it began sponsoring annual Lebanese conventions across the South that families from the Delta still regularly attend today. (These Lebanese conventions have long been famous as opportunities for mothers to scout out potential spouses for their children.)

Though many of the first American-born generation may have resisted the push to maintain a Lebanese identity, Carolyn Staton, a Vicksburg native and recent provost at the University of Mississippi, recalled growing up embracing her Lebanese heritage with delight:

> Every Sunday was Lebanese food. All during the week was Lebanese. How we knew to do the *dabke*, I don't know. Well, I know how we knew to do the *dabke*. Every New Year's Eve, the Lebanese community in Vicksburg rented the city auditorium. That was a big event. Now, the outsiders loved to be invited, but the Lebanese would end up doing the *dabke* and whatever. So the children learned the *dabke*, and then you'd go to weddings and people would do the *dabke*. But we did it so infrequently that we had to sort of relearn it every year. They would bring in bands from Shreveport that had the [Lebanese] instruments, and they would play at these New Year's Eve parties. So you got a smattering, and the culture would come to you that way. I loved it. (Staton 2007)

Pat Davis also remembered his growing up in a Lebanese community with a great deal of pleasure. Participating in Lebanese cultural traditions was an inherent part of life for the Davis family and other Lebanese families in the 1940s and 1950s. While Lebanese adults and children strove for Americanization, today some of the most memorable experiences in the lives of older Lebanese people in the Delta are of embracing their Lebanese identity. Pat Davis recalls:

> I remember as a youth we would always meet, it was on Fourth Street, which is now Martin Luther King Boulevard, and every Sunday about thirty or forty of all our Lebanese people would get together with the kids and they would dance and sing music and have kibbee and grape leaves and watermelon and fried chicken and all these things. The music was my daddy playing the mijwiz [a traditional Lebanese instrument consisting of two reeds put together], Gerald Abraham's father playing the mijwiz, and Sam Tony playing one darbukkah and John Tony playing another darbukkah, which is a drum, and that was our music, but it was beautiful. (Davis 2007)

Unfortunately, however, the retention of Lebanese cultural traditions had a downside. The protracted pace of assimilation into white society, which was partially a result of this retention of identity markers, slowed the process of acceptance, despite otherwise enthusiastic efforts to Americanize. During the years of peddling in the countryside and those years spent working and living in immigrant neighborhoods, the Lebanese were moderately successful at avoiding the bigotry experienced by blacks in the Delta, and once they began to gain the accoutrements of prosperity, such as automobiles, property, and larger homes in white neighborhoods, whites began to permit the Lebanese to climb the social ladder—although only so high. When the Lebanese community attempted to join traditionally white clubs or organizations, they quickly learned just how far they had—or had not—come. Although the Lebanese had now become welcome at most churches and public events, many exclusive organizations that had always been strictly "for whites only" remained so, giving notice to the Lebanese community that money had the ability to whiten only so much. Although the color line was now blurred, it remained drawn. For example, in colleges and universities across the state in the early 1960s young Lebanese students found themselves unable to join fraternities and sororities because of their Lebanese heritage. Country clubs and fraternal organizations like the Rotary, Kiwanis, and Lions clubs were no different. Not until 1960 was the stipulation that Syrians and Lebanese be excluded from the Vicksburg Country Club and other country clubs across the Delta dropped, even though the Lebanese had entered state politics as early as 1948 when Ellis Bodron of Vicksburg joined the Mississippi House of Representatives. Bodron went on to serve in the Mississippi State Senate from 1952 to 1984.

In the mid-1960s the white community began allowing certain Lebanese families and citizens to join their exclusive clubs and organizations. Lebanese/Anglo-American marriages were becoming more and more common and, in some places, accepted. After having lived in the Mississippi Delta for eighty years, the Lebanese people were finally being accepted by the dominant culture. The successful Lebanese assimilation into the white culture of the Delta came down to simple economics: as businesses grew so did Lebanese dollars. The Lebanese had become able to use their economic power to advance their social position in the white community. Mississippi senator Ellis Bodron recalled a conversation in which he advised Pete Nosser, a Vicksburg businessman, to exert that economic power:

Pete said, "You know I don't care about belonging to any clubs, but I've got daughters and primarily my sons-in-laws...." All of his sons-in-laws were non-Arab but were excluded from clubs because of their marriage to his daughters. Now Pete Nosser had four large supermarkets and was very successful. I said to him, "You buy a lot of things from a lot of different people—you're putting money in banks and you buy insurance. So don't [do it]. Determine who you buy from—a lot of them are influential at this club. You're in a position to correct the situation if you're not happy about it."

The situation began to change very shortly after that. You know, history hasn't changed a whole lot. There ain't nothing more important than economics. (Orfalea 1988)

Over the next twenty years, the social change for the Lebanese in the Mississippi Delta was significant. For example, by 1984 Shoupie Habeeb was the Vicksburg Country Club's president and the owner of the First Federal Savings and Loan in Vicksburg (Orfalea 1988). Habeeb also became the president of the Vicksburg Kiwanis and Rotary clubs, as well as president of the YMCA (Schechla 1985). Shoupie, incidentally, is the brother of Alfred Habeeb, whose family arrived in Vicksburg from the Lebanese village of Bishmezzine in 1920. Alfred went on to become the first Syrian-born immigrant in the South to attend medical school, and later became the senior anesthesiologist in the state of Alabama. In 1992, friends of Dr. Habeeb established and funded the Alfred Habeeb Endowed Chair in Anesthesiology at the University of Alabama at Birmingham (Chesnutt 2005).

THE LEBANESE TODAY

The Lebanese community today has fully assimilated into the dominant white culture, yet the economic, societal, and cultural contributions of the group are apparent in countless towns and cities across the region. The extent to which Lebanese are considered white today can be seen in a 2005 newspaper article written about the first black members accepted into the Greenwood Country Club. The article, from the *Greenwood Commonwealth*, describes Lebanese businessman Alex Malouf this way: "Alex Malouf, who founded and runs John-Richard, a home furnishings manufacturer and distributor, is a white member of the Greenwood Country Club" (Montgomery 2005). Although the article mentions the one-time exclusion of Catholics,

Jews, Asians, and Middle Easterners from the Greenwood Country Club, it never mentions the ironic fact that Malouf himself is Lebanese. Malouf, today, is merely "white." It is as if Malouf's "whitening"—perhaps because of his financial success, perhaps because of his Americanization—is complete. Another newspaper article, this time from the *Los Angeles Times*, actually attempts to define "whiteness" in the twenty-first-century Mississippi Delta and specifically mentions the Lebanese:

> "Are Lebanese white people?" we asked 71-year old Ned Holder, a former sheriff here. "Yes," he said, "although they're real dark." How about Italian Catholics; are they white? Sure. And Jews? Yes. What about the Chinese? "Yes," he said, "They go to the white schools." And Mexicans? "They're becoming more white. More of them are getting an education."
>
> Then what's a white person, we asked? After some confusion over the meaning of the question, he concluded that it was probably anybody "who isn't black."
>
> At Abe's Bar-B-Q in Clarksdale, I met a 19-year-old half Italian girl named Anna Brittain Antici who was a member of the elite Tri-Delta sorority at the University of Mississippi. She didn't seem to know or care that, not too long ago, her sorority wouldn't have anything to do with a girl with her name.
>
> But as I paid the check, I chatted with the Lebanese American owner, George P. Davis Jr., who was more acutely aware of the movable boundaries of whiteness. I asked him if he and his family were fully accepted as white folks in town.
>
> "I hope so," he said as he smiled, "but you never know." And, as he pointed to himself and the black employees working behind him, he added: "Let's just say it's gotten better for all of us." (Rodriguez 2007)

Lebanese and Delta cultures and traits have long shared a remarkable number of similarities. It is entirely possible, in fact probable, that that common ground between the two cultures played a part in Lebanese assimilation. For instance, hospitality is as great a part of Lebanese culture, "treasured as the 'most Syrian' of traits by the descendants of immigrants," writes Alixa Naff, "even after assimilation has distilled away all traditional bases for it" (Naff 1985). Friendships and community played essential roles in Lebanese immigration to Mississippi, a place where those cultural traits fit right in because of the southern emphasis on hospitality. But the cordiality and generosity of Lebanese hospitality extends farther than the parlor. The Lebanese are a people who are proud of their food culture, and, as with southerners, their tables are traditionally abundant. When people in the Delta consider the Lebanese, one of the first things that comes to mind is the food. Lebanese food in the Mississippi Delta is for a large number of Lebanese and non-Lebanese people just as much a part of southern food as is fried chicken. For example, Chafik Chamoun's incredibly popular Lebanese restaurant in Clarksdale, Rest Haven, is filled to overflowing every day at lunchtime.

For the Lebanese in the Delta, the sharing of meals and the breaking of bread means more than just eating. It is a community activity, one that reinforces familial bonds and reminds those attending of who—and what—is most important to them. The food, tied so closely to family and religion, is celebrated at every holiday and on most Sundays across the Delta in Lebanese households, and it is still as much a part of the Lebanese idea of community as it ever was. To be certain, a particular pride and joy is taken when a meal of grape leaves, kibbee, and tabouleh is shared with non-Lebanese friends and family, and every Thanksgiving and Christmas all of those dishes are proudly served alongside the turkey and dressing. Lebanese mothers enjoy passing down recipes and techniques for making Lebanese food to non-Lebanese wives ("Make sure you always bless your kibbee, honey," she would most assuredly say). Mary Louise Nosser of Vicksburg did not worry about the Lebanese food disappearing from her family's recipe book: "We always teach our in-laws when they marry how to make the Lebanese food," she said (Skipper 1983). By reinforcing the importance of these traditions, Lebanese families are able to retain some part of their cultural identity.

When introduced, Lebanese and Mississippians alike are liable to ask, "Who are your people?" or "To whom do you belong?"—that is, "Whose son or daughter are you?" or "Who are your relatives?"—making the family name a source of honor. Few things, if any, are more important within Lebanese and Delta society than a birth, a marriage, or the holidays, which provide the occasion for extended family to reunite, and Lebanese grandchildren across the state proudly refer to their grandparents with southern appellations such as Mamaw, Nanna, Memaw, Papaw, or Papa. Children nearly always call their mothers "Mama," and grown men and women alike call their fathers "Daddy." Yet, Arabic names are also ubiquitous. Lebanese grandchildren still call their grandmothers "Sitti" or "Sittu" and grandfathers "Jitti" or "Jido."

But, despite the retention of many Lebanese traditions, some are undoubtedly being lost. While endogamy—the practice of marrying exclusively within a social group—in the Lebanese community was once expected, Lebanese intermarriage today is the exception rather than the rule. Robert Thomas, Jr., a native of Leland now living in Baton Rouge, Louisiana, joked, "If I could wave a magic wand and choose, yes, I would choose a beautiful Lebanese woman as a wife. But I don't discriminate against any pretty ladies. If I had children, I would just like them to be aware of their history and heritage and how they got here, because it was not an easy trail by any means for our families" (Thomas 2007).

Each successive generation lessens the collective memory of Arabic words. Few Mississippi Lebanese know how to play traditional Arab instruments or dance the *dabke*. The traditional Lebanese religions within the Delta, being Greek Orthodox and Roman Catholic, are sometimes replaced with the religions of spouses. Yet churches like St. George Antiochian Orthodox Church in Vicksburg and St. Joseph's Roman Catholic Church in Greenville are still vibrant religious homes for a large number of Lebanese families, as well as for families of Italian, Irish, and German descent.

The Lebanese immigrants brought from the Mountain a desire for freedom and economic prosperity, as well as their language, music, food, and families. In the nearly 130 years since the first Lebanese immigrants began coming to Mississippi in search of the American Dream, they have assimilated into southern society and have shifted their identity from that which was once considered "foreign" to something more akin to "white." Nevertheless, the Lebanese here, in the "most southern place on earth," have created for themselves an identity that is simultaneously southern and distinctively Lebanese.

NOTES

1. Originally quoted in *The History of Syrian Trade in the American Colonies* (in Arabic), Part I, "1920–1921" (New York: Syrian American Press, 1929).

2. A detailed history of St. George Antiochian Orthodox Church can be found on the church Web site: www.stgeorgevicksburg.org.

LITERATURE CITED

Chamoun, Chafik. 2007. Personal interview. Clarksdale, Mississippi (April 6).
Chesnutt, David H. 2005. The American Society of Anesthesiologists *Newsletter* (June).

Cobb, James C. 1992. *The Most Southern Place on Earth: The Mississippi Delta and the Roots of Regional Identity*. New York: Oxford University Press.
Davis, Pat, Sr. 2007. Personal interview. Clarksdale, Mississippi (April 6).
Dollard, John. 1937. *Caste and Class in a Southern Town*. New Haven: Yale University Press.
Ellis, Mary H. 2003. *Cannonballs and Courage: The Story of Port Gibson*. Virginia Beach, Virginia: The Donning Company Publishers.
Ferris, Joseph W. "Syrian Naturalization Question in the United States: Certain Legal Aspects of Our Naturalization Laws," Part II, *The Syrian World* 2, no. 9 (1928).
Hale, Elizabeth Grace. 1998. *Making Whiteness: The Culture of Segregation in the South, 1890–1940*. New York: Vintage Books.
Jones, Lu Ann. 2002. *Mama Learned Us to Work: Farm Women in the New South*. Chapel Hill and London: University of North Carolina Press.
Mencken, H. L. 1926. *Prejudices: Fifth Series*. New York: Alfred A. Knopf.
Mohamed, Ethel Wright. 1987. "An Oral History of Southern Agriculture," National Museum of American History, Smithsonian Institution, Washington, D.C.
Montgomery, Susan. 2005. "Greenwood Country Club Makes Quiet Changes," *Greenwood Commonwealth* (November 20).
Naff, Alixa. 1985. *Becoming American: The Early Arab Immigrant Experience*. Carbondale: Southern Illinois University Press.
Nasif, Mildred Ellis. 1998. The Port Gibson *Reveille* (Thursday, August 27).
Orfalea, Gregory. 1988. *Before the Flames: A Quest for the History of Arab Americans*. Austin: University of Texas Press.
Rodriguez, Gregory. 2007. "Definitions of Whiteness amid the Delta Blues," *Los Angeles Times* (January 14).
Schechla, Joseph. 1985. "Dabkeh in the Delta," in *Taking Root: Arab-American Community Studies*, Volume II, ed. Eric Hooglund. Washington, D.C.: The American-Arab Anti-Discrimination Committee, ADC Research Institute.
Skipper, Deborah. 1983. "Lebanese-American Families Knit Future from Past," Jackson *Clarion-Ledger* (September 18), p. 1E, 4E cont.
Staton, Carolyn. 2007. Personal interview. Oxford, Mississippi (June 7).
Thomas, Frances Abraham, and Gregory Thomas. 2007. Personal interview, Vicksburg, Mississippi (April 14).
Thomas, Robert. 2007. E-mail correspondence (September 14).
Woodruff, Nan Elizabeth. 2003. *The African American Freedom Struggle in the Delta*. New Haven: Harvard University Press.

8

CHAI COTTON

Jewish Life in Mississippi

—STUART ROCKOFF

The comedian Lenny Bruce used to joke that everyone who lived in New York City was Jewish, even if they were Christian. What he meant was that the culture of the city was profoundly shaped by its Jewish population, who made up almost 30 percent of city residents in 1950. One could feel Jewish in New York just by living there and walking its streets. By this same logic, no one is Jewish in Mississippi, even those who worship in synagogues every week. Indeed, in many ways Mississippi Jews are an anomaly. They cling to a religion that rejects Jesus as the messiah in the cradle of the Christian Bible Belt. In a state that has long been rural and agricultural, Jews have congregated in Mississippi's towns and cities, owning stores and businesses instead of farms. Living among people who have long been rooted to their land, Mississippi Jews have moved around, often going from town to town in search of greater economic and cultural opportunities. In a state where life was defined by the racial line between white and black, Jews often lived in between these categories, even as they worked to fit into white culture.

Despite these differences, Jews have made a comfortable home for themselves in Mississippi. On the surface, their lives seem little different from other Mississippians, from their slow southern drawls to their enjoyment of such southern delicacies as fried chicken and barbeque. In the fall, they closely follow the football season of the Southeastern Conference, while praying that key games don't fall on the Jewish high holidays of Rosh Hashanah and Yom Kippur. They listen to Mississippi State's Jack Cristil, who has been broadcasting Bulldog football games on Saturday afternoons since 1953. On many Friday nights, Cristil speaks to a much smaller audience when he leads services at Tupelo's Temple B'nai Israel. Mississippi Jews closely identify with their home state. The writer David L. Cohn, who coined the famous description of the Mississippi Delta as beginning in the lobby of the Peabody Hotel in Memphis and ending on Catfish Row in Vicksburg, spent most of his life in Greenville. This son of Polish immigrants often wrote about his home state for such northern magazines as *The Atlantic Monthly*. Being Jewish did not prevent Cohn from becoming a widely read interpreter of southern life and culture. Although Jews have always been a miniscule minority in Mississippi, they have become an integral part of the state's economic, religious, and cultural life.

Beginning in the early nineteenth century, Jewish immigrants from Europe began to arrive in the Magnolia State, settling initially in towns along the Mississippi River. Concentrating in retail trade, these Jews became visible symbols of economic modernity and market capitalism in Mississippi, a role which brought them into civic leadership but also sometimes made them a target for those who opposed the state's economic changes. Mississippi Jews worked to lessen the cultural differences between themselves and their white neighbors, embracing Reform Judaism, which better fit their circumstances of living as a tiny minority in the Deep South. Perhaps most importantly, Mississippi Jews, at least outwardly, adapted to the culture of white supremacy, which brought them the economic and political benefits of whiteness. During the civil rights era, Mississippi Jews struggled over whether to respond to the issue as Jews or as white southerners, though most sought to avoid the conflict altogether. In recent decades, due to region-wide economic and demographic trends, the Jewish population of Mississippi has declined and become concentrated in the state's population centers.

PEDDLING ECONOMIC MODERNITY

The first Jews to settle in Mississippi lived in late eighteenth-century Natchez, though Jewish religious or communal life did not develop until the early nineteenth century when growing numbers of immigrants from Alsace and the German states began to settle in towns along the Mississippi River. Many came up from New Orleans carrying merchandise in packs or in wagons, going from farm to farm selling their wares. They first settled in trading towns like Natchez and Vicksburg that had sprouted along the Mississippi River. One of these Jewish immigrants was Bavarian-born Henry Seesel, who set sail for New Orleans to join his brother in Natchez in 1843. The two siblings peddled together in the area around Natchez. According to Seesel, "[T]here were a great many young men peddling, all of them making their home at Natchez." Indeed, the competition was so fierce that Seesel soon moved upriver to Vicksburg, where he continued his peddling.¹

These nascent Jewish communities often took several decades to blossom due to the tremendous amount of population turnover. Most of these Jewish peddlers and merchants did not stay in one place for very long, often moving to other towns in Mississippi and beyond in search of greater opportunity. Henry Seesel's journey did not end in Vicksburg, but took him to Ohio, Kentucky, and Louisiana, before he finally settled in Memphis in 1857. In Natchez, of the forty-nine Jewish household heads living in the city in 1870, only twenty-two still lived there in 1880. This instability no doubt hindered the effort of Natchez's Jews to build a permanent house of worship. Though Jews formed a congregation in 1843, it would be almost thirty years before they dedicated their first synagogue. Vicksburg had a similar delay, with Jews establishing a congregation in 1841, but not building a synagogue until 1870.²

This mobility spelled the end of certain nineteenth-century Jewish communities in Mississippi. Jewish merchants lived in Grand Gulf by 1838, though they soon abandoned the river port town due to disease and flooding. Woodville's Jewish community flourished in the late nineteenth century, when the town was known as "Little Jerusalem" due to its high percentage of Jews. By 1910, few if any Jews remained, and the synagogue was being used as a school. Summit first attracted Jewish settlement in the 1850s, and by one estimate, seventy-eight Jews lived in the town in 1878. After the arrival of the boll weevil, Jewish merchants closed their stores and moved to other towns seeking greater opportunity. In 1910, Summit's Jewish congregation, Ahava Sholom, disbanded due to its declining membership.³ This mobility and population turnover show that the development of Jewish communities in Mississippi was neither quick nor straightforward.

The nineteenth-century Jewish communities of Mississippi were dominated by merchants who sold dry goods, a general term referring to nonperishable, textile-based products like clothing and fabric. In reality, these merchants sold a wide assortment of goods. They were usually linked to Jewish-owned wholesale firms in New Orleans, who would ship their goods upriver to store owners throughout Mississippi. Jewish merchants often had a difficult time receiving credit from traditional sources, with the nation's leading credit rating firm Dun & Company usually assuming that Jewish storeowners were poor credit risks. In response, these merchants turned to fellow Jews for credit. These religious and often kinship ties gave newly arriving Jewish peddlers as well as small Jewish merchants access to goods without a large investment up front.

Historian Elliot Ashkenazi has examined how this credit system worked in antebellum Woodville, Mississippi. Located just ten miles north of the Louisiana border, Woodville was the seat of Wilkinson County and became the commercial center of the cotton plantations in the area. Jews had arrived in Woodville by the 1830s, opening stores that traded with the plantations. These Jewish merchants received their merchandise from Jewish-owned wholesale houses in New Orleans, which shipped the goods north on the river or later by rail. At the time of its bankruptcy in 1855, the New Orleans–based A. Beer & Company supplied twenty-one Jewish-owned stores in Mississippi with merchandise, including three in Woodville. One of these stores was owned by German-born Jacob Schwartz, who came to Woodville as a peddler in 1845. Two years later, he owned a modest dry goods store that sold primarily to small cotton farmers. One could find most anything at Schwartz's store, which sold everything from clothing to cowbells. The business had several ups and downs during the 1850s, dissolving and reforming with new partners three times in five years.[4]

The Jewish merchants of Woodville were closely integrated in the slave plantation economy, though they largely remained apart from its culture. In addition to selling goods to plantation owners, in several cases, they went into business with them. For a time, Jacob Schwartz co-owned a store with Felix Embree, a local planter. Jewish merchants Michael Simon and Joseph Kaiser took Wiley Bryan, another local planter, into their dry goods business. A German-born immigrant, Simon clearly aspired to the social and economic standing of the local planter elite, purchasing a small plantation and ten slaves by 1853, before moving to New Orleans in 1856. Yet Simon was largely an exception in his desire to mimic the southern ruling class. As early as 1855, local reporters for Dun & Company noted that the net worth of some successful Jewish merchants in Woodville was impossible to assess since they owned nothing but their store and its merchandise. The conspicuous consumption of the plantation economy certainly benefited Jewish merchants who sold them merchandise, but most of these immigrants remained apart from elite southern society and its open displays of wealth during the antebellum period. According to Ashkenazi, these Jewish merchants were "birds of passage" who used their time in Woodville to get started in their business careers before moving on to greater economic opportunities elsewhere. Thus, they had little interest in becoming part of local society, though this would change once Jews began to sink roots into Mississippi communities in the late nineteenth century.[5]

The business activities of these Jewish merchants can be seen by looking at one typical merchant family business, S. Bernheimer & Sons of Port Gibson. Samuel Bernheimer came to the United States from Austria, settling in Port Gibson by 1847, when he opened his retail store. By 1860, he was already worth about twenty thousand dollars. The Civil War did not seem to have a significant impact on his business; by 1870, Bernheimer was worth thirty thousand dollars.[6] Samuel's son Jacob eventually took over the business, which was still in operation in 1900. More than just a retail store, S. Bernheimer & Sons reflected the multifarious role that these merchants played in the state's economy. Bernheimer sold general merchandise to retail customers, including hardware like pipe, rope, paint, wire, and lumber; foodstuffs like bacon, meat, molasses, meal, and tobacco; as well as shoes. In addition to the retail business, Bernheimer would sell wholesale merchandise to stores in the small towns and rural areas of southwest Mississippi. Bernheimer was also a cotton factor, buying the crop from local farmers and accepting it as payment for debts. One of his sources of cotton was another Jewish merchant, Morris Gilston, who owned a store in nearby Martin, Mississippi. Bernheimer would often sell his cotton to a Jewish-owned cotton buying firm in New Orleans. Bernheimer bought his merchandise from a wide array of suppliers around the country. He bought paint from a company in New York City, shoes from a firm in Brockton, Massachusetts, and cheese from Sheboygan, Wisconsin.[7]

With access to East Coast markets and fashions, these Jewish merchants were often agents of modernity, selling merchandise that was not normally available in Mississippi. Their businesses sometimes bore the names "The New York Store" or "The Boston Store," which signified to customers that they offered more cosmopolitan goods than other stores in town. Mississippi and the rest of the South were undergoing tremendous economic change in the years after the Civil War. The expansion of the railroad helped to spread the market revolution throughout the region. More and more farmers moved away from subsistence agriculture to grow staple crops for the national market, forcing them to rely on merchants for their everyday needs. As the South began to move toward a capitalist, commercial economy, these Jewish merchants played an essential role in linking southern farmers to the national market.

Because of this role, Jews were closely associated with the coming of the market capitalist economy. As the old plantation order crumbled,

Jewish merchants settled throughout the state bringing the benefits of the new economic order. While their overall population numbers were miniscule, their presence was as visible as the signs outside of their stores or their ads in the local newspapers. In many places, like Meridian, Jewish merchants were celebrated as important builders of the community, but sometimes their connection to economic modernity aroused opposition. In 1876, an anonymous writer in the local newspaper in Columbus criticized the growing number of Jewish merchants in his town, accusing them of clannishness in both social and business relations. He also charged them with not investing in the community: "Does any Jew in Columbus own any real estate here? Does any one of the many clever Jews residing here own the residence in which he lives? In other words, does any Jew pay tax on any realty in this place? Do the Jews, as a class, patronize any grocery store in Columbus? Any boot and shoe store? Any clothing store?"[8]

One Columbus Jew answered these charges in a national Jewish newspaper published in Cincinnati, claiming that since real estate in Columbus was such a bad investment, Jewish merchants avoided it. He also criticized the merchandise in gentile-owned stores in Columbus, writing, "[D]oes any grocer in Columbus keep imported cheese in stock, Hungarian prunes, spiced sardelles, or any of the fancy groceries that are perishable? . . . Now the Jew not being accustomed to an unvarying diet of bacon and corn meal, and knowing of other luxuries in life than whisky [sic] and tobacco, wants these things for his table."[9] These Jews often had more sophisticated tastes than their native-born neighbors; their frequent travels to large cities and their economic ties to the country's financial and cultural centers often stood in stark contrast to the general provincialism of Mississippi.

These Jewish merchants' pursuit of their economic interests sometimes angered other Mississippians, especially when they appeared to violate the state's racial order. During the economic depression of the 1890s, some whites resented the growing economic power of Jewish merchants who had acquired land from poor farmers for nonpayment of debts. In southern Mississippi, this took on a racial cast, as many of these merchants rented to black sharecroppers. An underground group, known informally as "whitecappers" due to the hoods they often wore, targeted black sharecroppers and their Jewish landlords. During the elections of 1892, whitecappers began to force black renters from Jewish-owned farms in southern Mississippi. One whitecapping group in Lawrence County issued a proclamation stating their goal to "gain control of the negro labor, which is by right ours, that we may tend the soil under white supremacy, and under no circumstances will the negro be allowed to cultivate a Jew's ... land." They posted notices on sharecroppers' houses warning them to leave and stating, "This Jew place is not for sale or rent, but will be used hereafter as pasture." In Summit, they targeted H. Hiller, a successful Jewish merchant who owned four hundred small farms in the area. During a two-month period, whitecappers burned down twenty-seven sharecropper cabins on Hiller's property, and Hiller was unable to find renters to work his land. He eventually sold his business and moved to New Orleans.[10]

Although these incidents were short-lived and localized, they reflected the opposition of many white southerners to the changes brought on by the market economy. William Faulkner explored this ambivalence in many of his works. In *The Sound and the Fury*, Jason Compson explains his antipathy to Jews: "It's just the race. You'll admit that they produce nothing. They follow the pioneers into a new country and sell them clothes. ... I'll be damned if it hasn't come to a pretty pass when any damn foreigner that can't make a living in the country where God put him, can come to this one and take money right out of an American's pockets."[11] For men like Jason Compson, Jews were not Americans not only because of their foreign birth, but also because of their failure to work with their hands. Commerce was seen as unproductive and even harmful to the community. In Mississippi, though they were only a tiny percentage of the population, Jews and their stores were often the most visible symbol of commercial development.

This economic role of Jews cut both ways. While it could open them up to anti-Semitism, it also gave them entrée to the civic leadership of many Mississippi towns. Nowhere was this truer than Meridian, which emerged as a regional railroad hub in the years after the Civil War. A handful of German-born Jews lived in Meridian by 1869 as the newly named seat of Lauderdale County began its ascent. In the 1870s, Meridian flourished with the construction of the railroad through town, becoming a regional center of trade and industry. These Jewish immigrants embraced their adopted city, bolstering its economy and civic life. By the 1880s, Jewish merchants had established themselves in Meridian with many successful stores along Front Street. Israel Marks began a company with his three half-brothers: Sam, Levi, and Marks Rothenberg. Their operation, Marks, Rothenberg Company, became one of the largest wholesale grocery and dry goods businesses in the South. In 1899, they opened a mammoth five-story location. All four partners of the Marks, Rothenberg Company were leading citizens in Meridian. Levi Rothenberg was the president of Meridian's first bank, while Israel Marks played an instrumental role in establishing

Highland Park, donating much of the land for it. Marks served as president of the park commission from its formation until his death in 1914. Though remembered for many other civic contributions, the proprietors of Marks, Rothenberg Company are perhaps best known for building the Grand Opera House next to their downtown store. Completed in 1890, the opera house attracted performers from all over the United States to Meridian. Much of Meridian's downtown testified to the prominence of the city's Jewish community, including the Marks-Rothenberg Building, the Alex Loeb Building, the Threefoot Building, the Lamar Hotel, and many others. In most other Mississippi towns, Jews arrived and fit into the local economy and society; in Meridian, Jews were actively involved in the city's creation and development.[12]

Jewish merchants throughout the state became strong boosters of the local economy, often joining efforts to develop their towns. In Lexington, Morris Lewis founded the Lewis Grocer Company, which supplied wholesale groceries to stores across the state. Lewis became one of the leading businessmen in town, and worked to build up Lexington. In 1905, he was one of the founders of the local Merchants and Farmers Bank. He later helped to build a compress, oil mill, and ice factory in an effort to bring more industry to the town. He helped to fund the electrification of the town as well as its water and sewer system by putting together the necessary bond issue and purchasing many of the bonds himself. He also led the way in establishing the first community hospital in Holmes County.[13] In many other Mississippi towns, leading Jewish merchants played similar roles in the economic progress of the community.

Since Jews took on these roles of civic leadership, it's not surprising that so many were elected to local office. At least twenty-two Jews have served as mayors of seventeen different towns in Mississippi. Perhaps most notable was Sam Rosenthal, who spent forty-five years as the mayor of the small Delta town of Rolling Fork. Born in Brooklyn, New York, to Russian immigrant parents, Rosenthal had moved to Natchez with his family when he was three. When he was a young adult, he moved to Rolling Fork to work in his brother's clothing store. By 1924, he had been elected alderman. When the mayor resigned, his friend Fielding Wright, an ambitious local attorney who would later become governor of Mississippi, convinced Rosenthal to take over the office. Mr. Sam, as he was called, was soon elected to his own term, and reelected for the next four decades. Rosenthal helped to transform Rolling Fork, with new schools, libraries, a textile factory, and improved electricity. He was instrumental in saving people during the Great Flood of 1927 by organizing a mass evacuation of the town. He paved the roads of Rolling Fork in the 1930s with the help of the New Deal's Works Progress Administration. While he brought great progress to Rolling Fork, Rosenthal did not spend forty-five years in city hall by challenging the status quo. Like most other Mississippi Jews, he embraced the culture of the state, including its racial order.[14]

BECOMING WHITE MISSISSIPPIANS

In his 1941 classic, *The Mind of the South*, W.J. Cash described the southern Jew as an "eternal Alien" who refused to assimilate and thus stood out starkly in a region marked by its rigid conformity. According to Cash, southern Jews faced anti-Semitism as white southerners projected fears and anxieties about the South's changing economy and society upon these Jewish outsiders. As we have seen, Jews were often associated with the spread of the market economy, and opposition to these changes sometimes took an anti-Semitic tone. But Cash exaggerates the Jewish refusal to assimilate. Indeed, the story of southern Jewish life is in many ways the story of assimilation. Contrary to Cash's claims, most Mississippi Jews did not feel like outsiders. According to the Delta writer David L. Cohn, "I never felt alien there, nor was any attempt made to make me feel alien" and no Jew in Greenville "suffered any indignity or lack of opportunity because of being Jewish."[15]

This acceptance was not accidental. In Mississippi, soon after Jews arrived, they worked to fit themselves into the local economy and society. One of the first lessons they had to learn was race. Leaving countries where Jews were often seen as inferior, they arrived in a region that was obsessed with the color line. From their beginning in Mississippi, Jews were treated as white, and they claimed the social, political, and economic benefits of whiteness. Indeed, the white South's fixation with maintaining white supremacy precluded the rise of significant anti-Semitism, which was much more prevalent in the North.

Jewish assimilation in Mississippi was likely inevitable considering the minuscule number of Jews in the state. According to population estimates published in the *American Jewish Year Book*, the peak year of Mississippi's Jewish population was 1927, when 6,420 Jews lived in the state. This represented a mere 0.36 percent of the state's overall population. Since then, Mississippi's Jewish population has dropped significantly, and now represents less than one-tenth of 1 percent of the state's population.[16] Because

Mississippi Jews have always been an extreme minority, they have not been able to create the distinctly Jewish neighborhoods that existed in large cities like New York and Chicago. Even southern cities like Memphis, New Orleans, and Atlanta had smaller versions of these neighborhoods, where Jews could speak Yiddish, find kosher meat, and worship in the traditional Orthodox manner. Nothing like this ever existed in Mississippi, where Jews always had to interact with non-Jews as part of their daily life. For Jewish merchants catering to non-Jewish customers, learning English quickly and fitting into the local culture was essential.

This assimilation can first be seen in the Civil War. Most Jews in Mississippi at the time of secession had only been in the United States for a few years, and very few owned plantations or slaves. One might reasonably assume that these Jewish immigrants from the German states and Alsace would feel little connection to the Confederate cause, and seek to avoid the conflict. But instead, according to historian Robert Rosen, the Jewish immigrants who lived in Mississippi "flocked to the Confederate banner" and supported its ideological cause. These included Prussian-born Isaac Scherck who was living in Summit when he enlisted in the Third Mississippi Batallion. In a letter, he denounced the North as being filled with "bigotry and humbug." Simon Mayer of Natchez enlisted two different times, and explained in a letter to his brother that the Confederacy was "now battling for our rights and independence." Mayer's cousin, Oscar Levy, had only just recently come to Natchez from Landau, Bavaria, but nevertheless joined Simon in the fight. Jewish allegiance to the Confederacy even outlasted the war. In Vicksburg, Leon Fischel, who had served as an aide to General Albert Sidney Johnston, named his son Albert Sidney Johnston Fischel. The name has remained in the Fischel family for generations.[17]

This Jewish embrace of the Confederacy only grew as the mythology of the "lost cause" took hold in southern culture in the late nineteenth century. In Natchez, Jews could point with sorrowful pride at Rosalie Beekman, the seven-year-old Jewish girl who was the city's only casualty during the war, killed during a Union gunship's brief bombardment of the city. Mississippi Jews looked for ways to display their credentials as victims of northern aggression. While Jackson's Beth Israel temple actually burned down in 1872, in an official history of the congregation, the synagogue's destruction is mistakenly attributed to the Union's wartime torching of the city. Mississippi Jews also took part in memorializing those who died fighting for the Confederacy. Though he was not even in the country at the time of the Civil War, Polish-born George Bowsky donated a granite monument to honor the dead Confederates buried in Brookhaven's Rosehill Cemetery in 1924. Adopting the Confederate cause, whether in 1861 or 1924, was a crucial way for Mississippi Jews to show that they had become white southerners.[18]

In assimilating to southern culture, Mississippi Jews sought to diminish the differences between themselves and their white gentile neighbors without abandoning their religion. By the late nineteenth century, most Mississippi Jews had embraced Reform Judaism, which offered a style of worship more like the mainline Protestant churches in their towns. Jewish immigrants coming to the United States brought with them an Orthodox observance of Judaism. Such traditional practices as maintaining the Jewish dietary laws of *kashrut*, which preclude the eating of pork and shellfish and require that other meat be slaughtered in a particular way, could be extremely difficult to maintain in a place like Mississippi that existed on the periphery of American Jewish life. The prohibition against working on the Sabbath could be a severe detriment to Jewish merchants who found that Saturday (the Jewish Sabbath) was the day that most of their customers came to town to buy goods. As a result, most Mississippi Jews had to make accommodations. In Meridian, the small Orthodox congregation Ohel Jacob, founded in 1895, held its Saturday morning services at 6 a.m. so members would be able to say their Sabbath prayers before going to work at their stores.

The Jewish worship service changed as well. In traditional Judaism, worshippers sit in gender-segregated sections and pray out loud in a cacophony of Hebrew. Jews across America, but especially in the South, sought to refine the service, adopting elements of Christian worship, including mixed seating, choirs, sermons, and more prayers in English. These changes became known as Reform Judaism, which also represented a movement away from strict adherence to Jewish law and an increased focus on the larger ethical principles of the Bible.

While Reform was a national movement, it found especially fertile soil in the South and in Mississippi. One of the founders of Reform Judaism in America, Rabbi Isaac Mayer Wise of Cincinnati, actively recruited the congregations of the South to join his Union of American Hebrew Congregations. By 1907, almost 40 percent of the congregations affiliated with the Union of American Hebrew Congregations were located in the South, at a time when only 5 percent of American Jews lived in the region. Of the nineteen Jewish congregations in Mississippi in 1907, fifteen were Reform. By comparison, only about 24 percent of American congregations outside of Mississippi were Reform at the time. Thus Mississippi congregations were over three times as likely to be Reform than congregations in the rest of the county.[19]

Most of these congregations were not founded as Reform, but gradually adopted the philosophy. In Natchez, the Jewish congregation grew out of an Orthodox burial society founded in 1840. In the 1860s, the congregation still employed a *shochet*, a slaughterer of kosher meat, which ensured that its members would be able to follow the Orthodox Jewish dietary laws. Over time, a growing number of Jews in Natchez began to push for a more Reform style of worship. This debate came to a head in 1870 when the congregation was in the midst of building its first synagogue. One faction wanted to construct the sanctuary in the Orthodox manner, with the rabbi standing on a platform in the middle of the floor facing the pulpit. Another preferred the Reform style of having the rabbi on the pulpit facing the worshippers. Rabbi Isaac Mayer Wise, who traveled to Natchez from Cincinnati for the cornerstone laying ceremony, likely weighed in on this dispute, since the Reform group got its way. When the temple was dedicated in 1872, Congregation B'nai Israel had officially adopted Reform Judaism.[20]

A similar transformation occurred in Clarksdale. In the late nineteenth century, the first Jews to live in Clarksdale were immigrants from Eastern Europe, who were more Orthodox in their religious practices than the German and Alsatian Jews who had earlier settled in places like Natchez and Vicksburg. Founded in 1896, Congregation Beth Israel was an Orthodox congregation for its first few decades. But by the 1920s, a younger generation of native-born Jews wanted a Reform service with more English and a more American style of worship. Tensions became heated in the community and there was talk of a schism. As a result of this conflict, the leaders of Beth Israel pushed for the building of a new synagogue that would be able to house two different services at the same time, one Reform and one Orthodox. While Beth Israel officially became a Reform congregation, with Reform rabbis and services in the main sanctuary, its Orthodox members continued to meet in a smaller room in the synagogue for the next several decades.[21]

Reform Judaism, with its less onerous restrictions on diet and working on the Sabbath, better fit the lifestyle of Mississippi Jews. Its style of worship borrowed elements from mainline Protestantism, and so especially appealed to Mississippi Jews who sought to be accepted into the religious mainstream of their communities. By the late nineteenth century, as Jewish congregations were dedicating their synagogues, Christian ministers and elected officials regularly took part in the ceremonies. When Vicksburg's

Congregation Anshe Chesed dedicated its first temple in 1870, many local Christian ministers participated in the procession, as did Governor James Alcorn and several local officials. This interfaith spirit was also present in Natchez. When B'nai Israel's temple burned down in 1903, several local churches offered to lend their sanctuary to the congregation. While B'nai Israel's new temple was being built, the congregation met at the Jefferson Street United Methodist Church. Several non-Jews in Natchez donated money to the building fund. In 1957, when Tupelo Jews were raising money to build that city's first synagogue, over 40 percent of the donors were non-Jews. At the temple's dedication ceremony, the minister of the First Baptist Church as well as Mayor James Ballard spoke. By adjusting their religious practices, Mississippi Jews fit easily into the state's church culture, gaining the acceptance of their gentile neighbors.[22]

This desire to fit in could even push Mississippi Jews to become social pioneers. When the beloved rabbi of Meridian's Congregation Beth Israel died suddenly in 1950, the congregation asked his widow, Paula Ackerman, to take over as its spiritual leader, even though she had no rabbinic training. Ackerman became the first woman ever to lead a Jewish congregation, twenty-one years before the first female was ordained as a rabbi. The congregation wanted a leader who would be active in the larger community and become a respected part of the city's social and civic leadership. They did not want someone who would challenge the status quo, but rather someone who would fit well into white society in Meridian. When she had been the rabbi's wife, Paula Ackerman had performed this role beautifully. When she became Beth Israel's new spiritual leader, other church leaders and the local newspaper responded with fulsome praise. Throughout her three-year tenure, a search committee was interviewing rabbinic candidates, but was hesitant to hire someone who was foreign-born and had a heavy accent or someone who insisted on speaking out on such controversial issues as civil rights. Instead of being a radical act, the hiring of Paula Ackerman was essentially conservative and reflected the desire of Meridian Jews to be accepted by the rest of white society.[23]

Perhaps the most crucial element of Jewish assimilation in Mississippi was the issue of race, which dominated political discourse and social interaction in the state. In Mississippi, race almost always meant the difference between people of European descent ("white") and those of African descent ("black"). Whereas in parts of the North in the early twentieth century, Jews were sometimes perceived as belonging to a separate inferior race, their status as whites was rarely challenged in Mississippi. In the North, concepts of race were used to categorize and differentiate the large numbers of European immigrants coming through Ellis Island. These categories formed the basis of the 1924 National Origins Act which restricted the immigration of those groups, including Jews, who were seen as inferior. In the South, with its system of segregation, its ideology of white supremacy, and its far smaller number of immigrants, race remained a black and white issue. Thus Jews who settled in Mississippi had an easier time of proving their whiteness and achieving acceptance than did Jews in the North.

Indeed, Jews enjoyed tremendous acceptance in the South at least partly because of the racial prejudice directed against African Americans. Southern elites strived to create a common white racial identity among all nonblacks in the region that cut across class, ethnicity, and religion. Jews, though they had a different ethnic and religious background than most other southerners, were accepted as white. Thus southern racism helped to preclude the rise of significant southern anti-Semitism. Edward Cohen, in *The Peddler's Grandson*, his memoir of growing up in Jackson, Mississippi, writes, "I was grateful that we Jews were adjudged to be white ... We weren't Christian, but that wasn't determinative. All that mattered was that we weren't black."[24]

Jews in Mississippi and other parts of the South worked to ensure that they would be accepted into the white mainstream. Incidents such as the whitecappers of the 1890s, in which Jews were specifically targeted, unsettled many Jewish Mississippians. In the late 1930s and 1940s, the state was represented in Congress by two outspoken anti-Semites, Senator Theodore Bilbo and Representative John Rankin. Both men accused New York Jews of supporting communism and race mixing, but made a point of mentioning that not all Jews were a threat to the country. As Bilbo noted when accused of being an anti-Semite, "The Jews we got in Mississippi are ... some of the finest people we got. They're natives. They fought on our side in the Civil War."[25] Men like Bilbo also expected them to fight on the white South's side in the struggle over civil rights. Considering the fact that elected leaders like Bilbo and Rankin were quick to blame Jews for the problems they saw weakening America, Mississippi Jews sought to avoid any public criticism of white supremacy and "the southern way of life" whatever their true feelings might have been. As long as they supported the status quo, they were welcomed into the social and political leadership of their communities.

Despite this desire to be accepted as white Mississippians, Jews did not always enforce the informal rules of Jim Crow. Because of their economic position as peddlers and merchants, Mississippi Jews had regular interactions with black customers. According to sociologist John Dollard, who studied Indianola, Mississippi, in the 1930s, Jewish storeowners in town treated their black customers better than other white merchants. Jews were more willing to extend credit to black customers and to use terms of respect when speaking to them. Certainly, there was an economic incentive to treat their customers well, but as civil rights leader Aaron Henry noted, the Jewish merchants in Clarksdale were considered "the better of the white element that you had dealings with." The store owned by Edward Cohen's family in Jackson had a racially integrated bathroom and clerks called their blacks customers "Mr." or "Mrs.," which was very unusual at the time. As Cohen noted, "[W]e observed blacks' humanity, if not their equality."[26]

Indeed, these relationships were not equal. Like other upper-middle-class southern whites, Jews often employed black servants to care for their children and households. Some Jewish businessmen owned rental housing for blacks. While many Jews felt sympathetic toward the plight of blacks, they did not occupy the same class position. Jews were the employers, the landlords, and business owners; blacks were the employees, the tenants, and the customers. And most importantly, Jews were white. Thus whatever social graces were used, their relationship did not challenge the segregated status quo.

When the civil rights movement arose, Jews' loyalties and beliefs pulled them in conflicting directions. Their experience as a minority gave them a special insight into the plight of southern blacks that most other white southerners did not have. Thus, Jews were among the most racially progressive segments of the white South. And yet, because they were a minority, Jews in the South worked hard to fit in, to be accepted as insiders. In the South, this meant embracing or at least accommodating the culture of white supremacy.

Nationally, Jews were important allies and supporters of the civil rights movement. Jews had played a leading role in the creation of the NAACP in 1909, and several Jewish institutions and newspapers were outspoken advocates of racial equality. By one estimate, over half of the financial contributors to civil rights organizations were Jewish. A significant percentage of the northern white activists who joined Freedom Summer in Mississippi in 1964 were Jewish. National Jewish organizations like the American Jewish Committee, B'nai B'rith, and the Anti-Defamation League passed resolutions supporting the work of the movement.[27]

Membership in these groups could be a source of controversy in Mississippi. In 1952, the state chapter of the B'nai B'rith donated a film about tolerance entitled *The High Wall* to the state board of education. Even though the film focused on discrimination against a Polish family in the North, segregationist state senator George Yarborough and William Simmons, the head of the Mississippi Citizens' Council, raised a flap about the film in 1959, calling it integrationist propaganda. In response to their efforts, the state board of education banned the film. Simmons called the B'nai B'rith's Anti-Defamation League "one of the most aggressive and highly financed pressure groups for integration in this country" and accused it of having close ties with the NAACP. Sidney Rosenbaum of Jackson, the former statewide president of B'nai B'rith, defended the film and called Simmons's remarks anti-Semitic. In response to this controversy, the Mississippi State Sovereignty Commission, which investigated civil rights efforts for the state, opened a file on the B'nai B'rith. The Sovereignty Commission even sent investigators to spy on a regional convention of the B'nai B'rith Youth Organization in Biloxi in 1960, though all they found were excited Jewish teenagers who socialized and sang songs.[28]

Many Mississippi Jews were extremely uncomfortable with the visible role that Jewish activists and organizations were playing in the civil rights movement. According to Alvin Binder of Jackson, many Mississippi Jews resigned from B'nai B'rith after the national organization began to support the movement. In 1963, the Union of American Hebrew Congregations, the national organization of Reform Judaism to which most Mississippi congregations belonged, held a convention entitled "A Call to Racial Justice," and invited Dr. Martin Luther King to speak. In response, the board of the Jewish congregation in Greenville sent a letter of protest. The congregation's president wrote that the invitation to King "places undue and unnecessary pressure upon our already exposed people in this area of the country." The Greenville congregation was expressing their genuine fear that their close relationship with the white gentile community would be threatened if they were seen as sympathetic to the movement due to the civil rights activities of northern Jews.[29]

When northern Jewish civil rights workers came to Mississippi in the 1960s, local Jews tried to avoid any public association with them. One of these Jewish activists was Michael Schwerner, who came down to Meridian with his wife, Rita, in January of 1964 to try to get local blacks to register to vote. When Michael Schwerner met with Rabbi Milton Schlager of Meridian's Temple Beth Israel, the rabbi told the young activist to go back to New York since his presence would only hurt the black people he was trying to help. The Schwerners had little interaction with the Meridian Jewish community, who feared being associated with the New York activists. One local Jewish merchant, Alex Loeb, was willing to cash the Schwerners' paychecks from the Congress of Racial Equality, but he tried to do it without anyone knowing. Any support for these northern activists was usually done quietly and behind the scenes. After Schwerner was murdered along with Andrew Goodman and James Chaney in Neshoba County, Mississippi Jews became even more convinced that associating with these young northern activists would cause the most violent and reactionary forces of the South to target Jews. This in fact happened in 1967 and '68 in Jackson and Meridian, when a group of Ku Klux Klan members bombed local synagogues and the home of Jackson Rabbi Perry Nussbaum.[30]

Aside from the legitimate fear of speaking out, many Mississippi Jews were raised within the culture of white supremacy and not surprisingly shared the prejudices of other white southerners. This sentiment is best reflected in the pamphlet "A Jewish View on Segregation" that was written by an anonymous Jew from the Mississippi Delta and distributed by the Citizens' Council in 1957. The Mississippi-born author proclaimed himself to be a "Jewish Southerner, not a Southern Jew" and denounced national Jewish organizations like the B'nai B'rith and the American Jewish Committee for supporting integration. He went on to criticize other Mississippi Jews who sought to avoid the struggle over civil rights, writing that "the Jew who attempts to be neutral is much like the ostrich. And he has no right to be surprised or amazed when the target he so readily presents is fired upon." The author concluded that "any white Southerner, Christian or Jew, must do all he can to help maintain segregation." For Mississippi segregationists, there was no neutral ground; all whites, including Jews, were required to defend white supremacy. Jews had enjoyed the benefits of whiteness, and were now expected to defend its prerogatives.[31]

This pressure often conflicted with the religious teachings of Judaism, which stressed social justice and the common humanity of all people. Rabbis, as spokesmen for these religious values, were often caught in the middle of this struggle. Many sympathized with the movement, but felt pressure to remain silent by the opposition of their congregants and their fear of violent reprisals. In Hattiesburg, Rabbi Charles Mantinband often got into trouble with the members of Temple B'nai Israel for his outspoken comments on racial issues. In 1956, Mantinband gave a speech at a black college in Alabama in which he praised the NAACP and attacked segregation. The speech made the front page of the *Hattiesburg American*, which declared in a headline, "Local Rabbi Says Race Relations Stink." In response, his temple board called an emergency congregational meeting to try to convince the rabbi to stop speaking out on the civil rights issue. During the tense gathering, Mantinband refused to stop his activities, but temple members grudgingly voted to keep the rabbi since they realized that finding a replacement would be very difficult. Despite the unhappiness of his members, Mantinband continued his public support for civil rights, serving as president of the Mississippi Council on Human Relations in 1958. Tensions remained high throughout his tenure in Hattiesburg, with a number of threats being directed at the temple and its rabbi by local segregationists. Finally, in 1963, Rabbi Mantinband left Hattiesburg for a pulpit in Longview, Texas.[32]

While a few rabbis, like Charles Mantinband in Hattiesburg and Perry Nussbaum in Jackson, supported civil rights publicly, most did not want to risk the wrath of their congregants or the violent segregationists in their community. One Mississippi rabbi who did speak out defended the state, pleasing the Citizens' Council and many of his congregants, but angering many of his rabbinic colleagues. In Clarksdale, most members of Temple Beth Israel welcomed their controversial new rabbi, Benjamin Schultz, who arrived in Mississippi in 1962. Long an ardent anticommunist, Schultz defended Mississippi in the wake of the integration crisis at Ole Miss. He told his audience at a local women's club that "what America needs today is more Mississippi, not less," arguing that if the rest of the country followed Mississippi's lead, the communist threat wouldn't exist. Schultz's remarks were quoted prominently in the Memphis *Commercial Appeal* as well as the magazine of the Citizens' Council. Soon after, the rabbi received a congratulatory telegram from an official at the Mississippi State Sovereignty Commission. Other rabbis in Mississippi were horrified and moved to block any future statewide Jewish youth group events from being held in Clarksdale, yet they did not denounce Schultz publicly. Despite this controversy, most members of Clarksdale's Beth Israel were pleased with Rabbi Schultz, and he served the congregation until his death in 1978.[33]

Mississippi Jews made a comfortable place for themselves as white southerners, enjoying social acceptance and economic success. And yet as the historian Eric Goldstein has observed, there was a "price of whiteness," as this desire to assimilate racially often hindered the nurturing of a strong Jewish identity. Indeed, acceptance proved to be much more of a challenge for Mississippi Jews than did anti-Semitism. In Greenville, Rabbi Abraham Ruderman worried about the growing number of Jews marrying outside of the faith and the seeming indifference of their parents. In 1967, he wrote in his diary that "the number of Jewish partners with Christian children is appalling. At least a dozen children have been raised in the Church by their Christian mothers. To stand by supinely and watch one's children reared in a strange faith requires an indifference to one's faith that is hard to fathom." Intermarriage, long taboo in American Jewish culture, had become a fact of life for Mississippi Jews due to the relative scarcity of Jews in the state, which often made it hard to find a Jewish spouse. The significant social integration Jews enjoyed also fostered intermarriage.[34]

Faced with this demographic and social reality, Mississippi Jews worked to strengthen Jewish identity in the state, focusing much of their efforts on young people. A group of Jewish parents in Jackson, led by Celeste Orkin, created Mississippi Temple Teens by the early 1950s, which sought to create a Jewish social network across the state. This organization soon grew to include Arkansas, Louisiana, and western Tennessee, becoming known as the Southern Federation of Temple Youth. These programs mirrored earlier efforts in the Mississippi Delta, in which dances and other social events were held for young Jewish men and women across the region. This time, Jews sought to build permanent institutions that would help ensure the future generation of Mississippi Jews. Most notably, led again by Celeste Orkin, they worked to build a Jewish summer camp in Utica, the Henry S. Jacobs Camp, which continues to offer a unique and intensive Jewish experience to Jewish children from Mississippi and the rest of the Deep South.[35]

CHANGING TIMES, CHANGING COMMUNITIES

These efforts at strengthening Jewish identity became especially important as the Jewish population of Mississippi declined after World War II. From a peak of 6,420 Jews in 1927, the state's Jewish community had dropped to an estimated 4,000 by 1960. This decline has continued into the twenty-first century. According to the *American Jewish Year Book*, an estimated 1,500 Jews lived in Mississippi in 2005. No longer merchants scattered throughout the state, Mississippi Jews have entered the professional ranks and are now concentrated in just a few communities. Mississippi congregations are struggling to survive as most Jewish children raised in the state leave in search of greater economic and social opportunities.[36]

The Mississippi Jewish community has been transformed since 1945 as large-scale economic changes have reshaped Mississippi and the entire South. While the economic dislocations brought on by the Great Depression and the federal government's Agricultural Adjustment Act began the

8.1. Mark Perler, the lay leader of Temple B'nai Israel in Tupelo, is shown here holding the Torah. Photo by Bill Aron.

8.2. Cotton Sukkah made by the congregation of Anshe Chesed. Anshe Chesed, located in Vicksburg, is the oldest congregation in the state. Photo by Bill Aron.

8.3. Herman Kohlmeyer carries the Torah at the hundredth anniversary celebration of Port Gibson's Gemiluth Chassed congregation. Photo by Bill Aron.

8.4. Rabbi Judith Bluestein of Hattiesburg's B'nai Israel congregation. Photo by Bill Aron.

8.5. Joe Erber with Meyer Gelman, members of Ahavath Rayim of Greenwood, the last Orthodox congregation in the state. Photo by Bill Aron.

process, World War II was the watershed event that revolutionized the South's economy. Its most dramatic effect was to drain the region's farm population. Between 1940 and 1945, four million people, or 25 percent of the South's total farm population, left the land, joining the armed forces or moving to the city to work in the booming war industries. Those leaving the farm were laborers, tenants, and sharecroppers drawn by the greater economic opportunities that the war created. The southern farm population continued to decline after the war. In 1940, sixteen million southerners, 42 percent of the region's population, lived on farms. By 1960, only 15 percent of the South's population remained on farms, as technology such as the mechanical cotton picker replaced farmers and sharecroppers.[37]

With these structural changes to Mississippi's cotton economy, Jewish merchants lost much of their customer base. It was no longer economically feasible to operate retail stores in many Mississippi towns. Also, many sons and daughters of Jewish merchants went to college and chose to move to larger cities in the South and beyond. Southern Jewish life, once based largely in small towns, now mirrors the urban and suburban Jewish life of the North. Like other Americans, Jews have been drawn to the thriving areas of the sunbelt, like Atlanta and Houston, while states such as Mississippi, which have not been a part of this modern economic boom, have seen their Jewish populations plummet.

This decline is especially pronounced in the Mississippi Delta, which was once the center of Jewish life in the state. In 1937, the Mississippi Delta was home to forty-six different Jewish communities, ranging from 450 Jews in Greenville to single families living in places that were little more than wide places in the road. All told, about 2,300 Jews lived in the Mississippi Delta in 1937.[38] Over the last several decades, the Delta has seen a steep decline in its Jewish population. In 2005, no more than 300 Jews lived in the Delta, scattered in eight different communities, all of which were declining. Several congregations have closed, and the rest are struggling to remain open. Few Jewish children raised in the region have stayed, as the Delta no longer offers much economic opportunity. Jewish retail businesses have been undermined by the general economic decline of the region and the rise of chain discount stores. During the last few decades, most of these Jewish-owned stores have closed.

Clarksdale was once home to one of the largest Jewish communities in the state. According to a 1937 study, Clarksdale's 412 Jews ranked just behind Greenville's Jewish population. As one of the mercantile centers of the most fertile cotton-growing region in the country, Clarksdale thrived in the early twentieth century, but with changes in the cotton economy and the general decline of the Delta, the town is now a shadow of its former self. Jewish-sounding names are visible in sidewalk tiles in front of empty buildings or on faded signs, testament to Jewish retailers' former prominence in the community. Mirroring the decline of Clarksdale itself, the local Jewish community has withered to the point where the town's only congregation voted to disband and sell its synagogue building in 2003.[39]

A few hundred miles south of Clarksdale, Congregation B'nai Israel in Natchez, Mississippi, is facing a similar situation. The oldest Jewish community in the state, Natchez's Jews thrived in the nineteenth century. By 1900, about 450 Jews lived in Natchez, and their affluence is clearly reflected in the grandiose synagogue the congregation built in 1906. Soon after the building was dedicated, the area's cotton crop, which fueled the city's economy, suffered from boll weevils and low market prices, leading to a long slow decline in Natchez's Jewish population. By 1937, only 125 Jews were left. By 2005, ten remained. In 1992, the remaining members realized that they could not continue indefinitely and made arrangements with the Museum of the Southern Jewish Experience to preserve their building as a museum of Natchez Jewish history once they are no longer able to carry on as a congregation.

While the Jewish communities of the Delta and the river towns like Natchez and Vicksburg have declined, Jewish life has thrived in the state's capital, which is now the largest Jewish community in the state. According to a conservative 2001 estimate, 550 Jews lived in Jackson, more than twice the number of any other city in Mississippi. This shift has reflected the changing demographics of southern Jews, who are now far more likely to be professionals or corporate executives than retail business owners. Since Jackson is the medical and legal center of the state, it's not surprising that Jackson's lone Jewish congregation has been growing slightly in the twenty-first century. Yet even with this recent growth, most of the Jewish children raised in Jackson still end up settling outside of Mississippi after college.

As of 2008, there were active Jewish congregations in Biloxi, Cleveland, Columbus, Greenville, Greenwood, Hattiesburg, Jackson, Lexington, Meridian, Natchez, Oxford, Tupelo, and Vicksburg. Most all of these congregations, with the exception of Jackson, Biloxi, and Oxford, have been in decline for several decades. Jewish Sunday schools, which are an indicator of the number of children and thus the vitality of a community, only exist in five of the thirteen Jewish congregations in the state.[40] All except Jackson's are very small. While historians are always better at predicting the past than the future, these demographic trends will likely continue for the foreseeable future. If Jewish life in Mississippi ever experiences a resurgence, it will be tied to the overall growth and prosperity of the state. However out of place Jews might appear to be in Mississippi, the essential truth is that their experience has always been inextricably tied to the history of the state itself.

NOTES

1. Henry Seesel, "Memoirs of a Mexican Veteran" (Memphis: Jos. Samfield Printing Company, 1891), p. 18.

2. Ibid.; Teri D. Tillman, "Natchez Jewish Families, 1830–1900," Tillman Research Files; privately held by Tillman, Natchez, Mississippi.

3. Leo E. Turitz and Evelyn Turitz, *Jews in Early Mississippi* (Jackson: University Press of Mississippi, 1983), p. 3; Institute of Southern Jewish Life, Digital Archive, "Summit" and "Grand Gulf," http://www.isjl.org/history/archive/main_ms.htm.

4. Elliot Ashkenazi, *The Business of Jews in Louisiana, 1840–1875* (Tuscaloosa: University of Alabama Press, 1988), pp. 144–148.

5. Ibid., pp. 153–156.

6. U.S. Manuscript Census, 1860, 1870.

7. Information gleaned from the S. Bernheimer & Sons Papers, Goldring/Woldenberg Institute of Southern Jewish Life, Jackson, Mississippi. The collection only covers a few months from 1900, but offers a fascinating window into the business operations and connections of Jacob Bernheimer.

8. Quoted in *American Israelite*, November 27, 1876, p. 6.

9. Ibid.

10. William F. Holmes, "Whitecapping: Anti-Semitism in the Populist Era," *American Jewish Historical Quarterly*, Volume 63 (1974), pp. 244–261.

11. William Faulkner, *The Sound and the Fury* (New York: Vintage Books, 1954), pp. 237, 239.

12. ISJL Digital Archive, "Meridian," http://www.isjl.org/history/archive/ms/meridian.htm.

13. Robert Lewis Berman, *A House of David in the Land of Jesus* (Self-published, 2007), pp. 65–68.

14. State of Mississippi, House Concurrent Resolution No. 49, adopted March 11, 1981; "Mr. Sam recounts years as Rolling Fork mayor," *Delta Democrat Times*, November 1, 1976, p. 1; *Jackson Daily News*, October 30, 1949.

15. W.J. Cash, *The Mind of the South* (New York: Alfred A. Knopf, 1941), pp. 333–334; David L. Cohn, "I've Kept My Name," *The Atlantic Monthly*, April 1948.

16. Jacob Rader Marcus, *To Count a People: American Jewish Population Data, 1585–1984* (Lanham, MD: University Press of America, 1990), p. 107.

17. Robert Rosen, *The Jewish Confederates* (Columbia: University of South Carolina Press, 2000), pp. 38, 167, 172, 257–259.

18. Stuart Rockoff, "Playing Southern Jewish History Detective," *Circa*, Fall 2003, p. 9; *The Semi-Weekly Leader* (Brookhaven), January 13, 1934, p. 1.

19. *American Jewish Year Book, 1907–1908* (Philadelphia: Jewish Publication Society of America, 1907), pp. 115–118; 123–430.

20. "History of Temple B'nai Israel, Natchez, Mississippi," ISJL Digital Archive, http://www.isjl.org/history/archive/ms/HistoryofBnaiIsraelNatchez.htm.

21. "History of Congregation Beth Israel, Clarksdale, Mississippi," ISJL Digital Archive, http://www.isjl.org/history/archive/ms/beth_israel_clarksdale.htm.

22. Iuliu Herscovici, *The Jews of Vicksburg, Mississippi* (Xlibris, 2007), pp. 110–112; ISJL Digital Archive, "History of Temple B'nai Israel, Natchez," http://www.isjl.org/history/archive/ms/HistoryofBnaiIsraelNatchez.htm; "Dedication Book, Temple B'nai Israel, Tupelo, Mississippi," ISJL Archives.

23. Stuart Rockoff, "Not to Be Taken Lightly: Paula Ackerman and Temple Beth Israel of Meridian, Mississippi," *Jewish Education News*, Summer 2004, pp. 56–58; "Report of Pulpit Committee Congregation Beth Israel," October 26, 1952, Congregation Beth Israel Minutes, Meridian, Mississippi.

24. Edward Cohen, *The Peddler's Grandson: Growing Up Jewish in Mississippi* (Jackson: University Press of Mississippi, 1999), p. 145.

25. Edward S. Shapiro, "Anti-Semitism Mississippi Style," in David A. Gerber, ed., *Anti-Semitism in American History* (Urbana: University of Illinois Press, 1986), p. 146.

26. John Dollard, *Caste and Class in a Southern Town* (New Haven: Yale University Press, 1937), pp. 128–129; Clive Webb, *Fight Against Fear: Southern Jews and Black Civil Rights* (Athens: University of Georgia Press, 2001), p. 29; Cohen, p. 147.

27. Beth S. Wenger, *The Jewish Americans: Three Centuries of Jewish Voices in America* (New York: Doubleday, 2007), p. 294.

28. Memphis *Commercial Appeal*, October 22, 1959, clipping in Mississippi Sovereignty Commission Files, "B'nai B'rith and Film 'The High Wall,'" file #10-95-0, Mississippi Department of Archives and History; "B'nai B'rith Meeting at the Sun-N-Sand Motel, Biloxi, Mississippi," Reported by A. L. Hopkins, Investigator, December 30, 1960, Mississippi Sovereignty Commission Files, SCR# 10-95-0-23, MDAH.

29. "B'nai B'rith Meeting at the Sun-N-Sand Motel, Biloxi, Mississippi," Reported by A. L. Hopkins, Investigator, December 30, 1960," Mississippi Sovereignty Commission Files, SCR# 10-95-0-23, MDAH; Bernard Goodman, Hebrew Union Congregation, to Board of Trustees, Union of American Hebrew Congregations, November 7, 1963, Hebrew Union Congregation Archives, Greenville, Mississippi.

30. William Bradford Huie, *Three Lives for Mississippi* (Jackson: University Press of Mississippi, 2000), p. 52; interview with Alex Loeb, November 13, 2007, ISJL Oral History Collection; Jack Nelson, *Terror in the Night: The Klan's Campaign Against the Jews* (New York: Simon and Schuster, 1993).

31. Anonymous, "A Jewish View on Segregation," 1957, copy in ISJL Archives, Jackson, Mississippi.

32. Clive Webb, "Big Struggle in a Small Town: Charles Mantinband of Hattiesburg, Mississippi," in Mark K. Bauman and Berkley Kalin, eds., *The Quiet Voices: Southern Rabbis and Black Civil Rights, 1880s to 1990s* (Tuscaloosa: University of Alabama Press, 1997), pp. 215–229.

33. *The Citizen*, October 1962, p. 6; letter to Irv Schulman, Anti-Defamation League, March 15, 1963; letter to Southern Federation of Temple Youth Advisors from Rabbi

Robert Blinder, May 11, 1963, Benjamin Schultz Collection, American Jewish Archives, Cincinnati, Ohio.

34. Eric Goldstein, *The Price of Whiteness: Jews, Race, and American Identity* (Princeton: Princeton University Press, 2006); David B. Ruderman, "A Northern Rabbi Confronts the Deep South, 1966–1970," *The Jewish Quarterly Review*, Fall 2004, pp. 656–659.

35. Author interview with Macy B. Hart, October 6, 2006; Stuart Rockoff, "The Key to a Living Judaism: The Creation of the Henry S. Jacobs Camp," unpublished paper delivered at the Southern Jewish Historical Society Meeting, 2006.

36. Marcus, *To Count a People*, p. 107; *American Jewish Year Book*, 2006, p. 175.

37. Gavin Wright, *Old South, New South: Revolution in the Southern Economy Since the Civil War* (New York: Basic Books, 1986; reprint, Baton Rouge: Louisiana State University Press, 1996), p. 241; Numan Bartley, *The New South, 1945–1980* (Baton Rouge: Louisiana State University Press, 1995), pp. 8–11; 123.

38. *American Jewish Year Book*, Volume 40, 1938–1939, p. 250.

39. *Forward*, September 12, 2003, p. 23.

40. Author interview with Megan Roberts, Goldring/Woldenberg Institute of Southern Jewish Life, Jackson, Mississippi, October 3, 2008.

9

"CHAHTA SIYAH ÓKIH"

Ethnicity in the Oral Tradition of the
Mississippi Band of Choctaw Indians

—TOM MOULD

INTRODUCTION

Human habitation of the land that would become known as Mississippi dates back over ten thousand years. Today, only one indigenous group remains in any significant numbers: the Mississippi Band of Choctaw Indians. Spread across eight distinct communities in central Mississippi, the Choctaw are the only federally recognized tribe in the state.[1] There are approximately 9,660 tribal members, a number that has almost doubled in the past decade.

While the Choctaw are a politically and culturally coherent tribe today, distinguishing them as an ethnic group distinct from other native people in Mississippi is difficult until the mid-eighteenth century when the Choctaw began appearing in written records with a relative degree of consistency. Before then, indigenous people in the Southeast often lived in fairly loose confederacies, with groups both joining and incorporating other peoples in a dynamic mosaic of adaption, adoption, and reconfiguration. At least since the eighteenth century, however, the Choctaw have maintained a coherent ethnic identity, surviving both passive and aggressive acts to acculturate and eradicate them from the Mississippi landscape. Their perseverance contrasts sharply with many indigenous people in the Southeast who have struggled in the twentieth and twenty-first centuries to reclaim their ethnic identity.[2] Yet like all American Indian peoples, the Choctaw have had to confront the uncomfortable demands of determining who is and who is not a member of their tribe. The federal government issues Certificates of Degree of Indian Blood to certify the percentage of American Indian

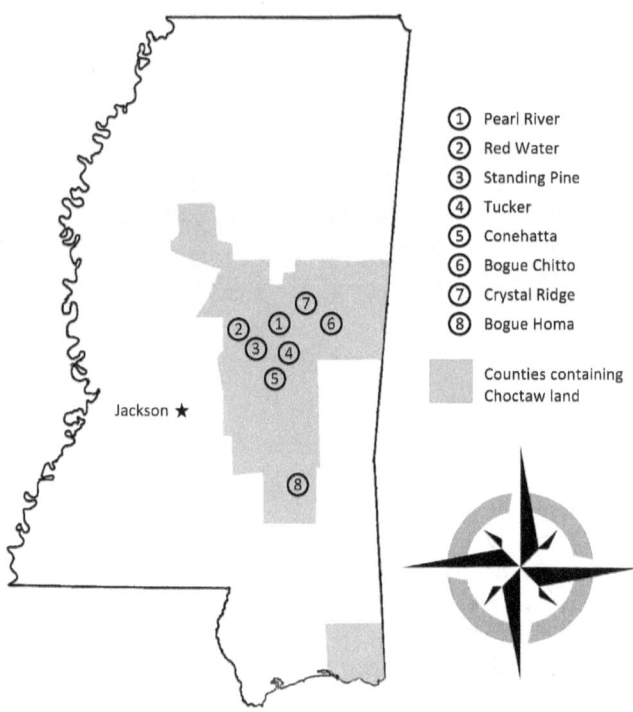

9.1. Map of Choctaw tribal land and communities in Mississippi.

blood of an individual belonging to a federally recognized tribe. Tribal governments then determine what percentage of blood is required for tribal membership. No other ethnic group in the United States has such official regulations for declaring and affirming ethnic identity.

HISTORY OF U.S./AMERICAN INDIAN RELATIONS

Considering the history of U.S./American Indian relations, the fact that any southeastern Indian peoples retain a coherent sense of ethnic identity today is a testament to their great perseverance. Federal policy towards the American Indians in the late eighteenth century was one of assimilation. For tribes in the Southeast, this meant they could remain east of the Mississippi but would be expected to give up their culture and adopt that of white colonists. The major tribes of the Southeast—the Choctaw, Cherokee, Chickasaw, Creek, and Seminole—did in fact incorporate customs and technologies of European colonists that they found useful, earning them the nickname The Five Civilized Tribes.[3] The process was one of adaption rather than adoption, however, and the tribes maintained an ethnic identity distinct from their new neighbors.

At the turn of the century, the growing demand for land by the relatively new European immigrants encouraged a shift in policy that demanded the removal of southeastern tribes to lands west of the Mississippi River in what is now Oklahoma. This policy became law in 1830 with the passing of the Indian Removal Act and resulted in what has become known as the Trail of Tears. Even with removal, however, assimilation remained the primary goal of federal policy. By the 1870s, the prevailing sentiment of how to deal with "the Indian problem" was captured in the common slogan "Kill the Indian, save the man," coined by Richard Henry Pratt. Pratt conceived of and executed the government policy to remove American Indian children from their homes and families, ship them to boarding schools, and assimilate them into mainstream Euro-American culture by cutting ties with their traditional cultures (see Churchill 2004, Ellis 1996, Prucha 1979). The policy was based on the fundamentally sound premise that American Indian culture was synonymous with American Indian identity. Eliminate Indian culture and eliminate the Indian.

More subtle and patient was the process of "killing the Indian" through blood quantum requirements. People were required to maintain a certain blood quantum, sometimes as high as 50 percent, in order to be an enrolled member of the tribe. U.S. officials realized that marriage between people of different ethnicities was common the world over and it would only be a matter of time before one American Indian after another dropped below the blood quantum requirement for tribal membership (see Campbell and Greymorning 2007, Tinker 2004: 39–43). Despite the American Indian Reorganization Act of 1934 and subsequent federal legislation such the 1975 Indian Self-Determination and Education Assistance Act that has returned governance to tribes, blood quantum continues to be used by many tribes to determine membership. The Mississippi Choctaw have the strictest blood quantum ratio of any tribe at 50 percent, a percent shared by only a handful of other tribes. In an age of federal grants, scholarships, and casino dividends, the Choctaw have found it useful and efficient to maintain strict blood requirements for who can call themselves Choctaw.

RACE AND ETHNICITY IN THE U.S. SOUTH

The history of U.S.–Indian relations provides one perspective for understanding the construction of Choctaw ethnicity. The history of race relations in the South provides another. To be clear, race and ethnicity are not synonyms. Ethnicity is defined primarily according to shared culture, race according to the presumption of shared genetics. Scientific study has made it abundantly clear that racial distinctions do not exist in the way that people have thought. Race, like ethnicity, is a social rather than biological construct, one that people have created to explain physiological differences between people primarily according to skin color, but including other facial and physical features as well. The concept of race has not disappeared, however. Common definitions for ethnicity include racial as well as cultural, national, religious, and linguistic heritage as criteria for describing a particular ethnic group. In other words, race still matters.

In the Southeast, race has served as a viable category for distinction and discrimination in legal, political, economic, and social systems. While recent studies have shed light on the complex stratification of race in the South in the nineteenth and twentieth centuries that recognizes multiple layers and categories, white and black nonetheless have dominated southern racial systems from slavery until the middle of the twentieth century. Yet within this social historical context, the Mississippi Choctaw managed to maintain a vibrant culture and coherent identity distinct from either white or black. Their solution was to isolate themselves from either group. Unaccepted as equals by whites and not wanting to be treated as poorly as blacks, the Choctaw drew their social boundaries tightly around themselves in the years following Removal and the American Civil War. Interaction was necessary for work and commerce, but contact was limited and rarely spilled over into the social sphere. While southern social systems may not have recognized a third ethnicity, the Choctaw did, and they cultivated their identity in contrast to their white and black neighbors.

Group identity can be established in many ways. Often, groups identify traits shared among their members in order to establish a coherent identity. As often, and simultaneously, groups may define themselves in contrast to other groups. That contrast can be directly oppositional, though it need not be.[4] The Mississippi Choctaw, for example, do not see their white and black neighbors as the antithesis of all that is Choctaw. However, contemporary Choctaw men and women do create and negotiate Choctaw ethnicity in the context of neighboring ethnic groups. The process is dynamic. The

9.2. Jake York telling stories to the youth during the Choctaw Language Immersion Camp. Photo by Tom Mould.

traits, symbols, and traditions that denote Choctaw ethnicity today are not the same as those used in the past. Nor are the neighboring ethnic groups. Historical shifts in the demographics, politics, and economics of the South have required constant negotiations with new neighbors and consequently shifting articulations of what it means to be Choctaw.

CHOCTAW ETHNICITY THROUGH THE ORAL TRADITION

Choctaw ethnicity can be usefully studied according to major events on the national and regional stage. First contact with Europeans, the Trail of Tears, the creation of a policy of self-determination, and the building of the first casino all provide useful vantage points to assess the development of ethnic identity. The more extended histories of treaties, alliances, government policies, and economic systems that brought Choctaw people in contact with non-Choctaw people also provide a useful lens for analysis. The picture that emerges from such study is useful but ultimately owes its structure, framing and focus of analysis to scholars outside the Choctaw community. It is possible, however, to place the Choctaw at the center of study, eschewing a historical events model of analysis for one based on those events and experiences the Choctaw themselves have deemed relevant by encoding them in their oral tradition. Myths, legends, supernatural stories, prophecies, histories, animal tales, and jokes all form an extensive oral tradition shared among men, women, and children. In these stories, tribal members often explore, create, and negotiate their ethnic identities in relation to other groups, whether other members within the tribe, other American Indians, or non-Choctaw neighbors. As a central part of the process for teaching the youth and interpreting the world, the oral tradition provides a relevant and effective focus for a study of Choctaw identity.[5] While the Choctaw oral tradition is vast, rich, and complex, a brief survey of the major narrative genres—origin myths, prophecies, historical legends, and *shukha anumpa*, or humorous tales—can nonetheless provide a useful overview of how tribal members themselves have conceived of Choctaw ethnicity.

Origin Myths

More than any other tribal stories, the origin myths of how the Choctaw came to be in Mississippi are shared frequently and known widely. There are two competing stories, one of migration to Mississippi from lands west, the other of emergence from a mound in Mississippi. The migration myth was first published in 1828 by the Reverend Alfred Wright and has been recorded and published consistently since.[6] It is a staple of the annual Choctaw Fair, where in 1996, the newly crowned Choctaw Princess Summer Saunders read the story to a mixed Choctaw and non-Choctaw audience.

> Good afternoon, ladies and gentlemen. Here is a story describing the settlement of the Choctaw people in Mississippi centuries ago.
> Many years ago, the ancestors of the Choctaws lived in the Northwest. In time, the population became so large that life there was difficult. The tribal wise men announced that a land of fertile soil and abundant game lay in the Southeast. The people could live there in peace and prosperity forever.

Under the leadership of two brothers, Chahta and Chikasa, our people set forth. At the end of each day's journey, a sacred pole was planted erect in front of the camp. The next morning, the pole would be found leaning one way or another. The tribesmen would travel in that direction for the day.

For months our people followed the sacred staff until they crossed the Mississippi River and reached what is now Winston County where they stopped during a heavy rain. The band that became the Chickasaws moved away from the main group, which was led by Chahta. We found our home. We'll call this place Nanih Waiya. Here we'll build our homes and a mound as the sacred burial spot for the bones of our ancestors.[7]

Summer Saunders continues reading, describing the history of the tribe up until the present day, crafting a story of perseverance in the face of desperate trials. The narrative is defiant and proud, as is her concluding statement: "We the Choctaw Nation of Mississippi, descendants of these strong people, are proud of the legacy of their courage and we welcome you to our nation with the Choctaw warrior's proudest boast: *Chahta siyah ókih*.[8] I am Choctaw." The boast dates back at least to 1896 and remains a common motto voiced throughout the tribe.[9]

In all of the versions recorded, two brothers lead their people eastward, only to be separated at the end of their journey. The result is a division of one tribe into two distinct nations, two distinct ethnic groups. While division is the result, the story nonetheless establishes a shared ethnic origin for the Choctaw and their neighbor, the Chickasaw. Ethnic identity is differentiated on the intertribal level, though specific differences are left unarticulated.

The same is true in the emergence myth, a parallel story of creation in which the Choctaw emerge from the sacred Nanih Waiya mound. Nanih Waiya figures centrally into both the emergence and migration myths and continues to hold great cultural and spiritual significance. One can visit the mound today, though there are two mounds called Nanih Waiya: the state park mound and the cave mound. The state park mound is of obvious human construction consistent with the mound builders of the Middle Woodland Period (A.D. 0–300). The cave mound, which lies about a mile away and has also been incorporated as a park, is held by many to be the sacred mound described in the myths. The emergence myth was first published in 1899 by Henry S. Halbert from Isaac Pistonatubbee and recorded again sporadically through the twentieth century.[10]

> A very long time ago the first creation of men was in Nanih Waiya. And there they were made. And there they came forth.
>
> The Muscogees first came out of Nanih Waiya, and they then sunned themselves on Nanih Waiya's earthen rampart. And when they got dry, they went to the east. On this side of the Tombigbee, there they rested. And as they were smoking tobacco they dropped some fire.
>
> The Cherokees next came out of Nanih Waiya. And they sunned themselves on the earthen rampart. And when they got dry they went and followed the trail of the elder tribe. And at the place where the Muscogees had stopped and rested, and where they had smoked tobacco, there was fire and the woods were burnt. And the Cherokees could not find the Muscogees' trail, so they got lost and turned aside and went towards the north. And there towards the north they settled and made a people.
>
> And the Chickasaws third came out of Nanih Waiya. And then they sunned themselves on the earthen rampart. And when they got dry they went and followed the Cherokees' trail. And when they got to where the Cherokees had got lost, they turned aside and went on and followed the Cherokees' trail. And when they got to where the Cherokees had settled and made a people, they settled and made a people close to the Cherokees.
>
> And the Choctaws fourth and last came out of Nanih Waiya. And they then sunned themselves on the earthen rampart and when they got dry, they did not go anywhere but settled down in this very land and it is the Choctaws' home.

Shared ethnic identity is less clear for these four tribes. Each is created separately from the other. However, all but the Choctaw attempt to follow their predecessor as if to reunite with them, suggesting a connection beyond a shared creator and shared site of emergence. As with Chahta and Chikasa, the trail is erased, this time by fire rather than water, and the groups are forced apart, each developing into a distinct tribe. A recent version told by Terry Ben reflects a more modern historical perspective by including the Seminole, thus encompassing all of the so-called Five Civilized Tribes of the Southeast.

An equally common shift in the emergence myth told today is from an *intertribal* focus to an *interracial* one.[11] In 1975, Wagonner Amos recounted a creation story of three men: "the Choctaw, the white and the black"

9.3. Nanih Waiya cave mound. Photo by Tom Mould.

(Mould 2004: 68–71). Harley Vaughn tells the story with a humorous twist, that the white man left the side of the mound undercooked by the sun, the black man stayed too long, but the Choctaw was cooked a perfect brown (Mould 2004:xxxix). The shift in narrative reflects a historical shift where the Choctaws' neighbors are no longer the Chickasaw, Creek, Cherokee, and Seminole but whites and blacks. In these stories, Choctaw narrators define tribal identity at the level of a racial category distinct from the two primary "races" of the South: black and white. The natural third race would be "red," which would indicate all American Indians. However, these stories portray *tribal* affiliation as far more relevant than a shared American Indian identity.

Prophecies of Preserving the Culture and the People

Prophetic movements among American Indians have often been characterized by charismatic leaders such as Neolin the Delaware Prophet, Tenskwatawa the Shawnee Prophet, Handsome Lake of the Seneca, and Wovoka who led the Ghost Dance Movement (see Mould 2003: 2–7). However, religious communities the world over have religious leaders who interpret their gods' messages, providing a compass for daily living. This socioreligious role was common among American Indians. For the Choctaw, prophets were known as *hopaii*, a term that has come to be equated with medicine man and witch doctor as the role has shifted and changed. While prophets are not clearly recognized among the Choctaw today, the prophecies of the *hopaii* of the past and elders past and present continue to be shared. The contemporary prophetic tradition is both heavily predictive and intensely moral. Through dire predictions of future loss, many of the prophecies critique social and cultural change in the Choctaw community. There is physical loss—loss of forests, loss of farmland, loss of land generally. There is also cultural loss—loss of social dances, loss of tribal clothing, loss of the language. This loss translates to a loss of Choctaw culture and by easy extension a loss of Choctaw identity. What it means to be Choctaw is deeply dependent on cultural traditions, many of which are performed as symbolic acts of identity. Not coincidentally, the traditions exhibited for non-Choctaw visitors at the annual Choctaw Fair—dancing, cooking, stickball, clothing, and the language—are the same traditions mentioned in prophecy as barometers of the health of the tribe. The loss of these traditions is a sign of the imminent demise of the tribe.

Billy Amos recounts the prophecies his mother told him growing up—predictions of new technological developments that would make life easier but would come with a costly trade-off.

> But at that time, some of the things in the future was going to come up. That's how they sit down and explained it. And some of the things that I saw today and in the past has come true. And most of them I haven't seen yet. But once in a while, they come up. So it's true.
> Back then ... what I was talking about was the sharecropping, that I was talking about.
> Same time was, we didn't have no electricity back then. Then we have to go and use a toilet outside. Or we have to tote water from the spring or wells. And that's how did we used to cooking.

Or maybe we didn't have no electricity on the stove. We had a fire on the stove. And we have to build a fire to make it cook. Every day. I don't care if it's hot, you still have to cook, unless you cook outside. Most of the time, some of them was cooking outside, like we do today, cook outside. And that's how they lived.

"But," she says, "someday, you'll be sitting inside a house, and they'll just put on the water and the water come in, in the house." And then electricity. "You just flip the button and the lights coming on."

We had a lamp to clean back then. Because I remember going to school, had to clean that lamp to get study. Clean it out every night. Lamp tops, you know; lamp globe in other words. Kerosene lamp.

And I can't believe that when she said that. "How can that be? Just put the water on the inside the house and it come on. And you got your hot water and cold water."

Well, we have to take a bath, we have to tote water from the spring or wells and then pour it in the wash tub, wash pot, and build a fire to heat it up, warm water to take a bath with. That's how did we go.

But like they said was, someday that you could flip the faucet, then you're ready to take a shower. And in a few minutes, you'd be finished taking a shower.

And I can't believe that. How that could be.

And then, I used to go out to TV, I mean movie. They had set up the tent; once a week that movie comes out. And then—I used to be crazy about it—so I have to go up there at night time, in the evening. Then I come back and I'm kind of scared coming down the road, but I go up there every week. And they had movies come out, chapter continued, movie. What happens, it goes off, then next week it continues. And I want to watch the whole chapter, I have to go up there.

She says, "Someday—you'll be running around, go up there walking, go see the white people's movie. But someday you going to be sitting in your own house, and going to watch them. You don't have to go out you just flip that button and you'd be watching the white people's movies, pictures in other words."

And I can't believe what she was saying.

But after all that time, there was . . . the first to come up was TV, black and white. And that's the way it was.

And beyond that, they got this VCR tape. What kind of movie you want, you just go to the store and rent it, and clicked it on, and then you can watch the movies, what you want to see.

9.4. Billy Amos, Bessie Morris, and Crystal Frazier chanting to accompany social dancing at the annual Choctaw Fair. Photo by Tom Mould.

But like I said, I don't know where they got the ideas, but in the future times that they look ahead of times and those things was come up.
"And the social dances is going to fade away," she said, "someday."
These are dancing on the weekend, Saturday night, they dance all night long in the ball field.
But they think it's going to be disappeared if they don't watch it.
So is the house dancing.
And today, that's where we at now, if we don't watch it.
So many things has changed.[12]

Electricity, running water, and movies—all would come to the Choctaw from outside the culture. In her description of theaters, Billy's mother specifically refers to "white people's movie." Despite their external origin, Billy expresses awe and excitement at the prospect of these modern conveniences. That excitement is tempered, however, by a trade-off. The VCRs and movies of mainstream white culture risk replacing the social dances and house dances of Choctaw culture.

The prophecies Harold Comby heard from his mother and the elders in the community are even more explicit about the link between the loss of cultural traditions and the loss of Choctaw identity.

> There are stories where the elderly used to say that there's going to be a time when you won't be able to recognize the Choctaw.
>
> And my mama says we're up to that point, because we're integrating with whites and blacks and other races.
>
> She said there was a lot of people that prophesized events like, she said, she has heard from her mother that her mother, her grandmother, used to tell her that they were going to have roads that were black, like asphalt. And they were going to have things that flew without being an animal. And the winter and the summer was going to switch.
>
> And she thinks that the time is now because, you know, at night, it's cool. And she says the days were going to get shorter. And, you know, when you think about it, it seems like the year goes on and on and on, quickly.

Harold introduces a theme that runs through many of the prophecies told today, a theme that dominates all others in frequency and relevance to the threat to Choctaw identity: intermarriage. In addition to the threat to identity due to the loss of culture, these prophecies warn against a direct biological threat of the loss of ethnic identity. Estelline Tubby explains:

> The most cultural thing, I was teached and we are teached in our Choctaw tribe is keeping the ... most one is about marriage. Well, we would like our children to marry whites, blacks or other tribes, but we are teached not to. 'Cause they don't understand our ways, and they don't understand our cultural ways.
>
> And, that's the main one we used to be teached: not to marry out of the tribe so they could understand our language.
>
> And my mom said, well, she really did tell us not to. Because, she said, "Look at the birds," she said. Cardinal, the mockingbird. And if you see sometimes around your house, the cardinals don't mate with the blue jays or mockingbird. God made that and they are beautiful, with female and male.

And she said just that.

And I don't know why she said that was, that, "When the children are mixed blood, they will never be Choctaw again."

And that's the way.

"But there are days coming, too, it's going to happen. But I'm talking to you as my children. I don't know about the future," she said, "but it may be going to happen."

And it has happened.

You see, when they say it like that, it usually happens.

Intermarriage with people of other ethnicities poses both a cultural and biological threat to ethnic identity. Estelline Tubby points out that the mandate against intermarriage is not an expression of racist ideology but rather a practical stopgap against the loss of culture and language. When a Choctaw person marries a non-Indian, English inevitably becomes the language in the home and the Choctaw language disappears (see Peterson 1972:1288). Choctaw traditions are also at risk of fading in the face of increased and sustained contact with the culture introduced by the non-Choctaw spouse.

Further, because the Choctaw use blood quantum as the primary indicator of tribal membership, intermarriage means the loss of legal status as Choctaw. Without tribal affiliation, people risk losing access to tribal lands and services. Louise Wilson quotes the prophecies she heard from her grandfather that "pretty soon there will be more mixed bloods than full." He explains to her: "You see the government giving us monies for this and that. Well, all that will be taken away" (Mould 2003: 168–169). Sally Allen describes a Choctaw woman who may not be able to keep her house on the reservation because she married a non-Choctaw man, a story she shares as a possible sign of the fulfillment of a prophecy that the Choctaw will once again be forced to move from their homes. She concludes ominously: "Choctaws will be dying out because of that interracial marriages" (Mould 2003: 75).

Many of these fears of the loss of tribal identity are captured in the prophecy of a Third Removal. In the middle of the nineteenth century, the U.S. government attempted a large-scale removal of the Indians in the Southeast, the brutality of which would be memorialized with the name "The Trail of Tears." The Choctaw were the first to be removed, beginning in 1830. A second major removal effort of the Choctaw occurred at the turn of the century. Choctaw prophecies describe a Third Removal, one that will once and for all remove the Choctaw from Mississippi. Most versions of this prophecy include signs that the Third Removal is imminent: large homes, paved roads, modern technology, day cares where kids are cared for by strangers, and general economic prosperity displayed in material wealth—all symbols of cultural change associated with a mainstream U.S. culture dominated by a white elite.

In many versions of the prophecy, the Third Removal will be accompanied by a war. Echoing the theme of cataclysmic cleansing and rejuvenation of other American Indian prophecies such as those of Wovoka and the Ghost Dance and Tenskwatawa the Shawnee Prophet, this day of destruction will bypass the Choctaw and return them to their homelands. The prophecy comes with an important caveat, however. Only those Choctaw who have maintained their ethnic identity and cultural traditions will survive. Charlie Denson recounts a series of predictions that culminate in the Third Removal and war.

> White people came. Told us how we're going to live. White man came and destroyed our people. Bible on left hand, gun on the right. Killed and raped our people.
>
> Now with this intermarriage. Choctaw prophet said white people will come and put us in bondage. We've been in bondage two hundred years now. Prophet predicted this. Someone came along, integrated our people, mixed it up. So that's where we come from. We got a lot of Negro, half Negro, half white. In the Bible it says we're not supposed to integrate. That's what the Bible told *me*.
>
> What we need is to study the Bible. To tell us how we come, where we go.
>
> My grandpa is ninety-five years old. He told me I would go into the army.[13]
>
> Moved to Arkansas. Second move to Oklahoma. Now we're in the third.
>
> My prophet told me we're going beyond Oklahoma. Past some island in the Pacific.
>
> China is going to come to the U.S. and give Choctaw land back to us. My grandpa told me that.
>
> He told me, if you're going to school, to seminary, high up in the sky, don't forget your language. If you quit your language, not speaking, you might get called on by the Chinese army. Because Chinese going to be here. "I want to hear the Choctaw language." If you can't speak none of your language, they going to kill you.

> He [God] don't want it to be integrated.
> That's coming up.

Survival depends on maintaining the language. The prophecy describes literal death for those who cannot speak Choctaw, making concrete what many understand metaphorically: that without the language, Choctaw culture and by extension Choctaw identity are at risk of disappearing. A common adage in Indian Country[14] and repeated frequently by the Choctaw Tribal Language Program staff is that a culture without its language is like a bird without its wings. According to these prophecies, the greatest threat to the language is intermarriage.

For most Choctaw, the mandate against intermarriage is handed down by prophets and elders. Charlie Denson adds biblical authority as well. Citing Christian scripture may seem paradoxical in the context of prophecies that laud the conservation of traditional culture against the influence of foreign agents. Yet while many Choctaw men and women mourn the loss of traditional Choctaw religious beliefs, few see Christianity as antithetical to Choctaw culture. The majority of the tribe is Christian, including Charlie Denson, who blames white people not for introducing Christianity, but for their hypocrisy of touting brotherly love while forcibly subjugating his people.

While language is the most common symbol of Choctaw identity evoked in the prophetic tradition, other cultural traditions are also mentioned. "If you're truly Choctaw, you would have a Choctaw shirt or Choctaw dress hanging up in your porch," recalls Linda Willis as she narrates the prophecy her grandfather told her of a great war. "That way they'll know that you're Indian living in that house, and they'll pass by you."

Prophecies of a Third Removal also reflect a deep fear of being separated from the land that was given to them by God. In one version of the creation myth told at the time of removal, the narrator quotes an emissary of the Great Spirit: "I give you these hunting grounds as your homes. When you leave them you die" (Claiborne 1964 [1880]:483–484). Land, life, and identity are intertwined. During removal, approximately six thousand Choctaw refused to leave Mississippi, choosing to eke out a living in the swamplands of Mississippi rather than leave for Oklahoma. The majority of those who remained again refused to leave as renewed pressure was placed on them at the turn of the century. Yet without legal claim to the land, the Choctaw were forced to invest their language and customs as the primary symbols of ethnic identity (see Kidwell 1986: 82). In the past fifty years, the tribe has reclaimed major tracts of land though legal claim and direct purchase, but the fear of the loss of land remains.

In all of these prophecies, Choctaws are contrasted with white and black people, a negotiation of ethnic identity on the level of race. These prophecies were recorded in the second half of the twentieth century, at the same time that the origin myth was shifting to reflect interracial rather than intertribal differences. The most recent prophecies hint at yet another shift in identity, one that recognizes American Indian as an umbrella ethnic group that includes the Choctaw. As the Choctaw have emerged from their local isolation in Mississippi and joined national American Indian organizations throughout the country, a growing recognition of a shared Indian ethnicity has emerged. Linda Willis recalls that Choctaw will need to put out their Choctaw shirt or dress to prove their "Indian" identity. The prophecies of a great war where Choctaw will be saved dovetail with similar prophecies of other American Indian tribes. At the Gathering of Nations powwow in New Mexico, Estelline Tubby heard a speaker talk about a day when all Indians would meet together again, and she wonders whether the Third Removal is part of this larger gathering (Mould 2003: 202). While the Choctaw will escape harm with their tribal traditions, other American Indians can presumably do the same with displays of *their* tribal traditions.

Such a shift is *not* evidence of pan-Indianism, a generic one-size-fits-all identity shared by all American Indians. This broader American Indian identity is based on shared indigeneity and shared historical oppression but not shared culture, which remains defined primarily at the tribal level.

Historical Legends

The stories of past historical events that continue to be shared today depict intratribal, intertribal, and interracial interactions, though the latter are confined almost exclusively to interactions with white people. John Hunter Thompson returns to the very beginning of the relationship with whites, the arrival of European colonists. His story serves as a moral rebuke regarding the alcoholism that continues to plague the tribe today.

> The Choctaws never really knew what liquor was until the white men brought it over. All they knew about the white man was that they came from the big water and came ashore.
>
> When the white man saw the Choctaws in the forest, they tried to speak to them, but had difficulty understanding each other. They

returned to their boat and came back with some whiskey and told the people to drink it; but the Chief said no, for he thought it was something that would kill them. So the whites left for the boat to return later to try again.

When they did return, they saw only a few Choctaws and asked them to come over and try the whiskey. This the Choctaws did. The whiskey tasted sweet to them so they continued to drink some more.

A little while later, the Choctaws started saying things that made no sense. This caused them to be unable to stand up straight. They would also fall down on the ground.

The white men saw this and went to their boat to get some more whiskey, leaving it on the shore for the other Choctaws to come and get it. The other Choctaws went and got it and soon everybody was drinking and getting drunk.

That's how the Choctaws started drinking.

Charlie Denson levels similar blame on whites for their immoral engagement with the Choctaw in the prophecies he shares. Whites fare no better in how they are portrayed in subsequent interactions with the Choctaw. They continue to use alcohol to trick the Choctaw out of their land—at Dancing Rabbit Creek where the treaty was signed that would remove the Choctaw to Oklahoma (Grady John 1998; Mould 2004: 154–155), and in individual interactions with unscrupulous land speculators.[15] Inez Henry describes a particularly blatant example of deception where two white men put a pen in the hand of her unconscious grandfather and signed his name on a deed of sale of his land (1986; Mould 2004: 156–157).

In contrast to these images of whites, the Choctaw appear as honest and trusting if somewhat prone to falling prey to the lure of alcohol and lofty promises. They are tricked and taken advantage of but remain resolute and persevering. Underlying this image of victimization and passive resistance, however, is the hint of subversion. The stories describe the Choctaw in Mississippi today as descendents of the men and women who either refused to leave during removal efforts in the nineteenth century or who sneaked back, both acts of willful resistance (Jake York 1997; Mould 2004: 155–156). In Inez Henry's story about her grandfather, her grandmother faced physical attack as she struggled to defend her husband, family, and land. And despite the powerful inroads Christianity has made into Choctaw life, Estelline Tubby describes how the Bogue Chitto community was able to resist periodic cultural purges attributed to overzealous missionaries, protecting one of the most powerful symbols of Choctaw identity today: stickball.[16]

> Other Indians have their own kind of religion. But I search for our Choctaw way, but no. Well, I asked one time, because, well, I asked my mother about it. I says, "Why don't we have our own way? I'm a Choctaw."
> I used to think, "I'm an Indian," so I want to be an Indian doing something.
> And she said, "Well, as far as I know, the Baptists said those are sins what we are doing."
> And I said, "Well, I thought God made everybody to worship in their own way, in our own tongue."
> But she didn't know either.
> But she told me this though. This is the way it started, as far as I know.
> She said that there was some religion people came here and they started one time to have school. My mother said that there was some religion that came out here and forced the Choctaws to give up their cultures and everything. And one of them, I think she said, was a Baptist. She just mentioned that name.
> And then, well, they'd been playing stickball and so on like that. And they told the men to bring all the stickball sticks. And it said it was a great big pile and they all burned it. And they burned a lot of things that the Choctaw had.
> And then they went on down to Bogue Chitto, I guess, and tried to do that too, but they said, "No. We will not listen to these people. We'll just keep our things and keep our culture the way it is."
> And now today, they are bringing it back from Bogue Chitto to here. That's how it is. Because those older people, older man and people, know about our culture. So that's how we got ours back. That's why we have it today.

In addition to pitting traditional Choctaw identity against the encroaching culture of white missionaries, Estelline Tubby's narrative highlights intratribal divisions of distinct communities where some communities are viewed as more traditional than others.[17] The current intratribal divisions resulted from the devastation of removal. After the signing of the Treaty of Dancing Rabbit Creek in 1830, Choctaw families remaining in Mississippi were promised 640 acres of land. Few families ever received that land, however; most were forced into undesirable swamplands as squatters.[18] Work as sharecroppers after the American Civil War dispersed Choctaws even farther. Not until a land purchase program beginning in 1921 after the Mississippi Choctaw had regained federal recognition were Choctaw families again able to live as neighbors in coherent communities.

During these years of relative isolation, Choctaw families maintained a sense of shared identity through the social gatherings that occurred a few times a year when people came together to play stickball, dance, and court potential spouses from outside their families and communities but from within the tribe.[19] Lillie Gibson tells a humorous story about walking to one of these gatherings when she was a young girl (see Mould 2004: 178–179). In 1949, these social events led to the formation of the Choctaw Fair, an annual event where each Choctaw community continues to assert its specific identity through displays of community products such as food, clothing, and crafts. Today, as in Estelline's story, Bogue Chitto is perceived to be the most traditional of the eight Choctaw communities in Mississippi, followed closely by Conehatta.[20] Pearl River, on the other hand, is home to the tribal government, museum, and high school, has more affluent neighborhoods, and is seen as the most progressive of the communities.

Intratribal ethnic identity based on one's community of birth continues to be used today to structure social relations, particularly in terms of expectations for traditional behavior. Community divisions also serve as political boundaries, with each community electing their own tribal council representatives. These boundaries were far more concrete in the past than today, however. Before removal, the Choctaw were divided into three major areas: Okla Falaya in the west, Okla Tannap in the east, and Okla Hannali to the south.[21] Near the beginning of the eighteenth century, the eastern and western areas were drawn into civil war by their respective French and British allies (Swanton 1931: 57). Louise Wilson recounts a story her grandfather John Hunter Thompson told her about the border disputes between these towns that continued beyond the war as a general practice of protecting one's hunting grounds. Violators who were caught were subjected to the painful torture of having blackberry briars pulled back and forth between their legs like a saw (Louise Wilson 1997; Mould 2004: 151–153). According to her grandfather John Hunter Thompson, the strategy was also used against neighboring tribes:

There were other Indian tribes near the Choctaws that they didn't know about. They hunted the small game and took it to their people.

The Choctaws found out, got angry, and told the other Indians to hunt somewhere else. This the other Indians did not do so the Choctaws and Muskogee, which is what they were called, started fighting.

It became a big war. The Muskogees were strong for they used bows and arrows while the Choctaws used blowguns.

This was told to me by my grandfather and father.

The Muskogee would travel at night to the Choctaw's house. They would knock on the door and when they opened the door they would kill them and run.

The Choctaws did the same to them.

When the young Choctaws went hunting in the forest, the Muskogee would hide, and they would catch the Choctaws. And they would gather some black bushes together and put it in between the young Choctaws' legs, and push it and pull it out like a saw. This would burn and cut the young Choctaws. They would have to crawl home.

The Choctaw found out and started doing the same to the Muskogee. This was the beginning of a big fight.

The Choctaw started wondering how they could go hunting without being caught by the Muskogees. They needed some place to hide.

A prophet told them that they should dig a hole and climb into it, when the Muskogees chased them and followed them in, hit them below the knee and beat them up.

So the Choctaws dug a hole near the stream deep in the hills. They did what the prophet said and this made the fight even bigger.

The Choctaws had help fighting the Muskogees by the whites. The whites helped them by giving them guns. The Muskogees left soon after this to live somewhere else.

This was a hard time for the Choctaws.

The relatively similar images of *inter*tribal and *intra*tribal relations displayed in these stories suggests that tribal differentiation was not as concrete and fixed as it is today, a conclusion supported by the historical record throughout the Southeast (see, for example, Galloway 1995 and Hudson 1976). Further, while the contemporary oral tradition recalls intertribal contact, it records little by way of clear distinguishing traits between groups. One exception is John Hunter Thompson's story, which paints the Muskogee (Creek) as aggressors and the Choctaw as defenders, an image again supported by the historical record, particularly if Thompson's story describes the Creek War of 1813.[22]

Shukha Anumpa

Shukha anumpa literally means "hog talk," though hogwash is a more meaningful translation. These stories are humorous and playful, inflated with exaggeration. This single genre of stories includes two categories of narrative distinguished by main character: either animal or human. Animal tales are some of the most frequently shared stories because of their appeal to both children and adults. The majority of the stories depict animals behaving in ways that illustrate appropriate and inappropriate behavior applicable to humans. In fact, many of these stories are used to teach the youth.

Animals regularly compete with one another, highlighting the talents and limitations of each animal. In one darkly comic story, a bear invites a rabbit over to supper. The bear is able to cut steaks from his side without harm and the two indulge in a particularly satisfying meal. The rabbit attempts to reciprocate, but his slim frame does not afford the same meat or protection as the bear and the rabbit ends up killing himself. The bear happily eats rabbit steak all the same.[23] The underlying message of many of these stories is a warning about adopting the ways of others. The result is ridicule, humiliation, and physical loss. Applied to humans, these stories echo many of the warnings evident in prophetic narratives.[24]

The stories of humans are naturally more explicit in describing relationships among people. Folk tales, tall tales, and the humorous stories of community members past and present draw humans into humorous interaction that reveal how Choctaw men and women construct a sense of ethnic identity through storytelling. The joke is the focal point in these stories. The goal: to make an audience laugh. Yet tucked away in these stories is a wealth of information about cultural traditions from the not-too-distant past that track the changes elders have seen over the course of their lifetimes. Gladys Willis refers to the process for killing hogs. Harry Polk describes how funerals were conducted before Christian rituals became more commonplace. Henry Williams explains how men courted women and the importance placed on hunting and stickball. Lillie Gibson describes the antecedent of today's Choctaw Fair, when families gathered in remote rural areas, set up temporary camps for the week, and ate, danced, and

Oral Tradition of Mississippi Band of Choctaw Indians   241

played stickball as they had for generations. These stories serve as reminders of cultural heritage and examples of cultural change. Unlike prophecy, however, they rarely carry a moral imperative and explicit critique of that change. One exception is with regard to the language. Jake York tells a story of a man who trains his dog with commands in Choctaw. His moral to the young boys and girls at the Choctaw language summer camp is explicit: "If a dog can learn Choctaw, then you all can learn, too" (Mould 2004: 186).

More often, however, the language is a source of humorous confusion as Choctaws and whites attempt to communicate. Gladys Willis tells a story about legendary funny man Ashman.

> They used to call Ashman. This is a Choctaw man. I think this was a Choctaw because when he met a white man, this Choctaw asked him, "Where are you from?" but in Choctaw. He said, "Katima ish minti," akamąno.
> The white man said, "What you say?" akamąno [he said].
> The Choctaw said, "Whatyousay minti miyah," atok miya ["He said he came from Whatyousay," so he said] [laughter].
> He thought he came from Whatyousay [laughter].
> That's the way it was.[25]

Language is a barrier for Choctaw and white interaction, as the most powerful symbols of group identity typically are, serving as borders differentiating one group from another. In this story, Ashman misinterprets the white man, directing the humor at the naïve Choctaw man. On the surface, the humor in Lillie Gibson's story of running water is similarly self-effacing. However, the humor rests on the pun Lillie plays, and while she pretends to be naïve, she is actually far more linguistically savvy.

> Mama got married. Well, our daddy died, and when she married a man, she married one from Conehatta, and so he already had a house. And so we had to move up here.
> And we didn't have no way to draw water; we didn't have no running water.
> So one day, a nurse, a home health nurse, came to my house, after we moved here, now.
> After I got married and we moved over here... when we moved over here, I got married.
> And so, she came around and asked, do we have running water.

And I told her, "Yes ma'am. We've got running water; if we run and go get it" [laughter].

As in prophetic narratives, modern technology is often equated with the culture of white people. Anxiety and confusion over cars, air conditioning, and running water suggest that despite the increasing interaction with their white neighbors, many of the older Choctaw continue to remain uncomfortable outside the safety of the relative isolation of their communities. Younger Choctaw are likely more comfortable with their white and black neighbors than their parents and grandparents, but that trend is not yet apparent in the oral tradition. Instead, the dominant image of the Choctaw that emerges in *shukha anumpa* parallels that of historical legends, commenting through humor rather than anger. Whites hold positions of power and material wealth while Choctaws remain relatively humble and naïve with flashes of underlying determination and perseverance.

Stories of Supernatural Encounters

Encounters with supernatural beings are unusual but not unexpected in the Choctaw community. The Mississippi woods remain home to mysterious balls of light, unusual animals, and any of a number of specific creatures such as *na losa chitto, kashikanchak, okwa nahollo, nishkin chafa,* or *bohpoli*. Virtually everyone in the community either has encountered one of these beings themselves or knows someone who has. The most common supernatural being people encounter today is *bohpoli*, also known as *k'wanokasha* or the little people. *Bohpoli* are generally described as being two to three feet tall, old, wizened, and often mischievous. They are said to look like Choctaw children in size, elders in all other respects. Also, they appear only to the Choctaw, the result of which is that sharing a story of one's encounter with *bohpoli* is tantamount to a declaration of one's ethnic identity. Since these stories are most often shared among tribal members familiar with *bohpoli* rather than non-Choctaw who may ridicule such beliefs, ethnic identity is negotiated more clearly on the intratribal rather than interracial level. Seeing *bohpoli* suggests not only that a person is Choctaw, but that they are fairly traditional in their beliefs, immersed and actively engaged in the culture rather than acculturated into mainstream skepticism of the supernatural. For many, knowledge of the supernatural is an important part of being Choctaw. One of the main problems with the youth today, according to Judy Billie, Regina Shoemake, and Sally Allen—all employees at the Choctaw Health Department—is their lack of understanding of tribal traditions, among them an understanding of supernatural beings and traditional Choctaw medicine. Knowledge of these traditions is a mark of Choctaw identity; *belief* in these traditions is a mark of *traditional* Choctaw identity, a privileged status in the community. This intratribal distinction is marked linguistically by the difference between "Chahta" and "Choctaw." Chahta is the Choctaw language spelling for the tribe. "Choctaw" reflects English spelling and pronunciation. Tribal identity expressed to non-Indians is *Choctaw* identity. Tribal identity expressed within the tribe, however, can be distinguished as Chahta *or* Choctaw, depending on how immersed a person is in the culture and therefore how traditional they are (see Thompson and Peterson 1975: 186–193). Seeing *bohpoli* is a mark of Chahta identity.

One's status as a traditional member of the community is elevated for those people who encounter *bohpoli* for reasons first explained in writing in 1895 by Henry S. Halbert: "Bohpoli, or kowi anukasha, is never seen by the common Choctaws. The Choctaw prophets and doctors, however, claim the power of seeing him and of holding communication with him. The Indian doctors say that bohpoli assists them in the manufacture of their medicine" (1895a: 57). David Bushnell records a more detailed description of how *bohpoli* leads young children away to be trained as doctors from Ahojeobe, a Choctaw man in Louisiana (1909: 30–31). In 1976, and again in 1996, Estelline Tubby narrated on audiotape the story of how her grandmother became a doctor.

> She had a good ways of becoming a medicine woman. She was fourteen when she saw the vision. That's when, I guess she was a young girl, went into the woods and looked around but ... And then after a while, she heard a lot of people was talking and laughing and all of this and that. But as she looked, she could not see nobody. But the voice was just looked like coming from behind the bushes but looked like they were just having a good time laughing and talking, but she couldn't make out on that talking either. She just stand there and listen.
>
> All in one sudden, there was a little whirlwind, you know, a little whirlwind, coming from that way, and came around to where she stand. And she did not see those flowers blooming, wild flower blooming. But when that whirlwind came and go around her, there was a lot of medicine blooms, flower blooms, you know, herbal. She mixed those herbal medicine, and herbs was the ones that was

9.5. Estelline Tubby at home. Photo by Allyson J. Whyte.

flowering. Those kinds were just in front of her. When she was looking, that whirlwind just whirled around and then went its way. And it disappeared, those things. But she had a vision of that.

And then after a while, she stand there, said, "What, what's happening to me?" And when she looked towards where she was coming from, a little trail, she saw a little old lady with, you know, those little black pots. She was holding that way, and she was walking slowly towards her. And she looked at it and she didn't know what that mean either. She got scared so she run off, before that old woman came.

And she went to her mother and told her all about what she had seen and heard and all of that. Her mother just smiled and seems happy when she heard that. And she said, "Well, as long as you live on this earth, you'll never be hungry."

And she was thinking, "Why I will not be hungry?"

And she said, "I think God has given you a good gift. And that will be yours always.

"And the people you hear is that you will be doctoring them, and they will be well again and will be happy and will be talking away and will be happy and laughing.

"And the whirlwind that you saw that flowering things before you, those are the medicines you will be using, in days to come.

"And then the old woman you saw with the black pot, that kind of a pot you're going to use for your medicine to boil. That's what's representing."

And she told her that "In days to come, you will be a doctor."

Claiming such privileged status in the community for oneself risks accusations of self-importance and excessive pride. Accordingly, people regularly describe how they came to know their encounter was with *bohpoli* and not some other supernatural being. After playing in an area thought to belong to the little people, Judy Billie found herself sleepwalking back to that spot and seeing a mass of strange people around her. The next morning, "[T]hey had to take me to a medicine man, and that medicine man told me that I was sleepwalking," she explains. "But they told me I was going out there to play with them. Those little people were around me, but I didn't know. And nobody knew" (1997). As a young teenager, Terry Ben saw a little man while out hunting one day. Scared, he ran away. Not only did his grandfather confirm what he saw, he revealed that had Terry stayed longer, he might have become a Choctaw doctor or received some other gift from the little man (1996). The interpretation of the encounter is socially expedient as well as practical. Many of the Choctaw supernatural beings can take similar forms. A ball of light, for example, could be *bohpoli*, *hashok okwa hui'ga* (similar to a will-o'-the-wisp), a medicine man, a witch, or, of course, just a light.

While narratives of encounters with the supernatural are still common, there is widespread concern in the community that the supernatural beings are slowly disappearing. They make their homes deep in the Mississippi woodlands. But as the woods are razed to make way for new housing developments and shopping centers, supernatural beings are being driven away. Increased development threatens the Choctaw supernatural beings and, by extension, Choctaw culture just as it threatens to precipitate the Third Removal in the prophetic narrative tradition.

Loss of habitat provides a practical explanation for the disappearance of the Choctaw supernatural. More disturbing is the possibility that lack of belief is equally to blame. A century ago, Choctaw doctors provided the primary care for the ailing in the tribe. Today, a modern hospital on the reservation serves the majority of the community. Some of the more traditional members of the tribe continue to visit Choctaw doctors, but the demand for their services has decreased considerably. Fewer doctors translates to a decreased need for help from *bohpoli*. If these fears are realized, stories of encounters with the supernatural, *bohpoli* in particular, will signify an increasingly elite group of traditional Choctaw.

SYNTHESIS

A genre-by-genre approach has been useful in avoiding the problems of premature summary where case-specific phenomena risk being portrayed as widespread pattern. However, summary and synthesis *across* genres, not just *within* them, is nonetheless a useful and appropriate concluding enterprise. Analysis of the oral tradition has revealed a negotiation of ethnic identity on intratribal, intertribal, and interracial levels, thereby providing a useful structure for synthesizing the ways Choctaw men and women negotiate ethnic identity in the oral tradition. At the risk of overstepping these bounds, however, it is also worthwhile to look beyond the oral tradition to how identity is expressed in daily life. Such comparisons are necessarily evocative rather than systematic, but provide a hint of the larger patterns that extend beneath and beyond the stories that people tell.

Intratribal

Intratribal identity reflects divisions Choctaw people perceive within their tribe and is negotiated at the level of both the community and the individual. In the past, communities were different enough to maintain strict boundaries, each with their own divisional chief. Distinct dialects developed and continue today, despite a radical reconfiguration of community boundaries after removal. Distinct community identities are maintained in stories told today and reflect in particular the degree of traditionality each can claim. Intratribal divisions according to degrees of traditionality can also be articulated among individuals in terms of fluency in the language and knowledge of tribal customs. One of the primary criteria in the judging of the Choctaw Princess pageant during the annual Choctaw Fair is knowledge of the tribal customs. Judges ask contestants questions about their values and what aspects of Choctaw culture they feel is most important in their lives.

Many young women vying for Choctaw Princess also make sure to greet the audience and judges in the Choctaw language. As the language disappears at an alarming rate, linguistic proficiency is a more and more powerful symbol of traditional Choctaw identity.[26] When Beasley Denson defeated Phillip Martin as tribal chairman in 2007, he immediately dropped the term "Chief" that Martin had used and adopted the title of "Mįko," a move explained in his first address to the tribe in the *Choctaw Community News* with the following headline: "Denson assumes title of 'Mįko'—Choctaw for Chief" (August 2007, 37 (8): 2). Denson had opposed Chief Martin with rhetoric that cast himself as a traditionalist committed to preserving Choctaw culture.[27] Denson's campaign slogan was "Chahta First," referencing traditional Chahta rather than Choctaw identity. His monthly column in the *Choctaw Community News* is the only place this spelling is used consistently in the newspaper.

Intratribal stratification is based not only on adherence to traditional beliefs but also on blood, as warnings against interracial marriage make clear. The explicit threat is from outside the community; the explicit identity negotiated is interracial. Yet Charlie Denson describes the result of intermarriage as people half one race, half another, often referred to within the community as "mixed-blood."[28] Concern over mixed-blood people and removal has a painful historical precedent. The Treaty of Dancing Rabbit Creek that would remove the Choctaw to Oklahoma was widely rejected by full-blood leaders of the tribe, most of whom went home once negotiations fell apart. The primarily mixed-blood leaders who remained agreed to sign the treaty, cementing a rift between full-blood and mixed-blood factions of the tribe that had been growing during the first half of the nineteenth century and radically altering Choctaw life in Mississippi (see McKee and Schlenker 1980, Wells 1986). The negative connotations of such mixing are reflected in the disdain for Choclish, the term coined to describe the mixing of Choctaw and English. Choclish is assumed to be the result of an inability to speak fluent Choctaw rather than the reverse or as a conscious act of code-shifting in order to signal the dual identity of the speaker, audience, or both. The disdain for Choclish can extend to the people who speak it, fueling intratribal divisions according to how traditional a person is.

9.6. A collection of Choctaw arts and crafts, including swamp cane baskets, small stickball sticks for decoration, and dolls. Photo by Tom Mould.

Intertribal/Racial

The oldest stories of the tribe describe a Choctaw ethnicity in contrast to neighboring American Indian tribes. This relationship was based primarily on a tribal and regional identity rather than a shared American Indian identity. In migration myths, the Choctaw and Chickasaw were brothers. The Choctaw were related to the other southeastern tribes as regional neighbors who sought reunification but were foiled by fire or rain. Nowhere in these early stories, however, is there a clear sense of some larger American Indian identity.[29]

More recent stories, however, suggest a growing recognition of a broader racial identity. As Choctaws have emerged from isolation over the past forty years, increased engagement both with other races—white and black—as well as with other Indian tribes has encouraged the adoption of a national racial identity as American Indians. In the past twenty years, the Choctaw have joined a number of regional and national American Indian organizations such as NASA (Native American Sports Association) and U.S.E.T. (United South and Eastern Tribes), while the Chahta Alla Youth

Council meets with American Indian youth groups across the country. Family vacations often include visits to other tribes throughout the country, particularly the Southwest. Dream catchers, Navajo quilts, and Hopi katchinas are displayed in Choctaw homes alongside tribal arts and objects such as quilts and cane baskets. Recent narrations of prophecies continue to focus on the Choctaw, but hint at the inclusion of other American Indians.

This shift has been slow, however. Many Choctaw members are acutely aware of the tendency of non-Indians to lump all American Indians together as a single homogenous group. Bobby Joe has a pat response when white people expect him to identify with every Hollywood Indian that shows up on TV and to understand their tribal language: "If you look at German. It look like your color. It look like you. You look at the French. French is the same thing. You look at the British. The British is the same thing. But, you could not understand German. You can't understand French. And you can't understand British. But yet, skin is the same color, same color hair" (Mould 2004: 203). Hulon Willis's solution to the problem is more efficient: avoid the umbrella term altogether and just call him Choctaw.

Interracial

Choctaw men and women use race as a means of categorizing their black and white neighbors in contrast to themselves. In the process, "Choctaw" takes on racial, not just tribal, significance. Black and white are not treated equally in the oral tradition, however. While blacks do appear in more recent versions of creation stories and in warnings against intermarriage, the dominant foils for Choctaw identity are whites, who symbolize both a specific historical and contemporary racial group and mainstream U.S. government, economics, and culture more generally. Narratives recognize blacks but do little to explore the relationship between the two groups that might impact the construction of Choctaw ethnicity. Louise Wilson points out the irony and racism of such omission in her account of a prophecy her grandfather told her that warns against intermarriage.

> He said pretty soon there will be more mixed than full. I believe that now because they did a statistics down at the health center. If you go down there, I see people I've never seen before.
> And he said, "These things will be coming."
> And he said, "You see the government giving us monies for this and that? Well, all that will be taken away."

> Well, I didn't know what monies he was talking about, but I guess he was talking about the services that's being provided, or the health care that's being provided or I know the welfare program, the social services used to have welfare given out. And all of these things, maybe that's what he was talking about.
>
> But he said, "You'll see these people doing that."
>
> And I thought, I did have a girl, a black friend when I was in Ohio, when I lived up there. I often wondered why, when I came back here, why are people so against black people?
>
> The white people, they [Choctaw] are not as against as much. In fact they bowed to them more. Even ones as poor as we were, Choctaws looked at them as higher.
>
> It was prejudice. Non-Indians treated them [blacks] differently. We were out in the fields together, helping each other to some extent.
>
> But still, my grandfather said you can be friends but no interrelations with them. We need to stay pure blood.

The prejudice against blacks extends to the Choctaw, many of whom adopted their view of blacks from whites and continue to harbor strong bias (see Kidwell 1986: 87). The rationale behind this bias reflects the assumption of a biracial South, as many Choctaw have worried that too close an affiliation with blacks would open them to the same virulent discrimination.

In her narrative, Louise Wilson suggests that bias *against* blacks comes in natural contrast to bias *in favor* of whites. The images of whites in the oral tradition are hardly positive, however, tending towards either wariness, scorn, or ambivalence. Where whites are unscrupulous, Choctaws are trusting. Where whites create and thereby advocate for modern convenience, Choctaws carefully and conservatively examine the trade-offs of replacing new with old, tribal with mainstream. Choctaw narrators describe respecting white technology but questioning white values. Differences in ideology are reflected in outward differences in appearance and culture, particularly in terms of language, clothing, and recreation, all visible symbols of ethnic difference.

There are, however, areas of convergence, where Choctaw identity overlaps with that of their non-Choctaw neighbors. Christianity binds these groups together. Until recently, farming has as well. For the most part, however, the oral tradition is silent on the overlaps among disparate ethnic groups. Daily life, on the other hand, reveals a Choctaw community far more similar than dissimilar to their non-Choctaw neighbors.

9.7. Storyteller and medicine woman Rosalie Steve (third row on left) and her family during a family birthday party. On the steps outside her church—Holy Rosary Indian Mission Church—in Tucker. Photo by Allyson J. Whyte.

Banaha, a mixture of corn and peas, symbolizes Choctaw ethnicity but daily meals are more likely to include biscuits, boiled vegetables, and fried chicken. While Choctaw Fair organizers work to bring American Indian music artists, the headliners are country music stars, and the daily listening regime of Choctaw youth is dominated by country, pop, and hip-hop. Stickball also serves as a clear symbol of Choctaw identity, but visit any of the Choctaw communities or attend a school event and one is far more likely to see basketball, baseball, softball, or football being played. This is not to say that ethnic identity is not expressed in daily life. Examples in the summaries above only hint at the myriad ways ethnicity is negotiated publically and privately in all aspects of life. The oral tradition, however, is more consistently conservative in how it portrays Choctaw identity, more likely to maintain ethnic divisions than to bridge them.

CONCLUSION

The Choctaw oral tradition depicts great dynamism in the construction of Choctaw ethnicity, tracking historical changes in the social, political, and economic demography of the landscape. When that change is critiqued, as it is heavily in prophetic narratives, the image is overwhelmingly bleak, marked by the loss of unique tribal customs and traditions that serve as the outward symbols of ethnic identity. The loss of those traditions therefore risks a loss of ethnic identity, the result of which is the figurative and, in some cases, literal death of the Choctaw.

Outside the oral tradition, there is a competing narrative, however, one publicized in glossy pamphlets and enacted in the lives of many tribal members today. The story describes a tribe that has gained financial wealth and stability, that is able to provide a broad range of social, medical, and educational assistance to its people. It is a tribe that, despite embracing many elements of mainstream U.S. culture, politics, and economics, continues to foster a distinct Choctaw identity, separate from their white and black neighbors as well as from other American Indian tribes. It is a story of gain, not loss, where four-bedroom homes and SUVs coexist with social dancing and stickball. Yet the conservative nature of the oral tradition generally, coupled with an ideology of caution woven into the fabric of prophecy specifically, poses a challenge to this narrative of compromise, adaptation, and cultural survival. In the oral tradition, mainstream culture is more often antithetical to Choctaw culture. Movies supplant social dancing, basketball supplants stickball, English supplants Choctaw.

This threat of acculturation from mainstream U.S. culture is consistently attributed to whites. In fact, other ethnic groups are generally absent in all but a few of the stories. Outside of creation stories, blacks only appear in stories that warn of intermarriage, a clear but singular threat to Choctaw ethnicity. Other American Indian tribes are only beginning to appear in the most recent versions of apocalyptic prophecies, but pose no threat to Choctaw identity at all. While fears of devolution into a generic pan-Indian culture plague many small tribes in the Southeast, the Mississippi Choctaw express no such angst in their stories. This does not mean they are not aware of the threat. Many members have opposed the hosting of intertribal powwows on the reservation because it risks blurring Choctaw culture with Plains Indian cultures. During the Choctaw Fair, American Indian arts and crafts are sold in a separate building from the swamp cane baskets, dolls, and beadwork made by Choctaw artists. For the Choctaw, ethnicity is based primarily at the level of the tribe, with broader American Indian identity emerging as a distant second. This tribally based ethnicity is contrasted most heavily with other racial groups, raising tribal identity to the broader category of race.

The most common vehicles for expressing Choctaw ethnicity are visible customs transformed into powerful symbols. Language is the most prominent, followed by clothing, social dancing, stickball, baskets, and medicine. Each of these symbols encodes ideologies and values that the Choctaw believe are integral to cultural survival.[30] Occasionally those values are made explicit, as when Odie Mae Anderson narrates a prophecy and critiques the introduction of day cares that supplant intergenerational child care so important to developing close family connections and respect for the elders. As often, however, these symbols operate directly as explicit manifestations of Choctaw ethnicity, allowing individuals to define the exact nature of ethnic identity for themselves. Ethnic identity will continue to shift temporally, regionally, and individually, as Choctaw people negotiate group identity in the context of new neighbors, new technologies, new trends, and new challenges. New generations of Choctaw will continue to declare their identity through stories as well as through tribally specific dances, sports, cooking and arts, declaring implicitly through them all: *Chahta siyah ókih.*

NOTES

1. The eight communities are: Bogue Chitto, Bogue Homa, Conehatta, Crystal Ridge, Pearl River, Red Water, Standing Pine, and Tucker. Crystal Ridge only recently received representation on the tribal council. There are also Choctaw communities in Ocean Springs near the southern border of Mississippi along the Gulf Coast and just across state lines to the north in Henning, Tennessee. Neither of these communities has tribal council representation, however.

2. Many American Indian people who avoided removal and stayed in the Southeast were forced to assimilate to survive. Government policies and laws restricted their ability to retain land and practice their customs and traditions. Today, many southeastern tribes are working to revive tribal traditions after generations of disuse. For a discussion of these efforts, see Paredes 1992, Sider 2003, and Williams 1979.

3. The designation "The Five Civilized Tribes" of the Southeast has been in use at least since the middle of the nineteenth century. The Removal Act of 1830 included these five tribes, all of whom had been allies with the new U.S. government and had been relatively open to adapting much of the technology of white colonists. The term continues to be used, particularly in Oklahoma where all five tribes have reservation lands.

4. Identity established in contrast to another group is regularly referred to as differential identity, a term coined and explicated by Richard Bauman in 1971, responding to the general assumption that folk groups and folklore is primarily a function of shared identity. A classic example of how identity can be constructed in direct opposition to another group can be found in Keith Basso's study of Apache jokes about white men

(1979). The image of the white man that emerges in these jokes has less to do with traits observed in white people than with traits Apache men believe members of their group *do not* or *should not* exhibit. If Apache people are reserved in their social greetings, white people are portrayed as outrageously forward. If Apaches value restraint in discussing health, whites are lampooned for constantly asking "How are you?" and "How are you feeling?" The critique may be accurate but it is also incomplete, focusing solely on traits that stand in opposition to Apache views of group identity.

5. Alan Dundes points out that folklore, such as a community's oral traditions, is a central tool for the creation and negotiation of identity: "Folklore is not simply a way of obtaining available data about identity for social scientists. It is actually one of the principal means by which an individual and a group discovers or establishes his or its identity" (1983: 259).

6. Versions of the migration myth include stories recorded by Wright (1828: 214), Gideon Lincecum (1861: 13), J. F. H. Claiborne (1964 [1880]: 483–484), Horatio B. Cushman, who published one version collected from missionaries who heard the story in 1820 (1899: 18–21) and another told by Israel Folsom (1899: 298–300), Henry S. Halbert from Peter Folsom via James Welch (1894: 215–216 and 1899: 228), Jack Gregory and Rennard Strickland (1972), Willard Keith Bacon from "a tribal elder" (1973: 2–3), Cynthia Thompson from John Hunter Thompson (1980), Tom Mould from Terry Ben (1996).

7. The version of the story Summer Saunders read was adapted by Nell Rogers for a longer performance dramatizing the history of the Choctaw nation in Mississippi. It most closely resembles the version recorded by Henry S. Halbert (1894, 1899).

8. The preferred orthography for the Choctaw language has shifted over the years. The text that Summer Saunders read from uses an older orthography that attempts to translate Choctaw sounds with English characters rather than diacritical marks and was spelled *Chahta siyah hoka"*. I have employed the current orthography in the text, thanks to the help of Curtis "Buck" Willis, Jr., at the Choctaw Tribal Language Program.

9. In 1896, Henry S. Halbert wrote: "There is hope for a people having such pride of race as the Choctaws, which they often evince by the expression 'Chahta sia hokat,' 'I am Choctaw'"(1895b: 540).

10. Halbert published the story in 1899 (229–230) and again two years later in 1901 (269–270). Since then the emergence myth has been recorded by David I. Bushnell from Pisatuntema (1910: 526), John R. Swanton from Olman Comby (1928: 1), and by Tom Mould from Terry Ben (1996) and Melford Farve (1997).

11. Despite the inaccuracy of the concept of race, the term continues to be used throughout the Choctaw community. I have chosen to adhere to native terms rather than introduce a more accurate term such as "interethnic."

12. A note about the transcriptions: all of the stories I collected are verbatim transcriptions from audio recordings. Accordingly, ellipses indicate pauses before a change of narrative direction, often after a false start, and not omitted words. Stories collected by other people in the past reflect each collector's distinct process for recording and transcription.

13. Charlie Denson did in fact join the army. He comments elsewhere that his grandfather was a medicine man and prophet. When he comments a few lines later that "my grandpa told me that," it carries the weight of prophecy.

14. "Indian Country" is a widespread term that maps culture as geography. Indian Country is generally not a specific place, though some use it to refer strictly to reservation land. More often, Indian Country encompasses all American Indians and issues relevant to indigenous peoples. Two of the largest national American Indian newspapers use the term in their title: *Indian Country Today* and *News from Indian Country*.

15. The use of alcohol to grease negotiations appears frequently in the historical record. J. H. Claiborne is particularly blunt in his assessment of the Choctaw in the nineteenth century whom he assesses were all too willing to barter away their possessions for whiskey (Claiborne 1844: 1–2, 5, cited in Kidwell 1986: 77). See also the more recent oral tradition (e.g., Mould 2004: 155–156).

16. The World Championship of Stickball is played every year during the annual fair, an event that draws a heavily Choctaw audience, scheduled late into the night after most non-Choctaw visitors have gone home. While stickball is almost entirely relegated to this one event each year, it remains a well-recognized symbol of Choctaw culture and identity. Stickball sticks are often proudly displayed in the homes of players, miniature stickball sticks hang from car rearview mirrors, and crossed stickball sticks are prominently displayed in the Choctaw tribal seal. Although women have begun to play the sport as well, the majority of the attention is given to the men who play the hard-hitting game as an explicit act of masculine, ethnic identity. Recently, some young men have reached back and evoked stickball players of the past by either tying horse tails to their waists as depicted in the famous and frequently reproduced painting by George Catlin of stickball player Tullok-chish-ko, translated as "he who drinks the juice of the stone" (1965 [1841]: 124) or painting their faces.

17. The story of Bogue Chitto saving stickball may reflect some degree of temporal condensation since the communities with formal designation today did not emerge on the Mississippi landscape until the twentieth century, yet the story reflects a missionary zeal more similar to the nineteenth century.

18. The primary blame can be laid on the shoulders of William Ward, the agent assigned to transmit applications for allotment to the War Department. He was by most accounts an incompetent drunkard who simply did not do the work assigned him. Another reason so few Choctaw received their land, however, was that some were afraid to register, fearing a trick to remove them from Mississippi once and for all. In the end, many of those who did receive their allotment lost it to unscrupulous land speculators.

19. Historically, the Choctaw were a matrilineal, exogamous tribe structured according to two moieties, each with between six and eight clans (see Swanton 1931: 55–84). While distinct clan identity is no longer recognized, exogamy outside one's community continues to be a concern, with some parents encouraging their children to date *across* communities rather than *within* them.

20. Bogue Chitto is regularly cited among tribal members today as the most traditional of the Choctaw communities, though Conehatta is often mentioned as well (this was true a few decades ago also; see Thompson and Peterson 1975: 189). Language surveys conducted in 1990 and 1997 suggest that Conehatta has a slightly higher percentage of fluent Choctaw speakers than Bogue Chitto (Fortune 1997b: 47). In both communities, older members of the community continue to speak the language, some of the oldest women continue to wear traditional Choctaw dresses on a daily basis rather

than for ceremonial occasions only, and people are more likely to cook under outdoor arbors than in other communities.

21. Okla Falaya translates as Long People, Okla Tannap as People of the Opposite Side, and Okla Hannali as the People of Six Towns. Although most agree on three primary areas, John R. Swanton argues that attention to town classifications suggests we must consider these areas as four distinct groups, adding a central group called Okla Chito, the Big People (1931: 55–56).

22. The Creek War of 1813 began after the Shawnee leader Tecumseh traveled through the Southeast attempting to form an Indian confederacy to fight against encroaching whites. The Choctaw refused, but the neighboring Creek took up arms and attacked Fort Mims in Alabama Territory. War ensued, with many Choctaw and Chickasaw aiding the U.S. Army. If Thompson's story references this period in history, then his description of whites helping Choctaws is likely inverted.

23. See versions recorded by John R. Swanton from Olman Comby (1928: 16) Gregory Keyes and Ken Carleton from Gus Comby (1990), and Tom Mould from Hulon Willis (2004: xxvii–xxx).

24. Animal stories deserve greater attention in understanding the construction of Choctaw identity. However, because of limited space, I must restrict my analysis to more explicit narratives of humans interacting with humans.

25. I have edited this story for clarity. Gladys Willis originally translated the question Ashman asks as "What's your name?" A few sentences later, she realizes her mistake, and retranslates the phrase as "Where are you from?" The unedited version is printed in *Choctaw Tales* (2004: 180). The portion I cut out fits between "... this Choctaw asked him ..." and "Where are you from?" and runs as follows: " ... this Choctaw asked him, 'What's your name?' I mean, in English it's 'What's your name'—'Katah chihohchifo,' akmąno. 'What you say?' 'Where are you from?' really. The Choctaw asked the white man ..."

26. Statistics compiled by the Choctaw Tribal Language Program show a dramatic drop in fluency in the language. In 1997, a survey of Choctaw language use by elders fifty-eight years old or older showed that 95 percent were fluent, 2.5 percent could speak "somewhat," and 2.2 percent could speak "hardly" (Fortune 1997a: 19). Three years later when the youth were surveyed, only 1 percent of four-to-five-year-olds were fluent, 7 percent had limited use, and 92 percent were nonspeakers ("Choctaw Language to be lost by 2005, According to Test Scores," *Choctaw Community News*, December 2000, 29 (7): 5).

27. Such polarizing politics are common in American Indian tribal politics historically as well as today. For a historical case study, the internal battles between factions often labeled traditionalist and assimilationist are well documented among the Cherokee in the lead-up to removal. The long-running struggle between the self-proclaimed Traditionalist Movement and the non-Traditonalists among the Hopi provide an equally instructive case study today.

28. "Mixed-blood" can have a negative connotation, though it remains in wide use in local communities. The term is also used in scholarly literature, though "biracial" or "multiracial" are increasingly chosen as more neutral terms. In an effort to avoid confusion and reflect the language of the historical documents and eras I am referencing as well as that of contemporary Choctaw, I have chosen to use the term "mixed-blood."

29. In 1975, Thompson and Peterson argued that "[o]lder Choctaws have probably never met any Indians other than Choctaws. For them, there is no word in Choctaw

that means Indian" (189). Younger members of the tribe are increasingly aware of other American Indians thanks to the mass media, the rise of intertribal powwows, and travel (189–190). The authors stress that Indian identity is not replacing tribal identity.

30. Edward Spicer notes those symbols have a logic within the culture if not among each constituent element: "A relationship between human individuals and selected cultural elements—the symbols—is the essential feature of a collective identity system ... In addition to land and language symbols, common constituents of identity systems are music, dances, and heroes. What makes a system out of identity symbols is not any logical, in the sense of rational, relationship among them. The meanings that they have fit into a complex that is significant to the people concerned. The meanings amount to a self-definition and an image of themselves as they have performed in the course of their history" (1971: 796, 798).

SOURCES CITED

Bacon, Willard Keith. 1973. Legends of Nanih Waiya. *Nanih Waiya* 1 (1):2–3.
Basso, Keith H. 1979. *Portraits of the "Whiteman": Linguistic Play and Cultural Symbols Among the Western Apache.* Cambridge: Cambridge University Press.
Bauman, Richard. 1971. Differential Identity and the Social Base of Folklore. *Journal of American Folklore* 84 (331):31–41.
Bushnell, David I., Jr. 1909. The Choctaw of Bayou Lacomb, St. Tammany Parish, Louisiana. Bulletin 48, Bureau of American Ethnology. Washington, D.C: Smithsonian Institution.
———.1910. Myths of the Louisiana Choctaw. *American Anthropologist* 12:526–35.
Campbell, Gregory R., and S. Neyooxet Greymorning. 2007. What's in a Label? Native American Identity and the Rise of a Tradition of Racism. In *American Indian Nations: Yesterday, Today, and Tomorrow*, edited by G. P. Horse Capture, D. Champagne, and C. C. Jackson. Lanham, MD: AltaMira Press.
Catlin, George. 1965 [1841]. *Letters and Notes on the Manners, Customs, and Condition of the North American Indians, Volume II.* Minneapolis: Ross & Haines, Inc.
Churchill, Ward. 2004. *Kill the Indian, Save the Man: The Genocidal Impact of American Indian Residential Schools.* San Francisco: City Lights.
Claiborne, John F. H. 1844. *Memorial,* 28th Congress, 1st session, February 19. H. Doc. 137.
———.1964 [1880]. *Mississippi as a Province, Territory and State.* Baton Rouge: Louisiana State University Press.
Cushman, Horatio B. 1962 [1899]. *History of the Choctaw, Chickasaw, and Natchez Indians.* Oklahoma: Redlands Press of Stillwater.
Dundes, Alan. 1983. Defining Identity Through Folklore. In *Identity: Personal and Socio-Cultural,* edited by Anita Jacobson-Widding, pp. 235–61. Atlantic Highlands: Humanities Press, Inc.
Ellis, Clyde. 1996. *To Change Them Forever: Indian Education at the Rainy Mountain Boarding School, 1893–1920.* Norman: University of Oklahoma Press.
Fortune, Jimmie C. 1997a. Mississippi Band of Choctaw Indians, a Tribute to the Choctaw Elders: A Demographic Profile: 1997. Blacksburg: Mississippi Band of Choctaw Indians.

———. 1997b. Mississippi Band of Choctaw Indians, Demographic Census. Blacksburg: Mississippi Band of Choctaw Indians.

Galloway, Patricia. 1995. *Choctaw Genesis: 1500–1700*. Lincoln: University of Nebraska Press.

Gregory, Jack, and Rennard Strickland. 1972. *Choctaw Spirit Tales: Tribal Folklore, Legend and Myth*. Oklahoma: Indian Heritage Association.

Halbert, Henry Sales. 1894. A Choctaw Migration Legend. *American Antiquarian and Oriental Journal* 16:215–16.

———. 1895a. The Choctaw Robin Goodfellow. *American Antiquarian and Oriental Journal* 17:157.

———. 1895b. The Indians in Mississippi and Their Schools. In *Biennial Report of the State Superintendent of Public Education to the Legislature of Mississippi, for Scholastic Years 1893–94 and 1894–95*, pp. 534–45. Jackson: Clarion-Ledger Printing Establishment.

———. 1899. Nanih Waiya, the Sacred Mound of the Choctaw. *Mississippi Historical Society*, pp. 223–34.

———. 1901. The Choctaw Creation Legend. *Mississippi Historical Society*, 4:267–70.

Hudson, Charles. 1976. *The Southeastern Indians*. Knoxville: The University of Tennessee Press.

Kidwell, Clara Sue. 1986. Choctaw Land and Identity, 1830–1919. In *After Removal: The Choctaws in Mississippi*, edited by Samuel J. Wells and Roseanna Tubby, pp. 64–93. Jackson: University Press of Mississippi.

Lincecum, Gideon. 1861. *Traditional History of the Chahta Nation*. Unpublished manuscript housed in the University of Texas Library.

McKee, Jesse O., and Jon A. Schlenker. 1980. *The Choctaws: Cultural Evolution of a Native American Tribe*. Jackson: University Press of Mississippi.

Nanih Waiya. 1975. Waggoner [Wagoner] Amos Tells Us a Story. 3 (1):21–24.

Paredes, J. Anthony. 1992. *Indians of the Southeastern United States in the Late 20th Century*. Tuscaloosa: University of Alabama Press.

Peterson, John H., Jr. 1972. Assimilation, Separation, and Out-Migration in an American Indian Group. *American Anthropologist* 74 (5):1286–95.

Prucha, Francis Paul. 1979. *The Churches and the Indian Schools, 1888–1912*. Lincoln: University of Nebraska Press.

Sider, Gerald M. 2003. *Living Indian Histories: Lumbee and Tuscarora People in North Carolina*. Chapel Hill: University of North Carolina Press.

Spicer, Edward H. 1971. Persistent Cultural Systems: A Comparative Study of Identity Systems that Can Adapt to Contrasting Environments. *Science* 174 (4011):795–800.

Swanton, John R. 1928. Choctaw Stories from Olman Comby, in English. Smithsonian Institution, National Anthropological Archives, Bureau of American Ethnology Manuscript Collection, 4132-b. Washington, D.C.

———. 1931. *Source Material for the Social and Ceremonial Life of the Choctaw Indians*. Bulletin 103. Bureau of American Ethnology. Washington D.C.: Smithsonian Institution.

Thompson, Bobby, and John H. Peterson, Jr. 1975. Mississippi Choctaw Identity: Genesis and Change. In *The New Ethnicity: Perspectives from Ethnology*, edited by J. W. Bennett. St. Paul: West Pub. Co.

Thompson, Cynthia. 1979–80. John Hunter Thompson on Things [interview with John Hunter Thompson]. *Nanih Waiya* 7 (1–2):25–31.
Tinker, George E. 2004. *Spirit and Resistance: Political Theology and American Indian Liberation*. Minneapolis: Fortress Press.
Tubby, Vernon. 1976. Estelline Remembers. *Nanih Waiya* 4 (1):114–18.
Wells, Samuel J. 1986. The Role of Mixed-Bloods in Mississippi Choctaw History. In *After Removal: The Choctaw in Mississippi*, edited by S. J. Wells and R. Tubby. Jackson: University Press of Mississippi.
Williams, Walter L. 1979. *Southeastern Indians since the Removal Era*. Athens: University of Georgia Press.
Wright, Alfred. 1828. Choctaws: Religious Opinions, Traditions, &c. *The Missionary Herald* 24:178–216.

INTERVIEWS

Allen, Sally [with Judy Billie and Regina Shoemake]. Interviewed by Tom Mould and Curtis Willis on June 3, 1997.
Amos, Billy. Interviewed by Tom Mould on August 1, 1999.
Amos, Wagonner. 1975. Interviewed by staff of *Nanih Waiya*. Published *Nanih Waiya* 3 (1):21–24.
Anderson, Odie [with Jeffie Solomon]. Interviewed by Tom Mould, Glenda Williamson, and Meriva Williamson on August 12, 1997.
Ben, Terry. Interviewed by Tom Mould and Rae Nell Vaughn on May 30, 1996.
Billie, Judy [with Sally Allen and Regina Shoemake]. Interviewed by Tom Mould and Curtis Willis on June 3, 1997.
Comby, Gus. Interviewed by Gregory Keyes and Ken Carleton on December 16, 1990.
Comby, Harold. Interviewed by Tom Mould and Liasha Alex on June 4, 1997.
Denson, Charlie [with Carmen Denson, Calvin Isaac, and Drain Sockey]. Interviewed by Tom Mould on March 12, 1996.
Farve, Melford. Interviewed by Tom Mould on July 10, 1997.
Gibson, Lillie. Interviewed by Tom Mould, Glenda Williamson, and Meriva Williamson on August 5, 1997.
Henry, Inez. Interviewed by Geri Harm on February 20, 1986, and October 28, 1988.
Joe, Bobby. Interviewed by Tom Mould on July 30, 1999.
John, Grady. Interviewed by Tom Mould on February 22, 1998; July 17, 1999; and January 15, 2000.
Polk, Harry. Storytelling session at Choctaw Language Immersion Camp recorded by Tom Mould and Liasha Alex on July 1, 1997.
Shoemake, Regina [with Sally Allen and Judy Billie]. Interviewed by Tom Mould and Curtis Willis on June 3, 1997.
Thompson, John Hunter. Interviewed by Cynthia Thompson in 1979. Published in *Nanih Waiya* 7 (1–2):25–31.
Tubby, Estelline. Interviewed by Vernon Tubby in 1976. Published in *Nanih Waiya* 4 (1):114–18.

Tubby, Estelline. Interviewed by Tom Mould on May 31, 1996; August 5, 1997, July 19, 1999; and July 22, 1999.
Vaughn, Harley. Interviewed by Tom Mould on May 31, 1997.
Willis, Gladys. Interviewed by Tom Mould and Rae Nell Vaughn on May 23, 1996.
Willis, Gladys. Interviewed by Tom Mould on August 6, 1997.
Willis, Hulon. Interviewed by Tom Mould on May 27, 1996.
Willis, Linda. Interviewed by Tom Mould on January 7, 2000.
Wilson, Louise. Interviewed by Tom Mould and Danielle Dan on June 10, 1997.
Wilson, Louise. Interviewed by Tom Mould on July 29, 1999, and January 11, 2000.
York, Jake. Storytelling session at Choctaw Language Immersion Camp recorded by Tom Mould and Liasha Alex on July 29, 1997.

SECTION III

Local Changes, Global Forces

The four groups discussed in this section have each become a presence in Mississippi since World War II, most as recently as the 1970s or 1980s. The Latino population, for example, has seen most of its increase only since the 1990s with a boom in growth following Hurricane Katrina, despite long ties between Latino countries and the ports of Mississippi and despite early history of workers from Texas and Mexico in the Delta. The movement of these new populations into Mississippi is linked to global migration patterns as well as Mississippi's growing ties to global communication (the Internet), globalized markets, and an increasingly attractive economy for outsiders.

These groups share with immigrants before them their ability to recognize economic opportunities and to fill market niches. For example, many Vietnamese were initially shrimpers or worked in the seafood industry. In the 1990s, many Latinos were drawn to the state to work in the poultry industry and after Katrina came to help rebuild the coast. Many immigrants from India came as professionals (physicians and engineers), but others from India found another economic niche operating small hotels throughout the state. The Mississippi they came to admits for more categories of identity than in the past. They come into a state in a time of changing social and economic structure and face challenges different from those who came before.

—*Editor*

10

THE VIETNAMESE IN MISSISSIPPI

—VY THUC DAO

INTRODUCTION

The Vietnamese who first arrived along the gulf shores of southern Mississippi were no strangers to difficult times and rough transitions. Having arrived as refugees from their native country during the middle 1970s, they had established a place for themselves in the humid, warm coastal areas that reminded them of their native land. Over time, they built homes, formed businesses, raised families, and became part of the larger fabric of Mississippi. Their steady engagement with the difficulties of migration and settlement provided a sense of pride and confidence for the Vietnamese. Yet, in the closing months of 2005, it is this same community that found their resilience tested by two significant, disturbing events: intense global competition against Vietnamese fishermen who had been supplying fresh seafood to the United States increasingly since the early 1990s, and the sudden catastrophic landfall of Hurricane Katrina in August of 2005.

Those living in communities along the Gulf Coast cities of Pascagoula, Gulfport, and Biloxi watched helplessly as Hurricane Katrina leveled their homes and transformed once-vibrant neighborhood streets into jumbled lanes of collapsed rubble. The storm brutalized Vietnamese shrimpers by destroying their boats and effectively canceling a productive shrimping season. While the swift, singular upheaval of a hurricane wiped out many of the Vietnamese quickly, the Mississippi community itself had already been struggling with an economic downturn within their community.

By the time Katrina hit, the core of the Vietnamese economy, shrimping, was in serious trouble. In 1991 the city of Biloxi, home to Mississippi's most populous region of Vietnamese, voted to permit offshore gambling. By 2005, nine casinos had been built, many of them encroaching on areas heavily populated by the Vietnamese. The result was that the Vietnamese found they were paying higher property prices and that new land purchases were now beyond their means (Le 2006). At the same time, competition from foreign markets made shrimping less profitable for the Vietnamese. Beginning in the late 1990s and escalating annually, enormous quantities of cheap, quality shrimp from foreign countries flooded the U.S. market and drove the price of domestic shrimp to record low levels (Cleveland 2003). As a result, American shrimping interests fell to less than 10 percent of the industry worldwide. Vietnamese shrimpers in Mississippi, who currently own approximately three-quarters of the fishing boats in the state, found that they were in direct competition with seafood powerhouses from China, South America, and, ironically, the country of Vietnam (USDA, GAIN Report 2007).

In the first case of calamity, the hurricane's destruction of homes along the Gulf Coast instantly transformed some Vietnamese residents who had arrived in the United States as political refugees into refugees once again. In the case of the changing economic world, Vietnamese American shrimpers today are locked into competition with their counterparts on the other side of the world, in a country that had once been their homeland.

Clearly, the story of the Vietnamese people in Mississippi is punctuated with such themes of revolving fortunes, twists of fate, and surprising turns of social, economic, and political situations. Currently, the number of people who identify themselves as Vietnamese or of Vietnamese descent in Mississippi is estimated at 4,835 (2006 American Community Survey). Prior to the storm, the 2000 census reported a population of 5,387 Vietnamese residents with the most concentrated communities located in the southern Mississippi areas of Biloxi, D'Iberville, and Gulfport (see Table 10.1). In order to ascertain how much population decline occurred after Hurricane Katrina, it is most useful to compare American Community Data estimates from 2004, the year before the storm, with the 2006 American Community Survey projected estimate of 4,835 people living in the area. In spite of poststorm population reductions, prestorm census figures had shown strong growth through three decades in the state.

These steady increases in the Mississippi Vietnamese have had a significant impact upon the commercial and cultural fabric of the state. In the minds of many nonresidents and casual observers of the South, and even to some locals, the state of Mississippi seems to present an unbroken terrain of Anglos and African Americans punctuated with historically French, Indian, and European influences. Yet, the Vietnamese contribute meaningfully to the ethnic landscape of the state and are themselves a diverse and dynamic group.

Table 10.1: Major Areas of Settlement in Southern Mississippi of Vietnamese			
	1980	**1990**	**2000**
Biloxi	472	1,936	1,707
D'Iberville	89	126	432
Gulfport	0	109	258
Ocean Springs	158	212	215
Pass Christian	12	269	193
Long Beach	0	172	171
St. Martin	Not reported	131	355
Pascagoula	35	94	116
Waveland	0	29	65
Gautier	0	28	74
Bay St. Louis	9	10	23
TOTAL in Mississippi	1,477	3,815	5,387
TOTAL in United States	231, 120	617,747	1,212,465

United States decennial census figures for the population of Vietnamese in Mississippi

In order to better understand the intriguing story of the Vietnamese in Mississippi, it is important to recognize that it began long before their first appearance in America. The following is a brief history of how many Vietnamese first came to refugee status as the country of Vietnam struggled with internal political strife, civil war, and American military intervention.

A LONG HISTORY OF MIGRATION

For some Vietnamese, arriving in the United States marked a second or even third migration. Long before they set foot on American soil, some immigrants had lived through arduous patterns of relocation and recovery within their own country. The country of Vietnam has a long history of occupation—Mongolian invaders, Chinese occupiers, and French colonists. The French began occupying Vietnam in the mid-1800s. In 1946, decades of long-simmering tensions erupted into war. Members of the national liberation, the Viet Minh, headed by communist revolutionary Hồ Chí Minh fought French and Vietnamese National Army forces under the emperor Bảo Đại. Independence for Vietnam came for the Viet Minh after eight grueling years of fighting, at which point international agencies intervened to broker a tentative peace agreement. A cease-fire agreement required that

France grant independence to their former colony, but also required that communist forces stay in the northern part of the country.

The agreement, then, split the country into the communist-controlled North, known as the Democratic Republic of Viet Nam (DRVN) and the nationalistic South, called simply the Republic of Viet Nam (RVN). The agreement included a three-hundred-day period when people could travel between the two territories. And, while some Vietnamese uprooted themselves to travel northward, the greater part of a million North Vietnamese settled into Saigon and other southern regions (Karnow 2001).

For many, this was the first migration. Those who migrated south often believed that their religious and economic interests diverged greatly from the communist regime. Catholics, the religiously affiliated, many anticommunist intellectuals and academics, along with the prosperous and wealthy, uprooted themselves and their families to the southern districts, effectively becoming refugees in their own country (Jacobs 2004). Tensions escalated within the divided country. Beginning in 1963 and escalating into 1965, the United States started military operations, what is called the Vietnam War.

When the war ended in 1973, the United States government began a chaotic draw-down of troops and financial support. As the U.S. withdrew, the North Vietnamese gained ground and swiftly captured many cities. The takeover of these cities rippled throughout the surrounding region of villages and resulted in a second large-scale migration of over a million people. Unlike the more orderly mass migration of twenty years earlier, this movement consisted of panicked villagers fleeing the encroaching northern offensive.

On April 30, 1975, the South Vietnamese capital city of Saigon collapsed under the pressure of revolutionary forces and the first phase of U.S.-led emigration was initiated. The flight of the Vietnamese is generally divided into two phases: the early days of April 1975 prior to the fall of Saigon until the end of 1977, and then a longer period from 1978 continuing into the early 1980s (Liu, Lamanna, Maurata 1979). Naturally, a large number of middle-class and educated Vietnamese had been working closely with U.S. military forces and had become familiar with the English language and American way of life. This group of people typifies the majority of first-wave Vietnamese to leave the country in the days prior to and immediately following the fall of Saigon (Herring 2001).

Two weeks prior to Saigon's fall and into the final days of April, over 90,000 Vietnamese evacuated by helicopter as ordered by President Gerald

Ford. As noted, the majority of evacuees were American military personnel, their families, and the Vietnamese affiliated with the collaboration and support of Western organizations, corporations, and the U.S. military (Karnow 1997). A sampling of 124,457 people from the 1975 cohort of refugees reveals that over 25 percent of the sample were college and university educated while nearly 50 percent held a secondary educational background (Montero and Dieppa 1982).

An additional 35,000–45,000 people left on their own by sea on small watercraft or other means during this time. The U.S. Navy often intercepted and directed these small groups toward military bases on Guam and in the Philippines. While 130,000 Vietnamese left in the year 1975 alone, the majority of refugees arrived after 1978 and included those from Cambodia and Laos and ethnic Chinese who fled when the new Vietnamese government enacted severe economic and social policies and placed thousands of people into reeducation camps. During this second phase of flight, the refugees, better known as "boat people," began arriving in large numbers to camps in Malaysia, Singapore, and other South Asian areas.

FINDING A PLACE IN AMERICA

Up until 1975 American cities had seen very few Vietnamese faces. During the late 1960s, the number of Vietnamese speakers in the United States was estimated to be only three thousand (Rumbaut 2007). That figure would rapidly increase as more and more Vietnamese arrived. The U.S. government expressed a major practical concern that so many refugees arriving at once would quickly settle in one or two major cities, and with their limited economic means would quickly create urban ghettos by crowding into a handful of metropolitan areas.

The government's plan then was to widely disperse the refugees throughout the nation. Charitable agencies, like Catholic Conference, became responsible for finding sponsorship for each Vietnamese family through churches, businesses, or individual families. In this way, over 130,000 Vietnamese were dispersed throughout the country in all fifty states (Do 1999). Despite the best efforts to conscientiously distribute refugees evenly in all states in 1975, the 1990 census estimates that over half of all Vietnamese resided in the state of California; by 2006, this figure was estimated at over 60 percent (American Community Survey). These

Table 10.2: Major Consolidated Metropolitan Statistics Areas (CMSAs) and Metropolitan Statistics Areas (MSAs) of Vietnamese Settlement; Census 2000

1. CALIFORNIA: Los Angeles-Riverside-Orange County	233,573
2. CALIFORNIA: San Francisco-Oakland-San Jose	146,613
3. TEXAS: Houston-Galveston-Brazoria	63,924
4. MARYLAND/D.C.: Washington, D.C.-Hagerstown-Baltimore, DC-MD-VA	47,423
5. TEXAS: Dallas-Fort Worth	47,090
6. WASHINGTON: Seattle-Tacoma-Bremerton	40,001
7. CALIFORNIA: San Diego (MSA)	33,504
8. MASSACHUSETTS: Boston-Worcester-Lawrence	32,792
9. NEW YORK/NEW JERSEY/PENNSYLVANIA/CONNECTICUT: New York-Northern New Jersey-Long Island	26,998
10. GEORGIA: Atlanta (MSA)	23,986

concentrated communities were created through secondary migration, which occurred as the refugees began to favor some states over others. In addition to this voluntary migration, people from Vietnam gained the right to petition to be reunited with family members who had been resettled in the United States. In this manner, many tens of thousands of Vietnamese were brought together once again.

The first groups who left Vietnam were surely refugees upon arrival to the United States, but very quickly demonstrated voluntary migration behavior as they sought to reunite with families, establish social and occupational networks, and patronize businesses that offered Vietnamese goods and services. As these settlers gradually achieved their primary objective of economic stability, they also found that their groupings had begun to coalesce into natural communities. In time, these communities will become the preferred sites for secondary migrations.

In Table 10.2, we can see how today the Vietnamese have largely settled into the following major metropolitan areas and have often developed highly visible, distinctive enclaves known as "Vietnam Towns." For states in the South, Vietnamese communities began to form most rigorously in the states of Texas, Louisiana, Oklahoma, and Florida. The first Vietnamese in Mississippi, then, arrived as a result of prescribed, sponsored settlement. Later-arriving Vietnamese came because of job opportunities, the need to be reunited with family, and the desire to be close to a growing, recognizable Vietnamese community.

THE VIETNAMESE IN MISSISSIPPI

The first Vietnamese families in Mississippi arrived in April 1975, most likely having evacuated during the weeks prior to the collapse of Saigon, or in the company of the nearly two thousand orphaned children evacuated during that same time period. In the state, newspaper accounts from late April 1975 indicate that over fifty refugee families had arrived in central Mississippi and were awaiting placement. During the years between 1975 and 1980, the majority of reports focused upon the stories of settlement and assignment of refugees in various cities across the state. Human interest stories such as "'Boat family' harbored safely now in Meridian" from 1979, or "Vicksburg gets special Christmas gift from Vietnam" from the same year typify the accounts regarding the Mississippi Vietnamese during this time.[1]

Families typically were placed in apartments while individuals might reside temporarily with sponsoring families, often associated with a local church. In short order, male heads of households would be employed, children would be enrolled in school, and families would receive outreach visits. In some areas, local high schools or community colleges would organize small language laboratories or English classes for adults. Otherwise many Vietnamese relief or sponsoring agencies would arrange for informal English tutoring.

It is estimated that in this manner, over fifteen hundred Vietnamese settled in Mississippi from 1975 to 1980 with the majority living in southern Mississippi[2]. Newspaper accounts report that the population rapidly swelled from twelve hundred in 1980 to twenty-three hundred by June of 1983.[3] Population growth continued at a slightly more subdued pace with a reported three thousand by 1987. However, the addition of over three thousand new residents caused considerable impact upon local schools, employment, social services, and community structures of worship.

Vietnamese Children in School

In response to the greater numbers of Vietnamese in Mississippi, the state reclassified fisherman as agricultural migrants and the children became eligible for migrant education programs. By 1977, Mississippi school districts received 2 million dollars to address the needs of 5,535 migrant students, of which approximately 1,000 were children of fishermen—mostly Vietnamese—and the funding grew over time.[4] Vietnamese children in Harrison,

Hancock, and Jackson counties became earmarked for migrant language programs due to their limited language proficiency. Of the roughly 750 children of all agricultural workers in the state of Mississippi in 1981, nearly half were Vietnamese students and had been enrolled in these school programs, which emphasized English acquisition, tutorials, and intensive content instruction in order to quickly streamline children into regular classes.[5] It would be interesting to compare the trajectory of these 1st, 1.5, and 2nd generation Vietnamese children during the 1980s with the settlement of a more recent migration group, Latinos.

These Vietnamese students soon impressed elementary and high school teachers with two distinguishing features—their rapidly growing numbers in the classroom and a zealous dedication to excelling in school. At Howard II Elementary School, the percentage of students who were Vietnamese soared from 3 to 41 percent from 1975 to 1983; by 1987, Vietnamese students comprised 10 percent of the Biloxi school system, and hundreds divided themselves among schools in Long Beach, Pass Christian, Ocean Springs, Gulfport, Gautier, and Pascagoula.[6] In general, teachers and administrators expressed glowing, perhaps effusive, sentiments regarding the academic prowess of Vietnamese students.[7] Most impressive to many observers was the fact that within a short time period, non-English-speaking elementary school students scored consistently well in high school, often earning accolades and scholarships to universities.

Sociologists have long observed that Vietnamese children rapidly adapt to American schools and often demonstrate a high achievement. However, these achievements are complicated by unexpected findings. Some researchers find that these children and adolescents face enormous challenges in everything from practical matters of language acquisition to more abstract negotiations of ethnic identity and acculturation issues. They find that while Vietnamese children show facility in schoolwork performance, they also demonstrate lower rates of self-esteem and a more pessimistic view of their future (Portes and Rumbaut 2001).

This reveals a paradox for educational researchers who usually correlate high self-esteem and optimism with higher academic achievement (Searle and Ward 1990). Further, zealous narratives of student "success stories" by teachers, students, and their family members often stymie seriously underperforming students who may suffer silently rather than risk embarrassment by expressing their need for academic support and help (Lee 1994). For many Asians, the notion that school success may serve as both a liberating resource and an oppressive device has been hotly contested and taken up as a central issue for many race and stratification scholars (Yang 2004).

To date, no one has studied these questions in Mississippi and so we do not know if Mississippi Vietnamese students also suffer from the high achievement/low self-esteem paradox.

Faith and Religion: Community Builders

One of the major voluntary agencies involved in refugee settlement had been the United States Catholic Conference due to the large numbers of Vietnamese Catholics. In 1979, the Catholic Diocese of Biloxi received a grant from the U.S. Department of Health to administer social services to the burgeoning community of eight hundred refugees.[8] The population grew such that by 1983, St. Michael's Catholic Church had eight hundred members in their congregation alone. In 1997, the city of D'Iberville opened the first Vietnamese parish in the state on land donated by the Biloxi diocese, the Vietnamese Martyrs Catholic Church. Both Catholic and Buddhist institutions thrive. In fact, the Vietnamese Buddhist Congregation, with its Chua Van Duc Temple, is located on Oak Street next to the Vietnamese Martyrs Catholic Church. Both congregations were damaged in Katrina, and by cruel coincidence the temple had celebrated the opening of its new building the day before the storm made landfall.

The churches are important because research of Vietnamese communities in neighboring Louisiana has found that that ethnic church attendance helps Vietnamese adolescents adjust and achieve in school and society. Church attendance seems to promote a supportive network and foster a positive ethnic identity. Vietnamese teenagers, then, receive encouragement toward high scholastic achievement and receive a cultural buffering against negative or overwhelming pitfalls associated with rapid acculturation.

Heading South Toward the Gulf

Attracted by the warm coastal climate, many Vietnamese found that areas along the Gulf Coast reminded them of their native country's weather. For some, the idea of working in the fishing industry, even in a tangential manner with oyster shucking and shrimp-picking duties, held great appeal.[9] Some refugees came into the United States with considerable fishing and seamanship skills, if little else, and gravitated toward southern Mississippi. Some agencies and governmental officials had hoped to capitalize on the congruence between the skill sets of Vietnamese refugees who had seafaring and fishing backgrounds with seafood companies who were in need of labor (Starr 1981). Few could have predicted, however, the enormous, perhaps even dominating, impact that the Vietnamese would have on the shrimping industries all along the Gulf Coast areas of Texas, Louisiana, Alabama, and Florida. Over 65 percent of the Vietnamese who live in Mississippi reside in southern Mississippi Gulf Coast areas.

THE VIETNAMESE IN BILOXI

The number of Vietnamese reported to have settled along the Gulf Coast doubled from 1975 to 1983, from roughly twelve hundred to nearly twenty-four hundred. During this time former refugees who had initially settled elsewhere began to gravitate toward Mississippi of their own accord, drawn by news that the local oyster and seafood plants were in need of workers. Quickly, these Vietnamese began the grueling, heavy work of oyster shucking and shrimp picking and found that a reasonable living could be made as a factory worker. Word of mouth spread among families and soon kinship groups developed around the cluster of seafood processing factories of Back Bay and Point Cadet. What did these Vietnamese settlers experience when they first arrived to work and live in the city that once billed itself as the "seafood capital of the world"?

Immigrants and the Mississippi Seafood Industry

In Biloxi, they are actually the third major group of immigrants to work closely with the seafood industry. In fact, many even settled into the same patterns of location and employment as those who came before them. During the first half of the nineteenth century, Biloxi cultivated a glowing, if sedate, reputation as a resort coastal city where cosmopolitan families in the South vacationed. Numerous beachfront attractions and grand hotels catered to the resort-minded tourists, and the abundant availability of fresh seafood had been an enticing amenity (Husley 2000). It was only in the second half of the century that Biloxi put forth a concerted effort to build a sustainable economic engine through the harvesting, processing, and shipping of Gulf Coast shrimp and oyster sources. Another chapter of this book details the unique ethnic history of Biloxi, which included the Polish, French Cajuns, Croats, Serbians, and Slavonians. Here we note that, like many other ethnic groups, the Vietnamese were drawn by their own fishing abilities and by economic opportunities. Within a short time, some Vietnamese who had made their livelihood from the sea began to pool monies and resources to strike out with their own fishing boats. In this way, many of these Vietnamese fishermen who had arrived with considerable fishing and seamanship backgrounds began to attract negative and even hostile attention from established Biloxian fishermen.

Gutierrez (1984) describes how the Polish were the first to arrive during the last two decades of the nineteenth century. Biloxi's small population of 1,540 during 1880 could not sustain the needs of the first cannery that opened in 1881. These first workers resided in bunkhouses manufactured by the canneries and in time constructed makeshift camps. Containing enclaves of workers, these came to be known as "bohemian camps" and awaited the seasonal arrivals of the Polish year after year. By the early 1900s, Biloxi had established several canneries and oyster dealers that required workers for landlocked plants as well as on boats.

French Cajuns from Louisiana, Croats from Yugoslavia, Serbs, and Slavonians made their presence known as they settled along the coast. They increased the population of Biloxi exponentially and helped generate the boom for seafood capitalization. Thus, the Vietnamese were following a well-worn path as they began living in the very same areas as the former bohemian camps first established by the Poles. Very quickly, businesses, shops, restaurants, and commercial services became available for the largely Vietnamese-speaking population. While researchers have observed that Biloxi preserves the strong traditions and cultural presence of the Poles, Slavonians, and French Cajuns, there seems to be a more complex absorption of the Vietnamese into the larger Biloxi community.

As previously noted, the first Vietnamese in the state of Mississippi were originally refugees fleeing from ravaging conflicts within their home country. Economic opportunity would further draw many more Vietnamese who had established themselves in Louisiana and Texas toward Biloxi. Starting off as oyster shuckers and shrimp pickers for processing plants, families began to establish themselves in the Back Bay and Point Cadet communities.

Gutierrez (1984) and later Schmidt (1995) depict the melding of the European and Cajun immigrant communities into the broader fabric of the city. In the earliest days, there seemed to have existed a benevolent curiosity between Biloxi locals and the colorful Polish groups who arrived by train every season. The boundaries of the bohemian camps were permeable to the residents and intermingling between the two groups became a common affair. The larger numbers of Yugoslavians and Slavonians that came into the city encouraged a more concentrated and continual settlement. Visibly and tangibly, the Cajuns, Yugoslavians, and Slavonians established an ethnic presence in Biloxi.

In contrast, the burgeoning relationship between the growing Vietnamese population and the city of Biloxi follows a more stressful path. In the next section we will explore the growing tensions and cultural negotiations as Vietnamese refugees become workers, shrimpers, and community members along the coast.

Rough Waters for Vietnamese Shrimpers

In 1983, two men spoke to a reporter and relayed very different sentiments regarding Vietnamese oyster shuckers and fishermen in Biloxi. Said one, "They saved the shrimp and oyster industry . . . I'd be out of business if it weren't for the Vietnamese," while the other remarked, "The industry is being saturated with Vietnamese . . . the federal government promised they would spread them out and they haven't done a damn thing."[10] While the comments were expressed with contrasting emotions, one person conveying positive and protective regard, the other antagonistic dismissal, both evaluations may ring true. The Vietnamese impact on the Gulf Coast seafood trade has evoked feelings of hostility and tension, appreciation and relief. How did the Vietnamese come to command such a large share of the shrimping industry in Mississippi? And what were the cultural, economic, and social consequences of such expansion?

While the initial groups of Vietnamese who arrived in Mississippi came as refugees, and would enter into the processing factories as paid laborers, other Vietnamese in Florida and Louisiana began entry into the more complex work of outfitting boats and going out to sea (Starr 1981). Almost immediately, conflict and suspicion arose from cultural misunderstandings and misinterpretations between the Vietnamese and "American fishermen" (a term that is still used to describe all non-Vietnamese fishermen despite the naturalized citizenship of many Vietnamese in the mid-1980s). Starr reports that disagreements and criticisms ranged from the cultural incomprehension Americans had at the Vietnamese custom of consuming "undesirable" or unappetizing catches in their nets (seaweed, squid, eel, mackerel, etc.) to heated accusations of illegal overfishing and the catching of undersized shrimp.

In some cases, Americans were reproaching the Vietnamese for adopting common practices among all fishermen, such as mixing legal-sized shrimp with undersized to profit from an otherwise mediocre catch. In other cases, bewildering clashes resulted from differing cultural customs. For native Vietnamese fishermen, barnacle-resistant paint was not made available for sale in Vietnam, thus necessitating the purchase or building of an entirely new vessel every few years. Such disposability inclined Vietnamese shrimpers toward a more casual attitude when it came to accidently bumping boats while mooring or moving. Americans who regarded their boats as permanent investments and "as important extensions of themselves" (Starr 1981: 232) felt enormously insulted by what they saw as cavalier and disrespectful behaviors. Hostilities from locals ran the gamut from refusals to sell ice and fuel to Vietnamese shrimpers to the delivery of death threats and violence (Draper 1996).

These tensions increased into the 1980s as more Vietnamese purchased boats and licenses. This trend of expansion is reflected all along the Gulf Coast with the fastest pace of activity occurring in Louisiana. In this state, nearly one in twenty fishermen were of Vietnamese descent and one out of every ten Vietnamese males were fishermen by 1990 (Bankston and Zhou 1996b). As early as 1980, angry confrontations occurred as fuel prices increased and local fishermen appealed to the government to limit the number of Vietnamese in state waters. In 1983, Mississippi issued one thousand commercial licenses for shrimping and fishing, of which three hundred were owned by Vietnamese. Of the forty-five hundred remaining licenses issued for recreational shrimping and fishing boats, a comparable number were also owned by Vietnamese but exact figures are unknown. Typically, accounts regarding the exact numbers of Vietnamese ownership of boats, licenses, and overall impact are imprecise, but estimates range consistently from 60 to 75 percent.

The entire seafood industry in the United States declined in the mid-1990s as imported shrimp drastically reduced the share of the American seafood industry on the worldwide market. This slowdown had been significant for the state in drastically reducing the number of shrimping licenses issued in the ten-year period from 1989 to 1999; Mississippi distributed only half the number of licenses, from 2,014 to 1,038. However, two domestic events delivered the most deadly blows to Mississippi shrimpers: the terrorist attacks of September 11, 2001, and Hurricane Katrina in late August of 2005 (Tilove 2005). While the first event drove up fuel prices to prohibitively expensive levels, the hurricane caused the most damage to infrastructure and real value assets. Over 5,000 boats had been damaged or sunk (NOAA report) during the 2005 hurricane season and slow recovery permitted only 306 boats to be ready on the opening day of the 2006 shrimp season in Mississippi, a decline from 633 the previous year (Ratcliff 2006). In time, and even with significant recovery, it is likely that there will be further erosion of the seafood industry due to ongoing global forces. Some scholars have already noted that the ethnic terrain of the Gulf Coast is rapidly evolving (Donato 2006) with Mexican and Latin American immigration and this will bring interesting demographic and economic changes. During a 2008 visit to Gollot Seafood, this author observed that several workers unloading incoming shrimp catches were from Mexico.

With the decline in the shrimp and seafood industry, the Vietnamese have gravitated toward finding work in the recovering casino and gaming industry. It would seem that the Vietnamese do not mourn this particular transition. Peter Nguyen, a former fisherman, said, "I don't want my children to become fishermen, I want them to go to college, because there is no future in shrimping." This stance eschews sentimentality regarding familial legacies. Unlike the observations of some historians (Schmidt 1995, Gutierrez 1984) who describe the strong emotional commitments of Polish, Slovenian, and French Cajun families to the seafood and fishing traditions of their forebears, the Vietnamese have viewed their participation as pragmatic adaptations to harsh economic conditions. Bankston (1996b), in his study of the Vietnamese fishermen in Louisiana, noted that one interviewee pointed out that fishing "is a hard and dirty job. I would not do this if I could do anything else. But what else can I do in America?" (46).

THE CHANGING VIETNAMESE FACE
The Vietnamese Family Structure

A commonly asserted characterization of the Vietnamese is that they place a high value upon the family. The Vietnamese themselves would say that family togetherness is highly prized and many would readily relocate across state lines to be close to one another. Again, fisherman Peter Nguyen explains, "I came here from Louisiana, where we were living, and when we [parents, brothers, and sisters] moved to Mississippi, my uncles and aunts and cousins all said, 'okay' and came along later."[11]

Vietnamese family structure is not easily explained by merely remarking that the Vietnamese practice ancestor veneration, or that the elderly and parental figures are accorded the highest levels of respect, or even that the Vietnamese nurture close relationships with extended family and encourage multigenerational living arrangements. Living in America has had profound effects on these complex customs and the Vietnamese have learned to renegotiate the upending of traditional gender roles and parental authority.

Vietnamese family structure may be explained by two cultural models that enormously influence family relationships and in particular gender roles. The East Asian model is based upon Chinese Confucian heritage and the Southeast Asian model derived from more indigenous customs. Confucian models supported the notion of multiple generations of families living together, headed by a patriarch, while the Southeast Asian model encouraged both patriarchal and matriarchal authority as well as more loosely organized households where families would live in proximity rather than directly under one roof. In 1991, Hirschman and Loi (1996) conducted an intriguing survey of 403 households in Vietnam as to living arrangements and familial relationships and found that many families blended traditions from both models while emphasizing the importance of parental relationships and an overall espousal of family as the most important social unit.

Strict gender roles distinguish husband-wife relationships in many Vietnamese families but even here, one may observe a complex interplay between economic and cultural factors. During the disconcerting process of migration and settlement, the traditional patriarchal family structure may be challenged by the need of Vietnamese women to find employment, thus becoming breadwinners as well as family caretakers. While this afforded many with liberations unknown to them before, such as the possibility of divorce from untenable unions, many found that the loss of the patriarchal structure actually reduced their parental authority and diminished their power in the domestic sphere (Marino 1998). Vietnamese mothers and fathers watched with great trepidation as their children swiftly learned English and, in their view, were increasingly at risk for becoming "Americanized" and potentially pulling away from traditional family roles.

In response to this erosion of family ties, Kibria (1990) found, Vietnamese women worked to temper their newfound power with deference to Confucian values by adopting strategies to maintain patriarchal structure. In particular, she reviewed how Vietnamese women cultivated extended social networks of female family members and other respected or resourceful Vietnamese women within their community. These circles of friends and family served as powerful Greek choruses that would provide advice, guidance, and, in some cases, direct intervention on behalf of a woman in need. For example, Vietnamese husbands who were seen as "shirking" their duties or abusing the deference naturally accorded to their position as head of the household may be admonished by elder women in the circle, or by the male relatives of the younger women.

In essence, the patriarchal arrangement remains intact while making way for inevitable challenges to this tradition. Vietnamese women reap more of the benefits of financial independence but maintain the custom of submissiveness in order to, ironically, champion their domestic authority. In a similar vein, the case of high-achieving Vietnamese girls also reasserts the traditional family structure of female submissiveness rather than challenging it as would be intuitively expected (Bankston 1995). In the home country of Vietnam, custom dictates that within a family, daughters must concede educational mobility to their brothers. With limited educational opportunities, resources are pooled for capable sons. Even families of wealth and means elect to promote male academic success while cultivating traditionally domestic roles for girls. Yet, their arrival in the United States has opened up opportunity structures for Vietnamese women and girls, and greater equality is compelled by economic necessity. Academic achievement in school is considered highly desirable for both sexes and Vietnamese girls often attain higher scores than their male counterparts. However, instead of serving as a threat to the traditional family structure, the success of teen girls is a marker of deep obedience to the patriarchal power because it reconceptualizes these achievements as contributing to the well-being of the family (Bankston 1995).

THE FUTURE

Thu Duong, a woman of both Vietnamese and Chinese descent, says that she believes that natural disasters often signify a message from heaven, a form of "karmic housecleaning." The end of one era ushers in the beginning of another. Great empires may crumble because citizens lived unwisely and leaders were corrupt, justifying a destructive phase to make room for future growth. Other times, it is simply a changing of the guard, an indication that occasional, catastrophic transformations are part of the natural state of order.

Hurricane Katrina made landfall in the tristate area of Louisiana, Mississippi, and Alabama where it is estimated that nearly forty-five thousand

Asian Americans lay in the path of destruction (Duong 2006). Perhaps it is likely that some of those citizens accepted the destruction of their homes and businesses with a sense of submission, a surrender to fate that may have been less than comprehensible to their non-Vietnamese neighbors. In either case, the storm reduced entire Vietnamese communities to ruin (AAJC report on Hurricane Katrina 2006). In particular two Vietnamese communities in Biloxi and New Orleans were similarly affected and reported parallel strategies in helping their residents recover—specifically, the use of religious organizations as a central hub for networking and aid.

Preliminary reports indicate that the Catholic Church and nonprofit arm of Mary Queen of Vietnam Community Development Corporation (MQVNCDC) principally spearheaded the recovery process of the New Orleans Vietnamese. Consequently, news accounts attributed the strong recovery of homes, businesses, and family repopulation in the region as due in large part to the efforts of the church (Dunbar 2006, Kromm 2006, Leong, Airriess, Li, Chia-Chen, and Keith 2007). Despite the dominance of MQVN, other Vietnamese organizations such as the local chapter of the National Alliance of Vietnamese American Service Agencies (NAVASA) and the Vietnamese American Association (VAA) played a role in post-Katrina mobilization.

In Biloxi, the Vietnamese organized around three major community touch points: the Vietnam Church of Martyrs, Vietnamese Buddhist Congregation of Biloxi, and the advocacy organization Boat People SOS. Currently, recovery for the Mississippi Vietnamese is regarded as modest. The 2000 U.S. Census for the hurricane-affected areas of Biloxi, Gulfport, and Pascagoula indicates a population of 4,264 Vietnamese; recent population projections estimate 2,500 currently. This is a return percentage of merely 60 percent compared to the touted 90 percent return rate in New Orleans. These differing recovery profiles are intriguing in that they invite a cautious comparison of these two southern Vietnamese groups. In particular, major challenges of recovery reported in Biloxi included the limited language capacities of the Vietnamese (Le 2006) and the confusion of local, state, and federal services that they needed to maneuver poststorm issues that the Vietnamese organizations in New Orleans were able to address within their community in a systematically organized manner through within-community interpreters.

Nevertheless, the recovery of the Vietnamese in southern Mississippi is under way and represents a bright beacon for the entire state. In the grueling work of rehabilitation and rebuilding, it is most important to remember that the Vietnamese community is more than a fascinating enclave nestled within a region of Mississippi; it is a crucible which reflects the economic and social conditions of the state. In Biloxi, when the lovely seaside town geared itself away from entertainment and leisure commodities and toward being an economically booming seafood powerhouse at the turn of the twenteith century, it did so powered by the healthy engine of migrant workers.

Now, as the city looks to come full circle back toward a gaming and entertainment industry, the Vietnamese are again proving to be integral to this process. In conclusion, all Mississippians should wholeheartedly cheer the recovery process for the Vietnamese, not so much because the loss of their community would leave a tear in the rich, cultural tapestry of the state, but because their fate is deeply intertwined with that of Mississippi.

NOTES

1. Elam, P. 1979. "'Boat family' harbored safely now in Meridian." *Clarion-Ledger*. December 8, A1; Sanders, L. 1975. "Refugees recall flight, begin building new lives." *Clarion-Ledger*. April 29; Smalhout, L. 1979. "Viet 'boat people' settle in Jackson." *Clarion-Ledger*. August 5, F1; Verongos, H. 1980. "Refugee teenagers just looking for a home." *Clarion-Ledger*. October 12, E1.

2. Pendergast, L. 1981. "Government assistance dwindling for refugees." *Clarion-Ledger*. April 19, A1.

3. Editorial. 1983. "New Americans: Vietnamese face many challenges." *Clarion-Ledger*. June 15, A14.

4. "State serves 5,535 migrants." 1977. *Clarion-Ledger*. May 1, A2.

5. Flynn, J. 1981. "Migrants in Mississippi: State tackles tricky problem of schooling transient children." *Clarion-Ledger*. December 26, A1.

6. O'Brein, J. 1987. Editorial. "Vietnamese among us adjust to tough challenges in new land." *Biloxi Sun Herald*, May 13.

7. Riley, S. 1983. "Language barriers past, Viet students excel." *Clarion-Ledger*. June 13, D1.

8. Riley, S. 1983. "Above all else, the Vietnamese have survived." *Clarion-Ledger*, June 12, A1.

9. Nguyen, Peter. 2008. Interview by author. July 28, Biloxi, Mississippi. Tape recording.

10. Riley, S. 1983. "Viets shuck living from oysters." *Clarion-Ledger*. June 12, E1; Riley, S. 1983. "Shrimpers want new Vietnamese arrivals banned." *Clarion-Ledger*. September 17, A1.

11. Nguyen, Peter. 2008. Interview by author. July 28, Biloxi, Mississippi. Tape recording.

WORKS CITED

Bankston, C. L. III. 1995. Gender Roles and Scholastic Performance Among Adolescent Vietnamese Women: The Paradox of Patriarchy. *Sociological Focus*, 28(2):161–176.

Bankston, C.L. III, and M. Zhou. 1996a. The Ethnic Church, Ethnic Identification, and the Social Adjustment of Vietnamese Adolescents. *Religious Review* 38(1):18–37.

———. 1996b. Go Fish: The Louisiana Vietnamese Ethnic Entrepreneurship in an Extractive Industry. *National Journal of Sociology*, 10(1):37–54.

Cleveland, B. 2003. "Mississippi coast shrimping industry declines as process fall." *Clarion-Ledger*. August 9, A1.

Coghlan, C. 1979. "'Boat people' await U.S. Christmas." *Daily News Staff Writer*. December 18, 3A.

Do, H. D. 1999. *The Vietnamese American*. Westport, CT: Greenwood Publishing Group.

Donato, K. S. Hakimzadeh. 2006. The Changing Face of the Gulf Coast: Immigration to Louisiana, Mississippi, and Alabama. Retrieved on May 17, 2008. http://www.migrationinformation.org/Feature/display.cfm?id=368.

Draper, Robert. 1996. "A Shrimp Tale." *Texas Monthly*, 24(10):136–147.

Dunbar, Tony. 2006. Update from New Orleans: The People's Approach. *Social Policy*, 36(4):40.

Duong, T. 2006. Hurricane Katrina: Models for Effective Emergency Response in the Asian American Community. *Asian American Justice Center*.

Elam, Peggy. 1979. "'Boat family' harbored safely now in Meridian." *Clarion-Ledger*. December 8, A1.

Flynn, J. 1981. "Migrants in Mississippi: State tackles tricky problem of schooling transient children." *Clarion-Ledger*. December 26, A1.

Gutierrez, C. P. 1984. The Cultural Legacy of Biloxi's Seafood Industry. Biloxi, Mississippi. Unknown binding.

Haines, D., D. Rutherford, and P. Thomas. 1981. Family and Community among Vietnamese Refugees. *International Migration Review*, 15(1/2):310–319.

Hein, J. 1995. *From Vietnam, Laos and Cambodia: A Refugee Experience in the United States*. New York: Twayne Publishers.

Herring, G. C. 2001. *America's Longest War: The United States and Vietnam, 1950–1975*. 4th edition. New York: McGraw-Hill.

Hidalgo, D. A., and C. Bankston III. 2008. War Brides and Refugees: Vietnamese American Wives and Shifting Links to the Military, 1980–2000. *International Migration*, 46(2):167–185.

Hirschman, C., and V. M. Loi. 1996. Family and Household Structure in Vietnam: Some Glimpses from a Recent Survey. *Pacific Affairs*, 69(2):229–249.

Husley, V. 2000. *Maritime Biloxi: Images of America*. Charleston, SC: Arcadia Publishing.

Jacobs, S. 2004. *America's Miracle Man in Vietnam: Ngo Dinh Diem, Religion, Race and U.S. Intervention in Southeast Asia*. Durham, NC: Duke University Press.

Karnow, S. 1997. *Vietnam: A History*. New York: Viking Press.

Kibria, N. 1990. Power, Patriarchy, and Gender Conflict in the Vietnamese Immigrant Community. *Gender and Society*, 4(1):9–24.

Kromm, C. 2006. Grassroots and Gumbo. *The Nation*, 283(8):22–26.

Le, U. 2006. The Invisible Tide: Vietnamese Americans in Biloxi, MS; An Update One Year After Hurricane Katrina. National Alliance of Vietnamese American Service Agencies. August 26.

Lee, S. J. 1994. Behind the Model Minority Stereotype: Voice of High and Low Achieving Asian American Student. *Anthropology and Education Quarterly*, 25(4):413–429.

Leong, K. J., C. A. Airriess, W. Li, A. Chia-Chen, and V. M. Keith. 2007. Resilient History and the Rebuilding of a Community: The Vietnamese American Community in New Orleans East. *The Journal of American History*, December: 774–779.

Lewy, G. 1980. *America in Vietnam*. London: Oxford University Press

Liu, W. T., M. Lamanna, and A. Maurata. 1979. *Transition to Nowhere: Vietnamese Refugees in America*. Nashville, TN: Charter House Press.

Marino, K. 1998. Women Vietnamese Refugees in the United States: Maintaining Balance Between Two Cultures. *The History Teacher*, 32(1):90–117.

Montero, D., and I. Dieppa. 1982. Resettling Vietnamese Refugees: The Service Agencies Role. *Social Work*, (27):74–81.

Nguyen, Peter. Interview by author, July 28, 2008, Biloxi, Mississippi. Tape recording.

Nguyen, T. H., and T. Q. Quan. 2007. *Vietnam Fishery Products Annual Report*. USDA Foreign Agricultural Service, Global Agriculture Information Network. June 29. Retrieved June 12, 2008, from http://www.fas.usda.gov/gainfiles/200707/146291702.pdf.

Noone, J. 1981. From Vietnam to the Mississippi Gulf Coast. Biloxi, Mississippi: The Catholic Diocese of Biloxi.

O'Brein, J. 1987. Editorial. "Vietnamese among us adjust to tough challenges in new land." *Biloxi Sun Herald*, May 13.

Oglethorpe, J. 1975. "S. Viets find new home." *Jackson Daily News*. October 17, A6.

Pendergast, L. 1981. "Government assistance dwindling for refugees." *Clarion-Ledger*. April 19, A1.

Portes, A., and R. G. Rumbaut. 2001. *Legacies: The Stories of the Immigrant Second Generation*. Berkeley, CA: University of California Press.

Ratcliff, B. 2006. "Good crop, lots of obstacles for Gulf Coast shrimper." *Mississippi Landmarks*, 2(3):6–7.

Riley, S. 1983. "Above all else, the Vietnamese have survived." *Clarion-Ledger*. June 12, A1.

———. 1983. Viets shuck living from oysters." *Clarion-Ledger*. June 12, E1.

———. 1983. "Language barriers past, Viet students excel." *Clarion-Ledger*. June 13, D1.

———. 1983. "Shrimpers want new Vietnamese arrivals banned." *Clarion-Ledger*. September 17, A1.

Rogers, L. 1980. "Coast Fishing Scene Shaken by Vietnamese." *Jackson Daily News*. May 13, D1.

Rumbaut, R. 2007. "Vietnam." Pp. 652–673 in *The New Americans: A Guide to Immigration Since 1965*, edited by Mary C. Waters and Reed Ueda with Helen B. Marrow. Cambridge, Mass.: Harvard University Press.

Rutledge, P. 1985. *The Role of Religion in Ethnic Self-Identity: A Vietnamese Community*. Lanham, MD: University Press of America.

Sanders, L. 1975. "Refugees recall flight, begin building new lives." *Clarion-Ledger*. April 29.

Schmidt, A. 1995. Down Around Biloxi: Culture and Identity in the Biloxi Seafood Industry. *Mississippi Folklife*, 28(1). Retrieved June 2, 2008, from http://www.olemiss.edu/depts/south/publish/missfolk/backissues/biloxi.html.

Searle, W., and C. Ward. 1990. The Prediction of Psychological and Social Cultural Adjustment During Cross-Cultural Transitions. *International Journal of Intercultural Relations*, (14):449–464.

Smalhout, L. 1979. "Viet 'boat people' settle in Jackson." *Clarion-Ledger*. August 5, F1.

Starr, P. 1981. Troubled Waters: Vietnamese Fisherfolk on America's Gulf Coast. *International Migration Review*, 15(1/2): 226–38.

"State serves 5,535 migrants." 1977. Editorial. *Clarion-Ledger*. May 1, A2.

Tilove, J. 2005. "Katrina Clouds Vietnamese Shrimpers' American Dream." *Newshouse*. September 4, 2005.

U.S. Bureau of the Census. 1980. General Social and Economic Characteristics for Mississippi.

———. 1990. Census Population and Housing; Summary File 1C.

———. 2000. Census Population and Housing; Summary File 2 PCT1.

U.S. Department of Agriculture. June 29, 2007. Foreign Agricultural Service. Global Agriculture Information Network (GAIN Report). Vietnam Fishery Products Annual Report. Prepared by Nguyen Thi Huong and Tran Quoc Quan.

Verongos, H. 1980. "Refugee teenagers just looking for a home. *Clarion-Ledger*. October 12, E1.

von Herrmann, D., ed. 2006. *Resorting to Casinos: The Mississippi Gambling Industry*. Jackson, MS: University Press of Mississippi.

Yang, K. 2004. Southeast Asian American Children: Not the "Model Minority." *The Future of Children* 14(2):127–133.

Young, D. C., and S. Young. 1992. Ethnic Mississippi 1992. In *Ethnic Heritage in Mississippi*, edited by Barbara Carpenter. Jackson, MS: University Press of Mississippi.

11

THE CHANGING FACE OF HINDU IDENTITY IN JACKSON, MISSISSIPPI

—DEVPARNA ROY AND LOLA WILLIAMSON

Hinduism, with close to a billion followers worldwide, is the third largest religion in the world after Christianity and Islam, and yet many Americans know very little about it. In this chapter, we look at the vast and heterogeneous religion of Hinduism by exploring how it is practiced by Indian Americans in Jackson, Mississippi, and how it serves as a cultural and identity touchstone. Hinduism is the oldest world religion still practiced today and encompasses many beliefs and styles of worship. This multifaceted quality can also be found in Mississippi as immigrants from different regions of India draw on their own particular traditions. The practices and beliefs may vary from temple to temple and from home to home. As such, Hinduism in Mississippi displays the same diversity as all religions do.

Unlike the Abrahamic religions of Judaism, Christianity, and Islam, Hinduism does not espouse a single belief system, creed, or scripture. Neither does it claim a founder. Hindus refer to their religion as *sanatana dharma*, which could be translated as the "eternal natural law." The tremendous diversity of Hinduism includes influences and traditions from four sources: the original inhabitants of India, who today are referred to as tribals, or *adivasis*; the Indus Valley Civilization (2500–1500 BCE); the highly developed Dravidian culture seen in South Indian Tamils today; and the Vedic religion of Aryan settlers (1500–500 BCE). Each of these traditions has in turn taken multiple forms. Close contact with Islam and Christianity has affected Hinduism as well. The resulting mélange is further transformed as people immigrate to other countries. Thus, as we look at Hinduism in Jackson, Mississippi, we must keep in mind that it is ever-changing and evolving as it settles into its new home. This brief introduction is a snapshot of Hinduism in Mississippi, which may look very different twenty years from now.

This chapter is the product of the collaboration of many people. While the authors are scholars, one of religious studies and one of sociology, the chapter could not have been written without the help of numerous practicing Hindus in Jackson and its surrounding communities. In January of 2007, the authors interviewed thirty first-generation Jackson Hindus—all of whom have lived in the Jackson area for a number of years—regarding their beliefs, values, and lifestyles. In July of 2008, Lekha Sunkara and Mangala Maddali, two students at Millsaps College, interviewed thirty second-generation Hindus from the ages of fourteen to twenty-nine, asking similar types of questions. In addition, Hindus involved in the founding of religious and cultural institutions provided historical data to the authors.

Today, immigrants and their descendents from many areas of South Asia reside in Mississippi, but we have chosen to focus solely on immigrants from the South Asian country of India. We narrow our focus further by discussing only the religious history and understanding of these Jackson-area residents. We do not discuss their economic, political, and other social contributions, of which there are many. An even finer focus comes as we examine only one religion: Hinduism. India is a religiously diverse nation, the home of eight major religious traditions: the Hindu, Jain, Sikh, and Buddhist traditions, which are all indigenous to India, and the Islamic, Christian, Parsi (an Indian form of the ancient Persian religion Zoroastrianism), and Jewish traditions, all of which have existed in India for well over a millennium, some even for two millennia. Several of these other religious traditions are represented in the Indian immigrant population of Jackson. In other words, not all Indians living in Jackson are Hindus. The Hindu tradition is by far the largest, however, both in India and among Indian Americans in Mississippi. According to 2001 census data, Hinduism comprises about 80.5 percent of the Indian population, or approximately 830 million people. A 2007 survey of religion in the United States performed by the Pew Forum on Religion and Public Life found that there are about 900,000 Hindus in the U.S., or about 0.4 percent of the population. Eight out of ten Hindus in the U.S. are foreign-born. Specific data is not available on Jackson, but according to people involved in the Hindu community, approximately 500 Hindu families reside in the Jackson area, with the first Indian Hindus arriving in Jackson in the early 1970s.

The 2007 Pew Forum survey concluded that Hinduism has the most stable identity of any religion in the U.S., with 90 percent marrying within their faith and eight in ten people raised Hindu remaining Hindu as an adult. It is likely that this will change as second and third generations of Hindu Indian immigrants embrace American culture. According to Vasudha Narayanan, scholar of American Hinduism, "Already we are seeing members of the next generation, who are assimilated, marrying into other traditions."[1] If Hinduism is to remain a vibrant religion in America, it must seek ways to pass its heritage on to future generations. In this chapter, we will look at attempts Jackson Hindus are making to maintain their Hindu identity by teaching their values, rituals, and beliefs to their children through family traditions and through establishing Hindu temples.

All religions are intertwined with culture, but Hinduism perhaps to a greater extent than many. Being Hindu means thinking and acting like a Hindu, which includes what we might consider "religious" aspects of daily life such as praying and performing rituals, but also includes cultural aspects, such as valuing family and education, respecting elders, and sharing Hindu scriptures and epic poems through storytelling, movies, and even comic books. The "religious" and the "cultural" are not separated in Hinduism. Many of those interviewed stressed this point. In fact, a person may self-identify as a Hindu, yet not attend a temple or pray within the home. Why? Because the person, simply by being born into a Hindu family, learns the important cultural values that are a part of Hinduism. For example, some of the people interviewed said that rather than praying or visiting a temple, they practice *karma yoga*, which means that they perform their work in the world well, without looking for praise or reward. Thus, we will look at rituals and beliefs, which many in the West associate with the term "religion," but we will also discuss values and daily life issues such as valuing education and choosing a life mate, for these are also part of what it means to be a Hindu. Part One will focus on the former and Part Two the latter. This is a division of convenience and not one that Hindus would necessarily make.

As we focus on Hindus of the Indian community in the Jackson metropolitan area, we realize that many important voices of the South Asian immigrant community are left out. This chapter serves as a humble beginning to what we hope will blossom into research on the religions and cultures of all areas of the South Asian immigrant populations, not only in Jackson, but in all of Mississippi.

PART ONE: HINDU PRACTICES AND BELIEFS
Negotiating Identity

While the United States is a predominantly Protestant country, Mississippi has an even higher percentage of Protestants than most states. According to the Pew survey referenced above, Evangelical, mainline, and historically black Protestant membership together comprise 81 percent of Mississippi's religious outlook. This means that, with only about five hundred Hindu families in the Jackson area, maintaining Hindu identity takes a certain amount of determined effort. People we interviewed felt that they have been welcomed by Mississippians, and yet admitted that sometimes they are misunderstood and proselytized. One man said, "I'd be lying if I didn't tell you I was anxious about coming to Mississippi. I was very pleasantly surprised. In eleven years, I can think of maybe a couple of occasions where people looked at me differently, but that's more my skin color. Being a physician, I interact with many people, and a lot of them know I don't belong to their religion. I've had several patients give me copies of a Bible and invite me to church, and I respectfully told them that I'm very comfortable in my faith."[2] A fifteen-year-old explained that she thought it was "fun to be the odd one out," because "you get special respect for being a Hindu." Another young person said, "It's weird for us because some people find our religion hard to understand. Some people are, I wouldn't say prejudiced, but scared of us because we do have different rituals than Americans here."

Almost all of the sixty people interviewed are very conversant with other religions, particularly with Christianity. Many first-generation Hindus were educated in Christian schools in India that had been established by the British. Many second-generation Hindus are also being educated in Christian schools in Jackson, such as St. Andrew's Episcopal School and Mississippi College. They, like their parents, are more conversant with Christianity than most Jackson Christians are with Hinduism. Interviewees stressed the openness and tolerance of the Hindu religion. One respondent said, "You have all these conflicts between Jews, Muslims, Hindus, and Christians, and every other religion. All this comes from lack of tolerance, you know. If you have tolerance, you will sit and try to understand the other person's viewpoint. To me, being Hindu is being a tolerant person, who understands, empathizes with all human beings, and treats them equally and with respect."

In India, Hindus learn religious values and practices by osmosis since they are surrounded by other Hindus. In Jackson, immigrants must create a Hindu environment if their religious values are to survive. Hindus in America meet the need for cultural and religious coherence by establishing temples that serve not only as places of worship but also as cultural centers that offer classes in Indian languages and celebrate political holidays, such as India's Independence Day. Many Indian immigrants are *more* religious than they would be in India because their ties to Hinduism help to create a sense of identity.[3] In fact, several Jackson Hindus noted that when they visit India, they notice that urban Hindus are losing many of the values that American Hindus are preserving.

Jackson Indians find that their distinctiveness as a cultural group distinguishes them to some extent from both non-Indian Americans and Indians in their home country. One woman said of her experiences visiting India, "I wear saris, but still they know I'm from the U.S. They just have a second sense. Sometimes they can tell by the footwear. Sometimes they can tell by the way we might treat the driver of the car. They're smart; they're very savvy. There are lots of telltale signs because we have lived here a long time, and we have picked up some of the American ways of conducting ourselves, and they pick it up immediately." A teenager spoke of changing her behavior depending on the group she was with: "In Indian functions I try to bring out my Indian identity and when I'm with American people, I generally don't bring out any Indian influence or culture. For example, when I'm talking to Indian people, sometimes a small Indian accent actually comes out. It's pretty funny. And when I'm with American people or talking to somebody else, I just switch back. So I guess I have two identities and they actually don't blend that much."

Since American Hindus live at the juncture of two worlds—a part of each and yet in a sense distinct from each—community is of utmost importance. One teenager put it this way: "I like to know that in this country, although I'm associating for the majority of the time with Americans, that I have a safe place, because Indian communities—well, I guess minority groups in general—tend to stick together. Even though I may not know some Indian adult, they're still always 'uncle' or 'aunty.' So I guess it's just a nice safe feeling to have a strong Indian community." Groups from particular areas of India, who may speak a different language and have different customs than people from other areas, fill the need for a "safe place" by occasionally gathering for picnics or cultural or religious events.

11.1. A typical Saraswati Devi *puja*. Photo by Greg Williamson.

As an example of how religious and ethnic identities are reinforced through these gatherings, we will look in detail at an event organized by and for Hindus from the northeastern province of West Bengal. The event—a celebration of Saraswati Devi, goddess of learning, language, and music— took place in January 2007 in the community room of an apartment complex. Saraswati Devi is worshipped throughout India and is a favorite deity for students during exam time who pray to her for success. People of West Bengal have a particular affinity for this day of worship. Nobody is to touch a book on the day of Saraswati Devi's *puja* (worship) because the books are set aside for her special blessing. The *puja* is performed in the month of Magh (January–February). Since Hindus use a lunar calendar to determine the time of religious holidays, dates vary slightly from year to year.

Entering the community room, one sees rows of shoes lining the wall by the entryway. Some women are in the side kitchen setting up lunch and foods for the *puja*. Almost all Hindu events—cultural and religious— include a vegetarian meal, lovingly prepared that day. Other women sit in front of the altar and watch while the men talk casually in the back of the room. Children come and go, playing outside for awhile and then coming in and sitting with their mothers for awhile. In the front two women perform the *puja*. One woman reads from a notebook, at times reciting words and at times chanting prayers and praise to Saraswati Devi. At the center of the altar sits a framed image of the goddess decorated with a garland of flowers. Saraswati Devi is depicted playing a stringed instrument with two of her four hands, the other hands holding a book and prayer beads. Students place their textbooks and musical instruments around the altar. Offerings of food adorn the altar as well.

The *puja* lasts for about two hours, during which more people arrive and sit down near the altar behind the two women celebrants. One woman performs various acts of worship while the other recites from the text. Worship includes scattering flower petals, waving incense, and blessing the books and musical instruments. Near the end of the service, there is an *arati* (lamp-waving ceremony) during which one of the women celebrants waves a ceremonial oil lamp made of brass before the altar as the group stands and watches. After the *arati*, she walks with the lamp around the front of the room to allow people to place their fingers above the flame, after which they touch their eyes or head, the flame's heat providing a benediction. Finally, the celebrants distribute *prasad* (blessed food) from a tray. People receive the *prasad* with the right hand and, eating it, receive Saraswati Devi's blessing.

After the *puja*, the women uncover warm pots of food and everyone helps themselves to Indian home cooking. After lunch, the music begins. First, two men sitting on the floor play their instruments: a sitar (a type of Indian string instrument) and tabla (a type of Indian drum). Then the women begin to sing various songs, sometimes alone and sometimes in groups of two or three. The world-renowned poet, composer, novelist, and artist Rabindranath Tagore is Bengali, and some of his songs are beautifully performed by one of the women. The music and singing last for several hours. It is a full and satisfying day.

Hindu Temples

A second-century Tamil woman poet wrote, "Do not live in a town where there is no temple."[4] Hindus believe that temples make the land in which they dwell sacred. In India temples are found in every village and in every neighborhood of large cities. People always have a sacred haven to go to where they can feel, see, and touch God, represented in a particular form. If there is no physical structure, a tree, a river, or a rock can represent the holy, and worship occurs at all of these sites. It must have been difficult for Indian immigrants to come to Mississippi where no designated Hindu holy place existed. In the early 1970s when immigrants began to settle in the Jackson area, Hindus would gather in people's homes to worship together. Over time, as more Indians arrived, the need for a place set apart from the cares of the world became obvious. One of these early Jackson immigrants described the difficulty she faced raising a daughter before the temples were built. She said she had a real "eye-opener" when her daughter, at the age of five, was facing severe identity problems about being both Indian and American at the same time. She explained that most Americans in the Jackson area were not familiar with Hinduism or Hindus at that time. When invited to a school function, the mother announced that she was from India. Later, after going home, the girl said, "Mom, how can you say that? I'm not an Indian. I am American." The mother realized that it was important to start some cultural activities. Now, the daughter, who is a lawyer, "is very proud to be Hindu. She is more like me. She doesn't pray every day but she has, you know, basic Hinduism knowledge."

Jackson has three temples that accommodate the needs and worship styles of all Jackson Hindus. The first temple, located in Brandon, was founded in 1990 and is called simply the Hindu Temple. The other two temples opened in 1998. The Sita Ram Hindu Temple, located in Jackson proper, serves the needs of immigrants from the area of Punjab primarily, although it is open to anyone. The third temple is the Shree Swaminarayan Temple, and most of its congregants are from the western Indian state of Gujarat. In addition, Mississippi is home to the ISKCON New Talavana Dham, a farm community founded by Bhaktivedanta Swami Prabhupada in the early 1970s in the town of Carriere in southern Mississippi. About fifty people live on this twelve-hundred-acre property where they farm and worship the form of God known as Krishna. We will focus here on the histories and styles of worship of the three temples in the immediate Jackson area. Even though each of the temples has its own style of worship, many Hindus freely visit all of the temples for different occasions.

The Hindu Temple

The Hindu Temple, located on the south side of the Ross R. Barnett Reservoir near Flowood and Brandon, serves the religious and cultural needs of Jackson-area Hindus by providing a place for individual and family worship, for congregational worship on Hindu holidays, and for gatherings in celebration of Indian holidays that are not necessarily religious. The elaborate 3,500-square-foot temple was consecrated during a five-day ceremony on May 22–26, 2010. The space that previously served as a temple next to the current structure will be used for the more secular community gatherings so that the new space can be reserved just for worship. The Hindu Temple is more ecumenical than the other two Jackson temples. Three major deities of India are found in the main sanctuary: Lord Balaji (also known as Venkateshwara, a form of Vishnu), Lord Shiva, and Lord Rama (believed to be an incarnation of Vishnu who is the subject of the Hindu epic, *Ramayana*). Other gods and goddesses are located in subtemples within the building. It employs two full-time priests. One of the priests, Shri Ram Babu, is from the South of India and speaks four southern languages. The other, Shri Kirit Joshi, is from Gujarat, and speaks Gujarati and Hindi. Both are learned in Sanskrit, the ancient language that is used in Hindu ritual worship and which is considered to be sacred by Hindus. Both also speak English. Between them, they are able to meet the needs of many of the Hindus in Jackson. The board of the temple plans to eventually hire a third priest.

Most Hindus do not worship congregationally on a regular basis. Instead they visit the temple, individually or as a family, on special occasions, such as birthdays. The priest performs a *puja* for whoever requests it. At the end of the ceremony, the priest offers *prasad* to the worshippers, as we have already seen in the case of the Saraswati Devi *puja*. The priest also offers the flame that has been used in the worship to the people attending, and they receive the blessing by extending their hands over it and then touching their eyes or foreheads. In addition to the flame, the priest offers the devotee *thirtham* (consecrated water) and *prasadam* (consecrated food). Jackson-area Hindus also simply visit the temple to pray quietly. As a college student explained, "There's something about going to a place of worship. Even if it's just within your own house, there's that sense that you've set apart a place in your life to be holy, to be sacred. And the very fact that you do that, it means something. I believe that God is everywhere and therefore everywhere is sacred and you can connect with God everywhere, but in a way, going to the temple means that by designating this place as sacred, you've taken the first step yourself. You've made it easier for yourself to get into a spiritual way of thinking."

All Hindu deities are associated with a *vahana* (vehicle), an animal or bird upon which the deity may ride. The *vahana* is offered due worship along with the presiding deity. They are displayed prominently along with the gods and goddesses in temples and are suggestive of the nature of the power that is expressed by the gods. In the Hindu Temple, for example, Vishnu's *vahana* Garuda, a mythical figure that is part eagle and part human, can be found in a small sanctum opposite the larger sanctum of Lord Venkateshwara. Upon entering the temple, Hindus first pray to Ganesha, the elephant-headed deity who is considered the "remover of obstacles." He is traditionally petitioned before beginning any new venture, such as taking a trip or opening a business, but also before performing any other worship. Then the person may pray to each of the deities, who represent different qualities, such as abundance, in the case of Lakshmi, devotion in the case of Hanuman, or learning, as we have seen, in the case of Saraswati. A person may also choose to just pray to their *ishta-devata*, or chosen deity. While monotheists, such as Christians, Jews, and Muslims, have traditionally referred to Hindus as polytheists, many Hindus do not understand their own religion that way. Rather, the different deities represent different aspects of one God. As one college student put it, "I'm really just praying to one God, even if I'm standing in front of a statue of Shiva. It's really just God."

The Hindu Temple draws large crowds on special holidays. One of these is called *Navaratri*, or "Nine Nights." This is a traditional time for worshipping the goddess in her many forms. The temple celebrates this occasion with a *garbha*, a graceful dance in which some move in one direction, creating a large clockwise circle, while others move in a counterclockwise circle. Both men and women participate, and those who are physically unable to dance sit along the sides where they enjoy watching. This is a favorite holiday for young people. It is a beautiful sight to behold everyone decked out in their finest silk saris and *salwar kameez* (loose trousers and long shirts), dancing for hours to the accompaniment of a host of live musicians. This is just one example of the many festivals that occur over the course of a year.

The Brandon Hindu Temple is among the finest in the United States—the result of many years of work and about four million dollars. The long process of finding land and building a temple began in 1983 when a committee was formed as part of the Indian Association of Mississippi (IAM). Since people of different faiths, including Muslim, Sikh, Jain, and Christian, belong to the IAM, in 1986 some of the members decided to form a separate legal entity called the Hindu Temple Society of Mississippi. In 1990, the earlier Hindu Temple was consecrated.

After much deliberation over how to "Indianize" the temple, the Hindu Temple Society decided to convert it to a community hall and to begin construction of a new temple that would meet the requirements of Hindu

11.2. *Arati* for temple blessing. Photo by Ramrao Takkallapalli.

11.3. Blessing temple. Photographer unknown.

scriptures. Traditional temples in India are dedicated to a single deity. This is possible since there are many temples. However, a single temple in the United States must meet the needs of Hindus who come from different areas of India and who may worship different deities. This is why in American temples one finds an array of deities.

11.4. *Kalash*. Photo by Sheola Takkallapalli.

In the case of the Brandon Hindu Temple, the architecture itself also accommodates different Hindus by combining aspects of temple design from both the North and the South of India. The more intricate designs that adorn both the inner and outer walls are inspired by southern Indian temple architecture. Traditionally these designs are carved in rock, but this arduous labor takes many years. In the United States, the repeated designs are made with molds in wet cement and even this, by American standards, is time consuming. Eight *shilpis* (artisans) from India worked for four years to complete this design work. *Shilpis* must be trained under a Master *Shilpi* or a *Sthapati* (architect) for many years and must be brought from India as the training is not available in the United States. Designing and constructing a temple is a religious activity that draws on ancient Hindu texts called the *Atharva Veda*, among the oldest scriptures of the Hindu tradition. The architect of the Brandon Hindu Temple is Subramanian Thangam, and he and the *shilpis* are followers of Ganapathi Sachchidananda Swamiji, a guru of some renown. This guru has visited Jackson three times, most recently in August of 2008.

The Hindu Temple has seven towers and each of these towers is topped with a *kalash*, an ornament shaped like an inverted pot. Energy and power are believed to enter the temple through the *kalash*. During the opening ceremony, the priests "enlivened" the *murtis*, or statues of the deities, some of which were transferred from the old space and others of which were shipped from India. The older *murtis* are crafted in the style of South India and the new statues in the style of North India, again adding to the ecumenical flavor of this large temple. The priests enlivened the *murtis* through repeating certain mantras, after which they performed an *abhisheka*, or ablution, of the different *kalashes*. Worshippers who visit the new temple circumambulate each of the deities. They may also circumambulate the temple itself and the entire compound. This is an important form of Hindu worship that was not possible in the original structure and is a unique feature for a relatively small temple such as this.

The Sita Ram Hindu Temple

The Sita Ram Hindu Temple is open to anyone, but it offers a particular style of worship to which immigrants from the area of Punjab in northwestern India are accustomed. As Indira Bhowal, one of the founders of the Sita Ram Hindu Temple, explained it, "Just as there are different churches that all share similar beliefs but have different ways of expressing their beliefs, so Hindus have some variance in the way they worship." In 1997, a group of families began to meet in people's homes and in spare rooms of offices to practice their religious beliefs by singing *bhajan* (prayer to deities) together. Eventually, a committee began to search for a public and permanent location. In 1998 they bought a former Popeyes Chicken restaurant on Highway 80 in West Jackson, which had burned down three years prior and had been sitting in ruins ever since. It took many hours of dedicated work to turn this roach- and rat-infested remains of a building into a house of worship. It began with about fifteen families, and today it is supported by about fifty families.

Mr. Som Budhraja arranged to bring *murtis*, statues of deities, from India. The *murtis* in the Sita Ram Hindu Temple are made of white marble in contrast to those originally found in the Hindu Temple near Brandon, which are made of black marble, deriving from the tradition of South India. Just as in all Hindu temples, the *murtis* were enlivened during a *Prana Pratishta* ceremony held in November 2001. A priest from the Swaminarayan Temple performed this ceremony for them as they did not yet have a priest of their own. Indira Bhowal tells the story of how they finally found a priest for the temple: "We didn't find a full-time priest until 2002. I decided to go to the motel across from the temple and ask the Indian owner if he knew of a priest. He said, 'There is a guy whose father is coming from India, and he knows how to do all this worship.' So we asked this man, Mr. Mehta, and he agreed to be our priest. Every morning he comes to perform the washing and feeding of the *murtis* and then again in the evening. Some of

11.5. Sita Ram. Photo by Greg Williamson.

the older members in our group helped him learn how to do *puja* the way they wanted it done. He's a very nice man, and everybody is pleased."

Members visit the temple mainly on Sundays because that is when they have time off from work. This temple celebrates some religious event almost every month. In fact, in April there are three festivals. Singing *bhajans* and *kirtans* is a favorite activity during these gatherings. *Bhajans* are devotional songs, some of them deriving from "poet-saints" of the Middle Ages, such as Kabir, Mirabi, Surdas, and Tulsidas. *Kirtans* are also expressions of devotion to God. These are simple songs performed in a call-and-response fashion, with lead singers and musicians beginning, and the congregation responding by repeating the same words. The singing is accompanied by musical instruments. The *harmonium* consists of a keyboard on which the musician plays a melody with one hand while bellows are squeezed with the other hand to create the sound. Sometimes an electric keyboard replaces the harmonium. The beat is kept with drums called *dholak*, on which leather is stretched across the ends. This is one of several drum instruments used in Indian music, and learning the various traditional beats is a long process that requires years of study to become proficient. During the *bhajans* and *kirtans* in the Sita Ram Temple, a person often plays small hand-held cymbals as well.

All of the main deities of Hinduism are worshipped at the Sita Ram Hindu Temple. Its name, however, derives from Ram (a well-loved incarnation of Vishnu) and his wife, Sita, who are the heroes of the epic called the *Ramayana*. The story of Ram's banishment to the forest, the abduction of his wife by the evil Ravana, and the battles that ensued between Ram's and Ravana's armies is the most popular scripture of Hinduism.

The Swaminarayan Temple

The Swaminarayan Temple opened in 1998, the same year the Sita Ram Temple was established. While anyone can attend this temple, it is primarily for people from the western state of Gujarat. When talks are conducted at the other temples, they may be in English or the language of the visitor giving the speech, and the words are often translated into one or more languages. "Sermons" are a regular feature of services at this temple, and they are always presented in Gujarati. The Swaminarayan Temple stresses its Gujarati heritage, and classes in Gujarati are held on Sundays as part of the Sunday school for children. This temple is somewhat different from the other Jackson temples, which are not associated with any particular guru. The Swaminarayan Temple would not exist if it were not for its tie to a guru named Pramukh Swami. He is part of a *parampara*, or guru lineage, that goes back to the founder of the sect, Sahajanand Swami, also known as Swami Narayan (1781–1830). Swami Narayan and other gurus in his lineage are considered by their followers to be divine incarnate. As is the case with most Hindu gurus, several lines of descent result as different people claim to be the successor of a guru. One of these lines of descent brings us to the present guru of the people who attend this temple. They belong to an organization called the Bochasanwasi Akshar Purushottam Sanstha, or BAPS.

BAPS has a million followers around the world. It is very popular among Gujaratis who come to America, even though it makes up only about 5 percent of the population of Gujarat. Scholar of American Hinduism Raymond Brady Williams found that one-third of the 224 American BAPS followers whom he surveyed became members *after* their arrival in the United States and that 80 percent of first-generation immigrants in BAPS became more interested in religious matters after coming to the United States.[5] This speaks well for the organization's role in helping to maintain a strong Hindu heritage in the U.S. BAPS considers itself to be a "sociospiritual organization" that addresses all the needs of its members. It stresses charity, and responds to crises with donations and services. During the Katrina crisis, for example, Jackson temple members collected money for victims and delivered hot food to New Orleans for a week.

Many who attend this temple have the last name of Patel. This does not mean they are all cousins. The name "Patel" evolved from the word "pat," which refers to a parcel of land. The Patels are descendents of landowners or farmers or record keepers of these parcels of land. Business is "in their blood," so to speak, and many Patels who immigrate to the U.S. are hotel owners. According to the Asian American Hotel Owners Association, which has more than eight thousand members, 60 percent are named Patel.[6] Mississippi is no different from the rest of the U.S., with Patels comprising the majority of its Indian hotel owners.

BAPS members of Jackson are similar to other American BAPS members in their enthusiasm for religious practice. They place a strong emphasis on maintaining Hindu moral and cultural values. As one man explained when we visited the Swaminarayan Temple, "We have to give our children our values. If we don't have a temple, our children will lose those values. Pramukh Swami says, 'If you lose your children, no matter how much wealth you have, you've lost everything.' Even children who are raised here, they're still Indian American; they're not American American. So we have to teach them what it means to be Indian American." Many Jackson *satsangis*, as they refer to themselves, follow their guru's advice and avoid television and the Internet, except for watching news or DVDs that are religious or uplifting in nature. Some we spoke to simply did not have a television. Most follow a vegetarian diet and avoid onions and garlic as well. Teenagers, as in almost all Hindu families, do not date. People who attend the temple follow their guru's advice in regards to spending family time together every day. Many pray together on a daily basis. Others simply make sure they have time to talk every day in the midst of hectic lives. Family dinners are also stressed. "The family that prays together and dines together, stays together," one Swaminarayan follower told us.

The temple houses many of the same popular deities that are found in the other temples. A difference is that the Swaminarayan Temple also has *murtis* (statues) and pictures of their guru lineage, of which Pramukh

Swami is the fifth. These are worshipped and bathed and fed in the same way the deities are. A special chair is set aside for Pramukh Swami, on which his picture rests, but on which he sits when he visits Jackson.

The Swaminarayan Temple holds weekly services on Sunday evening, which approximately two hundred people attend. Special holidays draw about three hundred people, and very special occasions, such as Diwali, the "Festival of Lights," will draw over five hundred people. Unlike the other two Jackson temples, the Swaminarayan Temple has "sermons" every week. A typical *sabha*, or assembly, includes *kirtans* (as discussed above), a sermon (given by a layperson in Jackson; in larger centers, given by trained *sadhus* or "saints"), a video of Pramukh Swami, and then the *arati*, or waving of lights. Children and teens join their parents for the *arati*, but attend classes during the rest of the service. The classes are divided up according to age and gender. BAPS members maintain strict separation of the genders at religious functions. Males and females sit on separate sides of the room, and eat in separate rooms following the service. In fact, women often plan and hold their own religious celebrations. Otherwise, they would not have a chance to lead a service or give a talk. Women are not allowed in the physical presence of their guru because he is a strict celibate. Even so, there are more women involved with BAPS (about 60 percent) than men. Women have faith in Pramukh Swami and receive guidance through his books and in dreams, and so they do not feel the need to be with him physically. Pramukh Swami has visited the Jackson temple several times. Even though he has a million followers from around the world, several people said that he remembers everybody's name, as well as the names of family members. Having a living guru ties the members of this group together, creating a family-like bond among them.

Religion in the Home

Worshipping in a temple plays a secondary role to worshipping within the home. Overwhelmingly, it is women who perform the daily worship. Although some men may light a candle and say a prayer in the morning, women almost invariably view performing *puja* as their role in the family. Men, on the other hand, often spoke of their role as performing *karma yoga*, the yoga of action. One professor pointed to his books in his office and said, "They are the way I worship."

Almost all Hindu homes have an altar. Some altars are simple with a single deity represented along with a candle, while others are elaborate with

11.6. Home *puja*. Photo by Greg Williamson.

pictures and small statues of many deities and sometimes gurus as well. In some homes an entire room is set aside for daily worship. Many of the homes we visited had *puja* altars in the kitchen pantry, with some shelves housing a deity, and other shelves serving as storage space for the implements needed such as candles and incense. The daily rituals that women (and sometimes men) performed varied. Everyone of all ages, however, stressed that a person must bathe before performing any kind of worship. The simplest form of daily worship is to light a candle or, more often, turn on an electric light on the altar. More complicated worship involves chanting *shlokas*, verses, to one or more deities. A few of the people we visited spend a full hour in ritual worship, chanting and making offerings to deities on the family altar. The simpler forms of worship are more common. Many pointed out that they simply do not have the time that their parents had to devote to worship. One family we visited has a *puja* in their laundry room, which is on the way to the garage. That way they can stop and say a short prayer on their way out the door before they begin work or school. A simple prayer is viewed as enough, and this attitude is something they want to pass on to their children. As one woman said, "I just want to give my daughter a foundation. Simple things, like on religious holidays, do something.

Wake up; pray to God; don't forget where you're from. You don't have to do like my grandmother and have some elaborate nine- or ten-step process of offerings. Just close your eyes and think about God. On a holiday, do something. We don't have a priest come. But don't ever be in a phase where you don't do anything."

PART TWO: HINDU VALUES AND BEHAVIORS

Existing research on the first generation of immigrants looks at the activities they undertake when transmitting traditions and rituals to the next generation. As Joshi[7] has argued, though, much of this scholarship does not consider "lived religion," which refers to everyday behaviors and practices rather than formal worship or rigid rules. As he puts it, "Lived religion encompasses not only ritual practices but also principles and tenets internalized and applied in daily interactions and decisions." In this section, as an exploration of the "lived religion" of Indian Americans in Jackson, we will examine the values that our respondents hold in high esteem, such as human warmth in relationships, tolerance for non-Hindu others, and respect for education. We will also try to understand how young Indian Americans view the practices of dating and arranged marriage, and how they go about finding life partners.

Caring Relationships

When we visited people's homes where children were present, respect for elders was obvious. Teenagers and college-aged young adults offered tea or food to their parents and to us as we were talking. This is something that would be rare in a European American home. Many respondents expressed the view that their children, even when grown, would consult them about decisions. As one woman said, "My daughter is twenty-one, but she still has to get my permission to go anywhere. The main thing, though, is that everyone in the family has to be very caring for each other." This caring is expressed through the willingness of family members to sacrifice their time and material goods to help their aging parents or to give their children the best education possible.

Many spoke of warmth and depth in human relations outside of the family as well. It is expressed through dropping everything when a friend is in need, or through readily opening one's doors to receive others. Some felt that interaction among Indian friends had a more informal tone than European American interactions. They expressed how they can drop in on a friend any time without even calling. With a tinge of chiding, one respondent talked of how European Americans ask, "How are you?" and then walk away without waiting to hear the answer. One woman stated, "When it comes to relationships between neighbors in India, it's in the culture to be friendly, to be informal, to help. Whereas here in the United States you may not know the neighbors at all and you cannot feel really comfortable in going and saying, 'Can I borrow this?' In India, it is very common." A physician spoke of this quality of human warmth in relation to his patients. He said, "The most important thing about being a doctor is to spend a lot of time with the patient, answering questions until he is satisfied. If I rushed people out so I could see more patients, I wouldn't feel good in my heart. It's a cultural value—that respect for human beings. When people leave you, they should feel very happy."

Tolerance for Non-Hindu Others

Another quality held in high regard among Jackson Hindus is tolerance. In fact, most of our interviewees mentioned tolerance, broad-mindedness, or flexibility as forming the core of Hinduism's identity. One male respondent said, "To me, a Hindu is a tolerant person, one who understands, empathizes with all human beings, treats them equally and with respect." He felt his Hindu identity blended easily with his American identity because "my view of Hinduism is one that makes me a citizen of the world. I feel that. I am not concerned or upset about other religions. I am very tolerant. And hence I can go to a church." A woman commented, "Prayer is the main theme of any religion. So we are all common that way. So I can identify with any religion. I have no problem going to church and praying to Jesus because I know he is God." Another woman expressed that she was tolerant of other religions when she was growing up in India. Then she came to America where she experienced religious intolerance from other people, but still she did not give up the value of tolerance. She said, "It is very hard when other people are intolerant to teach tolerance to your children or yourself for that matter. I had to struggle hard. I had to struggle for a long time in order to come to the point where I say, no matter, I don't mind if someone else is intolerant but I won't give up my tolerance because it's such a valuable thing."

Transmitting Knowledge

Most respondents stayed in touch with Hindu culture through learning stories from parents and grandparents. One young woman reported, "When I was little, my mom used to tell me Hindu mythological stories. I loved those. Every night when I went to sleep, my mom used to tell me a story, and that's how I know those stories." Comic books that relate the religious stories and the biographies of Hindu saints, such as the very popular *Amar Chitra Katha* series, were important for both first- and second-generation Hindus. The television series *Mahabharat* and *Ramayana* (based on two of the greatest Hindu epics) were very influential in India when they were shown there several years ago, and many second-generation Hindus own tapes of these series. Bollywood films are world-famous, and many of our younger respondents said that they *loved* Indian movies. One young man said, "Because I came here when I was four years old, and I never got to study Indian history, I watch movies like *Lagaan, Legend of Bhagat Singh, Jodha Akbar*, those that tell the history of India, *Ashoka*. I've learned so much from them."

It is important to note that, besides listening to bedtime stories, reading Indian comic books, and watching old television series and Indian films, many Indian American families in Jackson also watch several Indian television channels through satellite TV. This helps them stay in touch with the current events in their home country. Indian Americans in Jackson are also fortunate because they get to watch current Indian hit films on the big screen several times in a year.

Most of our interviewees indicated that education received a high priority in their families and in their lives. Several young adults said that the tremendous emphasis placed on education by their parents is a part of Hindu culture: "Indian parents expect way more of their children than normal parents. Indian parents expect their kids to be the best out of the best. I don't blame them. All of them expect that, not just one." Another young woman said, "Our parents always stress education in our family. We can't talk about anything else. Education is first, then marriage and everything else comes after that."

Some indicated that the emphasis on education was prominent because they wanted a better life. For example, a young man, on his way to becoming a physician, said, "I think all Indian parents believe that education is a way to success in the future, to attaining money and other things needed for a comfortable future." Another young man said, "I think it's related to the fact that they've come here with an opportunity to make their kids' lives better than their own when they were growing up."

Hindu parents are determined to help their children financially so that they can get a good education. One woman said, "There was absolutely no talk of me even stopping after college. I had to go on to professional school. The best part about it is that they try to pay for your education and try to make sure that you're not in debt when you come out. I know my family's done that for me, and I know a lot of other Indian families have done that for their kids. They make sure that their kids don't have to worry about the monetary part so long as they just study. My parents put a big emphasis on me not working during school. I did work during summers and stuff, but while I was studying, there was absolutely no working, so I could concentrate only on my studies."

Views on the Caste System

The caste system has been an integral feature of Hinduism for millennia. Traditionally, each Hindu belongs to the caste into which she or he was born for life. The hierarchical system of social stratification consists of four large groups called *varnas* and thousands of subgroups called *jatis*. *Brahmins* (priests) are located at the top of the caste system. Below the *Brahmins* are the *Kshatriyas* (the warrior *varna*), and below the *Kshatriyas* are the *Vaishyas* (the *varna* that engages in business). The *Shudra varna* (the caste that serves the other three castes) is the lowest category. Outside of the varna system are the untouchables or *dalits*.

When people were asked how they felt about the caste system, the general opinion was that it is no longer important. One man held this opinion: "What I do not like about the caste system is how dogmatic it is, how you have a birthright to be born into a certain caste and have a total inability to climb from one caste to another. I think that is where the caste system went wrong. The caste system was originally simply to identify the nature of work that a person was doing." Most respondents said that they did not identify with their caste background. Some of those who *do* identify with their caste background are Brahmins (the highest Hindu *varna*), but they stressed that they did not discriminate against other castes. A fifty-eight-year-old Bengali woman stated, "It's my privilege that I am Brahmin but I don't think I am superior to non-Brahmin." Similarly, a fifty-six-year-old Maharashtrian woman said, "I am Brahmin and I am proud of it and I don't discriminate against anyone who is a non-Brahmin." A third woman, a forty-seven-year-old Tamil Brahmin woman said, "I very strongly identify myself with my caste. I don't know if that's right or wrong, but I guess that's the way I've been raised."

Dating and Marriage Practices

Bollywood films are generally about "boy meets girl" and fantastic romances, but the custom of dating is foreign to the Indian Hindu culture even today, and we found that most of our first- and second-generation Hindus did not date either. Most of the first-generation Hindus met their life partners through the system of arranged marriages, but their children had mixed views about the custom of arranged marriage.

Most second-generation Hindus interviewed said they did not date. When asked if they dated, most young men and women responded with a prim "no." They were not always opposed to the idea, but it did not figure into their activities. One woman said, "Well, I prefer not to right now. It's not that I think it's a sin or anything. I just don't, because I have a lot of things I need to focus on, and I prefer not to have any distractions. I just haven't found anybody that I like that I'd choose over focusing on my studies."

A very few did choose to date, but they were cautious about getting into relationships. One young man said he would get into relationships only with someone who has "high family values." A young woman said that she did date but there was "no sex, no kissing, no touching, that kind of thing. Going out to dinner, go watch the movies together, that's fine. There are lines that can't be crossed."

If they did not date, how would they find marriage partners? Would they opt for arranged marriages? What were their opinions about arranged marriages? Opinions varied widely. Some had reservations about arranged marriages: "I believe in them as a last resort. Sometimes they've been successful and sometimes they've been unsuccessful." Another said, "Arranged marriage, it's a big gamble, a big risk. I don't like arranged marriages at all." Yet some young persons approved of their parents finding potential life partners for them. A young man said, "To me, arranged means my parents will talk to me about it and will not just fix everything. They'll ask me if I like the girl or not. It's kind of a misconception people have. They think it's forced." Another young woman said that she didn't agree with "parents coming home and saying to me, you have to marry this boy or you don't marry anybody at all. What I don't mind is, them saying, here's a prospective guy, check him out."

CONCLUSION

It is hoped that this brief snapshot (captured in 2007 and 2008) of first- and second-generation Indian Hindu Americans in Jackson, Mississippi, has conveyed a sense of what it is like to be a Hindu in the South in the age of globalization. In this chapter, we have seen how Jackson Hindus negotiate their Hindu identity by teaching their values, rituals, and beliefs to their children through family traditions and through establishing Hindu temples. Hindu communities crystallize around temples, and we have seen how the three temples in Jackson cater to the needs of different Hindu communities.

As Furseth and Repstad[8] note, religion frequently increases in importance as a result of migration. It may strengthen the feeling of fellowship and revitalize religious traditions. This is certainly the case with Jackson Hindus, who have established three temples in Jackson to serve the roughly five hundred Hindu families who live in this region.

Based on our interviews, we can conclude that Jackson Hindus belonging to the first generation have been successful in transmitting their values, beliefs, and customs to the second generation through means such as that of bedtime stories, Indian comics, old television series, Indian films, and satellite TV. We did not find any significant differences between the first- and second-generation immigrants in their values, beliefs, and practices. But will the second generation play as strong a role in maintaining Hindu religious beliefs and practices as their parents did? This is a question that will require further research in the future.

NOTES

1. Andrea Useem. *Religious News Service.* "Hindus Thrive as Buddhists Struggle to Pass on the Faith." Feb. 25, 2008. Available at http://pewforum.org/news/display.php?NewsID=15035. Accessed August 11, 2008.

2. The thirty interviews conducted by the authors of first-generation Hindus were anonymous; the thirty conducted by Millsaps students of second-generation Hindus from the ages of fourteen to twenty-nine are on deposit with the Mississippi Oral History Project. The authors have chosen to keep all names anonymous for the purpose of this chapter.

3. Raymond Brady Williams. *Religions of Immigrants from India and Pakistan: New Threads in the American Tapestry.* New York: Cambridge University Press, 1988, 11.

4. Auvaiyar. Quoted in Vasudha Narayanan, "Creating the South Indian 'Hindu' Experience in the United States," in Raymond Brady Williams, ed., *A Sacred Thread:*

Modern Transmission of Hindu Traditions in India and Abroad. New York: Columbia University Press, 1992, 147.

5. Williams. *Religions of Immigrants from India and Pakistan*, 177.

6. http://www.hotel-online.com/News/PR2004_3rd/Jul04_PatelHotel.html. Accessed August 14, 2008.

7. Khyati Joshi. *New Roots in America's Sacred Ground: Religion, Race, and Ethnicity in Indian America*. New Brunswick, NJ: Rutgers University Press, 2006, 8.

8. Inger Furseth and Pal Repstad. *An Introduction to the Sociology of Religion: Classical and Contemporary Perspectives*. Burlington, VT: Ashgate Publishing Co, 2006, 172.

12

FILIPINAS IN THE DEEP SOUTH

Reading Domestic Oral Narratives as Sites
of Politicization and Community Building

—LINDA PIERCE ALLEN

Of the population for the state of Mississippi, totaling over 2.9 million, roughly 4,000, or .13 percent, are Filipinos.[1] The Filipino communities in the northern and coastal areas of the state are facilitated by the presence of military bases such as the Naval Air Station in Meridian and Keesler Air Force Base in Biloxi; these bases produce transitory populations of traditional Filipino military families and fairly typical representations of the Filipino immigrant family living in rural areas in the United States. The communities in south Mississippi, however, incorporating the greater Hattiesburg area and the surrounding cities of Columbia, Sumrall, Purvis, Petal, Ellisville, Laurel, and spanning even as far north as Jackson, are atypical. Despite the presence of Camp Shelby, an army base located in Hattiesburg, the Filipino community in south Mississippi is largely a Filipina community, comprised mainly of first-generation Filipina immigrant women married to white American men. Sprinkled throughout rural Mississippi, this community of women found one another across county lines, through dry counties and wet counties, in Chinese restaurants and Catholic churches, in hospitals and universities, and in markets sifting through pigs' feet and chitterlings in search of oxtail and tripe. Spread over a ninety-mile radius centered on "the Hub City" of Hattiesburg, these women forged ties across distance, dialects, and provincial differences to create a community that would initially provide a social network, and eventually establish critical systems of support. Creating a women's network ultimately geared towards Filipina survival in the Deep South, these women invoke the spirit of the *Babaylan*: in keeping with Leny Mendoza's description of the *Babaylan*, they are "keepers of wisdom, folk therapists, folk philosophers," and "transmitters of culture" who "stabilize social structures" (148).[2] Serving as healers, leaders, and community builders, bringing strength and balance to one another, Filipinas in south Mississippi have created a network that honors, celebrates, and embodies Filipina culture. Having traveled across miles and specific cultural divides in order to find one another, they *became Babaylan*, serving one another in their efforts to adjust to life in Mississippi.

COMMUNITY-BASED RESEARCH

Oral narratives of some of the longest permanently settled Filipinas in south Mississippi are housed at the University of Southern Mississippi Center for Oral History. These narratives were collected through personal interviews I conducted with community members in order to chronicle the living history of Filipinas in the Pine Belt. All interviewees consented to donate their material to the university for use in research, for the preservation of historical memory and the documentation of historical record. It is important to note that interviewees maintained editorial control over the digital record: I followed their directions on when to stop recording so they could speak "off the record," and when to go back and erase material they would rather keep private. Interviewees were also able to place restrictions on their donations, such as stipulations on the duration of personal anonymity or the date of public accessibility. While some of the women asked to remain anonymous and some did not, I have chosen to maintain the anonymity of all of the interviewees referenced in this article for the sake of consistency as well as privacy.

The information in this article is based on an analysis of these oral narratives, along with my own membership and participation in the community over the past six years. My personal knowledge as a community insider helped to guide some of the serious ethical considerations driving the research, such as: which of the community's "secrets" were okay to reveal, and which details should be kept private; how much detail I can provide about ongoing domestic violence interventions without putting people in jeopardy; what kind of information will help women as opposed to placing them further at risk; and how I can analyze the culture of Filipinas in south Mississippi critically, while representing them fairly, accurately, and in a manner of which they can be proud. In my attempt to provide enough useful information to the reader that still honors the community, I listened to the various wishes of the participants both off the record and outside the realm of the interview, and censored information accordingly. As a result, this article can provide only a partial picture of life in the Filipina American Society of Mississippi—a glimpse into a complex, thriving, and continually evolving community.

PHILIPPINE–U.S. RELATIONS

Filipina Americans are unique amongst immigrant women because of the history of colonialism between the United States and the Philippines that connects the two countries in meaningful ways. At the turn of the last century, the Philippines allied with the United States in the war against Spanish oppression that held the Philippines, along with several other countries, captive as colonies under Spanish rule. In a surprising twist, the United States ended the war through a treaty with Spain that effectively transferred "ownership" of the Philippines to the States. Stunned by this betrayal, the Philippines immediately declared war on the U.S. in a fight for independence. The Philippine-American War ended with a U.S. victory, rendering the islands an "unincorporated territory" of the U.S., to be occupied and colonized by the States for almost the next fifty years. As a colony of the United States, the Philippines became economically, militarily, demographically, and culturally tied to the U.S.: during the first half of the last century, migration patterns, legal and educational institutions, and even social infrastructures in the Philippines were influenced by U.S. colonization. When colonialism finally ended, the Philippines began the long-term project of "decolonization"—working to reimagine and rebuild a national identity (and its corresponding institutional structures) in the wake of independence. Today, the Philippines still exists in a neocolonial relationship with the U.S.; in other words, many of the aforementioned ties to its most recent colonizer remain intact, to varying degrees, despite the fact that it is no longer a protectorate of the U.S. Of course, neocolonialism collides with the project of decolonization in ways that complicate the ongoing affiliation between the two countries. This unique history marks the profound, meaningful connection between the nations, made even more convoluted by continuing transnational migration.[3]

In the midst of these complex, ambiguous relations, Filipinas who migrate to the States and become "Filipina Americans" experience a strange amalgamation of conflicting cultural identities. One of the earliest members of the Filipina community in south Mississippi describes this hybrid identity as a liminal state, existing in between two cultures. She acknowledges that, while she is "still a Filipino," when she goes home she doesn't exactly "think like [a Filipino] anymore. And then when I'm over here, I'm not an American, I don't think like them also."[4] Like many other ethnic minority immigrants, Filipina Americans occupy a hybrid space, wherein they are neither recognized (nor do they self-identify) as solely Filipina nor solely American: they are neither, yet both. While much has been written about the hybrid identity of the minority immigrant,[5] the hybrid identity of Pinays[6] is further complicated by the ongoing neocolonial relations between their home and adopted countries. Similar to other colonized countries, in the aftermath of colonialism Filipinos were faced with the task of recovering a national identity—institutional and cultural—independent from its former colonizers. This process of identity reconstruction defines the struggle to decolonize—a conflicted, ambivalent struggle that continues long after the actual period of colonization has ended. To complicate matters further, over the past several decades the world, and certainly U.S.-Philippine relations, has moved towards neocolonialism, a modern-day form of colonization that relies on international economic strategies to continue the indirect rule of formerly colonized countries. Given the complicated political history between these two countries, the hybrid identity of the Filipina American emigrant becomes even more complex.

FILIPINAS IN SOUTH MISSISSIPPI

Unlike the abundant Filipino communities populating the West Coast, the comparatively tiny population of Filipinos in the Deep South exists within much smaller family structures. Traditional Filipino families extend far beyond the immediate, nuclear family, including a strong sense of extended familial, sibling, and filial obligations. Although the subtropical climate of the Magnolia State and the hospitality for which the South is known are familiar to Filipinas, the separateness, individuation, and isolation of the American nuclear family is not. Nostalgic for the fellowship of the large, Catholic Filipino family and the company of village life in the provinces of the Philippines, Filipinas in south Mississippi have actively worked to reconstruct a familiar sense of community in the rural South. In order to find one another across cities and counties, this tiny population of Filipina immigrants in south Mississippi was forced to overcome any internal divisions they may have carried over from differing regional, communal practices throughout the Philippines. The rural nature of the state helped to bridge cultural differences, bringing Filipinas from various provinces together to form a diverse, yet common sense of community.

Many of these women are bonded by their membership in a global network of OCWs—overseas contract workers mostly comprised of domestics (maids and nannies), entertainers, nurses, and health care professionals. Filipina OCWs are mainly single women who enter into the international labor trade in order to help support their families back home, and effectively bolster the Philippine economy with their remittances in the process. Away from home, family, and country, OCWs are often exploited in order to meet the demands of an increasingly greedy international market. In south Mississippi, several members of the Filipina population began their original emigration as OCWs before they married and settled in the States. The strength and resiliency they developed while working overseas as lone, young women is embodied in the matrifocal[7] community they have built in the rural South. Today, there are Filipinas working in many different types of professions throughout south Mississippi, although the dominant careers are commensurate with the national as well as international average: the majority of Filipinas living abroad work as nurses and domestics, adhering to an overtly feminized culture of service to others.[8] Other Filipinas hold various positions in the professional industry, retail, and education, although the number of military wives (and retired military wives) in the Filipina population is also notable.

While many of these women began their emigration as OCWs, all of them are *Balikbayan*. Tied to their homeland through family as well as cultural roots, *Balikbayan* are Filipinos permanently residing abroad (regardless of nationality or acquired foreign citizenship). The *Balikbayan* population consists of OCWs, immigrants, and expatriates, all of whom live in exile from their homeland. Yet, aside from place of residence, what defines the *Balikbayan* is her enduring connection and sense of obligation to her mother country. For *Balikbayan*, the channel they opened with their initial immigration remains a viable passageway between their lives in America and their homeland and family in the Philippines. For *Balikbayan* in Mississippi, these bilateral channels allow for a continual, albeit temporary, return to one's homeland, as well as the possibility for family members to visit and sometimes immigrate to the United States. Most of the Filipinas in south Mississippi travel back home to the Philippines frequently, making regularly scheduled trips, spending long visits with family and countless extended relatives. Many of their husbands and children have accompanied them on these visits, creating a new generation of Filipino American children who develop a sophisticated sense of transnational identity at a young age. Ties to the homeland are also maintained as parents and other relatives from the Philippines come to Mississippi to visit for several months at a time. When Filipinas themselves are not traveling through this channel, their "*Balikbayan* Boxes" are: the practice of sending home packages containing gifts and items that may be expensive or difficult to acquire in the Philippines is a popular one for *Balikbayan* across the United States. Comprising a very active *Balikbayan* community, Filipinas in south Mississippi remain connected to their country of origin even decades after settling permanently in the United States.

THE ROLE OF FOOD IN FILIPINO AMERICAN CULTURE

Food has always played an important role in the establishment of Filipina communities; in Mississippi, however, Filipino food preparation initially presented some challenges. In my interview with one woman who came to settle permanently with her American husband in south Mississippi in 1972, she described what life was like as the lone Filipina in the Hattiesburg area.[9] As "the first Filipina," charmed by the city's one Chinese restaurant at that time, she witnessed the slow growth of the Filipina population and is considered the founding mother of the now thriving community. Within five years, there were three Filipinas living in the area, and together they began to connect with the transitory Filipino populations at the naval base in Meridian. By 1978, there were still no Asian markets available offering necessary ingredients, so the women learned to make *everything* from scratch. Many Americans today are familiar with the thinly wrapped Filipino egg roll called *lumpia*; although the recipe for making *lumpia* is rather simple, the process becomes far more complicated when the *lumpia* wrapper is not available for purchase at any grocery store. Whereas today the Internet has facilitated the easy exchange of ingredients and refrigerated goods that may be otherwise difficult to acquire, prior to the advent of the Internet the acquisition of Asian ingredients in rural Mississippi was difficult, to say the least. In order to eat familiar foods from back home, these women not only had to learn how to make the dishes—they had to learn how to make the ingredients. Using cookbooks, recipes learned from phone calls back home, and recipes acquired from Filipina wives stationed at the naval base, they taught each other to make their own *lumpia* wrapper, *siopao*, and *hopia*, along with more standard fare such as *pancit*, *adobo*, and

12.1a and 12.1b. Signs announcing one of the major get-togethers of Mississippi Filipinos, the annual Christmas party. One is from 2004 and the other from 2008. For privacy reasons, no Filipinos are pictured in the photos. Photos by Linda Allen.

empanada.[10] The need to make every single ingredient—including bean sprouts, which you could not find back then and had to be cultivated from fresh *munggo*[11] beans—gave cooking "from scratch" a whole new meaning. Although the work was tedious and difficult, the taste of home was necessary for new immigrants experiencing culture shock.

Food is central to Filipino culture, and the preparation of the food—down to the making of each ingredient—helped to facilitate the production of a Filipino community.[12] As more women arrived in south Mississippi in the 1980s, it became easier to divide the difficult cooking tasks. As the women came together to cook foods from home once a week, the Filipina American community became established. This community was essential to the women's ability to survive and thrive in small, rural towns so far from home. Several of the earliest Filipinas recall the need to see others

12.2. The front of the brochure for the 2004 Christmas pageant for the Filipino-American Society of Mississippi. Photo by Linda Allen.

Dedication

So many of us left home and traveled across oceans to begin here anew. The winds were not always calm as we struggled to create a feeling of home in this foreign land. We left loved ones behind and were torn away from everything familiar as we chased promises and dreams. Others of us, though born here, were raised with a sense of nostalgia for our home away from home. Longing for our past, we hold onto traditions, maintain languages and preserve recipes in order to recreate the type of community that we value so dear. All of us maintain ties to our homeland; we go back for extended visits, we write letters, we send and receive packages in order to sustain our cultural ties. Together we work to build a new community; together, we strive to create a new home.

We have reached across oceans, across provinces, across dialects in our attempts to establish a sense of "home" for ourselves here in Mississippi. Yet, in the midst of all of our searching, we ultimately found home in the most basic place of all: in each other. "Home," for us, is found in our potlucks, party planning, rehearsals, and birthday celebrations. Home lies within each auntie who shows up late because she's on "Filipina Time," each young child who wants to learn the Tinikling, and each new member, recently relocated to Mississippi and searching for a Pinay community. Home is the laughter that breaks out when we miss a step, or collide during dance rehearsal; it is the support we give one another when we have suffered a loss, or a great victory. "Home," for us, is the Filipino American Society of Mississippi. We give thanks for one another, and we welcome you into our home.

The Filipinos

12.3. Dedication written by Linda Allen for the 2004 Christmas pageant. Photo by Linda Allen.

who looked like them, spoke their language, and shared their culture. Even differences in dialect became insignificant compared to the comfort the women felt at seeing "the same kind of face" as their own.[13] The process of building community was slow, but even in the early days when there were only three women, they persevered. Despite the initial challenges, the need to maintain a sense of themselves and their cultural practices as Filipinas was too important to forego. Eventually, as the women began to acculturate to Mississippi life, they became Filipina *American*—a cultural hybrid, not entirely one or the other. Their hybridity is reflected in the food, which serves as a marker of Filipina American communal identity. For a New

Year's Eve party, for example, south Mississippi Filipinas might make the traditional *pancit* dish, containing long noodles to celebrate long life at the start of the New Year, alongside such traditional New Year's fare as black-eyed peas, greens, and cabbage, thought to bring good luck and prosperity throughout the South.

THE SIGNIFICANCE OF THE KITCHEN

As they worked to build community, Filipinas congregated in the familiar space of the kitchen. The very idea of the kitchen as a purely domestic space is challenged by Filipinas who rely on this space to engage in community building and facilitate the exchange of information. Almost every Filipino community activity takes place through a communion over Filipino food; entailed in this communion is ongoing conversation, including an acknowledgement (and recovery) of cultural history and a dispersal of news significant to the community. The kitchen is crucial for beginning stages of community development, as it provides the opportunity to bridge regional differences. When one of the more than 90 million citizens of a seven-thousand-island archipelago arrives in Mississippi, social, linguistic, and ethnic variation is practically inevitable. Seeing how dishes like *karé karé* or *pinakbet*[14] are prepared differently in Quezon City versus northern Luzon, or in the province of Cebu versus Iloilo, often leads to discussions on the cultural differences between Tagalogs and Ilocanos, or Visayans and Ilonggos—ethnic groups in the Philippines hailing from different regions and speaking different languages and dialects.[15] Informal conversations over foods from back home help to unite the women across differences; although not every dish prepared is Filipino food, it is understood that the real incentive for coming together is the communion over foods from "back home." Yet even later, as these early, purely social gatherings transformed into planning meetings for community events such as the Philippine Independence Day celebration or the annual Christmas pageant, the kitchen remained the primary site of activity.

TSISMIS

The Tagalog word for "gossip" is *tsismis*—pronounced "chis-miss"—but, as in most cases, the English translation is not exact; *tsismis* carries more weight, more import than simple gossip. *Tsismis* is the discourse that serves to sustain Filipina communities, especially in rural areas such as south Mississippi. It is part of the membership code for the community, although much of the information shared belongs to a larger, global society as well as to this local group of women. *Tsismis* provides subtext and context to this inherently transnational *Balikbayan* community, effectively politicizing the group. While most of the women would not identify themselves as part of a political cooperative per se, in this hybrid, neocolonial immigrant community still struggling (often ambivalently) to decolonize its people, *tsismis* is always political. And in southern Mississippi, these politics have played out in serious ways over the past thirty-eight years.

PEN PALS

Both oral histories and community *tsismis* reveal that a disproportionate number of Filipinas first came to south Mississippi as either pen pals or some variation thereof. The term "pen pal" signifies something particular in the Filipina community: the modern-day version of the "mail order bride," the burgeoning pen pal industry, bolstered by the advent of the Internet, has supplanted mail orders by finding ways around tougher immigration laws intended to curb the international "wife" trade. Because pen pals have yet to carry the visibility and the accompanying stigma of mail order brides—although they are actually quite similar in practice—they are still sometimes viewed with more legitimacy within certain circles in the community. As it turns out, the reason a largely first-generation Filipina community dominates south Mississippi is precisely because many of them were brought to the South as pen pals, at once creating both the necessity for a very specific, supportive and political community organization and an incredibly complicated political economy for Filipinas in Mississippi. Pen pal communities differ significantly from traditional Filipino communities in the United States, for obvious reasons: they are entirely matrifocal, always interracial, and always first-generation; almost all of the husbands are local whites, previously divorced at least once, and there is usually a considerable age gap between the spouses, who have produced a new generation of American-born *mestizo* and *mestiza* children who are already seeming to expand standard notions of *mestizaje*, even at their young ages.[16]

Certain variations of the pen pal ritual allow prospective grooms to circumvent much of the standard practice entirely, bringing the man directly to a pool of eligible women in order to select a bride to marry and take back with him to the United States. These women are sometimes located through personal contacts, as was the case with one of the earliest Filipinas in south Mississippi, whose eventual husband came to the Philippines with a Filipina friend who was married to an American.[17] In this instance a lonely, divorced American military veteran, impressed with the Filipinas whom he had met in the past, came to the Philippines specifically looking for a young wife. Although his Filipina friend had accompanied him to introduce him to one young woman in particular, when that woman was not interested he turned his attention to her cousin. Although he was fifty-three years old, and the young cousin was only eighteen, he asked her if she would like to accompany him to America. In this way, the prospective groom is proposing more than just marriage: he is proposing a new life in the famed land of opportunity, and the prospect of someone helping herself and her family financially. The young woman was finishing her second year of college, yet she was well aware of the promise of the American dream. She explains that, in the Philippines, "you hear about America, how beautiful it is: America, a land of opportunity," and acknowledges the economic lure of a country where "everybody has a car" and a color TV. Nevertheless, when offered the prospect of immigrating to America in exchange for marriage to a man who "looked like MacArthur," she was initially reticent. She recalls that at first she said, "no, I don't know," but after he called a family meeting she was persuaded by her parents and seven brothers and sisters that this was too great an opportunity to let pass. Ironically, the local Filipino police chief ran a background check on the young woman because he was looking out for the best interests of the American man rather than his own female citizen. The couple met each other in the month of May, married in June, and came to the States in July. The woman recalls the wedding as "just a simple ceremony, civil, nothing elegant, nothing extravagant. . . . No fairy tale."

Another variation of the pen pal comes in the example of a Filipina OCW living and working in Japan to support her family of seven back home.[18] In this case the prospective groom was a divorced American serviceman also stationed in Japan, who frequented the club where the OCW was performing nightly as a singer. The man kept purchasing expensive American gifts from the military base and delivering them to the apartment shared by several of the singers. The gifts were not addressed to anyone in particular; rather, they were intended as an offer of courtship for anyone in the apartment who might be interested. He jokingly referred to the gifts as "bait," intended to lure a potential spouse. Although there was a considerable age difference, as he was forty-five and she was twenty-four, the Filipina saw potential in this "nerdy-looking" man who had already "slimmed down" his formerly heavy frame in response to teasing from his friends. The two had to struggle through a language barrier: she was fluent in Tagalog and Japanese, and spoke a little Spanish, but was just beginning to learn English at that time. She recalls, "I didn't know when we were dating, he kept on telling me let's do this paperwork. I didn't know he had a plan for the States." After dating him for six months, her OCW contract expired and she returned to the Philippines. He then surprised her by calling her from the Manila airport and announcing he was in town. She recalls, "It's just like he had a plan already. He said, 'Let's go take a picture,' like every time we go we have to take a picture, like he's giving a history, because he had to document everything." With considerable documentation, he applied for a visa for the Filipina, completely unbeknownst to her. She remembers, "He came to the house ... I didn't know he was waiting for the visa. He thought it came that month because he already sent it off. He stayed like three weeks, waiting for the visa."

Although both of these examples resulted in twenty-year marriages, with the former only ending when the young Filipina was widowed and the latter still going strong, not every pen pal bride finds a happy ending in the United States. The danger in the pen pal relationship is that the young woman is making a huge gamble: in exchange for the opportunity for a new start and the ability to help her family back home, she must trust her very life to the hands of a virtual stranger taking her thousands of miles away from everything familiar. Once in the United States, she is essentially at the mercy of her new husband, with few options in the event the marriage fails. She usually arrives in the U.S. without knowing how to drive and has few to no contacts in her new locale. Both the financial expectations of her family back home and her immigration status depend on her remaining in her marriage; even her devout belief in Catholicism discourages her from divorce. One of the women to whom many look as a leader in the south Mississippi Filipina community acknowledges that the pen pal marriage is "a risk you take."[19] Although she came to the United States as a pen pal herself, she says she would "never recommend" it to anyone else and, in fact, has refused to serve as a contact for prospective grooms searching for pen pal brides. Just as the Filipina women have formed a strong network of support for one another, the local men have formed a network to assist one another in finding Filipina wives; yet, the men's network relies on the assistance of the women who are willing to help them make contact with relatives and friends from back home. Instead of assisting the men seeking pen pals, this Filipina leader has devoted a lot of her time to helping new immigrants adjust to their lives in Mississippi.

DOMESTIC VIOLENCE IN PEN PAL MARRIAGES

Since the pen pal bride is at the mercy of a virtual stranger with somewhat questionable intent, there is widespread potential for spousal abuse. Although the new bride is largely unaware of this potential, domestic violence within pen pal marriages is a not-so-secret occurrence among the Filipina community members in Mississippi. It is a "secret" that is fairly common knowledge, one that is rarely discussed openly but constantly shared with one another—a fact that is voiced, just not very loudly. It is acknowledged, yet denied by those Filipinas who are seen as exceptions. A woman who ends up in a successful pen pal marriage is thought of as "one of the few lucky Filipinas" because her husband is "good to her."[20] Although the plight of the "unlucky" Filipina pen pal is far more common, the women usually lower their voices and slow their speech when they talk about those situations. There's not a silence about it, exactly, because it is softly spoken— it's almost a shame, and a denial of that shame at the same time because so many of the community members themselves are somehow implicated in the abuse (as either victims, or contact persons who helped facilitate what they thought was just a marriage of opportunity). Of course, the ambivalence surrounding the position of Filipina pen pals is irrevocably yoked to the ambivalence intrinsic to the neocolonial position of Filipina subjectivity. It is exposed not only in the slowed speech and lowered voices, but in the act of *tsismis* itself—the urge to reveal that which is both urgent and ugly, to give (soft or quiet) voice to the not-so-secret, to render unofficial common knowledge "official" community gossip.

When a young woman immigrates to this new land with hopes for greater opportunities, she is often surprised by what she encounters. Women who grew up in well-populated cities describe feelings of isolation after moving to a rural area absent *any* nearby neighbors, much less familiar Filipina faces. Women who marry very young often arrive without knowledge of basic cooking skills, not to mention that of recipes from back home. One woman remembers losing "a lot of weight" and feeling like she was "starving" because she "didn't know how to cook."[21] Others are surprised that the life they encounter is not commensurate with the one their new husbands had described to their families prior to the marriage. Far from home, local men are often able to misrepresent themselves and their intentions for their prospective brides. After several failed marriages to American women, one local man in his mid-fifties decided he wanted a young Filipina wife. With around sixty thousand dollars gained from an insurance settlement from a work-related injury, he passed himself off as a wealthy American. "Bragging about how much money he spent while he was there, he was like a king: he had a driver . . . he gambled in the casino like he was a millionaire. He showed everybody he had money."[22] Spending money by the tens of thousands, he promised a comfortable life to a loyal Filipina willing to dote on him in America; however, when his bride arrived in Mississippi where he lived a modest life, he put her to work at his roadside fruit stand and began his regimen of verbal abuse and physical violence to maintain control over her and make her stay.

In addition to misrepresentations of financial wealth, pen pals also fall prey to distortions of the prospective groom's emotional stability and hidden chemical dependencies. Having been divorced several times already, many of the men are either very lonely and suffering from depression, or bitter and searching for a submissive woman and a relationship over which they can maintain total control. It is no surprise that the frequency of alcoholism among pen pal husbands is disproportionately high, especially considering the ways that it corresponds with both depression and abuse. Such addictions are easily hidden during the pen pal courtship, only to be unveiled after marriage and migration, much to the surprise of the bride, who often remains married to her alcoholic spouse for the duration of his life.

Like alcoholism, the frequency of mental and physical violence as a means to control Filipina women is unfortunately also very high in pen pal communities. In one example, after a verbally and physically abusive man's pen pal bride escaped to relatives in another state, he returned to the Philippines to seek out yet another Filipina wife.[23] This time he searched for someone with no contacts in the States, and someone even younger; although his new bride was in her twenties (as opposed to his fifties), she could easily pass for sixteen. His abusive behavior became even more coercive with this younger wife, whom he manipulated into staying with him for several years despite her life of daily torment. In another example, one of the variations of the pen pal bride, a young woman met a much older, thrice-divorced Mississippi man who was working overseas and represented himself as a kindhearted and generous older man searching for a wife who could take care of him.[24] After he brought her to the States, he would leave her for a month at a time to return to his work abroad; completely isolated in her new country, the woman had to survive off the one hundred dollars a month with which he left her to live. Although she was literally struggling to survive on this menial amount of money, the husband used mental and physical violence to frighten the woman into staying in the marriage.

In addition to the threat of physical beating, there are several reports of the threat of gun violence against Filipinas in south Mississippi. In one instance, the husband of a pen pal threatened to "commit suicide if she left him"—but only after he took her life as well.[25] In another case, a Filipina's husband would hold a gun to her head and threaten her life in order to force her to stay in the marriage.[26] In many other examples, the women are virtually imprisoned in their homes by their paranoid, abusive husbands. After bringing his pen pal bride to the States, one man "would never let her off his sight," lest she attempt to leave. He brought her to become "a glorified maid," and to serve him with all of the privileges afforded in marriage as well.[27] Another woman, married to a retired man, recalls that for their first year of marriage, he "never went anywhere, he never left me alone in one year, never."[28]

Global Economics in Local Communities

An awareness of the complexities of pen pal communities in Mississippi can help us better understand their role in Mississippi, U.S., and international politics. As the long arm of the U.S. constabulary reaches around the globe, one consequence of U.S. militarization is its impact on the growing sex industry. As Venny Villapando explains, "Many of the Asian countries affected by the revived mail-order bride business have a history of U.S. military involvement" (324).[29] U.S. soldiers continue to provide an increasing demand for sex trade workers overseas; in response to this demand, impoverished women provide the supply that promises to lift them out of economic squalor. Many retired soldiers, having long stereotyped all "Asian" or "Oriental" women as the servile sex trade workers often supplied to U.S. military bases overseas, then contribute to the trafficking of women through "mail-order" or "pen-pal" catalogues. Although *Babaylan* is literally translated as "one who serves" (Mendoza 148), the notion of Filipinas as *servile* is actually counter to the spirit of the *Babaylan*, who symbolize powerful revolutionary community leaders demanding honor, respect, and the decolonization of women's bodies.

While the demand for pen pal brides originates locally, the supply is influenced by economics globally. Pen pal communities inherently foreground the connection between the local and the global, and politicize the domestic space by the very nature of their existence. Because the overwhelming majority of those who bear the brunt of globalization are "third world"[30] women, any discussion of Filipina pen pals must account for the sexual division of labor in the production of transnational capital.[31] In fact, the very nature of the Filipina and Filipina American feminism, or peminism[32] that is central to Pinay studies[33] engages the inequalities of power in the international economic order. As Delia D. Aguilar asserts, "[T]here [is] no way we could speak of Asian/Pacific women without at the same time implicating unequal power relations between the North and the South" (162).[34] In this self-proclaimed apolitical group of Filipinas, the personal is on a crash course with the political, as the machinations of local pen pal networks are at work within the global political economy. Because gender shapes economic divisions of labor, both with patterns of migration in general and with the sexual trafficking of women specifically, a peminist analysis (and, specifically, an analysis of the feminization of wage labor) is critical to any discussion of globalization.

Understanding the "Supply-Side"

In the supply and demand of pen pals, the demand-side is clear: the desire for young, servile, dependent women is often appealing to the older, divorced men who seek pen pal brides. The supply-side is far more complicated: the motivation of young, vibrant Filipinas to marry considerably older American men who are practically strangers to many of them is tied to globalization and patterns of migration. As Raquel Z. Ordoñez explains, it is not coincidental that the growing mail-order bride industry, which has been extensively critiqued as "the 'wholesale commodification'[35] of Filipino women in particular and of Third World women in general," is "occurring simultaneously with the globalization of the world economy and the exodus of Filipino women as overseas contract workers" (122).[36] It is important to remember that several of the Filipina women in south Mississippi began as OCWs, becoming unofficial pen pals in the process. Pen pals and OCWs share the *Balikbayan* sense of financial obligation toward their families back home, an obligation that is grossly exploited by "for-profit" corporate agencies. Economically restrictive and exploitative "structural adjustment programs" (SAPs) implemented by the World Bank, the International Monetary Fund, and other international lending agencies, most often in their own interests and at the expense of many nations' impoverished masses, contribute to the labor trade by displacing women from their homes and jobs. SAPs often transform traditional self-sustaining agrarian economies into systems of cash-crop production and production of consumer goods for export, effectively creating landless, dependent populations who are forced to migrate in order to make a living wage. As Grace Chang explains, as a result of SAPs, "women who were once small farmers have been forced to do home work, to migrate to the cities to work in manufacturing and the electronic industry, or to migrate overseas to do nursing, domestic work, sex work, and 'entertainment'" (135).

The labor trade, marked by a sexual division of labor born out of the worldwide feminization of poverty, exploits women's desires to break themselves, and their families, "away from the vicious cycle of prevailing poverty and unemployment besetting the country" (Ordoñez 133). For pen pals in the United States, part of the lure comes from the promise of the American Dream, and the stories that confirm "there are really some good Americans that really treat their wives [well]."[37] Moreover, with the existence of women's oppression globally, many women view the possibility of domestic violence as a risk in *any* marriage, which does not serve as a unique deterrent to the pen pal arrangement. Even one of the opponents of pen pal marriages concedes, "But it's true, I mean even here even if they hadn't met as pen pals you still have some cases [of domestic violence], so how would you know that even if you had known someone for years, and you get engaged [the same thing might not happen]."[38] The success stories provide hope, and the potential to break away from poverty and provide help for family members back home is difficult to refuse.

Ironically, the very cycle of poverty from which they are hoping to break free—a poverty that is often internalized and associated with the very fabric of one's national culture—has itself (in the case of the Philippines and many other "developing" nations) been perpetuated by an international corporate capitalism which thrives on the inequalities embedded in monopolies. In their attempts to respond to the feminization of poverty, networks of OCWs end up further entrenched in the cycle of exploitation while simultaneously helping to sustain the machinations of corporate empire. As Miriam Ching Louie explains, "[W]omen increasingly find themselves being the first contributors and the first victims of economic restructuring schemes around the world. Women are the 'first hired and first fired' in development policies, exploited through the 'feminization of labor' and the 'feminization of migration'" (122).[39]

COMPLICITY AT HOME

With SAPs working against them, women become trapped in a system wherein their relatives' livelihood, as well as their home country's economic sustainability, becomes dependent upon their exploited labor. Not only are "approximately 30 to 50 percent of the entire Filipino population dependent on migrant worker remittances" (Chang 136–137), the majority of which are sent from female family members in particular, but "NGOs estimate that remittances sent home by Filipina overseas workers run between six and seven billion U.S. dollars a year" (Ching-Louie 125). In this way, the economic development strategies of sending countries, which often develop out of concessions to multinational corporate terrorization in the first place, participate in the global abuse of their laboring daughters. As Chang blatantly asserts, "The Philippine government has been unable to protect its own female citizens abroad and apparently has given up any intention of doing so. The trade in women from the Philippines has proven immensely profitable to the Philippine government and entrepreneurs, and highly 'economical' to the governments that recruit them and the elites who employ them" (148).

By depending on their daughters' labor to support their national economy, the Philippine government is grossly exploiting the *Balikbayan* sense of obligation to send funds to support families back home; moreover, by encouraging their daughters to become pen pal brides, Filipino families are exploiting the financial incentives of marriage. As Lena Edlund and Evelyn Korn explain, "A woman can either work in a regular job or be a prostitute. If she holds a regular job, she marries; if a prostitute, she does not. Hence, the female choice is couched in terms of whether to be a wife or a prostitute" (212).[40] Limiting their daughters' choices to markets that generate the largest remittances, Filipino families who agree to trade their young, often teenage daughters for marriage to complete strangers old enough to be their fathers not only affect the daughters specifically, but the sex trade broadly. As Edlund and Korn again explain, "The price of marriage conditions the market price for sex, which, generally speaking, would affect the tradeoff between marriage and singleness" (12). The effect on the market price for sex notwithstanding, *any* price paid for our daughters is too high.

RESISTANCE AND COMMUNITY BUILDING: INVOKING THE *BAYANIHAN* SPIRIT AND THE *BABAYLAN* TRADITION

It should be no surprise that a system that can only be described as the trafficking of women results in the commodification and subsequent abuse of women's minds and bodies.

The Filipino American Society of Mississippi, a self-professed social and cultural club, has a history of "rescues," or domestic interventions for which they have come together, raised money, and brought in law enforcement in order to extract pen pals from households with abusive husbands who solidly believe they have "bought and paid for" personal maid service, sex slaves, and the right to terrorize their wives. The complexity involved in such rescues ranges from the logistical—raising funds to remove the woman, finding a protected, sometimes out-of-state location to which she can be delivered, and filing appropriate documents with law enforcement, divorce attorneys, and immigration—to the psychological and sociological, such as convincing the victim of abuse to leave, convincing the devout Catholic woman to divorce her husband, reckoning with the complex financial obligation the woman usually feels towards her family back home, and dealing with her fear of deportation and her husband's constant threats to her citizenship. The rescues are further complicated by inevitable divisions within the community itself, exacerbated by varying degrees of risk, fear, and bravery, conflicting obligations, cultural and class differences that originate back home and are then carried overseas, and limited resources. The history of the organization's rescues lives on through *tsismis*, but the impetus for the rescues themselves is born out of the *Bayanihan* spirit, which not coincidentally comes from a rural tradition of helping others in the Philippines. The word "*bayani*" is Tagalog for hero, and in the rural tradition, the *Bayanihan* spirit would inspire community members to help neighbors who were moving to a new location.

The *Bayanihan* spirit was invoked in south Mississippi by one brave woman, willing to risk her own safety in order to help a fellow Filipina in need—literally moving her to a new location.[41] Although this brave woman was also the "first Filipina" in the Pine Belt, acknowledged as the founding mother and one of the leaders of the community, for many years she felt like "the oddball" because she *wasn't* a pen pal. In this community of women who mostly came from the provinces and entered into arranged marriages in an attempt to escape from poverty, an upper-class, educated woman who lived a life of privilege with maids and cooks in the Philippines, and married for love, had entirely "different stories" from the rest of the community. She concedes, "In the old days I was very snobbish," and remembers of the woman who first called her for help that "she was friends with everybody. And I would be the last one she'd call: I was a last resort." Long suffering from intense spousal abuse, and very seldom allowed to leave the house, the caller had become terrified for her life after her husband took out an insurance policy on her and threatened to kill her in order to collect the settlement. When asked why this woman called her, "the last resort" remembers, "I thought she [was] friends with the others. But apparently she was calling for help, nobody wanted to help her. I didn't know that until later." The rest of the community was too fearful to act, and rightly so—the one woman who did help had to put her own safety at risk in order to offer assistance. She was even followed, and eventually chased down the highway, as she rescued this woman from her abusive husband. Moreover, some of the pen pal husbands were discouraging their wives from getting involved. The rescuer was even chastised for her success, as "one of the husbands of the Filipina girls" told her what she did was "foolish." She insists, however, that if given the choice she would do it again, explaining that "many times I act because it has to be done." The "pleading" in the caller's voice, which she described as a "really, really pitiful voice," was what persuaded her instantly. Coming home directly from Sunday Mass at the Catholic Church and hearing this woman's "really sad voice" on the telephone, whispering cries for help, urged her to immediate, albeit dangerous action.

The successful actions of this one woman then inspired the community to come together and support each other through future crises as well as successes—to become a true *Bayanihan* community. The "last resort" became the first woman to turn to, no longer the oddball in the group. After a couple of solo rescues, she remembers "another one that we spirited away," which entailed "a community effort." There have since been other brave women who have stepped up to help others; none of the women see themselves as leaders, but all of them identify their desire to help others.[42] As one leader explained, giving to others creates a mutually beneficial relationship, which works towards building a strong community. She states, "I like to help people. It's just...I would have never made it if nobody helped me here, I mean, to survive."[43] The *Bayanihan* spirit is very much alive in the Filipino community in south Mississippi; the community's founding mother hopes this spirit will be one of the elements of Filipino culture that will endure throughout future generations in America.

Concern for the basic survival of others also embodies the tradition of the *Babaylan*, the shamanistic healers, diviners, and priestesses indigenous to precolonial Philippine culture. Leny Mendoza describes the *Babaylan* as a woman who will "[i]ntercede for the community and individuals" (148). Political in nature, the *Babaylan* were considered a danger and a threat to the Spanish colonial mission and *Babaylan* women began to be retributively murdered, which eventually drove them underground. Like the *Babaylan* from oral history and legend, the modern-day Filipina subversive intercedes for her community and individuals in local as well as global contexts. In Mississippi, she too operates underground and anonymously, fearful of retribution from the domestically violent, as well as from a system that perpetuates the acceptability of the idea of Filipina bodies available for sale and ownership. She fights for herself, as well as for her sisters who *are* being retributively battered, and sometimes murdered once they assert their rights as free-thinking human beings rather than stereotypical incarnations of the mail order bride. Her subversive actions continue to pose a danger and a threat to the neocolonial mission that barters her body to service militaries, sustain national economies, and satisfy an aging patriarchy in its second or third exhibition of a midlife crisis. Filipinas in south Mississippi are fighters.

REVISITING THE KITCHEN

Filipina American community events do not foreground these politics, and their purpose is neither to educate nor inform others about the perils of transnational, neocolonial relationships in the markedly raced and gendered state of late capitalism. But the politics are always already present, part of the cultural memory that we all inherit, which continues to live on in sites of female community-building such as car trips and kitchens. A space for socializing, eating, teaching, and learning, as well as the necessary communal preparation and cooking of some of the more complicated or laborious recipes, the kitchen represents an empowering site, a space for female solidarity, the exchange of critical domestic information, and active community planning. For Filipinas in south Mississippi, *the kitchen is the site of rescue*. It is ironic that the domestic role long rebuked by Western feminists for its gendered expectations—a woman's place in the kitchen—is located as the central space for Filipina women's empowerment in this necessarily political organization. Active for its own sake—namely, the survival of many of its members—the Filipina American Society of Mississippi not only provides service to one another, but works to ensure that its members continue to learn and appreciate the complex cultural (living) history of the community.

NOTES

1. The Mississippi state population (2,938,618 as of 2008) is based on the U.S. Census Estimate. The Filipino population (3,845) is cited in Jennie L. Ilustre, Olivia J. Quinto, and Ted Regencia, *Philippine News*, 13 Sept 2005. http://www.philippinenews.com/news/view_article.html?article_id=d06a03896c5d6589f4382c035853d34f.

2. *A Book of Her Own: Words and Images to Honor the Babaylan*. San Francisco: T'boli Publishing, 2005.

3. For an introduction to Philippine-American colonial and neocolonial history, see the following: (1) E. San Juan, Jr., *After Postcolonialism: Remapping Philippines-United States Confrontations*. Lanham, MD: Rowman & Littlefield, 2000. (2) Oscar V. Campomanes, "The New Empire's Forgetful and Forgotten Citizens: Unrepresentability and Unassimilability in Filipino-American Postcolonialities." *Critical Mass* 2.2 (Spring 1995): 145–200. (3) Vincente Rafael, ed., *Discrepant Histories: Translocal Essays on Filipino Cultures*. Philadelphia: Temple UP, 1995. (4) Sharon Delmendo, *The Star-Entangled Banner: One Hundred Years of America in the Philippines*. Rutgers UP, 2004. (5) Daniel B. Schirmer and Stephen Rosskamm Shalom, eds., *The Philippines Reader: A History of Colonialism, Neocolonialism, Dictatorship, and Resistance*. Boston: South End Press, 1987.

4. Anonymous Personal Interview #3. Center for Oral History, University of Southern Mississippi. 29 March 2007. The interview subject referred to herself as "Filipino" (in the masculine form) rather than "Filipina" (the feminine form) because she was using "Filipino" as a universal term.

5. For the preeminent study of hybridity, see Homi Bhabha, *The Location of Culture*. New York: Routledge, 2004.

6. "Pinay" is the colloquial term for Filipinas and Filipina Americans (the masculine form of the word is "Pinoy").

7. Literally translated as "focused on the mother," matrofocal cultures, groups, or societies are centered on women and led by a mother, mother figure, female head of household or group leader(s). Interestingly, most Filipina Americans in south Mississippi exist largely within patrifocal group structures—dominated and led by men—with the exception of their participation in this society of Filipinas. While the women of this community are often not the "head of household" in their marriages, they certainly constitute the leadership of the Filipina community.

8. Catherine Ceniza Choy has done extensive work which connects "Americanized nursing training in the Philippines during the U.S. colonial period" to the "feminized, highly educated, and exportable labor force" and marks the Philippines as "the *world's* top exporter of nurses" (82–83). "Asian American History: Reflections on Imperialism, Immigration, and 'The Body.'" In *Pinay Power: Peminist Critical Theory*. Ed. Melinda

deJesús. New York: Routledge, 2005. 81–97. For Choy's comprehensive, transnational study, see *Empire of Care*. Durham: Duke UP, 2003.

9. Having not yet learned to drive, she had yet to discover the Filipino populations brought in by military bases in Meridian and Biloxi.

10. *Siopao* is a steamed bun stuffed with meat; *hopia* is a sweet bean- or bean paste-filled pastry; *pancit* consists of long noodles stir-fried with vegetables and sometimes various meats and/or seafood; *adobo* is a method of cooking meat braised in soy sauce, garlic, and vinegar; and *empanada* is a savory meat-stuffed pastry.

11. Also spelled *mongo*; known as "mung" beans in English.

12. As Fred Gardaphé and Wenying Xu explain, "In the United States, relationships between food and ethnicity bear historical, social, cultural, economic, political, and psychological significance. In other words, ethnic identity formations have been shaped by experiences of food productions and services, culinary creativities, appetites, desires, hunger, and even vomit" (5). "Introduction: Food in Multi-Ethnic Literatures." *MELUS* 32.4 (Winter 2007): 5–10.

13. Anonymous Personal Interview #5. Center for Oral History, University of Southern Mississippi. 2 April 2007.

14. *Karé karé* and *pinakbet* are both Filipino dishes; the former is an oxtail stew cooked with vegetables in a peanut sauce, while the latter, which is also spelled *pinacbet*, is a vegetable stew usually cooked with pork and/or shrimp and shrimp paste.

15. The Tagalogs are the largest Filipino ethnic group, dominating present-day Manila, and the term "Tagalog" refers to both the people and the language. The Tagalog language is also the basis for the national language of the Philippines, otherwise known as "Filipino."

16. "Mestizo" and "mestiza" are the respective masculine and feminine terms for mixed-race. "Mestizaje" describes the unique experiences and conditions of the mestizo/a.

17. Anonymous Personal Interview #3.

18. Anonymous Personal Interview #2. Center for Oral History, University of Southern Mississippi. 28 March 2007.

19. Anonymous Personal Interview #3.

20. Ibid.

21. Ibid.

22. Ibid.

23. Ibid.

24. Anonymous Personal Interview #4. Center for Oral History, University of Southern Mississippi. 30 March 2007.

25. Ibid.

26. Anonymous Personal Interview #4.

27. Anonymous Personal Interview #5.

28. Anonymous Personal Interview #3.

29. "The Business of Selling Mail-Order Brides." *Making Waves: An Anthology of Writings by and about Asian American Women*. Ed. Asian Women United of California. Boston: Beacon Press, 1989. 318–326.

30. The terms "first" and "third world," as well as "developing," "lesser developed," and "developed" nations are problematic for the ways in which they participate in colonial

structures and rhetoric, as well as global, hegemonic representations and rankings, without acknowledging the complicity involved every time we invoke such terms unproblematically. I use these terms for lack of a more appropriate alternative; however, the quotation marks are intended to acknowledge this problematic.

31. See Grace Chang, "The Global Trade in Filipina Workers." In *Dragon Ladies: Asian American Feminists Breathe Fire*. Ed. Sonia Shah. Boston: South End Press, 1997. 132–134.

32. The term peminism, borrowed from Melinda deJesús, denotes a Filipina (and Filipina American) feminism that acknowledges the ways in which the Filipina diaspora operates within an increasingly globalized political economy.

33. "Pinay studies" refers to the academic study of the lives, experiences, and culture of Filipinas and Filipina Americans. See note 15.

34. "Lost in Translation: Western Feminism and Asian Women." In *Dragon Ladies: Asian American Feminists Breathe Fire*. Ed. Sonia Shah. 153–165.

35. "Commodification" describes the act of treating someone or something like a commodity for sale or exchange.

36. "Mail-Order Brides: An Emerging Community." In *Filipino Americans: Transformation and Identity*. Ed. Maria P. P. Root. London: Sage, 1997. 121–142.

37. Anonymous Personal Interview #3.

38. Ibid.

39. Rhacel Salazar Parreñas adds, "Migrant Filipina domestic workers depart from a system of gender stratification in the Philippines only to enter another one in the advanced capitalist and industrialized countries of the United States and Italy [who have the largest populations of Filipino migrants to Western countries]" (105). See Parreñas, "Migrant Filipina Domestic Workers and the International Division of Reproductive Labor." In *Pinay Power*. Ed. Melinda deJesús. 99–116. Neferti Xina M. Tadiar also concurs, arguing, "Filipinas suffer the consequences of, even as they create the conditions for, the national and international structures and processes that constitute the commodified identity *Filipina* in the warring world market" (375). See Tadiar. "Filipinas 'Living in a Time of War.'" In *Pinay Power*. Ed. Melinda de Jesús. 373–385.

40. "A Theory of Prostitution." *Journal of Political Economy* 110.1 (2002). 181–214.

41. Anonymous Personal Interview #5.

42. Anonymous Personal Interviews #3, #4, and #5.

43. Anonymous Personal Interview #3.

13

THE GENESIS OF A NEW ETHNIC GROUP?

The Meanings of Latino/Hispanic Identity in South Mississippi

—BRIDGET ANNE HAYDEN

INTRODUCTION

Mississippi has been best known in migration studies for its iconic role as a source of out-migration, particularly of African Americans. It was among the ten states with the smallest population change between 1950 and 2000. If the states are ranked by the size of their populations, it is one of only three states that had its highest ranking in 1900. At that time it was the twentieth most populated state; by 2000 it ranked thirty-first (U.S. Census 2002: 28–29). Since the last decade of the twentieth century, however, the state has increasingly become home for immigrants from Latin America. This is creating a new ethnic presence in the state. This population as yet remains comparatively small and is not well known, with almost no published research available on Latinos in Mississippi. This article is a small step towards filling that gap, with a particular focus on the southern part of the state.[1]

In order to get a handle on how we can understand Latino[2] identity in Mississippi, I will look at how identity can be understood in terms of demographics, the analysis of differences within the population, and, finally, the "Latino imaginary," or the self-representations of the group itself.[3] Each of these dimensions, or aspects, of how identity is experienced is only briefly defined now, but will be discussed in depth later in this essay. Demographic analyses group people together by a trait such as ethnicity, regardless of whether people self-identify with that trait. This makes a group visible by giving it a name, but it does not necessarily represent the way people think of themselves. In contrast, analytic approaches disaggregate the population into constituent parts, for example by class, gender, place of settlement, education, or national origins. The third approach, the "Latino imaginary," refers to how the community sees itself. This alludes to the way in which a sense of unity is created despite diversity of experiences. This is the dimension that reflects a group's sense of self-identification.

In this essay, I will first provide a brief history of Latino immigration to Mississippi and then use the three dimensions of Latino/Hispanic experience to reflect on how Latinos in south Mississippi are becoming an ethnic/racial group in a place where they were relatively invisible until recently.

THE LONG HISTORY OF A NEW POPULATION

We can say that the first Spanish influence on what is now Mississippi was Hernando de Soto's expedition through the region in the early 1540s. The Spanish retained a presence in the southernmost part of the state through the colonial period. However, until the last decade of the twentieth century the influence was small and only a few hints remain, for example in place names, surnames, and hot tamales, which are common in the Delta. Even so, Latinos participated in the economic development of the state throughout the twentieth century. This history reminds us that Mississippi has always been linked to regional, national, and international processes and policies.

The first known records of Latino migration to Mississippi date to the first decade of the last century. By 1904, Mexican migrants were recruited to Louisiana and Mississippi for agricultural work (Garcia 1981, cited in Chamberlain 2003: 223 fn 19), and in 1908 there were Mexicans in Lumberton. There they worked in the lumber industry in south central Mississippi (Weise 2008). Even so, their primary destination prior to the 1970s was to the Delta to work in cotton harvests. Records of Delta planters indicate that they requested assistance from the Illinois Southern Railroad to recruit "negroes from Puerto Rico, or white laborers from Portugal and Italy" (Brandfon 1964: 600) as early as 1903. At the end of the nineteenth and beginning of the twentieth centuries, southern states attempted, with relatively little success, to attract immigrants from the migrant streams then settling in the North and West. This desire for immigrant labor coincided with the well-known emigration of labor from the South to work in the industrial North during and after World War I. Although this migration slowed during the Great Depression, it continued until the 1960s (Kirby 1983: 591–593), and Mississippi lost population in the decades between 1910 and 1920 and 1940 and 1960. However, even as it lost population, between 1910 and 1930 Mississippi gained "white population of Mexican origin," which increased from 89 to 1,221 (Gibson and Jung 2002). This pattern was shared with states to the west and bordering the Delta (Arkansas, Louisiana, Oklahoma, and Texas), rather than the other states in the Southeast. Thus, it seems to reflect labor migration to the Mississippi Delta.

In the 1920s, Mexicans and Mexican Americans came to have a stronger presence in the Delta (Weise 2008). Before the Great Depression, a major problem for Delta cotton planters was the availability of labor for the harvest. One solution was to bring workers from Texas. In the 1920s, there were four types of cotton harvest labor: sharecroppers, blacks from nearby towns, blacks from outside the Delta, and "Mexicans," a category that included both Mexicans and Tejanos (Mexican Americans from Texas) (Whatley 1983: 907). Weise's research shows a significant use of Mexican (including Texan) workers in the 1920s. For example, in 1925 a priest in Clarksdale found Mexicans on every plantation in his parish (Weise 2008). Although most of these migrant farm workers would leave after the harvest, some remained and settled in Mississippi. Others left families in Mississippi while the men continued on the annual cycle of seasonal agricultural work in other states (Weise 2008).

Racial and ethnic identity was an important and sometimes contentious issue as new immigrants were integrated into the social system of the Delta in the early twentieth century. It was not clear how immigrants would fit into the system that was based on strong social distinctions between black and white. Brandfon argues that the planters' lack of interest in integrating Italian workers into white society and the deferential behavior expected of plantation workers resulted in Italian immigrants being classified with other nonwhite racial and ethnic groups, which included "Chinese, Mexicans, Indians, and Negroes" (Brandfon 1964: 610). "By replacing the Negro in the same type of work and under the same conditions, the Italians assumed the status of Negroes. One blended into the other, and southern thinking made no effort to distinguish between them" (Brandfon 1964: 610). In this example, we can see how racial and labor categories were coconstructed. It is reasonable to suppose that most Latino workers who came to Mississippi (whether from Texas, Puerto Rico, or Mexico), at least to the degree that they performed low-status work, were also classified as nonwhite. One difference between black Mississippians and these immigrants would turn out to be the degree to which the latter could mobilize resources to question their classification.

Weise demonstrates that racial classification, and consequent access to places, was a significant concern for Mexicans/Mexican Americans in the Delta in the 1920s. In 1926, Bolivar County ruled that children of these families could not attend the white Gunnison school and instead hired a Mexican teacher for a separate Mexican school. After the teacher left in 1928, some students attended the white school until 1930 when the school board began enforcing the ruling excluding them. A Latino resident, Rafael Landrove, turned to the consulate in New Orleans, which appealed to the governor of Mississippi, who intervened on behalf of the Mexican residents. This was important, since access to education in the white school system was key to economic and cultural mobility.

Between the 1940s and the 1960s, the United States developed a guest worker program, eventually called the Bracero Program, to use Mexican workers to make up labor shortages in agriculture. This program was most active in the southwestern states, but growers in the Mississippi Delta also brought in braceros, as these guest workers came to be called. The program involved federal oversight of labor conditions. Southern planters sometimes preferred to find workers, including Mexicans and Mexican Americans recruited from Texas, independently to avoid that federal regulation of their labor practices. Tejanos were more likely to come as family groups and even integrate into local white society in the Delta, an option not available to them in Texas, while braceros came as single men (Weise 2008). By the 1960s, widespread adoption of mechanical pickers reduced the demand for labor in cotton production. As a consequence, the Delta no longer figured in the annual cycle for migrant farm workers, and most Tejanos also left the state (Weise 2008).

There was relatively little demand for Latino labor in the state in the 1970s and 1980s. An important route to Mississippi for Latinos at that time was through higher education, as some Latin Americans who came to study in the state's universities, including the University of Southern Mississippi's English Language Institute, remained after graduation. Other people moved to the state as members of the military or spouses of United States citizens. During these years, the Latino population was small and tended to be integrated into the surrounding native-born community. Subsequent decades have seen increased numbers of a more diverse population of Latinos. This new cohort of immigrants has been more visible and less completely integrated into preexisting communities in the state.

Historically, however, the Southeast was not a major destination for immigrants to the United States. Beginning in the late 1980s, Latin American immigrants have chosen a wider range of destinations within the United States. In particular, greater numbers have moved to the Midwest,

Great Plains, and southeastern United States. For example, in 1960 only 4 percent of all recent immigrants settled in the South (excluding Florida and California), while in 2000 it was 15.9 percent. The diversification of destinations has been particularly marked for Hispanics with the lowest levels of education (Liaw and Frey 2007): the percentage of immigrants without a high school diploma in the South rose from 2.5 to 17.5 (Borjas 2004:41). As more low-wage workers immigrated to the South, the class status of Latinos in states such as Mississippi became more diverse. For example, in addition to professionals, immigrants began arriving to work in the poultry industry in central Mississippi. In southern states other than Texas and Florida, the percentage of immigrants who were professionals or technical workers fell from 46.8 in 1960 to 22.5 in 2000 (Borjas 2004:20) as the percentage who were laborers rose from 5.7 to 13.8. The importance of labor in the immigration of this period also meant that more adult men came than women or children.

On the Mississippi Gulf Coast, the number of Latino immigrants began to increase with the rise of the casino industry in the 1990s. However, the population remained relatively small, and much of the immigration to the state in that decade was in the northwestern and central parts of the state. Hurricane Katrina and its aftermath marked a new epoch in the history of Latinos in south Mississippi as there was a demand for Latinos to help with cleanup and reconstruction. In addition, the post-Katrina era brought a change in the national and class origins of immigrants on the coast. Prior to Hurricane Katrina, the immigrants contracted to work in the casinos tended to be from middle-class and university educated backgrounds. Typically they were contracted from South America or Costa Rica, joining a small population of Hondurans with deeper roots in the region as a result of the banana trade that connects New Orleans, Gulfport, and the Caribbean. Immigrants who came after Hurricane Katrina are more likely to be from Mexico and to have been working class or rural in their home country. Their larger numbers have also created a more visible community.

As the population of Latinos has increased in the past two decades, their reception in the state has been mixed. Despite the increase in immigration since the 1990s, the actual numbers of Latinos in the state remains relatively small. For the state as a whole, according to the 2000 census, only 1.4 percent of the population was Hispanic or Latino. The two towns, according to the same census data, with the greatest percentage of Hispanics were Forest (13.2 percent) and Morton (14 percent); after that the next highest was Yazoo City (7.3 percent). Most towns had well under 3 percent

Hispanics, and thirty-one of the seventy-two places listed as an "Urban Cluster" had less than 1 percent Hispanic population. Latinos' visibility and presence in the popular imagination seems greater than their physical numbers. In the following sections I will examine the meanings attributed to this ethnic category and the implications of it for Latinos in the state.

AGGREGATION AND STEREOTYPES

My research so far suggests that light-skinned Latinos may experience less discrimination than other Latinos, particularly if they speak English well. In this case, Mississippians may not realize they are Latino, since they are considered white. In addition to skin color there are other differences among Latinos. People from Latin America do not typically come to this country thinking of themselves as Latino or Hispanic at all. Instead this identity is first imposed on them through a process called aggregation. Aggregation refers to the way in which society may recognize commonalities among individuals and group them together (for example, by demographic variables such as sex, age, or race) regardless of whether those individuals perceive themselves as having a group identity.

Aggregation can lead to stereotypes by bringing together into a single group people who may have nothing else in common, eliding the diversity of backgrounds, experiences, and values. The aggregating approach to studying an ethnic group, exemplified by the census statistics just cited, makes the population visible. In effect, aggregation creates the population by counting and naming it. The attention may be positive (e.g., "hard workers") or negative ("taking our jobs"), but the sociologist Flores suggests that "the means and result are usually the same—stereotyped images offering up distorted, usually offensive, and in any case superficial portrayals of Latino people" (2003: 98). An example of a negative repercussion of aggregation is when people assume someone is not here legally because he or she looks Latino. Even people from Latin America can fall victim to the errors of inaccurate aggregation. For example, some are surprised to learn that not all Latin American immigrants speak Spanish, since speakers of indigenous languages, such as Maya and Mixtec, have also come to the United States, including Mississippi.

Flores's concern over the insulting and flattening nature of most stereotypes is reflected in the reactions many Latinos have experienced from non-Latinos in Mississippi. Many have encountered common stereotypes of "Latin" and "undeveloped" countries, including the idea that their home countries must lack basic infrastructure and sanitary conditions, images of poverty, and the belief that they must like to dance. Other reactions toward Latinos in general are shaped by particular perceptions of Mexico because people in the United States usually know more about that country than other parts of Latin America. For example, people often assume that the cuisine of all Latin America is spicy and like what they have grown to know as "Mexican" food, erasing not only the variation between national cuisines but also the cultural diversity of Mexico itself.

Other forms of aggregation are related to Latinos' perceived status and role in the United States. Legal status is an important source of differentiation among Latinos. A person's access to resources varies greatly if one is a citizen, has legal residency or a work permit, or is undocumented. Even one's ability to participate in social activities, go shopping, or attend church can be affected by legal status. Undocumented immigrants are sometimes afraid to go out because of the dangers of detention and deportation. This means they are likely to limit their activities in order to remain safe. Public representations of the population focus mostly on undocumented immigrants, and this perception of immigrants as law breakers colors many people's reception of the entire population. In the experiences of the Latinos I've met, non-Latinos often assume that people are undocumented if they appear to be Latin American (if they are darker skinned, but also if they do not speak English well or have a strong accent). In recounting the travails of his dealings with the police when his car was stolen, a Peruvian man on the coast commented, *"Tengo este problema,"* "I have this problem":

> There still exists the idea that because you are Hispanic you are illegal, immediately, now automatically the authorities, the police or whatever person, says: "No, Hispanic, illegal." Why? Why do all Hispanics have to be illegal? No, it isn't like that. That is, some Americans or authorities haven't educated themselves.

He makes three important points: not everyone is here under the same legal conditions, people should educate themselves against stereotypes, and there are situations in which legal status is not relevant. He had difficulty reporting the theft of his car because the police wanted to know his immigration status, a fact that should have been irrelevant.

There is no uniform experience among Latinos/Hispanics of their reception in south Mississippi. Although complaints about discrimination and prejudice are common, it is also frequent for people to report that they have not encountered discrimination personally for a variety of reasons. Many have experienced the state of Mississippi as *tranquilo* (calm, untroubled) and like it for that reason. *Tranquilo* means different things, depending on an immigrant's experience of other places. I interviewed a Salvadoran who emphasized peacefulness, lack of violence, and people's honesty or lack of crime in Mississippi. This reflected his experiences of El Salvador as the opposite (because he had experienced both war and a kidnapping), in addition to his relatively tranquil experience of Mississippi. Similarly, some immigrants who come from large metropolitan areas find even the relatively large urban area of Gulfport and Biloxi quiet in comparison. Others used the word *"tranquilo"* to refer to the relative safety from prejudice, arrest, and deportation that they had felt in the state before immigration enforcement seemed to increase in 2008. Professionals seem less likely to experience discrimination than working-class immigrants. It also is likely that negative reactions to immigrants increase when the population becomes larger and more visible.

Although negative reactions from U.S. citizens are noted, some immigrants recounted how well they were received. This is particularly true in their capacity as workers. Some Latinos argued that undocumented immigrants are the hardest workers because they have little recourse, while those who are here legally have more options. In other words, the perception that Latinos are better workers than either whites or blacks seems to reflect the equation of "undocumented" with the entire population. Several people pointed out that in this context being a good worker essentially means one is exploitable and unlikely to claim rights. For them, then, this was not a positive aspect of their reception despite the fact that being a good worker is an apparent compliment.

Another problem with the representation of Hispanics as good workers is that the acceptance of Latinos as *workers*, generally assumed to be temporary, reflects a one-dimensional image of the people who comprise that population. A lack of awareness of the diversity of the population or knowledge of Latinos in other dimensions of their daily lives (for example as parents, students, athletes, or artists) results from their exclusion from the larger communities in which they live. A Latino store owner in the Pine Belt region of south Mississippi commented on this problem when he told me he had never seen a Fourth of July parade. He has an image of them, in our conversation he itemized the component parts of the day, and he would like to see the celebration. He said he knows little about any U.S. holidays, other than Thanksgiving, and he wishes he did because he wants to know the country and community in which he lives better. He suggested that the Latino community should be invited and included, with a cultural explanation, in public celebrations such as holidays, parades, and homecomings. He also felt the town should reach out to include immigrants in recreational sports and similar activities, sites and times of community building that would help immigrants to integrate and assimilate in their new home.

Politics and marketing are other key domains in which the aggregating dimension of social reality is important (Flores 2003: 98). Latinos do not yet have a significant political presence in the state, but they are increasingly important as consumers in addition to producers. This can be seen in the sale of basic ingredients such as *masa harina* (corn flour used for tortillas and tamales) in grocery stores and the growth of "Spanish" or "Mexican" stores that cater directly to the needs of the Latino population. These carry diverse cultural goods: foods, music, movies, clothing, religious items, and other products. These ethnic stores generally reflect the fact that most Latino immigrants in the state are now from Mexico; however, in some cases the merchandise is more varied. At least one store in East Biloxi, for example, carries several types of sour cream for the slightly different tastes of Salvadorans, Hondurans, Guatemalans, and Mexicans.

The category of Latino/Hispanic is created outside the population, at least initially. Latin American immigrants arrive identifying by nationality and sometimes by regions within their home countries, and not usually as a larger ethnic group. Even Latinos who arrive from other parts of the United States and are citizens do not necessarily identify with a larger category or with immigrants; for example, they may identify as Tejano, Puerto Rican, or Cuban American. Even so, this aggregation can be used by newly defined Latinos once they become accustomed to the concept. It may be that self-aggregation is most likely or necessary in places, such as Mississippi, with relatively low numbers of people. In remembering early efforts to organize Latino community activities on the Gulf Coast, a woman from Bolivia commented that she couldn't "be" Bolivian because she'd have been the only one. In other words, she couldn't act as part of a larger social group based on that identity. She had to reimagine herself as "Hispanic" in order to create a community under the aegis of the Catholic Church's Hispanic Ministries. People on the coast and in Jackson formed socially active groups based in the church and rooted in a common language. On the coast, this included people from Spain as well as Latin America under the umbrella term of "Hispanic."

The new immigration of the last two decades made the population more visible in Mississippi. In doing so, it changed the meaning and experience of being Hispanic because it altered the composition of the population. The earlier Latinos in central and southern Mississippi were largely professionals or married to professionals and United States citizens. The new Latinos are largely working class, often rural, with lower levels of formal education. The earlier Latinos of the 1970s and 1980s were more often from South America, with some Cubans and more educated Central Americans. The recent Latino immigrants are more likely to be Mexican. The increased population made Latinos more visible; however, the tendency of non-Latinos to perceive Hispanics/Latinos as an aggregate has the effect of separating them from the larger community and equating people who would otherwise have little in common. The earlier professional immigrants and the laborers who immigrated after them would not have shared a common identity in their home countries. Therefore the aggregating tendency does not increase understanding either between Latinos and non-Latinos or within the Latino population itself.

ANALYTIC DIFFERENCES IN EXPERIENCES

The fact that there is no necessary basis for a common self-identification among people often lumped together—as Hispanics are often grouped—is recognized by Latinos in Mississippi when they mention the importance of such differences as legal status, economic class, race or ethnicity, urban vs. rural origins, and even religious affiliation. These distinctions help us to analyze the differences among the members of a demographic group and are therefore examples of what is called the analytic dimension of identity. This approach helps us approximate the experiences of being Latino without assuming that all Latinos are one unified community. The analytical perspective pushes us to recognize important social differences that shape people's experiences. In other words, it can help us to avoid stereotypes. However, if we are not careful, the analytical perspective can lead to new stereotypes about subgroups. It is best if the analytical categories are meaningful to the people themselves. I focus on differences that Mississippi Latinos themselves have identified as important.

One of the most important differences among Latinos at this time is legal status. There is a complex range of possible statuses, including native-born citizens, those with legal residency, those who entered the country legally (who may be here in a variety of conditions and degrees of legality), and those who entered undocumented. Those with legal status or who entered legally are often of a higher social status in their home countries than those who enter "over the border," or illegally, although they may occupy the same jobs in the United States. Legal immigration entails the resources to obtain a passport and visa. Among the requirements for a visa to the United States are bank accounts, a good job, and other evidence that you will not want to stay to work in the United States. In some cases, for example in the casinos prior to Katrina, people were recruited to work in their home countries through programs giving them work visas for a specified period. These programs sometimes cost the employee as much as two thousand dollars, which resulted in a select group of people with greater resources being able to participate in such programs. So, the life experiences and class standing of immigrants vary before they come to the United States, and those differences continue to be influential in this country. Although Latino workers may all seem alike to the untrained U.S. eye, to immigrants themselves the differences of education, class, rural/urban origin, and nationality are more evident.

The privilege of legal status can be seen in the contrast between the often severely restricted lives of the undocumented and the relatively greater freedom of movement and social life of others. The undocumented are also more vulnerable to mistreatment and less able to defend their rights. A man from Honduras contrasted his home country and his experience living on the coast in this way:

> Ah, one is the entrapment. It is not easy to move about, and so that isolates you. You are frozen like you cannot stretch your hands or go where you want like in your own place because of the fear always. Because you are in territory where you think that someone is going to grab you or ... Because you an immigrant, because many people say to you—you fight your fear because you have come here to fight and maintain your identity as much as possible outside of the society's public space, do you understand? So they will not be able to see you, only from work to the house, and this was extremely, very hard for me because I was accustomed to being free.

This experience of feeling imprisoned by fear and the need to be invisible is common for many undocumented immigrants. Those who do not fear deportation are less restrained by fear, although they may still find their use of space severely constrained by long work hours that leave little free time or by transportation problems, if they do not drive or do not have a car.

The practical effects of legal status are significant in shaping lives, but are not necessarily important in self-identification. However, at least some among the undocumented perceive that those who are U.S. citizens or have legal status consider themselves better. For example, one man from Mexico living in the Pine Belt reported having seen people on television talking against undocumented immigrants and added that "some Latinos identify as Americans, they attack Latinos for being immigrants, or they are illegals, or they don't have papers, or they take jobs." After some discussion of this issue with the interviewer, he stated:

> If a person is able to have papers here, if they see you they don't greet you. They speak Spanish, but they are from here now. They have residency here. They don't want to see someone like us.
>
> Interviewer: They want to create a separation?
>
> There is a separation among us. They don't want to believe it, but there is a separation. It is rare the person who has a building and has papers who is good to one. When they have papers, they feel they are from here. But they are not really from here because the day the United States wants to remove the Latinos from the country, they'd have to leave just like us.

Not all legal residents and citizens would recognize themselves in this description, but some do express sentiments regarding undocumented immigrants that warrant his interpretation of the situation.

Some legal and citizen Latinos espouse the same attitudes towards extralegal immigration that many non-Latinos do. They resent those who come illegally for sullying the reputation of all Latinos. Others, however, are pleased with the growth of the Hispanic population and the increased availability of foods and Spanish-language venues, and they participate in community activities fully. In Mississippi, some long-standing Latino residents also saw themselves as positioned to bridge the divide between the cultures for less experienced newcomers and organized accordingly, creating, for example, both the Mississippi Hispanic Association and the Gulf Coast Latin American Association.

Color and class also can shape Latinos' experiences. Race in Latin America is not typically conceptualized in the same way as it is in the United States, but color is important even so. In the United States, our race is defined without regard for our class position. In Latin America, a person's class position and behavior can influence how other people define his or her race. In many Latin American countries racial terms typically are more numerous than in the United States and racial descriptions of a person are often more flexible, varying for the same person in different contexts. Latinos can be any color, but when they come to the United States they can find themselves placed in a new racial framework. Some people commented on their confusion or discomfort when they first arrived and were asked to put themselves into racial categories. "What are you?" was one of the first things one Peruvian woman remembered being asked.

In Mississippi, there are both indigenous peoples from Mexico and Guatemala and Spanish-speaking people from Latin America as well as Latinos from other states and ones born and raised in Mississippi. There is a wide range of skin colors and other physical traits included in this population. On the one hand, some people interviewed noted that because they have light skin they are often perceived as white by non-Latino Mississippians—unless and until they speak with an accent. On the other hand, immigrants from indigenous communities often see Hispanic/Latino as a race/class term referring to nonindigenous Latin Americans and not themselves. In their home countries indigenous Latin Americans had a lower status and different social identity than Spanish speakers. Latino/Hispanic is a category that both the white and indigenous immigrant may come to adopt in the United States. However, if they do so it means they have accommodated to U.S. ethnic and racial forms of classification and developed new forms of solidarity.

There are other forms of social differentiation, in addition to nationality and race/ethnicity, that immigrants bring from their home countries. These too may divide the community and lead to different experiences of immigration. For example, urban immigrants may have different customs than rural ones, reflecting either more formal education or more cosmopolitan experiences. This can mean that they have cultural knowledge that helps people adjust to life in the United States more easily. In addition, some Latinos answered questions about "identity" and "community" with discussions of values and religion that they believed made them different from other Hispanics. For example, one Mexican man answered my question about identity first by telling me that he has done everything legally, always using his real name. In that response, he clearly differentiated himself from the representation of "immigrants" as all undocumented. When I clarified that the question was about community, he said that he does not identify with other Hispanics very much because he thinks of himself primarily in terms of his religion. As a "Mexican Baptist," he does not feel that he has very much in common with Catholic Latinos. Frequently outsiders assume that a common ethnic identity means that people will share perspectives and interests; however, Latino/Hispanic identity can sometimes be little more than a shared census classification.

ETHNIC SOLIDARITY AND HOMELANDS

The final dimension of Latino/Hispanic reality that I will examine is the "Latino imaginary," that is, self-representation and identification. The term "Latino imaginary" draws on the idea of nations being "imagined communities." This is the idea that our society's institutions and the narratives we the people create, the stories we tell about ourselves, help people "imagine" that they have something in common with all others in our group or nation—people we will never meet.[4] "Imaginary" does not mean that a group does not exist; instead the word is meant to focus our attention on collective meanings and representations. Our task is to think about how a collective identity is created, rather than assume it must exist just because it has a name. Flores suggests that Latino ethnicity is a form of solidarity built on a memory of struggle, oppression, and pain as well as hope. This imaginary refers, he says, "first of all, to home countries in Latin America, the landscapes, life-ways, and social struggles. . . ." (2000). In addition to being Latino, one also has a national identity based on the country or countries of origin of oneself or one's family. Consequently, the "we" of being Latin American or Latino is filtered through "particular national optics." Finally, migration plays a prominent part of the Latino imaginary in the United States. This is in part because non-Latinos typically assume Latinos must be immigrants and in part because Latin American immigration has grown so rapidly in the past few decades.

Although identity as Latino is initially imposed because people arrive as citizens of specific countries or members of indigenous ethnic groups, for people I have interviewed in Mississippi the experience of coming to see themselves as Latinos often is an experience of growing solidarity.

Although not all Latinos are immigrants, the idea of immigration and empathy with the difficulties experienced by the most disadvantaged of the immigrants become part of the meaning of the identity for many people. For example, a Peruvian woman who is in the country legally and married to a United States citizen stated that although she felt that she had a good life, she was not happy because she watches a lot of television and sees the discrimination happening in the country. It hurts and bothers her to see discrimination against Latinos who are "working to make an honest living." My interviews with Latinos in Mississippi suggest that one of the primary occasions when identification as Hispanic/Latino across class and legal status arises is in recognition of the need for immigration reform or in the desire to combat racism and discrimination. Expressions of being Latino in the interviews I have collected are frequently accompanied by a call for justice for immigrants, particularly the undocumented. Thus, although not all Latinos are immigrants, recognition of the plight of immigrants and the less well off does seem to be an important dimension of the shared history and hopes that Flores (2003: 100) describes as the basis for a Latino imaginary.

An excellent example of how solidarity forms the basis for Latino/Hispanic identity is professional Latinos who organized on both the coast and in Jackson in the 1990s. They did not do this because they identified themselves as part of the same social group as the new immigrants. Instead, they acted out of solidarity and a sense of responsibility to ease the way for the new immigrants by using their 1) knowledge gleaned from a longer experience in the United States, 2) generally higher levels of education, and 3) facility with the English language. They saw that they could act as mediators between the dominant society and the new residents. Although one organizer emphasized that he would not turn away people from other racial or ethnic groups, in each case the organizations were clearly formed around a common Latino identity rooted in language and geography. One woman reflected on the decision to form an identity based on solidarity:

> There are thousands of Hispanic people who don't want to know anything because they have been here many years. They don't want to go to the [Catholic] masses [in Spanish], they don't want anything. What they want is to separate themselves. But we cannot separate ourselves. We have to give spirit, what we have learned, what we have been able to do; and what we can best do with the experience that we have in this country is give that experience. And hope that they

accept it, because there are times when they don't accept us, because we have been here for years. They say, "No, that one? She thinks she is an American."

What she rather perceptively adds to her sense of responsibility to do what she can for the Hispanic community is recognition of potential divides and the fact that language or regional origins alone do not necessarily a community make.

In addition to this solidarity and a history that recognizes the importance of immigration, Latinos share an understanding of cultural traits that they have in common beyond the differences in customs, vocabulary, and foods. There are differences between countries and regions of the same country. When I have been with groups of Latinos of mixed national origins in Mississippi, these differences are a frequent topic of conversation as people learn how things are said or done in different places. However, in interviews people repeatedly gave very similar answers about cultural traits believed to be broadly shared among all Latin American countries and therefore Latinos. The biggest area of agreement can be glossed as "human warmth" or "openness."

Many of the Latinos in Mississippi who were interviewed perceive Latinos to be more open and warm, in contrast to a more reserved and private U.S. character.[5] The most common trait that is felt to distinguish Latinos and Latin America from the United States is a focus on personal relationships, especially within the family. For example, one man put it this way:

> To me the culture here is very individualistic, it is a little cold. The family doesn't occupy the same place that it has in our country, it is like in a second plane. Here everything is what is close, closest to the person, to the individual rather than the family. The family still exists, more in some than in others, it is more—it has a different importance. Here it is like everyone follows his own path and let's say once in a while is in contact with his or her family, but it isn't fundamental.

One woman described it in this way:

> Latin families, we are very united, more sentimental, more worried about each other. American families, they are—we say cold because when their children turn sixteen, seventeen years old they give them

the option to choose. Either you work, or you study. But at that age the children begin to be more independent.

Latin Americans represented their families as caring for children more and longer; e.g., children don't move out when they turn eighteen. They said that families and neighbors were closer and social relationships more open in Latin America. Americans can be generous and helpful, but Latino immigrants found them less welcoming: you have to make an appointment to visit a U.S. home, one man said. Nobody knocks on your door here, others noted. Another long-time resident, who now feels her culture is as much Unitedstatesian[6] as Latin American, explained it by contrasting how she would act in even her U.S. in-laws' house and the house of her Venezuelan sister. In her sister's house she would make herself at home and feel free to go into the kitchen and get something out of the cupboard or refrigerator, while in a U.S. home, even her mother-in-law's, she would ask permission. She expressed understanding and appreciation for the ways in which she sees Unitedstatsians as also giving, but distinguished it stylistically from the Latino's: the Unitedstatsian would help, for example, by participating in volunteer activities, but maintain a more private and less expansive home and sense of family.

Although the Latino presence in south Mississippi is relatively small and recent, and despite the fact that subgroup (especially national, but also class and religious) identities are in some way primary for most people, Latinos do express a sense of being a group and some consensus of what that means. The Latino imaginary, that is, the definition of commonality from within the group, is one of solidarity in the face of what are believed to be unjust immigration and labor practices and a belief that there are some basic values and a style of relating to other people that are different between the United States and Latin America.

CONCLUSIONS

The category of Hispanic/Latino, then, is defined both externally and internally. Externally, the ethnic category is inflected with racial and class meanings in addition to legal ones. At the current moment, for first generation (i.e., those who were born abroad) Latinos, immigration politics are clearly an important element defining the group from the outside. The future of the population depends in part on what happens with immigration reform because this will dictate whether people can continue to come or stay in the state. Furthermore, politics and popular sentiments regarding immigration, Latin America, and Latinos will define the environment within which Latinos either do or do not define their common identity and their relationship to other ethnic groups in the state.

The conditions for a Latino/Hispanic ethnic identity are quite recent in Mississippi. Although Latinos are not new arrivals to the United States, in the past three decades the population and its distribution have changed dramatically. This gives Latinos increased importance and a new cultural dynamic. The histories of this immigrant group vary by nationality and by region of settlement in the United States. Consequently the meanings of being Latino/Hispanic are different in different parts of the country. For example, in some places Latinos are assumed to be Cuban or Salvadoran instead of Mexican. In a place like Mississippi that does not have a long-standing, multigenerational Latino community, the terms Latino and Hispanic have fewer preexisting connotations and they were considered interchangeable by almost everyone interviewed in my research. The politics of the name and the identity have largely bypassed the state. It remains to be seen to what degree and in what ways a Hispanic/Latino imaginary will consolidate as new generations are raised here.

It is unclear how the different Latino social groups within the state will develop and to what degree they will continue to create a Latino imaginary. Lighter-skinned and legal immigrants could merge with the rest of the white population or identify with a Hispanic community that is generally thought of as being darker-skinned. One storeowner in the Pine Belt recounted to me that his son did not want to go to his parents' Central American home in the summer of 2008 because there were too many "Mexicans" there. In other words, this relatively privileged "Latino" youth did not identify with the darker and lower-class majority of Latino immigrants or those apparently like them in Latin America. His use of the adjective "Mexican" to refer to Salvadorans in their own country reflects an acceptance of the aggregating tendency of many non-Latino Mississippians who cannot tell Latinos apart and assume them all to be undocumented Mexicans. On the other hand, there are also light-skinned Latinos very actively involved in the development of a common identity and solidarity organizations. With time, a common sense of being Latino that crosses class and national lines could develop or the category could come to be composed primarily of darker-skinned Latinos. Or, some other option might develop. It also may be that the meanings of being Latino vary or will vary in different areas of the state where the demographic patterns of settlement differ. These are topics for future research.

NOTES

1. This chapter is based on data from two research projects directed by the author. In the first, immigrant youth (Rosa Gomez, Owen Fernandez, Kency Yanes, and Harim Yanes) collected oral histories from twenty-nine Latin American immigrants who survived Hurricane Katrina. The second project is research conducted by the author between 2007 and 2009, with the assistance of two student research assistants, Zachary Wilborn and Arabella Daniels, in the summer of 2008. This research was on experiences of Latin American immigrants in Mississippi and included both interviews and participant-observation research (i.e., a more in-depth and informal interaction with people in their daily lives). All participants are referred to with pseudonyms here to protect their privacy. I also thank Melissa Johnson, Shana Walton, and Julie Reid for their comments on different drafts of this article. To the degree that it now reads clearly, the credit goes to them.

2. In this article, the terms "Hispanic" and "Latino" are used interchangeably, reflecting the usage of most of the people I have known and interviewed in Mississippi. In contrast, in other parts of the country the choice between these terms is often politically significant, although there is variation in what the words mean to different people. For example, "Hispanic" is often associated with official contexts, such as the census, while "Latino" may represent a preferred form of self-identification. For some people, "Hispanic" is associated with more conservative politics and "Latino" with liberalism. Even the boundaries of who is considered Latino/Hispanic are variable. Sometimes people from Spain are included as "Hispanic," sometimes not. Others have argued that "Latino" should refer to Spanish-speaking people in the United States and "Hispanic" should be used to talk about people throughout the Americas. "Hispanic" is sometimes thought of as the more restricted term, referring to use of Spanish, while "Latino" is construed as more encompassing, referring to people (and their descendents) from any "Latin" country, including those colonized by the French and Portuguese. In Mississippi, there is not typically a clear distinction between the terms, even among people who call themselves Hispanic or Latino.

3. The term "Latino imaginary" is borrowed from the sociologist Juan Flores (2003) who develops these three dimensions of identity as a way of understanding the diverse meanings of Latino identity. Throughout this chapter I rely on his framework for understanding Latino identity formation on the national level to interpret the situation of this new ethnic group in Mississippi.

4. This use of the idea of the imaginary draws from the work done by Anderson (1990).

5. Although Mississippians see themselves as distinct from the other regions of the country in this regard, Latinos I interviewed did not make this distinction and most had not lived in other parts of the country so their generalization about the United States was based on their experiences in Mississippi.

6. My use of the word "Unitedstatsian" is inspired by the Spanish word *estadounidense* (from Estados Unidos, the Spanish for United States). I use it in recognition of the fact that people from Latin America are also Americans.

SOURCES

Anderson, Benedict. *Imagined Communities: Reflections on the Origin and Spread of Nationalism*. New York: Verso. 1990 [1983].

Borjas, George J. The Rise of Low-Skill Immigration in the South. In University of Kentucky Center for Poverty Research Discussion Paper Series. 2004. Accessed http://www.ukcpr.org/Publications/Immigration_in_the_South_1.pdf.

Brandfon, Robert L. The End of Immigration to the Cotton Fields. *Mississippi Valley Historical Review*. 50:4:591–611. 1964.

Chamberlain, Charles D. *Victory at Home: Manpower and Race in the American South during World War II*. Athens, GA: The University of Georgia Press. 2003.

Flores, Juan. The Latino Imaginary: Meanings of Community and Identity. In *Identities: Race, Class, Gender, and Nationality*. Linda Martin Alcoff and Eduardo Mendieta, eds. Malden, MA: Blackwell. Pp. 96–104. 2000 [2003].

Garcia, Mario T. *Desert Immigrants: The Mexicans of El Paso, 1880–1920*. New Haven, CT: Yale University Press. 1981.

Gibson, Campbell, and Kay Jung. Historical Census Statistics on Population Totals by Race, 1790 to 1990, and by Hispanic Origin, 1970 to 1990, for the United States, Regions, Divisions, and States. Population Division, U. S. Census Bureau. Working Paper Series No. 56. September 2002.

Kirby, Jack Temple. The Southern Exodus, 1910–1960: A Primer for Historians. *The Journal of Southern History*. 49:4:585–600. 1983.

Liaw, Kao-Lee, and William H. Frey. 2007. Multivariate Explanation of the 1985–1990 and 1995–2000 Destination Choices of Newly Arrived Immigrants in the United States: The Beginning of a New Trend? *Population, Space and Place*. 13(5):377–399.

Mato, Daniel. On the Making of Transnational Identities in the Age of Globalization: The US Latina/o-"Latin" American Case. In *Identities: Race, Class, Gender, and Nationality*. Linda Martin Alcoff and Eduardo Mendieta, eds. Malden, MA: Blackwell. Pp. 281–294. 2000 [2003].

Stuesse, Angela Christine. Globalization "Southern Style": Transnational Migration, the Poultry Industry, and Implications for Organizing Workers across Difference. Ph.D. dissertation, University of Texas. 2008.

U.S. Census Bureau. Demographic Trends in the 20th Century. Census 2000 Special Reports. 2002. http://www.census.gov/prod/2002pubs/censr-4.pdf.

Weise, Julie. Mississippi. In *Latino America: A State-by-State Encyclopedia*. M. Overmyer-Velazquez, ed. Westport, CT: Greenwood Press. 2008.

Whatley, Warren C. Labor for the Picking: The New Deal in the South. *The Journal of Economic History*. 43:4 (Dec. 1983): pp. 905–929.

POSTSCRIPT

Celebrating Heritage and Recognizing Complexity and Change in Mississippi Culture

—SHANA WALTON

Throughout this volume the appearance of chapters neatly divided, one group per chapter, has made "ethnicity" seem to be a simple fact—just a way people identify themselves now or maybe just where their ancestors originated. Groups of people are presented as if they have always existed, sharing identity through clear labels: Jewish, Chinese, Hindu. The reality, of course, is much more complicated. Take, for instance, the story of the Lebanese in Mississippi in this volume. As author James Thomas explains, most of the people who now self-identify as "Lebanese" had ancestors who came to the U.S. when the country of Lebanon did not actually exist. Technically, they were citizens of Syria. Some were identified as Turks because in the nineteenth century, when many immigrated to Mississippi, much of that area of the Middle East was under the control of the Ottoman Empire. So, people researching their Lebanese history often turn to documents about "Syrians" or even "Turks" (see Thomas, this volume). The story is similar for the people we label "Croatians" in Biloxi. At various times, these same people have called themselves "Slavonians" or "Dalmatians," depending on what part of their heritage people were referencing or what point in history is being cited (see Schmidt, this volume). Even the seemingly straightforward idea of the "Scottish" becomes complicated when you realize that at the time of heavy immigration in the eighteenth and nineteenth centuries, many of the people we lump together as "Scots" very much saw themselves as distinct cultural groups (see Ray, this volume), with divisions among religions and between those who spoke Gaelic and those who did not.

German identity provides a good case study of how we use simple labels to cover complex histories. The label "German" was the third most common listing on the 2000 census form for ethnic identity in Mississippi.

A good many of those claiming German ancestry had families who immigrated in the early 1800s, but the country we think of as Germany was not even unified as a single nation until a decade after the U.S. Civil War. At that time of immigration, most of our "German" ancestors probably identified nationally as "Prussians" or "Bavarians," or members of some other German-speaking kingdom. When people more than a hundred years ago said they were "Deutsch," they could easily have been referring to their common language, not their country. Even "Deutsch" wasn't unifying, however, because some varieties are only barely mutually intelligible. Today Germany is a political reality with a culture that Americans find meaningful (at least as a stereotype), and people use that label, that country, as a point of ancestral origin rather than, say, writing in "Bavarian." Indeed, the fact that their ancestors might not have considered themselves "German" is actually not important. People are using the labels to indicate political, social, and cultural categories that are salient today, and because they are trying to communicate their intentions to contemporary citizens, it doesn't matter that their ancestors might not have understood or approved. Using the word "German" calls upon current general understandings, a known entity, knowledge shared by other Americans, while using the word "Bavarian" will mean little to many Americans. Almost all Americans "know" that Germans are clean, well-organized, eat sauerkraut, and build fast cars. In short, the label "German" is meaningful in a way that the label "Bavarian" is not.

Far from being a straightforward fact, then, ethnicity is, instead, a complex, elusive, changeable concept—not a fixed reality. Of course, the irony is that while ethnicity is actually historically contingent and mutable, its attractiveness often rests on its promise of historical depth and authenticity. The search for ethnicity is one way people claim something intangible but real and meaningful in their lives. "Race" is no less of a complex or illusive concept. This chapter looks at the differences between "ethnicity" and "race" as labels, times when ethnicity and race function in the same way, the special place ethnicity has in Mississippi identifications, and the search for ethnic labels and meaningful identity among nonhyphenated Mississippians.

ETHNICITY AND RACE

A wonderful discussion of ethnicity in the U.S. South, with clear, simple definitions, can be found in the introduction to *Ethnicity*, Volume 6 of the *New Encyclopedia of Southern Culture*. In that introduction, Celeste Ray (also an author for this volume) writes:

> As culturally constructed notions, racial identities are imposed generally by those with whom one does not share a designation. Ethnic identity one traditionally learns at a grandparent's knee. Ethnicity lies in folktales, in tying fishing nets, in conceptions of the supernatural, in the music that delights multiple generations simultaneously, in the foods that mean home. Ethnic identities are cultural identities, and as such they are dynamic and renegotiated in different contexts and periods. Some consider southern identity shared by black and white southerners (as opposed to "southern blacks and whites"), an ethnic identity within the United States.... Southern culture, or the multiple southern cultures of the South's many subregions, is a complex amalgamation of disparate ethnicities and traditions from around the globe. After centuries of blending, the sum is undoubtedly greater than its parts but is hardly a finished product. (Ray 2007: 2)

Ray leaves us to conclude that although we commonly use national designations such as Filipino or Vietnamese to signal ethnic identities, we can't conflate nationalities with ethnicities. Ethnicity is intimately connected to what anthropologists call "enculturation"—how you know what behavior is appropriate, how you think families should act toward each other, what kinds of foods taste good to you, possibly how you worship or even which colors you think go together well. She also implies that ethnicity is, to some degree, a choice, while race is "imposed" by outsiders.

Simply put, race is usually framed as biology or presumed biology. We often think of race as being about skin "color" or hair texture or facial shape. But scientists tell us that our common perceptions are inaccurate. There is more variation within a "race" than between any two races. That is, the people who get classified as one "race" can show more physical variation than do people of "different races." If race were real, then skin color would correlate with other genetic features that would come packaged together, making these people a distinct group. But this is not the case. There are some differences. For instance, the disease sickle cell anemia is linked to African Americans, and to some this appears to be a "racial" disease. But it turns out that only African Americans whose ancestors were from central and western Africa carry the sickle cell trait. Southern Africans are no more likely than European Americans to have sickle cell. In addition, people from Turkey, Yemen, and Greece can be carriers of sickle cell trait. Sickle cell is place-based, but not race-based. Analysis of mitochondrial DNA—the DNA inherited solely through the mother's line—allows researchers to trace a person's "biogeneology," the area of the world his or her ancestors are from. This test works against the idea of unifying "races" because it turns out that people from, say, Europe or Africa will not share a single marker, but instead have markers that vary by the place on the continent where their ancestors lived. There is no gene for "race." From the view of biologists, anthropologists, and sociologists, biological "race" is a fiction.[1]

But, of course, race is also very real. If you grew up only a generation ago, your "race" determined where you went to school and what type of job you might have. Despite the scientists' assertion that "race" is a nebulous, confusing category, the fact remains that very few people are actually confused about what "race" they are. Although more people are choosing mixed-race categories, most people in Mississippi continue to see themselves as members of a race. And the racial disparities in Mississippi remain stark. According to the 2009 American Human Development Project, which drew on data from the United Nations Human Development Report, if you are black in Mississippi, you will, on average, earn ten thousand dollars a year less than a white person in the state and die four years sooner (Burd-Sharps et al. 2009: 10). Mississippi also celebrates many black sons and daughters as writers, artists, business and political leaders. In fact, Mississippi has not only the largest number of black elected officials, but also the highest proportion of such leaders in the nation (Bositis 2001). The larger point is that race in Mississippi matters and continues to matter. As we start the twenty-first century, race continues to shape where Mississippians go to school, where we go to church, and who our friends are.

SHIFTING IDEAS OF RACE AND ETHNICITY

But race wasn't always a great social cleaver. In fact, race as we know it was only invented a few hundred years ago. As recently as the 1600s and 1700s, the Europeans and Native Americans in what is now Mississippi didn't necessarily see themselves as "white" or "Indian." The Europeans saw themselves as French or English or Scottish, or perhaps as Bretons or Gaelic. The Native Americans saw themselves as Natchez or Choctaw or any of a dozen other groups. For generations after arriving, Africans forcibly brought to the Americas saw themselves not as "slaves" or "black," but as Kongo, Mandingo, Wolof, or members of dozens of other cultures (Hall 2007, Ray 2007). In those days, the labels "white" or "black" didn't have the meanings they have today. Identities like Irish, Greek, Italian, and others might be referred to as a "race." But by the time Mississippi became a state, and as slavery increased in importance to the economy, the concept of a society with two races came to dominate political as well as everyday talk and ideas. This had a powerful warping effect on ethnic or cultural identity. This is the time historians now refer to as Mississippi's "closed society." The phrase, introduced by historian James Silver, refers to the state having a racial "caste" system, in which admission to "white" society was closed to blacks and vice versa. The idea also refers to the way Mississippi, with its particular history, was "closed" off from other prevailing currents and thoughts in American society and culture, as it was locked in its racial struggles. During this time people began to submerge their cultural, national, or ethnic identity and "choose" one of the two available racial identities—or have a racial identity foisted upon them. Some groups that were not of Western European origin, like the Lebanese and some of the Jews, were grouped into the "white" category (Rockoff and Thomas, this volume). Other groups, like Latinos, often became associated with "black" (Hayden, this volume). Other groups were more problematic. For instance, the Chinese in the Delta and the Choctaws in the eastern part of the state never fit into either category and always remained between black and white (Mould, this volume; Erwin Jones and Quon, this volume).

For our purposes, we will divide Mississippi social/cultural history into three phases (Peacock and Matthews 2005). The first phase is from the 1500s, the time of Spanish and French exploration, until 1793, when the cotton gin was invented and, simultaneously, more Indian lands were appropriated or "opened up" for European settlement. For more than 250 years the area we now think of as Mississippi was a frontier region with a very diverse population and multiple languages spoken. Some of this early diversity was explored in the first volume of *Ethnic Heritage in Mississippi* (Carpenter 1992). During many of those years the area was controlled by the French (and then the British and then the Spanish), but there was always a variety of people passing through, especially people trading up and down the river. Multiple Native American groups called the region home, and by 1719 the French had brought in enslaved people from Africa. Many of those Africans still spoke West African languages. For 250 years after the European invasion of North America, the Mississippi region remained diverse to say the least. In the days when Biloxi was a fort and Natchez was an outpost, a traveler down the Natchez Trace could easily hear French, Spanish, English, West African, and many Native American languages.

The second phase is the "closed society" (Silver 1964). During this time, from 1793 to the end of the Civil Rights Movement, Mississippi was part of what came to be "invented" as the U.S. South—both a region and a concept (Peacock 2005) and maybe its own ethnic group (Reed 1982). Using the word "invented" does not mean that the South isn't a real region or that the Civil War didn't historically and culturally separate the South from the rest of the United States. The South was a distinctive geographical region marked by a plantation economy, legal slavery long after the rest of the U.S. outlawed slavery, and then by a legal apartheid system (sometimes called Jim Crow). Using the word "invented" refers to the fact that the South is more than just its history in the American imagination. By turns, and depending on your point of view, the South was/is a place of romance and mystery (gracious plantations and genteel lifestyles, blues music, juke joints, down-home food, and good manners) or the shame of the nation (lynchings, violence, evil planters, and amoral sheriffs). Neither of these sets of stereotypes ever captured the complexity of the groups who made up Mississippi. Even during this "closed society" time, groups came and established themselves in Mississippi. These groups had the complex task of negotiating an identity in a binary caste society (see Rockoff, Erwin Jones and Quon, Mould, Thomas, all in this volume). In addition, despite relocation efforts by the U.S. government, thousands of Native Americans remained in Mississippi, and they also had an anomalous identity in this black-white world.

The third phase has been just in the last thirty years. After the fall of segregation and the increase in diversity in the economy in the South, Mississippi entered a new, global identity phase. One of the largest groups to arrive during this most recent wave has been the Vietnamese. Many were relocated here after the Vietnam War and others migrated to the prime fishing and warm climate later or from other parts of the U.S. Latino immigration increased starting in the 1980s and 1990s as poultry processing became a growth industry in Mississippi and demand for labor rose (Striffler 2005). Latino immigration accelerated after Hurricane Katrina created an unprecedented demand for construction labor (Hayden, this volume). Other groups, such as East Indians, have also begun to find Mississippi an attractive destination (Roy and Williamson, this volume). For good or ill, global communication links and ease of travel have made it easier for Mississippians to meet and draw toward them people from other countries. For example, the increasing number of Filipina brides are in turn (re)creating a Filipino community (Allen, this volume).

Today people are layering on ethnic labels, in addition to racial labels. There are at least three reasons why we see people using more ethnic labels.

One clear reason people are reaching for more ethnic labels in this state is simply because as diversity is increasing, racial labels just don't work. As this volume points out in Section II, there have always been groups that have been "between black and white," but the assimilation pressure has always been to merge with one of the dominant racial categories. In the case of Mississippi, Lebanese and Jewish residents became "white." The plasticity of racial categories allows for such expansion. At one time, "white" was limited to the British and specific Northern Europeans, but gradually the label came to include Italians, Greeks, and even the Irish (Ignatiev 1996). But the label was never flexible enough to include Asian or Native American groups. They always remained outside. In the post–Jim Crow era, there is less pressure to be either black or white, and now there are even more groups who don't fit the labels, including the Vietnamese, Filipinos, and East Indians. Latinos/Hispanics, for example, can be either black or white. People from Cuba or the Dominican Republic are often labeled "black" by outsiders, while most people from, say, Spain are considered "white." Many Latinos from Central and South America also self-identify as Native Americans, further confusing the picture. Racial categories alone, then, are clearly not sufficient tools for socially classifying people in modern Mississippi.

The second reason for the growth of increasingly numerous labels in Mississippi, as in America at large, is a reaction to the social and political empowerment of African Americans. After African Americans fought for equal rights and protection in the Civil Rights Movement of the 1950s and 1960s, many then turned to questions of identity. The quest for identity became immortalized in the television miniseries *Roots*. Broadcast in 1977, this television series was about an African American, Alex Haley, who was trying to trace his family origins through six generations. About that same time, some people rejected the racial label "black" and began asserting a point-of-origin label, "African American," instead. Today many people use the labels interchangeably, but others see their usage as marks of social awareness and political positioning. That is, to some people it signals something about you and your beliefs if you choose to say "African American" instead of "black." The search for place-of-origin identity by African Americans began a wave of hyphenated identity by others in the U.S.

The third reason is the trend toward ethnic revitalization that began in a wave of renewal in ethnic identity in the 1980s (Alba 1990). Often "white" seemed to be a less meaningful category than, say, Irish American or Italian American, and across America, many white Americans sought to reconnect with their European heritages. These are the people for whom ethnicity is a choice. They participate in an ethnic identity to the extent that it's meaningful, but don't have to suffer from outsiders labeling them or judging them. During these last three decades we have witnessed a revival of interest in ethnic heritage among Mississippians of European descent. Visible signs include how the St. Patrick's Day parades and Celtic festivals in the state have grown into events that attract thousands (Ray, this volume).

Mississippi caught the national ethnic revival wave at a time when great changes were under way socially and politically in the state. Jim Crow segregation was collapsing and at the same time new waves of immigrants were finding their way to the Magnolia State. And just as alternative identities were suffocated by the creation of a narrow black-white society, its collapse created some breathing space for Mississippians to assert more complex identities.

FINDING AND CLAIMING IDENTITIES

Over the last thirty years, people of both African and European heritage have started to publicly reach for more specific ancestral identities. This is easier for people of European ancestry. Because there has always been a subset of people in the state interested in ancestry and genealogy, the state libraries have excellent genealogy collections and record archives. Mississippi's planters were often obsessed with lineage. For example, the famous Percy family of Greenville, which ran a virtual plantation empire for a century in the Mississippi Delta, liked to trace their origins to "Hotspur Harry" Percy who fought alongside of (and then against) England's King Henry IV and was later immortalized in Shakespeare's play about the king. Other Percys claimed their lineage extended all the way to Percys who fought with William the Conquerer at the Battle of Hastings (Wyatt-Brown 1996). Mississippi's European heritage is much like the European heritage of much of the United States, with the predominant ancestral categories being German, English, and Irish, although Mississippi has a wide range of other European ethnicities represented (Ray, this volume).

Trickier to find are ethnic identities among people of African heritage. Africans who were enslaved and brought to the New World mostly came from an area of west and central Africa that today supports more than a dozen countries, an area roughly the size of the continental U.S. minus California. Researchers can narrow it down some because most of the west and central Africans were brought from the Senegambia region. But that doesn't help much. People from Senegambia spoke more than a dozen languages, had different religions, rituals, holidays, and distinct ways of counting who was or was not kin. For example, at the time of the transatlantic slave trade, areas of Senegambia had been Muslim for generations because of centuries of interactions with traders from the Near East. Others in Senegambia practiced nativistic or polytheistic religions. Some were farmers or herders and vast areas were rural, while others from the region were urban dwellers who came from large and wealthy west African cities.

New research is piecing together the range of ethnic identities held by the people captured and sold into slavery and brought to the New World (Hall 2007). Between 1719, when the French brought over the first African slaves to build Fort Rosalie, until the early 1800s when the slave trade (but not slavery) was banned, many of the slaves came directly from Africa to the New World. They brought with them their language, customs, and beliefs. Some of these Africans came to Mississippi. By the time Mississippi became a state, the ban against bringing slaves from Africa was in effect. So, during all of the time that Mississippi was a state, the enslaved people brought in were the children and grandchildren of Africans who had themselves been born into slavery. This internal slave trade brought people down the Natchez Trace to places like Fork of the Roads in Natchez from eastern U.S. states like Virginia or Tennessee (Barnett and Burkett 2001). To consider African ethnicity, then, in terms of specific geographical heritage, we must consider the origin points of both the enslaved Africans brought directly to the region and those of the Africans brought to other parts of the U.S., whose descendents wound up in Mississippi.

What historian Gwendolyn Midlo Hall (2007) has found in her groundbreaking work on African American identity is that ethnicities were sometimes recorded, often at the initiative of the Africans themselves. She found that between 1719 and 1820 the eighteen most common ethnicities among Louisiana's enslaved Africans are (in decreasing percentage of frequency) Kongo, Mandingo, Mina, Senegal/Wolof, Igbo, Bamana, Chamba, Yoruba, Kanga, Aja/Fon/Arada, Fulbe, Calabar, Hausa, Moor/Nor, Ibibio/Moko, Kisi, Makwa, and Edo (Hall 2007: 43–44). Hall's work looks specifically at the ethnicities of Africans in Louisiana. Louisiana has a slightly different history, but what we can take from this is that the Africans were from widely varied groups and worked to self-identify by their language or ethnic heritage even as they were ripped from all normal surroundings. Much work remains to restore the links between African Americans today and specific African geographic heritages. Today the label "African American" stands as an umbrella term for the descendants of multiple and varied cultures who were brought to the New World.

Approximately one-third of Mississippians are descended from Africans. Clearly, at this point, there is no straightforward way for most of those Mississippians to claim a country of origin or an ancestral language without doing a lot of guesswork. Ethnicity as a concept must be flexible enough to encompass group identities in cases where people create community, lineage, and heritage from the tools at hand and must recognize populations that form community based on core values or traditions beyond birth country, like place-based identities (see Young and Crowe, this volume) or practice-based, such as music or religion (see Jackson; Ray, this volume).

THE PARTICULAR MEANING OF ETHNICITY IN MISSISSIPPI

Ethnicity, of course, is more than just whether your ancestor fought at the Battle of Hastings or came from a particular country in Europe or Africa. Ethnicity is equal to neither ancestry nor country of origin. In other words, if you see someone on St. Patrick's Day wearing a "Kiss Me, I'm Irish" badge, you don't necessarily conjure up an image of, say, Cork or Belfast. Nor is ethnicity about authentically re-creating a past. For example, many African Americans are keenly interested in which countries their ancestors might have lived in, and they might adopt clothing or learn some west African drumming. But very few would actually want to practice, for instance, preferred first-cousin marriage like many west African groups. Similarly, while many in the Mississippi Hibernian Society enjoy donning a kilt for special occasions, few want to wear a kilt every day. Nor do most want to add haggis to their regular diets. The ethnicity movement is not about "authenticity." Instead, you might say, as researcher John Jackson does, that ethnicity today is about "sincerity" (Jackson 2005). That is, the ethnicity movement is about connecting to the past to seek meaningful identities in a contemporary context.

Connecting to meaningful identities is what the ethnicity revival in Mississippi has in common with the larger ethnic revival movement. In other words, this is one way Mississippi is showing itself to be wholly a part of a larger American cultural and social movement. Beyond the fact that almost all Americans are doing this, it seems important to also reflect on what ethnicity might uniquely mean in Mississippi. Why have ethnic identifications increased in the state? Are all people claiming ethnicity? Who is or isn't? How do the growing numbers of immigrants to Mississippi in the last generation influence the state's culture? Can we celebrate ethnic identity without overlooking other social divisions? If ethnicity is growing, are we beyond "race"? Are we beyond being "southern"? Is the idea of being "southern" losing its power? Or, from another perspective, what does "ethnicity" mean in a context where social interactions are still marked by racial divisions? When is an "ethnic" identity meaningful and when is it not?

We can only draw limited conclusions at this point. We know that Mississippi is returning to the kind of diversity that marked the early years of the territory. We know that even as people reach for new identities they cling to the old, and identities are being layered on in complex ways. A person can be "white," "southern" and "Jewish" all at the same time, drawing on different understandings to navigate changing social situations. If we have several labels, is one more meaningful? In other words, which is most important?

The label "southern" is probably safe. "Southern" remains a meaningful category in the South for people of all races and many ethnicities (Griffin and Thompson 2003; Griffin et al. 2005). So, if the pollsters are correct, future generations will certain identify as "southern." There can be no doubt that race remains a dominant social category. But there is also no question that the wave of new immigrants and the changing demographics are chipping away at the power of "race" to define people. One of the most optimistic predictions is that the resurgent interest in ethnicity will eventually lead to race being de-emphasized or even rendered meaningless as a social category. Perhaps race labels will be seen by future generations as only a vestigial remnant of something that was once essential but eventually evolved into a mild curiosity or conversation point. The less optimistic or perhaps dangerous possibility is that ethnic categories will harden, take on negative connotations or social rankings, and become a source of strife. Ethnic differences have never been a major source of tension in the U.S. South, but in other parts of the world—for example, Bosnia, Rwanda, or Sri Lanka—ethnic differences have led to bloody conflicts. Mississippi has seen some ethnic discord. One example was the conflict in the 1980s between the new Vietnamese immigrant shrimpers and the more established Cajun and Croatian shrimpers (Dao, Schmidt, this volume). Those tensions have mostly evaporated as economic space was made for everybody to make a living. Probably neither extreme—the loss of race, nor the hardening of ethnicity—is likely.

With the embracing of a wide range of ethnic labels, one change we can chart is that Mississippi is looking (and sounding) more like American states outside the South. Like Americans everywhere, Mississippians are embracing—and claiming for themselves—a mainstream national trend to celebrate ethnic heritage. The biggest impact this might have is on how "southern" gets defined as we move into the future. As we southerners take on a plethora of labels and complexly layer identities, the concept of "southern," can be freed from its former tight association with regional politics or racial positioning (either black or white). There was a time when celebrating southern heritage would automatically evoke political or racial stances (often Confederate flags). Now, "southern" seems to embrace a wider variety of ethnicities and races and looks to be on a path toward evolving in the same way as labels like Irish or Greek or Lebanese. These are what some people call "costless" ethnicities (Waters 1994). In other words, claiming such an identity does not in any way foreshorten your ability to interact across all racial, regional, or ethnic groups nor preclude your participation in any particular activity nor forecast what type of political or social positions you might take. The face of Mississippi is changing, and the labels are changing as well. This evolution will be in process for the next few generations, but it is possible that in the future the labels "southern" or "Mississippian" will not signal someone from a biracial world, but merely that you say "y'all" and know that tea should be iced.

NOTE

1. This paragraph is only a brief summary of what researchers know about race. For a thorough but easily understood discussion of the core concepts of race, see "Race: The Power of an Illusion," a documentary and Web site sponsored by California Newsreel and PBS (2003), and "Race: Are We So Different?," an educational project by the American Anthropological Association (2010), which can be seen at www.understandingrace.org.

WORKS CITED

Alba, Richard. 1992. *Ethnic Identity: The Transformation of White America.* New Haven: Yale University Press.
Barnett, Jim, and H. Clark Burkett. 2001. "The Forks of the Road Slave Market at Natchez." *The Journal of Mississippi History*, Vol. LXIII, Fall, No. 3:169–187.
Bositis, David A. 2001. "Black Elected Officials: A Statistical Summary 1999." Washington, D.C.: Joint Center for Political and Economic Studies.

Burd-Sharps, Sarah, Eduardo Borges Martins, and Kristen Lewis. 2009. "A Portrait of Mississippi: Mississippi Human Development Report." American Human Development Project of the Social Sciences Research Council. Retrieved from http://www.measureofamerica.org.

Carpenter, Barbara. 1992 (2009). *Ethnic Heritage in Mississippi*. Jackson, Miss.: University Press of Mississippi.

Griffin, Larry J., and Ashley B. Thompson. 2003. "Enough About the Disappearing South? What About the Disappearing Southerner." *Southern Cultures*, Fall 2003.

Griffin, Larry J., Ranae J. Evenson, and Ashley B. Thompson. 2005. "Southerners All?" *Southern Cultures*, Spring 2005.

Hall, Gwendolyn Midlo. 2007. *Slavery and African Ethnicities in the Americas: Restoring the Links*. Chapel Hill: University of North Carolina Press.

Ignatiev, Noel. 2008. *How the Irish Became White*. New York: Routledge.

Jackson, John L. 2005. *Real Black: Adventures in Racial Sincerity*. Chicago: University of Chicago Press.

Peacock, James, and Carrie Matthews. 2005. *The American South in a Global World*. Chapel Hill: University of North Carolina Press.

Ray, Celeste. 2007. "Introduction." *New Encyclopedia of Southern Culture: Ethnicity*. Chapel Hill: University of North Carolina Press.

Reed, John Shelton. 1982. *One South: An Ethnic Approach to Regional Culture*. Baton Rouge: Louisiana State University Press.

Silver, James. 1964. *Mississippi: The Closed Society*. New York: Harcourt, Brace & World.

Striffler, Steve. 2005. *Chicken: The Dangerous Transformation of America's Favorite Meat*. New Haven: Yale University Press.

Waters, Mary. 1990. *Ethnic Options: Choosing Identities in America*. Los Angeles: University of California Press.

Wyatt-Brown, Bertram. 1996. *The House of Percy: Honor, Melancholy and Imagination in a Southern Family*. Oxford: Oxford University Press.

CONTRIBUTORS

Linda Pierce Allen is an associate professor of English at the University of Southern Mississippi specializing in multiethnic, postcolonial, critical race and feminist literature.

Carl L. Bankston III is a professor of sociology at Tulane University. A specialist in ethnicity, immigration, and education, he has written numerous books. His most recent book is *Public Education, America's Civil Religion: A Social History*, coauthored with Stephen Caldas.

Milburn J. Crowe was born in Mound Bayou, Mississippi, in 1933. After working in Chicago, he returned to Mound Bayou in 1967 to run the family restaurant and serve as unofficial town historian, devoting much energy to documenting the history of the town his grandparents helped settle. He helped found the Mound Bayou Historical Foundation and was active in the Bolivar County Historical Society and the Mississippi Historical Society. Mr. Crowe's work was recognized with the Mississippi Humanities Council Achievement Award. He passed away in 2005.

Vy Thuc Dao is a graduate student in sociology at Tulane University. She is currently writing her doctoral dissertation, which is a comparative study of the Vietnamese communities in New Orleans and Biloxi.

Bridget Anne Hayden is an associate professor of cultural anthropology at the University of Southern Mississippi. Her research includes work on migration and globalization in Central America as well as looking at Latino groups in Mississippi.

Joyce Marie Jackson is an associate professor of anthropology at Louisiana State University. As a folklorist and ethnomusicologist, she specializes in African American culture and the peoples of the African diaspora.

CONTRIBUTORS

Emily Erwin Jones is the university archivist at the Charles W. Capps Jr. Archives at Delta State University. She runs the university's oral history program and has helped archive the largest collection in existence of interviews with Mississippi Chinese. In addition, she has organized collections on civil rights, black farmers in the Delta, and Mississippi Italians.

Tom Mould is an ethnographer and folklorist who teaches in the Department of Sociology and Anthropology at Elon University. He is the coeditor of *Choctaw Tales*, along with former chief Phillip Martin, and is the author of *Choctaw Prophecy: A Legacy for the Future*.

Frieda Quon, now retired, was for many years a librarian at Delta State University; her work included directing the university's Instructional Resouces Center. Her family members were Chinese immigrants to the Delta, and she served as an interviewer for the university's Chinese in the Delta oral history collection.

Celeste Ray is a professor of anthropology at the University of the South. She is the author of several books on ethnicity in the southern United States and edited the volume on ethnicity for *The New Encyclopedia of Southern Culture*.

Stuart Rockoff is a historian and the director of the history department of the Goldring/Woldenberg Institute of Southern Jewish Life. He also serves as the vice president of the Southern Jewish Historical Society and is working on a general history of Jewish life in the South.

Devparna Roy is a sociologist who is assistant professor in the Department of Anthropology and Sociology at Hobart and William Smith Colleges. While teaching at Millsaps, Roy helped conduct some of the first research on Mississippi's Hindu community.

Aimée L. Schmidt, a native of Mississippi, is a folklorist and serves as events coordinator at the Rialto Center for the Arts, George State University.

James Thomas is a historian who also serves as the managing editor of *The New Encyclopedia of Southern Culture* at the Center for the Study of Southern Culture at the University of Mississippi. A Lebanese and native Mississippian, he is one of the first historians to document the state's Lebanese community.

Shana Walton is an anthropologist who teaches in the Department of Languages and Literature at Nicholls State University. Her research focuses on race and ethnic identity in the U.S. South.

Lola Williamson teaches in the Department of Religious Studies at Millsaps College. A specialist in Asian religions, her book *Transcendent in America: Hindu-Inspired Meditation Movements as New Religion* was published by New York University Press.

Amy L. Young is an associate professor of anthropology at the University of Southern Mississippi. Young is an archeologist who specializes in historical and urban archaeology in the southeastern United States.

INDEX

Page numbers in *italics* refer to illustrations.

Abraham, Haseeb George, 177
Ackerman, Paula, 205
Adams, John, 37
African Americans: ancestral identity of, 360–61, 362; Chinese and, 153; Choctaw and, 250; church and, 78–79; in the Delta, 43; ethnicity and, 5–6, 13, 361–62; farm system and, 107; Jews and, 198–99, 206–10; Lebanese and, 176–78, 182–84; lynching and, 177; oral tradition of, 78; out migration and, 333; in the Piney Woods, 74, 75, 76–77; population of, 21–22; race relations and, 77, 176–78, 182–84; religious music and, 79–86, 95–96; rural to urban shift of, 106; secular music and, 86–96. *See also* slavery
Agricultural Adjustment Act, 211, 214
Aguilar, Delia D., 211
Alba, Richard, 7
Al-Bayan, 178
Alcorn, James, 205
Al-Hoda, 178
Allen, Linda, 10
Allen, Sally, 232, 242
Alvarado, Luis de, 33
American Human Development Project, 356
American Indian Reorganization Act, 221
American Jewish Committee, 207, 209
American Jewish Year Book, 201, 211
Amos, Billy, 228–30, *230*
Amos, Wagonner, 226

Anabaptists, 55–56
Anderson, Odie Mae, 253
Antici, Anna Brittain, 189
Anti-Defamation League, 207
Appalachia, 43
Appalachian Regional Commission, 43
archeology and descendant communities, 101–2, 103, 104–5, 106
architecture, 109–11
Arkansas River Valley Emigration Company, 147
Ashkenazi, Elliot, 196
Asian American Hotel Owners Association, 298
Athenian Society, 65
Audubon John James, 41–42
Austin, George, 34

Ballard, James, 205
Bank of Mound Bayou, 100, 103, 104, 112–13, 116
Banks, Charles, 100, 103, 104, 112–13, 116
Bankston, Carl, 8, 13
Bảo Đại, 265
Baraka, Amiri, *Blues People*, 86
Barhanovich, Yankie, 59
barrelhouse circuit, 89–91
Baxter, Robert, 44
Beekman, Rosalie, 202
Ben, Terry, 226, 245
Bernheimer, Jacob, 197
Bernheimer, Samuel, 197
Beth Israel, 204, 205
Bhowal, Indira, 296
Bienville, John Baptiste LeMoyne, Sieur de, 39

Bilbo, Theodore, 206
Billie, Judy, 242, 245
Biloxi, Miss.: Cajuns in, 57–58, 123, 124, 127–28, 274; casino industry and, 133–34, 138; Catholicism and, 129; history of, 125–27; Hurricane Katrina and, 134–36; seafood industry and, 123, 124, 126–28, 132–33, 139–40; race relations and, 122; Vietnamese in, 272–74
Biloxi schooner, 128
Biloxi Shrimp Festival, 58, 60
Binder, Alvin, 208
Blessing of the Shrimp, 60, 123, 130–31
Bluestein, Judith, 213
B'nai B'rith, 209; *The High Wall*, 207–8
B'nai Israel, 24–25, 204, 205, 209
Boat People SOS, 279
Bochasanwasi Akshar Purushottam Sanstha, 298
Bodron, Ellis, 187–88
Bohemians, 42
Bowsky, George, 202–3
Bracero Program, 336
Brandon, Gerard, 51
Branfon, Robert L., 335
British, 36, 41, 43
British Petroleum, 139–40
Bruce, Lenny, 193
Bryan, Wiley, 196
Budhraja, Som, 296
Bushnell, David, 243

Cajuns: in Biloxi, 57–58, 123, 124, 127–28, 273, 274; in the Gulf Coast region, 42; in the Piney Woods, 44; seafood industry and, 128–29
Carroll, Charles, 51
Cash, W. J., *The Mind of the South*, 201
Catholic Conference, 267
Causey, Hugh F., 158–59
Cavat, Rebecca, 40
Cedars of Lebanon, 185
Celtic Heritage Society, 55
CelticFest Mississippi, 55
Chamoun, Chafik, 174–75, 177, 190

Chan, Jachin, 162
Chaney, James, 209
Chang, Grace, 325
Charles Auguste, 147
Cherokee tribe, 221, 226
Chester, Peter, 37
Chickasaw tribe, 37, 221, 225, 226
Chinese: assimilation of, 156–68; businesses of, 150–51; church and, 156–57, 160–62, 166–67; cultural preservation and, 168; in the Delta, 149–50; education, *155*, *156*, 155–60, *159*; funerals of, 163–64; immigration of, 22, 25–26; migration of, 148; race and, 153, 154, 155–56; recruitment of, 147–48; sense of community among, 154; social lives of, 162–65; weddings of, 164–65
Chinese Exclusion Act, 148, 155
Choctaw Community, 247
Choctaw Fair, 224, 228, *230*, 238
Choctaw Tribal Language Program, 234
Choctaw tribe, 9, 22, 37, 76. *See also* Mississippi Band of Choctaw Indians
Chu Lin, George, 164
Chua Van Duc Temple, 77
Citizen's Council, 77, 208; "A Jewish View on Segregation," 209
Civil Rights Movement, 77
Clapton, Eric, 88
Cleveland Chinese Mission School, 159
Cobb, James, 146
Cohen, Edward, 207; *The Peddler's Grandson*, 206
Cohn, David L., 193–94, 201
Coleman, Caroline, 176
Comby, Harold, 231
Coney, Wakefield "Big Moody," 91
Congregation Anshe Chesed, 205, 212
Congress of Racial Equality, 209
Costa Ricans, 337
Côte des Allemands, 61
Covacivich family, 132
Creek tribe, 221. *See also* Muskogee tribe
Cristil, Jack, 193
Croatians, 58–60, 127, 273

Crowe, Milburn, 9, 13, 14, 98, 102, 104, 105
Cruso, William, 63

Danes, 69
Danish Folk Society, 69
Dao, Vy, 9
Davis, George P., Jr., 189
Davis, Jefferson, 111
Davis, Joseph, 89–99, 111
Davis, Pat, 182, 186
de Soto, Hernando, 32–33, 38, 63, 334
Deepwater Horizon spill, 139–40
Delta blues, 87
Delta region, 42, 43, 145–47
Democratic Republic of Viet Nam, 266
Denson, Beasley, 247
Denson, Charlie, 233–34, 236, 247
D'Iberville, Miss., 36
Diehl, Martha, 57
Diehl family, 57
Dill family, 57
Doiron, Elizabeth, 166
Dollard, John, 207; *Caste and Class in a Southern Town*, 182
Dong, Fay, 157
Dong, Juanita, 154
Downey, James C., 82
DuKate, W. K. M., 126, 127
Dunbar, Scott, *From Lake Mary: Scott Dunbar*, 88–89
Dunbar, William, 37
Dunkers. *See* Old Order German
Duong, Thu, 278
Durkheim, Émile, 78

Eastland, Jim, 164
Edlund, Lena, 326
Ellis, Commour, *179*
Ellis, George, *179*, 181
Ellis, James, *179*, 181
Ellis, Michael, *179*, 181
Ellis, Nazera, 181
Ellis, Sam, *179*, 181
Ellis family, *180*
Ellison, Ralph, 86
Elmer, F. William, 126

Embree, Felix, 196
English, 21, 22, 23, 29–30, 37, 40–41, 43
Erber, Joe, *213*
Ethnic Heritage in Mississippi, 4–5
ethnicity: ancestral identity and, 360–63; defined, 6–7, 8, 10, 122–23, 222, 353, 354, 355; place and, 356; race and, 8, 353, 354–56, 359–60
Europeans, 10, 22, 25, 30, 46, 70

Fattouh, Ameen Naseef. *See* Nasif, Ameen
Fattouh, Elias Naseef. *See* Nasif, Ellis
Faulkner, William, *The Sound and the Fury*, 199
Filipinas, 358; acculturation of, 316–17; community and, 312–13; cultural identity of, 312–13; domestic violence and, 321–23, 325; economic conditions of, 313; economic obligations of, 313, 326; food and, 314–17; global economic influences on, 323–25; importance of kitchen to, 317, 329–30; as pen pals, 318–23; rescue efforts and, 327–29; in south Mississippi, 309–10; tsismis and, 317–18. *See also* Filipinos; Philippines
Filipino American Society of Mississippi, 327
Filipinos: cultural identity of, 313–14; gatherings of, *315*, *316*; population of, 309. *See also* Filipinas; Philippines
filles de la cassette, 37
Fischel, Albert Sidney, 202
Fischel, Leon, 202
Five Civilized Tribes, 221, 226
Fleur de Lis Society, 58, 123–25, 129, 135
Flores, Juan, 338, 346, 347
folk group, membership in, 124
Ford, Gerald, 266–67
Fort de la Boulaye, 35
Fort Louis de la Mobile, 35
Fort Rosalie, 36
Fort Saint-Pierre, 36
Frazier, Crystal, *239*
Freedom Summer, 207
French, 33–37, 38, 39–40, 43

French and Indian War, 37
Friends of the Poor, 66
Furseth, Inger, 307

Gaiter, Simon, 99–100
Gathering of Nations, 235
Gelman, Meyer, 213
German Fest, 62
German prisoners of war, 61
Germans: in the Delta, 43; immigration of, 22, 23, 24–25, 29–30, 32, 37, 61–62, 353–45; in the Piney Woods, 44
Gibson, Lillie, 238, 240–43
Gilston, Morris, 197
Gleeson, Eric, 210
Goldring/Woldenberg Institute of Southern Jews, 10
Goldstein, Eric, 210
Gollot, Richard, 27, 131–32
Gong, Penney, 162
Goodman, Andrew, 209
Gorenflo, William, 126
Governor's Commission on Recovery, Rebuilding and Renewal, 136
Grafton, Michael, "Hip Hop Ain't Nothing But the Young People's Blues," 94
Great Britain, 37
Great Day at Bude, 95
Greeks, 44, 65–67
Green, Benjamin, 98, 99, 111, 112
Green, Benjamin A., 104, 115
Greenville Chinese Cemetery, 163
Greenwood Commonwealth, 188
Griffith, Clark, 136
Guatemalans, 7–8
Gulf Coast Italian American Society of Mississippi, 344
Gulf Coast Latin American Association, 344
Gulf Coast region, 42, 46
Gulfhaven Mennonite Church, 56
Gutierrez, C. P., 273
Gwin, Peter, 57

Habeeb, Alfred, 188
Habeeb, Shoupie, 188

Halbert, Henry S., 225, 243
Hall, Gwendolyn Midlo, 361
Handsome Lake, 228
Harrison, Alferdteen, 105
Hattiesburg American, 209
Hayden, Bridget, 9
Henry, Aaron, 207
Henry, Inez, 236
Henry S. Jacobs Camp, 211
Hermann, Janet Sharp, 112
Highlands & Islands Association, 55
Hiller, H. 199
Hindu Temple (Brandon, Miss.), 291–96, *294, 295*
Hindu Temple Society of Mississippi, 293
Hinduism, 284, 285, 286
Hindus: caring relationships and, 302–3; caste system and, 305–6; Christians, 287; cultural preservation and, 288, 304; dating and marriage and, 306; education and, 304–5; Hurricane Katrina and, 298; population of, 285; religion in the home and, 300–302, *301*; Saraswati Devi puja, 289, 289–300; sense of community and, 288; temples of, 290–300; tolerance for non-Hindus of, 303
Hirschman, C., 277
Hispanic. *See* Latinos
Hồ Chí Minh, 265
Holder, Ned, 189
Holloway, A. J., 134, 136
Hondurans, 337
House, Son, 88
Howlin' Wolf, 88
Hungarians, 60
Hurricane Camille, 135
Hurricane Katrina, 36, 134–36; Hindus and, 298; Latinos and, 261, 337, 358; Mennonites and, 56; seafood industry and, 275–76; Vietnamese and, 263, 278–79
Hurst, E. H., 77

Iberville, Pierre Le Moyne, Sieur d', 125
immigration to Mississippi, 15, 16, *17*,

17–21, *19–21*, 23, 23–24; postbellum, 44; undocumented, 18; to the United States, 15–16, *17*
India. *See* Hindus
Indian Association of Mississippi, 293
Indian Removal Act, 221
Indian Self-Determination and Education Assistance Act, 221
Indians (Asian), 261, 285, 358. *See also* Hindus
international sex trade, 323–24
Irish, 23, *50*; Catholicism and, 39; in the Delta, 43; in the Gulf Coast region, 47; immigration of, 25, 37, 47–52; in the Northeast hills, 43; in the Piney Woods, 44
Irish Travellers, 68–69
ISKCON New Talavana Dham, 291
Italians: in the Delta, 43, 146; immigration of, 22, 27, 30, 44–45, 63–65, 335; race and, 335

Jackson, John, 362
Jackson, Joyce, 9, 13
Jackson, Judge, *The Colored Sacred Harp*, 82
Jackson, Miss., 38
James, Elmore, 88
Jews, 10, 193–94; assimilation of, 201–11; businesses of, 195–96, 197–98, 214; civic leadership and, 199–201; civil rights movement and, 207–10; in the Civil War, 202–3; economic influences on, 211, 214; immigration of, 24–25, 194; intermarriage and, 210–11; mobility of, 195; NAACP and, 207; peddling and, 194–95; politics and, 200–201; population decline and, 211, 214–16; race and, 205–6; race relations and, 198–99, 206–10; Reform Judaism and, 194, 203–5
Joe, Bobby, 249
Joe, Edward, 149
Joe, Ray, 164–65
Johnson, Bunk, 90
Johnson, Robert, 87–88
Johnston, Albert Sidney, 202

Jolliet, Louis, 33
Jones, Emily Erwin, 9
Jones, Lu Ann, *Mama Taught Us to Work*, 175
Jones, Richard M., 90
Joshi, Khyati, 302
Jue, Bobby, 149–50
Jung, John, 160–61; *Chopsticks in the Land of Cotton*, 151

Kaiser, Joseph, 196
Kaqchikel, 8
Kibria, N., 277
Kiché, 8
King, B. B., 87
King, B. J., *The Sacred Harp*, 82
King, Martin Luther, Jr., 208
Kirit Joshi Shri, 292
Know-Nothing Party, 51
Kociuszko, Thadeus, 60–61
Kossuth, Lajos (Louis), 60
Krewe of Killarney, 51
Ku Klux Klan, 77, 209
Kwan, Randy, 165

La Fayette, Marquis de, 60
La Louisiane, 33, *34–35*, *36–37*, 61
La Salle, René-Robert, 33, 41
Labor Day Weekend Blues Festival, 95
Landrove, Rafael, 336
Latinos: aggregation of, 338–39, 341; casino industry and, 337; as consumers, 341; in the Delta, 335; demographic analysis of, 333; ethnic identity of, 349–50; family and, 348–49; guest worker program and, 336; Hurricane Katrina, 29, 30–31, 261, 337, 358; imagery and, 333–34; immigration of, 23–24, 28–29, 336–37; legal status of, 342–44; migration of, 334–35; politics and, 341; population of, 22, 261; race and, 335–38, 339–40; self-identification of, 7–8, 346–49; skin color and, 338, 339, 345; stereotypes and, 338–39; undocumented immigrants among, 339, 343

Law, John, 36–37
Le Moyne, Jean-Baptiste, 35
Lead Belly, 90
Lebanese: assimilation of, 183–85, 187–90, 191; businesses of, 182; cultural preservation and, 185–87, 190; in the Delta, 146; foods and, 178; immigration of, 22, 26, 143, 172–73; music of, 178; peddling and, 173–78, 181; race and, 182–84, 189; race relations and, 176–78; social acceptance of, 182
Lee, Frieda, 154
Lee, Herbert, 77
Leflore, Greenwood, 40
Leflore, Louis, 40
Lescau, Marie-Anne, 37
Levy, Oscar, 202
Lewis, Dorothy, 85
Lewis, Julia, 82–84
Lewis, Morris, 200
Lincoln, C. Eric, 78
Little, William, *The Easy Instructor or a New Method of Teaching Sacred Harmony*, 81
Living Cities: The National Community Development Initiative, 136–38
Lockwood, Robert Junior, 88
Loeb, Alex, 209
Loewen, James W., *Mississippi Chinese: Between Black and White*, 25
Loi, V. M., 277
Long, Worth, 80, 92–95
Longfellow, Henry Wadsworth, *Evangeline*, 57–58
Longino, Andrew Houston, 63, 64
Lopez, Lazaro, 126, 127
Los Angeles Times, 189
Lou, Lisa, 165
Louis XV, 37
Lum, Martha, 158
Lum v. Rice, 155, 156, 158–60

Maddali, Mangala, 285
Mafri, Abu Anees. *See* Thomas, George
Mafrij, Anees. *See* Thomas, Ernest

Malouf, Alex, 188
Mamiya, Lawrence H., 78
Mantinband, Charles, 209–10
Mardi Gras, 40, 130
Maritime & Seafood Industry Museum, 128, 135, 140
Marks, Israel, 199–200
Marks, Levi, 199
Marks, Sam, 199
Marquette, Jacques, 33
Martin, Phillip, 247
Mary Queen of Vietnam Community Development Corporation, 279
Maycock, James, 126
Mayer, Simon, 202
Mazda, Ahura, 88
McCoy, Laughlin, 53
McRae, John, 53
Mehta, Mr., 296–97
Memphis Commmercial Appeal, 210
Mendoza, Leny, 329
Mennonite Disaster Service, 56
Mennonites, 44, 56
Mexican Americans, 336
Mexicans: in the Delta, 146, 335; education and, 336; Hurricane Katrina and, 29; immigration of, 22, 23–24, 28–29, 62. *See also* Latinos
Mirsky, Richard M., 84
Mississippi: Americanization of, 41–42; attraction of immigrants to, 334; cultural regions of, 42; ethnic influences on, 3–4; farming in, 45; history of, 32–38, 357–58; immigration to, 15, 16, 17, 17–21, 19–21, 23, 23–24, 30–31; out-migration and, 333; population growth in, 21–22; poverty in, 46; prevalence of religions in, 287; race and, 5, 357–58; Territory of, 38; undocumented immigrants in, 18
Mississippi African American Historic Preservation Council, 102
Mississippi Band of Choctaw Indians: acculturation of, 252; alcoholism and, 235–36; arts and crafts of, 248; Cholish

and, 247; Constitution of, 155, 158; ethnicity of, 222–23, 246–47, 250–51, 253; intermarriage and, 231–32, 234, 247, 249–50; intertribal relations and, 235, 239; intratribal divisions among, 237–38, 243; language preservation by, 234; membership in, 219–20, 221, 232; oral tradition of, 224, 251–52; origin myths of, 224–27; prophetic traditions of, 228–35; in the Piney Woods, 76; race and, 143, 222, 235, 248–50; race relations and, 235–37, 242, 250; religion and, 234, 237; Shukha anumpa and, 240–42; supernatural stories of, 242; Third Removal prophesy and, 232–34, 245; Trail of Tears and, 232; tribal lands of, 220, 234–35. *See also* Choctaw tribe

Mississippi Board of Immigration and Agriculture, 16; *Hand-Book of Mississippi*, 44

Mississippi Coastal Research and Extension Service, 134

Mississippi Council on Human Relations, 210

Mississippi Division of the American Legion, 56

Mississippi Gaming Control Act, 133

Mississippi Hibernian Society, 49, 51, 362

Mississippi Hispanic Association, 344

Mississippi Humanities Council, 116, 168

Mississippi Migrant Alliance, 29

Mississippi Negro Business League, 113

Mississippi State Sovereignty Commission, 208, 210

Mississippi Temple Teens, 211

Mitchell, Emil, 67

Mitchell, Kelly, 67

modernization theory, 107–8

Mohamed, Hassan, 177

Mokarzel, Salloum, 175

Montgomery, Ben, 98–99

Montgomery, Isaiah T., 98–99, 100, 111, 112, 113, 114

Montgomery, Little Brother, 89–90

Montgomery, Mary, 98

Montgomery, Thornton, 113

Montrose Academy, 54

Morton, Jelly Roll, 89

Mould, Tom, 9

Mound Bayou, Miss., 8–9; archeology at, 14, 100, 104, 105, 108, 116–18; economic independence and, 107; economy of, 113, 114–15; history of, 98, 99–101, 111–15; modernization and, 115, 118–19

Mound Bayou Historic Preservation Council, 103, 105

Mound Bayou Loan and Investment Company, 113

Mound Bayou Normal and Industrial Institute, 112

Moving Forward, 136–38

Mullin, Herbert J., 130

Munsif, Al, 181

Murray, Albert, 86

Muskogee tribe, 226, 239. *See also* Creek tribe

NAACP, 207, 209

Naff, Alix, 189; *Becoming American*, 174

Nanih Waiya cave mound, 227

Narayan, Swami, 298

Narayanan, Vasudha, 286

Nasif, Ameen, 173

Nasif, Ellis, 172–73

Natchez, Miss., 36, 37, 38, 40

Natchez Hibernian Society, 51

Natchez tribe, 36

National Alliance of Vietnamese American Service Agencies, 279

National Geographic, 57

National Tartan Day, 57

Native American Sports Association, 248

Nelson, Charles, 89

New Urbanism, 137

Newsome, Sam, 80

Nguyen, Peter, 276

Northeastern Hills region, 42–43

Nosser, Mary Louise, 190

Nussbaum, Perry, 209

Oakley, Giles, 89, 90
Ocean Springs, Miss., 34
Odum, Howard, *Southern Regions of the United States*, 45–46
Old Biloxi, Miss., 35, 36
Old Order German, 56, 57
Orange Order, 51
Ordoñez, Raquel Z., 324
Orkin, Celeste, 211
O'Rourke, Michael, 52
Overseas Contract Workers, 313, 324–25

Parker, Mack Charles, 77
Patmian Society, 65
Patton, Charley, 88
Pearl River South Singing Convention, 84
Peloso, Berardo, 63
Perler, Mark, 212
Pew Forum on Religion and Public Life, 285, 286, 287
Pew Hispanic Center, 47
Philippines, 9–10, 311
Piaggio, Henry, 63
Pine Lake Fellowship, 56
Piney Woods, 42, 43–44; African Americans in, 44, 74, 75; ethnic groups in, 76; geography of, 75–76; race relations in, 77; racial composition of, 76–77; religious music and, 79, 95–96; secular music and, 86–87
Pistonatubbee, Isaac, 225
Polish, 126, 271
Polk, Harry, 240
Prabhupada, Bhaktivedanta Swami, 291
Pramukh Swami, 298, 299–300
Pratt, Richard Henry, 221
Presley, Elvis, 87
Prévost, Antoine-François, *Manon Lescaut*, 37
Pruitt, Joe, 92
Pruitt, Tommy "T-Bone," 91–92
Pruitt, Verta, 92

Quan, Robert Seto, *Lotus Among the Magnolias: The Mississippi Chinese*, 26
Quon, Frieda: on the Chinese Church, 160–62; on Chinese in Mississippi, 154; Chinese oral history and, 9; on education and, 157; family business of, 151–54, 152; on her father, 148–49, 150; wedding of, 164–65; weddings of children of, 165
Quon, John Paul, 157, 164–66, 168
Quon, Lisa, 166
Quon, Shannon, 165, 166
Quon, Trey, 165, 166

Ram Babu, Shri, 292
Rankin, John, 206
Ray, Celeste, 8, 354
Reed, Shelton, 9
Reinecke, George F., 124
religious music: gospel, 80–81; sacred harp, 81–86; spirituals, 79
Repstad, Pal, 307
Republic of Viet Nam, 266
"Reviving the Renaissance," 136
Rockoff, Stuart, 9
Rolling Stones, The, 87, 88
Romani, 67–68
Roosevelt, Theodore, 100
Roots, 359
Rosen, Robert, 202
Rosenbaum, Sidney, 208
Rosenthal, Sam, 200–201
Rothenberg, Levi, 199
Roy, Devparna, 9
Ruderman, Abraham, 210–11
Russians, 25

Sacha, Bob, 57
Sacred Heart Church, 60
Sahajanand Swami, 298
Saunders, Summer, 224–25
Scherck, Isaac, 202
Schlager, Milton, 208
Schmidt, Aimée, 8, 13, 273
Schultz, Benjamin, 210
Schwartz, Jacob, 196
Schwerner, Michael, 208–9
Schwerner, Rita, 208
Scothern, William B., 109–10

Scots-Irish, 49; immigration of, 21, 47, 52; in the Northeastern Hills, 43; in the Piney Woods, 44
Scott, Walter, 54
Scottish, 37, 43, 53–55
secular music, 86–96
Seeligman, John O., 125
Seesel, Henry, 194–95
selective tradition, 75
Seminole tribe, 221, 226
September 11, 2001, 275
Serbians, 59, 127, 273
Seu, George, 148–49, 150, 161
Seven Years War, 37
Shepherd, Ted, 161
Shoemake, Regina, 242
Shui Tuck Hi, 152–53
Sidney, C. W., 156
Sillers, Walter, Jr., 158
Simmons, William, 208
Simon, Michael, 196
Singleton, Theresa, 102, 105
Sita Ram Hindu Temple, 291, 296–98, *297*
slavery, 37, 43, 44, 76, 106
Slavic Benevolent Association, 59, 123–24, 129, 135, 140
Slavonians: in Biloxi, 123, 124; in the Gulf Coast region, 42; immigration of, 44, 58–60, 273, 274; seafood industry and, 59–60, 126, 127, 128–29
Silver, James, 357
Smiley, A. C., 84, 85
Smith, Floree, 85
Southern Federation of Temple Youth, 211
Spanish, 32–33, 36, 37–39, 43, 334
St. George Antiochian Orthodox Church, 185, 191
St. Joseph's Roman Catholic Church, 191
St. Mary's Basilica, 39
St. Michael's Roman Catholic Church, 59, 130, 135, 271
St. Patrick's Day Parade, *50*
St. Peter's Catholic Church, 52
Stanton Hall, *48*
Starvin Chain, 90
Staton, Carolyn, 186

Steps Coalition, 138
Steve, Rosalie, *251*
Sunkara, Lekha, 285
Swaminarayan Temple, 291, 298
Swartzentruber Amish, 56–57
Sweet Potato Queens, 51
Swiss, 37
Syrian World, 178
Syrians. *See* Lebanese

Taft, William Howard, 159–60
Tagore, Rabindranath, 260
Taylor, W. E., 82, 83, 84
Tejanos, 336
Tenskwatawa the Shawnee Prophet, 228, 233
Thomas, Emma Ellis, 181
Thomas, Ernest, 181
Thomas, George, *180*, 181
Thomas, Gregory, 174, 177, 183–84
Thomas, James, 9, 353
Thomas, Robert, Jr., 191
Thompson, John Hunter, 235, 238
Thornell, John, 168
Trail of Tears, 221, 232
Tran, Liem, 132
Treaty of Dancing Rabbit Creek, 238, 247
Treaty of Paris (1763), 37
Treaty of San Lorenzo, 37
Truman, Harry, 62
Tubby, Estelline, 231–32, 235, 236–37, 243–45, *244*
Tuck Chon. *See* Seu, George

Union Church, 54
Union of American Hebrew Congregations, 203, 208
United Nations Human Development Report, 356
United South and Eastern Tribes, 248
United States: guest worker program of, 336; immigration to, 15–16, *17*; Philippines and, 311; policy on American Indians, 220–21; policy on Vietnamese, 267–68

United States Catholic Conference, 271
University of Southern Mississippi: Center for Oral History, 310; English Language Institute, 336

Vaughn, Harley, 227
Vick, Newitt, 36
Vicksburg, Miss., 36
Viet Minh, 265
Viet Nam War, 266–67
Vietnamese: assimilation of, 273; in Biloxi, 123, 124, 131–33, 272–74; casino industry and, 28, 263–64, 276, 280; education and, 268–71; family and, 276–77; gender roles and, 277–78; in the Gulf Coast region, 4; history of, 265–67; hostility towards, 274–76; Hurricane Katrina and, 138, 263, 275–76; immigration of, 22, 23, 30, 263, 266–68, 358; population of, 264, 265, 279; religion and, 271; seafood industry and, 27–28, 261, 263, 264, 271–73, 274–76; U.S. refugee policy and, 267–68, 268
Vietnamese American Association, 279
Vietnamese Buddhist Congregation, 271, 279
Vietnamese Martyrs Catholic Church, 271, 279
Villapando, Venny, 232
Ville De St. Lo (ship), 147

Walder, William, *Southern Harmony*, 81–82
Washington, Booker T., 100, 104, 113, 114
Washington, Miss., 38
Waters, Mary, 7
Waters, Muddy, 87, 88
Welsh, 43
White, Benjamin, *The Sacred Harp*, 82
White, Joyce, 84
Williams, Big Joe, 88
Williams, Henry, 240
Williams, Raymond Brady, 298
Williamson, Lola, 9
Williamson, Sonny Boy, 88
Willis, Gladys, 240, 241

Willis, Hulon, 249
Willis, John, 61
Willis, Linda, 234, 235
Wilson, Charles Reagan, 63
Wilson, David, 80–81, 91, 92–95
Wilson, Deborah, 80
Wilson, Louise, 232, 238–39, 249–50
Wing, Luck, 150
Wise, Isaac Mayer, 203, 204
Wong, Frances, 157
Wong, Raymond, 168
Wovoka and the Ghost Dance, 233
Wright, Alfred, 224
Wright, Fielding, 200

Yarborough, George, 208
York, Jake, 223, 241
Young, Amy, 9, 13, 14, 98, 102, 103, 104
Yugoslavians, 273, 274

www.ingramcontent.com/pod-product-compliance
Lightning Source LLC
Chambersburg PA
CBHW030602230426
43661CB00053B/1814